THE FAMILY AND CHILD MENTAL HEALTH:

Selected Readings

Edited by
John Touliatos
Byron W. Lindholm, Jr.
Auburn University

MSS Information Corporation
655 Madison Avenue, New York, N.Y. 10021

This is a custom-made book of readings prepared for the courses taught by the editors, as well as for related courses and for college and university libraries. For information about our program, please write to:

MSS INFORMATION CORPORATION
655 Madison Avenue
New York, New York 10021

MSS wishes to express its appreciation to the authors of the articles in this collection for their cooperation in making their work available in this format.

Library of Congress Cataloging in Publication Data

Touliatos, John, comp.
   The family and child mental health.

   1. Child mental health--Addresses, essays, lectures.
2. Family--Addresses, essays, lectures. I. Lindholm,
Byron W., joint comp.   II. Title.   [DNLM:
1. Affective disturbances--In infancy and childhood--
Collected works.   2. Child behavior disorders--
Collected works.   3. Family--Collected works.
WS 350 T723f 1973(P)]
RJ111.T6   614.5'832'08   73-6770
ISBN 0-8422-0306-0

CONTENTS

PREFACE

Most approaches to the study of children acknowledge the impact of the family on child mental health. In most cases, the family provides the child with his earliest experiences and is the primary agent for his socialization. The family lays the foundation for the development of personality structure and dynamics, self-concept, and stimulus-response interactions.

This series of readings was initiated to incorporate the growing concern for the role the family plays in the etiology, prevention, and treatment of behavior problems. Heretofore, no other book of readings has dealt with this aspect of child mental health.

J.T.
B.L.

The Meaning of Psychological Health

Marie Jahoda

THERE IS HARDLY a term in current psychological thought which is as vague, elusive, and ambiguous as the term "psychological health." That it means many things to many people is bad enough; that many people use it without even attempting to specify the idiosyncratic meaning the term has for them makes the situation worse. As Stafford-Clark [1] has recently pointed out, psychological health is most appropriate in Humpty-Dumpty's vocabulary when he is at his most mischievous behavior in a conversation with Alice. "When *I* use a word," Humpty-Dumpty said in a rather scornful

[1] David Stafford-Clark, *Psychiatry Today*, Penguin Books, London, 1952.

SOCIAL CASEWORK, 1953, Vol. 34, pp. 349-354.

7

tone, "it means just what I choose it to mean—neither more nor less." On that basis he explains that "glory" means "There's a nice knockdown argument for you." To wring the term "psychological health" from Humpty-Dumpty's vocabulary is a first step toward putting it where it ultimately belongs—into psychological theory. It may take some time before we can achieve this final goal. But perhaps we can be somewhat more explicit than Humpty-Dumpty about the reasons, however idiosyncratic, that prompt us to make "glory" mean a "nice knockdown argument."

What I propose to do here is, first, to examine critically some current connotations of the term "psychological health" in order to eliminate them from further discussion. I hope that the arguments I shall use in this context will have little idiosyncratic flavor. This will lead me, next, to a description of the psychological categories within which one has to search for a meaning of psychological health. And, finally, I shall describe the more concrete content that we have selected at the Research Center for Human Relations—perhaps arbitrarily—for research on this problem.

Inappropriate Connotations of Psychological Health

1. *The Absence of Mental Disease.* There is widespread agreement that the absence of mental disease is a necessary, though not a sufficient, condition of psychological health. The value of such consensus for our task here is, however, more apparent than real. To use it presupposes that we have a clear concept of mental disease. This is, of course, not so. In a recent discussion [2] among psychiatrists, psychologists, and social scientists the question of what constitutes a psychiatric case was intensively debated but not answered. One of the major difficulties in using the absence of mental disease as a criterion for psychological health is the existence of the vast no man's land between those who are unquestionably ill and those who are definitely healthy.

[2] See *Interrelation between the Social Environment and Psychiatric Disorders*, **Proceedings of Conference on Mental Health**, Fall 1952, Milbank Memorial Fund, New York, 1953.

Many so-called "unadjusted" persons are found in that area. This fact reminds us that if and when we arrive at a concept of psychological health, this concept will have to permit statements about different degrees of psychological health rather than be limited to an oversimplified dichotomization.

2. *Statistical Normality.* Perhaps the most misleading popular connotation is based on the assumption that psychological health is what the majority of people do, feel, or are. Cultural anthropologists, however, have provided us with a vast range of data on very different forms of human behavior which are statistically normal in different societies. In our own culture, many things are done by a majority which we hesitate to call psychologically healthy; for example, experiments have abundantly demonstrated that under conditions of hunger, people tend to see food objects where there are none. That the majority responds in such fashion may be perfectly understandable; but this is very different from regarding as psychologically abnormal those who, in spite of their hunger, maintain the ability to perceive correctly.

In another sense, too, statistical normality begs the question of psychological health. There are, of course, innumerable aspects of human behavior amenable to statistical research. Which of these should be selected as indicators of psychological health? The question as to whether psychological health is the statistical norm will be an interesting research problem, once we have a suitable concept. It is against our knowledge of the social influences on human behavior to reverse the procedure so as to define psychological health by what the majority of people are.

3. *Psychological Well-being.* Much research has been done, based on standardized personality tests and interviews, to identify persons who are happy, do not worry, are free from tension and conflict, and so on. These highly desirable states have then been taken as indicators of psychological health. Underlying this notion is a naïve optimism about this world. If somebody is unhappy, worried, or in conflict, this view holds there must be something wrong with him psychologically. Those who suffer misfortune and deprivation are by this stand-

ard unhealthy. This view was apparently already prevalent some 1500 years B.C., when the friends of Job told him that the reasons for his utter misery must be sought in himself. As will become clear later on, it is more appropriate to regard Job, whose clear view of himself and of the world in which he lived was never disturbed, as one of the psychologically most healthy persons described in the literature of the world.

4. *Successful Survival.* Related to the notion that psychological health manifests itself in well-being is the notion that it can be inferred from a person's success in mastering the vicissitudes of life. Such social Darwinism is subject to criticisms similar to those outlined above. It can easily be taken *ad absurdum.* Under a totalitarian regime, for example, it may well help psychological survival to become completely apathetic to external events. Under less extreme circumstances it may foster psychological survival to perceive wrongly that one is accepted by one's peers when this is actually not the case. It would be difficult indeed to justify either behavior as psychologically healthy.

Toward a Positive Concept of Psychological Health

From this sketchy examination of some connotations of psychological health we conclude that the absence of mental disease is too vague a guide for discovering meaning in psychological health. What is needed is an approach that can, but need not, include the statistical norm; that can, but need not, include feelings of well-being; that can, but need not, include successful survival.

Now there is a common element in all the objections raised so far against some suggested criteria of psychological health: *these criteria are inappropriate because they neglect the social matrix of human behavior.* If we lived in the "Good Society" that Gilbert Murray has defined as one in which the fortunes of men are unequivocally related to their merits and efforts, the statistical norm, a feeling of well-being, and psychological survival might be suitable criteria for psychological health. In proposing a concept of psychological health we must, however, never forget that the Good Society is an ideal construct rather than reality. As an ideal construct, the Good Society has a place in thinking about psychological health in the following way: first, we note that even in this ideal construct, conflicts and problems are not excluded. We assume conflicts and problems to be inevitable in every human life; that is, we assume that every human being has to overcome the difficulties that arise in his efforts to establish a workable arrangement with the environment in which he finds himself. Second, we note that the actual world in which we live is not altogether the opposite of the Good Society. In some situations and for some people merit and effort are related to their fortunes. Without systematic research on a given environment there is no way of telling whether and to what extent it will reward psychological health. It follows that we must not conceive of psychological health as the final state in which the individual finds himself, for this state is dependent upon external events over which he has no control. Rather we should think of it as a style of behavior or a behavior tendency which would add to his happiness, satisfaction, and so on, *if things in the external world were all right.* Psychological health, then, manifests itself in behavior that has a *promise* of success under favorable conditions. This, in the broadest sense, is what I want to propose as the meaning of psychological health.

Before describing behavior tendencies that have this quality of increasing individual satisfaction if the environment does not interfere, let me emphasize again the formal characteristics of our approach: psychological health or its absence manifests itself in the way a person handles the problems and conflicts of life; it cannot be inferred from the result of behavior for the psychic economy of a person because of the nature of possible external events but only from the behavior itself; further, psychological health is a truly *social psychological* notion. The unit of analysis when investigating psychological health can never be the individual in artificial isolation. It must be simultaneously the individual and the social matrix within which he is observed. One of the basic research questions

9

in this whole area is: what are the psychologically relevant attributes of an environment which permit the manifestation of psychologically healthy behavior?

Problem-Solving and Need-Free Perception

There are undoubtedly several behavior tendencies that fulfil the formal requirements of our approach to psychological health. Perhaps somewhat arbitrarily we have selected two behavior tendencies for closer study: problem-solving and certain cognitive tendencies. Neither of them in itself should be regarded as indicating psychological health. They are twin criteria: only if certain modes of problem-solving coincide with certain modes of cognitive tendencies can we speak of psychologically healthy behavior.

Psychologically healthy modes of problem-solving. The approach to realistic life problems created by environmental conditions is a highly complicated process which extends over some time. It might help to distinguish the various dimensions of this process if I take an example from a current study at the Research Center. In a relatively new community in a certain county many of the residents complain about the problem created by the fact that people let their dogs run loose; the dogs destroy young plants, dig up grass seeds, frighten babies, and are generally experienced as a nuisance. We have asked a sample of women among other matters whether they regarded the dogs as a problem, and if so, how they handled it. Let me give you a feeling for the variety of ways in which this problem is tackled.

Mrs. A: "Sure it is a nuisance; it worries me more and more as the weather gets better. I can't let the baby out in the yard. But there isn't a thing you can do about it."

Mrs. B: "I was very annoyed in the beginning. I thought of building a fence, but that was too expensive. If I had known the owner, I would have spoken to her. But I didn't feel like starting off with a fight with a neighbor. Now I've got used to it. It doesn't annoy me that much any more."

Mrs. C: "I discussed it with my husband; we decided to tell the Civic Association that they should hire a dog-catcher. I haven't

yet been to a meeting, but I will go when I have time."

Mrs. D: "What do I do? I continuously have my eye on the window. When I see one coming I rush out and shush it away. It's a nuisance; but I guess I'll get used to it."

These examples should suffice to illustrate three dimensions of the process of problem-solving. First we note that these women differ according to the *stage* to which they have taken their problem-solving efforts. The first woman, who said "There isn't a thing you can do about it," has not gone beyond admitting that the dogs do present a problem. The second woman has gone a step further; she is at the stage of considering solutions such as putting up a fence or talking to the neighbor. The third woman has decided how to handle the problem, but she has not yet implemented her decision; the fourth is in the arduous process of implementing her solution: chasing away every dog as he approaches. Admission, consideration, decision, and implementation are, then, four stages of problem-solving. In actual experience people need not be conscious of this logical sequence. In any case, it appears that different people have a tendency to stop their problem-solving at different stages of the process. It seems fair to assume that those who habitually carry the process to the stage of implementation have the best chance to eliminate the problem under favorable external conditions.

The next dimension is the *feeling tone* that accompanies the process. Some of the women, at whatever stage they left their problem, "had got used to it" or felt better about it; others worried just as much or even more in spite of having implemented a decision. This is, of course, understandable, if the implementation did not solve the problem. Psychologically more revealing is the case of the women who after a while felt better about the problem even though it continued to exist. They learn to accept passively whatever difficulty confronts them, perhaps because the strain of facing a problem is too great. They seem to have a low tolerance for problem-facing. We infer that such passive acceptance is not promising of success even under favorable conditions. Rather such persons will become shallow and nondescript in their needs and desires.

A third dimension in the process of problem-solving is the *directness or indirectness* with which a person approaches the root of the annoying experience. The woman who decided to ask the Civic Association to hire a dog-catcher, who would presumably eliminate all stray dogs or at least establish rules and regulations, went directly to the heart of the matter. If circumstances are favorable, the problem will disappear once and for all. In sharp contrast is the woman who rushes after every single dog. She is dealing with the recurring symptom of the nuisance rather than with its basic root; she will have to repeat her action, day-in, day-out. The chances of her feeling happy about the situation even under favorable circumstances are indeed slim.

Each of these three dimensions of the problem-solving process is influenced by both the individual and the relative "goodness" of the environment. In all their logically possible combinations these dimensions permit sixteen different modes of problem-solving. As the maximum degree of psychologically healthy problem-solving we regard that combination which includes a tendency to go through all stages, where the feeling about the problem is determined by its actual continuation or elimination, and where the attack on it goes directly to the root rather than indirectly to symptoms.

Psychologically healthy cognitive processes. A psychologically healthy mode of problem-solving does not contain in itself a definite promise of success, even if there are no external barriers. The chances may be negligible indeed if a person's cognitive habits are unhealthy, that is, if he is accustomed to see what he likes or fears or needs instead of what there is to be seen, independent of his needs. To stay within the previous example: suppose a woman wanting to solve her problem approaches a small, powerless Civic Association that is deliberately ignored by the other residents. Such a misperception of social reality will probably lead to failure. If this misperception is based solely on lack of information, it can be quickly remedied, of course. However, if the woman is so deeply involved with that organization that she needs to see it as the center of social life, correction of the misperception will be more difficult. Here we are dealing with a distortion of a person's cognitive relation to the social environment, which is rooted in special needs. The absence of such distortion in the end product of perceptual and cognitive processes we regard as the second psychologically healthy behavior tendency.

Recent experimentation has, of course, abundantly demonstrated the close interdependence of needs and percepts. An over-enthusiastic interpretation of this vast array of fascinating experimental data often tends to overlook one simple fact: what these experiments demonstrate is as a rule a statistically significant relationship and never a correlation of plus 1. An adequate psychological interpretation must account for the deviant minorities as well as for the hypothesis-confirming majorities of experimental subjects. I submit that the distinguishing attribute between those who do and those who do not confirm the hypothesis of need determination in perception is what I call a psychologically healthy cognitive tendency.

George Klein [3] has actually demonstrated the existence of this differentiating tendency in an experiment which he reported at a meeting of the American Psychological Association. He compared the perceptual performance of thirsty and not thirsty persons. The differences were relatively small, in spite of the obvious difference in need. When he isolated in both the experimental and the control group those who demonstrated a tendency not to be distracted—in an entirely different task—he discovered that this factor distinguished the performance of his subjects to a much greater extent than the experimental condition of thirst.

Something akin to this ability we have in mind when talking about cognitive processes free from need distortion.

Let me, in conclusion, state once again what I see as the meaning of psychological health: a person is psychologically healthy

[3] George S. Klein, "Need and Regulation," paper presented in a symposium on "The Measurement of Human Motives," Washington, D. C., 1952.

11

to the extent that he manifests behavior tendencies that would raise his general level of satisfaction *under favorable circumstances.* Two such tendencies—there may be others—have been suggested: a certain mode of problem-solving and cognitive processes relatively free from need distortion. The implication of this approach is that we recognize the possibility of environmental circumstances that prevent a vast majority, if not all human beings, from behaving in a healthy way; its greatest challenge is the identification of those environmental conditions in our society which permit human beings to live in a healthy way.

RESEARCH DEFINITIONS OF MENTAL HEALTH AND MENTAL ILLNESS[1]

WILLIAM A. SCOTT

A serious obstacle to research in the area of mental illness lies in the lack of a clear definition of the phenomenon to be studied. The term "mental ill health" has been used by different researchers to refer to such diverse manifestations as schizophrenia, suicide, unhappiness, juvenile delinquency, and passive acceptance of an intolerable environment. Whether some or all of these various reactions should be included in a single category of "mental illness" is not clear from a survey of the current literature. Theories describing the nature and antecedents of one sort of disturbance rarely relate it to another, and there is a paucity of research evidence indicating the extent to which such manifestations are empirically intercorrelated.

In the face of such ambiguity it would appear useful to attempt an organized review of the various definitions of mental illness which are explicit or implicit in recent research, with a view toward highlighting their commonalities and discrepan-

cies on both a theoretical and an empirical level. Such a presentation might help students concerned with causative factors to assess the comparability of previous research findings on correlates of "mental illness," and also point toward some next steps in research to discover the degree to which these diverse phenomena represent either unitary, or multifold, psychological processes.

The research criteria for mental illness to be reviewed here are subsumed under the following categories: (a) exposure to psychiatric treatment; (b) social maladjustment; (c) psychiatric diagnosis; (d) subjective unhappiness; (e) objective psychological symptoms; and (f) failure of positive adaptation. For each category we shall review studies which appear to have employed the definition, either explicitly or implicitly. This will be accompanied by a critical discussion of the adequacy of each definition, together with an assessment, based on empirical data where possible, of the relation between this and other definitions. Finally, we shall attempt to summarize the differences among the definitions, by indicating their divergent approaches to certain basic problems in the conceptualization of mental illness and health.

MENTAL ILLNESS AS EXPOSURE TO PSYCHIATRIC TREATMENT

The most frequently used operational definition of mental illness, at least in terms of the number of studies employing it, is simply the fact of a person's being under psychiatric treat-

[1] This review was prepared for the Survey Research Center, University of Michigan, as background material for that organization's national survey of mental health, sponsored by the Joint Commission on Mental Illness and Health. The writer is indebted to Dr. Gerald Gurin of the Survey Research Center, and to Dr. Fillmore Sanford, formerly of the Joint Commission, for their contributions to the ideas presented here. Also appreciation is due the following researchers for their suggestions and for data from current studies which they provided: Harry Beilin, John Clausen, Benjamin Darsky, John Glidewell, Marie Jahoda, Morton Kramer, Thomas Langner, Charles Metzner, M. Brewster Smith, and Shirley Star.

PSYCHOLOGICAL BULLETIN, 1958, Vol. 55, pp. 29-45.

ment. And this definition is usually restricted to hospital treatment. rather than outpatient service. Nearly all the ecological studies (e.g., **3**, **16**, **22**, **30**, **35**, **50**) and most of the studies correlating mental illness with demographic characteristics (e.g., **5**, **19**, **29**, **41**, **47**) use this as a criterion. They obtain their information from hospital records or, in unusual instances (e.g., **28**), from psychiatrists in the area who furnish information about persons treated on an outpatient basis.

Such a definition of mental illness is operational rather than conceptual, but its implicit meaning for the interpretation of research results is that anyone who is regarded by someone (hospital authorities, relatives, neighbors, or himself) as disturbed enough to require hospitalization or outpatient treatment is mentally ill, and people who do not fit into such diagnoses are mentally healthy. Use of hospital records, moreover, requires that the criterion of the nature of the mental illness be the diagnosis which appears on the record.

Shortcomings of such an operational definition are recognized by no one better than its users. The reliability of psychiatric diagnosis is of course open to question, and any attempt to determine correlates of particular kinds of mental disturbance must take into account the large error inherent in the measuring process. (One study of the association between diagnosis at Boston Psychopathic Hospital and previous diagnoses of the patients at other hospitals showed only 51 per cent above-chance agreement between the two [cf. **15**, pp. 42–43].)

If "under the care of a psychiatrist" is to be regarded as the criterion of mental illness, one must realize the automatic limitation on the size of the mentally ill population that such a definition imposes. Kramer (**34**, p. 124) has estimated that the maximum possible number of mentally ill, under such a definition, would be less than 7,000,000, given the present number of available psychiatrists.

It has been suggested by both sociologists (**7**, **10**) and physicians (**17**) that different rates of hospital admissions for different geographical areas may indicate more than anything else about the areas the relative degree to which the communities tolerate or reject persons with deviant behavior (**11**). Or as the Chief of the National Institute of Mental Health puts it: researchers using hospital records are dependent on the public's rather uneven willingness to give up its mentally ill members and to support them in institutions (**17**); this in addition to the admittedly unstandardized and often substandard methods of record-keeping used by the various hospitals is likely to render incomparable prevalence and incidence data from various geographical areas.

The effects of such differential thresholds for admission in various communities are difficult to estimate, since they cannot be uniform from study to study. In 1938 a house-to-house survey in Williamson County, Tennessee, yielded nearly one person diagnosed as psychotic, but never having been in a mental hospital, for every hospitalized psychotic from the county (**48**). By contrast, Eaton found in his study of the Hutterites (**14**) that more intensive canvassing by psychiatrists did not yield a larger number of persons deemed psychotic than did a more superficial count based on community reports.

Eaton's study *did* yield higher proportions of neurotic diagnoses the more intensive the case finding procedure became, and this observation relates to the finding in New Haven that neurotics under outpatient treatment came disproportionately from the upper socioeconomic strata (28). At first consideration, such differential rates seem readily attributable to the cost of psychiatric treatment, but Hollingshead and Redlich prefer to seek an explanation in the greater social distance between lower-class neurotics and the psychiatrists than in the case of middle- and upper-class neurotics. Whatever the sources of rate differences, it is clear that such correlations as have been reported make one wary of the hospital admissions or outpatient figures as indicative of the "true" incidence of psychiatric disorders. Thus the criterion of exposure to psychiatric treatment is at best a rough indicator of any underlying conceptual definition of mental illness.

MALADJUSTMENT AS MENTAL ILLNESS

Adjustment is necessarily determined with reference to norms of the total society or of some more restricted community within the society. Accordingly, one may conceptually define adjustment as adherence to social norms. Such a definition of mental health has an advantage over the preceding in encompassing a range of more-or-less healthy, more-or-less ill behavior, rather than posing a forced dichotomy. The operation for assessing mental health by this criterion might ideally be a community (or other relevant group) consensus concerning a given subject's degree of adjustment. This has been approximated by at least one set of studies (1, 2).

Rather than assess consensus by pooling many divergent individual opinions, it is possible to assume that a law or other visible sign of social norms constitutes the criterion against which adjustment is determined. Such reference is employed in studies of suicide (12, 26) or juvenile delinquency (25) or divorce (39, 53) as indicants of maladjustment. While the operational criterion may become dichotomous in such cases (whether or not the person comes in contact with the law), this is not necessarily so. Gordon (21) has suggested considering the "biologic gradient" of suicide, extending from contemplation of the act to its actual accomplishment.

Finally, it would be possible to assess degree of adjustment with reference to some externally defined set of requirements for a given social system. Thus a work situation might be seen as demanding a high level of productivity from all its members, and the degree of adherence to this standard becomes the criterion of adjustment, without reference to the individual opinions of the group members or to the manifest norms of the group. This criterion of conformity to the requirements of a given social structure has not been explicitly employed by any of the researchers covered in the present review, but it has been hinted at (37) and remains a possibility, provided that the structural requirements of a social system can be determined independently of the members' behaviors.

Theory of social structure suggests that these three criteria of adjustment would tend toward congruence: The demands of a particular social system lead to the development of social norms, which are expressed in laws or customs and also in the individual participants' notions of what is acceptable behavior. Lack of congruence may be taken as evidence of cultural lag, of poor correspondence between manifest and latent function within the social structure, or of defensive psychological processes within the participating individuals. Since all of these factors supporting discrepancy do occur within most social systems, the criteria may be expected to yield somewhat different results.

When maladjustment is assessed by community consensus, one finds considerable divergence of opinion among various segments of the public regarding what constitutes good and poor adjustment. The Minnesota Child Welfare studies (1) showed differences in criteria for assessing adjustment among different occupational groups in the community. Teachers tended to emphasize standards different from those emphasized by ministers, who in turn displayed some differences from a more heterogeneous group of community adults. Beilin concludes that it is meaningless to discuss "adjustment" in the abstract or to contemplate the prediction of "adjustment" in general. One must specify *adjustment to what, adjustment to whose standards* (2). Lindemann reflects this relativistic conception of mental health when he states: "We find it preferable not to talk about a 'case' in psychiatry— rather we try to assess functional impairment in specific situations as viewed by different professional groups in the community. So a 'case' is really a relationship of possibly pathogenic situation and appropriate or inappropriate behavior to that situation. It is often a matter of arbitrary choice whether such a person becomes an object of psychiatric care" (38, p. 130).

Thus, though adjustment appears a more conceptually adequate criterion of mental health than does exposure to treatment, the necessity for considering different personal frames of reference and the demands of different social structures poses seemingly insurmountable obstacles to the establishment of mutually consistent operational definitions. All such difficulties which lie "hidden," as it were, under the psychiatric treatment criterion, come to the fore to plague the researcher trying to establish a criterion for adjustment which applies to the treated and nontreated alike.

PSYCHIATRIC DIAGNOSIS AS CRITERION FOR MENTAL ILLNESS

There have been a few studies in which entire communities or samples of them have been systematically screened, either by direct examination (44, 48) or by evidence from community records or hearsay (13, 14, 54). Here the criterion for mental illness or health need not be dichotomous, but can be divided into several gradations. Such intensive case-finding can be expected to increase the yield of persons classified as neurotic (34, p. 124) over that provided by the criterion of exposure to treatment, but whether the psychotic group is thereby increased will depend on the community (34, p. 124; 48) and, of course, on the standards for diagnosis employed by the particular investigator.

The lack of standardization of diagnostic procedures and criteria contributes to the incomparability of mental illness rates derived from such studies (34, p. 139; 55). So long as the criterion of assessment is largely dependent on the psychiatrist's subjective integration of a different set of facts for each subject, nonuniform results can be anticipated. Expensive and unreliable though the method may be, it at least places the judgment regarding

16

mental illness or health in the hands of professionals, which is not the case when adjustment is the criterion. And though hospitalization is in part determined by the judgment of professionals, *who* is sent to the hospitals for psychiatric diagnosis is, for the most part, out of the hands of the psychiatrists. As Felix and Bowers (17) have observed, it is the community rather than the clinician that operates the case-finding process today, and this will continue to be so until diagnostic examinations are given regularly to all people.

Mental Illness Defined Subjectively

It has been maintained by some that a major indication of need for psychotherapy is the person's own feeling of unhappiness or inadequacy. Conversely, the degree of mental health may be assessed by manifestations of subjective happiness, self-confidence, and morale. Lewis (36) quotes Ernest Jones to the effect that the main criterion for effect of therapy is the patient's subjective sense of strength, confidence, and well-being. Terman (52, 53) has used a "marriage happiness" test, composed largely of subjective items, and Pollak (43) has suggested that old-age adjustment be assessed in terms of the person's degree of happiness or well-being in various areas of his life.

That such criteria of mental health correlate somewhat with independent diagnoses by physicians has been indicated in two sorts of studies. In the Baltimore Eastern Health District (9), cases diagnosed psychoneurotic were found to express complaints about their own physical health; it is suggested that persons who report chronic nervousness can be classified as suffering from a psychiatric condition. Rogers has maintained that a marked discrepancy between one's "perceived self" and "ideal self" constitutes evidence of psychiatric disturbance (45), and some empirical studies lend support to this position. When Q sorts of subjects' self concepts are compared with Q sorts of their ideal selves, it is possible to distinguish psychiatric groups from non-psychiatric groups on the basis of the degree of discrepancy between these two measures (4). Furthermore, progress in therapy (as judged by the therapist) tends to be associated with increasing similarity between the patient's self concept and ideal self (46).

Though subjective well-being is an appealing criterion for mental health in ordinary daily living, it might be presumed that under some circumstances psychological defense mechanisms could operate to prevent the person's reporting, or becoming aware of, his own underlying unhappiness and disturbance. Jahoda (33) has rejected happiness as a criterion for mental health on somewhat different grounds: Happiness, she says, is a function not only of the person's behavior patterns, but of the environment in which he moves. If one wants to relate mental health to characteristics of the environment, then one must not take as a criterion of mental health something that already presupposes a benign environment. "There are certain circumstances in which to be happy would make it necessary first to be completely sick" (33, p. 105).

Such objections to this criterion imply that it is possible to find persons who are mentally ill by some other criterion, yet who nevertheless report themselves as happy or self-satisfied. Empirical demonstration of this implication is not available at present. In fact, while one study predicted defensively high Q sorts for the self concept of paranoid psychotics, they were found to have a greater discrepancy between self- and ideal-sorts than normals, and no less discrepancy between these measures than psychoneurotics (4).

MENTAL ILLNESS DEFINED BY OBJECTIVE PSYCHOLOGICAL SYMPTOMS

It is generally accepted almost by definition that mental illness entails both a disordering of psychological processes and a deviation of behavior from social norms (6). The latter aspect of disturbance may be assessed as maladjustment to one's social environment (discussed above); the former aspect can presumably be assessed by psychological inventories aimed at the assumedly critical processes. The distinction between the psychological inventory approach and the subjective assessment procedure discussed above is not really a clear one. Subjective well-being may be regarded as one of the psychological processes which becomes disordered. Yet more "objective" measures of psychological process, which do not require the subject's verbal report of his degree of happiness, are frequently preferred, both to guard against purposeful distortion and to tap areas of disorder which may not be accompanied by subjective counterparts.

Such "objective" psychological inventories may represent various degrees of manifest purpose. For some, the objective of assessment is transparent, and the only reason they are not classed as devices for subjective report is that they stop just short of requiring the subject to report his over-all level of well-being. Such a manifest-level inventory is Halmos'

questionnaire concerning the respondent's difficulties in social relations (24).

At a somewhat less obvious level are such inventories as the MMPI, the War Department Neuropsychiatric Screening Battery, and the Cornell Medical Index, which require subjects to check the presence of various subjective and objective symptoms (e.g., "I smoke too much."). Once validated against an accepted criterion, such as psychiatric diagnosis, these are frequently used as criteria themselves. Rennie constructed a composite instrument of this type to assess his respondents' levels of mental health in the Yorkville study (44); at the same time, a validity analysis of the index was undertaken, by correlating each item with independent psychiatric diagnosis on a subsample of the respondents. On the basis of their experience with such a composite instrument, one of Rennie's colleagues (Langner, personal communication, August 1956) suggests caution in abstracting parts of previously validated batteries, since the item validities are sometimes not maintained when they are used out of context of the total instrument.

An adaptation of the psychiatric screening battery approach for use with children is suggested in the work of the St. Louis County Public Health Department (20). It involves obtaining information about symptoms from the children's mothers rather than from the children themselves. Naturally, the symptoms covered must be of the "objective" type ("Does Johnny wet the bed?") rather than of the "subjective" type ("Does Johnny worry a lot?"). As validated by an outside criterion (teachers' and psychiatric social workers' ratings of the child's level of adjustment), the number of symptoms reported by the mothers appears to be a promising index of the child's mental health.

A general characteristic of the types of psychological inventories reviewed so far is that each item in the battery is assumed, a priori, to involve a "directional" quality, such that one type of answer (e.g., "yes" to "Are you troubled with nightmares?") may be taken as indicative of psychological disorder, and the opposite answer as indicative of normal functioning. Thus the index of disturbance is computed by adding all the positive indicators, weighted equally. That alternative methods of test construction may yield equally, or more, valid indices of mental illness is indicated by the extensive investigations of McQuitty (40).

McQuitty proposes several different methods of diagnostic test scoring, each based on explicit assumptions about the diagnostic procedure which the test is supposed to represent. One of the simplest assumptions, for example, is that an individual is mentally ill to the extent that his psychological processes deviate from the culturally modal processes. Thus, any type of multiple-alternative test may be administered to a group of subjects representing a "normal" population. Each alternative of each item is then scored for its "popularity." The score for a subject is then computed by adding the popularity scores of the items he checks (McQuitty calls this the T method of scoring); a high popularity score is taken as evidence of mental health (by this "typicality" criterion).

An alternative assumption proposed by McQuitty as underlying the diagnostic procedure might be that mental health is manifest to the degree that the subject's responses conform to *any* pattern of answers represented by a significant number of community people, regardless of whether that pattern is the most popular one. Such an assumption leads to a scoring procedure (H method) whereby a subject's index of "cultural harmony" is based on the degree to which his responses to different questions "go together" in the same manner as do the responses of all people in the sample who check the same alternatives he does.

Elaborations on these basic procedures provide for differential weighting of responses depending on their degree of deviance (WH method), and correction for "linkage" between successive pairs of items (WHc method).

The Bernreuter Personality Test and the Strong Vocational Interest Inventory were administered by McQuitty to a group of mental patients and to a group of university students; they were scored by different methods, the scores for the two tests were correlated, and the mean scores of the two groups compared. Results of the comparisons indicate that: (a) when appropriately scored, the Strong can discriminate mental patients from normals, though not so well as the Bernreuter; (b) better results are obtained if, instead of treating each answer as a separate, independent measure, it is evaluated in terms of the pattern of other answers with which it occurs (WHc scoring method); (c) within the Bernreuter, those items which correlated best with the total score (McQuitty's WHc method of scoring) and provided the best discrimination between patients and normals tended to be of the "subjective" type (i.e., they depended on the subject's introspection, as in "Do you often have disturbing thoughts?") rather than the "objective" (items which an observer could report, such as "Do you talk very much?"); (d) different scoring procedures appeared differentially appropriate for the "subjective" and "objective" items; (e) when the "subjective" items were scored by the method most appropriate to them (i.e., the method which best discriminated patients from normals), and the "objective" items by their most appropriate method, the correlation between the two scores on the same group of subjects was about zero, indicating that two independent dimensions of mental health were being tapped by these two sets of items.

A separate study reported by McQuitty (40) indicated that the simple T method of scoring (based on the popularity of the subject's responses) both subjective and objective items significantly discriminated groups of school children classified on the basis of independent criteria of mental health. There is considerable evidence from these studies that, especially with respect to those traits measured by the "objective" items, the person may be regarded as mentally ill to the extent that he deviates from the dominant community pattern.

The foregoing studies provide a certain amount of evidence that measures of mental illness according to psychometric criteria relate to two of the criteria discussed earlier—maladjustment and psychiatric diagnosis. That such concurrent validation may yield somewhat different results from studies of predictive validity is indicated in Beilin's report of the Nobles County study (2). Two indices of student adjustment predictors were constructed, one (the "pupil index") based on students' responses to five different instruments, and the other (the "teacher index") based on teacher ratings. Both were concurrently validated against juvenile court judges' nominations of delinquent youngsters and against teachers' descriptions of the youngsters. Four years later the mental health of the youth was assessed by a number of different criteria—community reputation, interviewers' ratings, self-assessment, and an adaptation of the Rundquist-Sletto morale scale. The predictors correlated significantly with only some of the subsequent criteria, and all of the correlations were at best moderate. The "pupil index" correlated better with the interviewer's rating than with the community reputation criterion; while the "teacher index" correlated better with the subject's subsequent community reputation than with the interviewer's rating. Or, stated more generally, the psychologist's predictor predicted better to a psychologist's criterion, and a community predictor predicted better to a community criterion. Though the time span (four years) between the predictor and criterion measures may have been such as to allow for considerable change in the subjects, one is nevertheless reminded by these results that various criteria for mental health are not necessarily highly correlated.

In summarizing the various studies of mental health and illness defined by psychological testing batteries, we may note that many of them lack an underlying conception of the nature of mental illness from which to derive items and scoring procedures (a notable exception being McQuitty's measures), that some of them challenge the notion of the unidimensional nature of mental health, and that their degree of correlation with other criteria, such as adjustment or psychiatric diagnosis, depends on the nature of the criterion.

MENTAL HEALTH AS POSITIVE STRIVING

A radically different approach to the assessment of mental health is indicated in the definitions proposed by some writers with a mental hygiene orientation. Gruenberg suggests that, though failure to live up to the expectations of those around him may constitute mental illness, one should also consider the person's failure to live up to his own potentialities (23, p. 131). Frank speaks of the "positive" aspect of mental health—healthy personalities are those who "continue to grow, develop, and mature through life, accepting responsibilities, finding fulfillments, without paying too high a cost personally or socially, as they participate in maintaining the social order and carrying on our culture" (18). In a less exhortative tone, Henry (27) discusses successful adaptation of the person in the "normal stressful situation." He sees many normal situations as situations of inherent stress. Some individuals in them develop mental disease, while others may develop out of them a more complex, but more successful, personality. It is this successful coping with the "normal stressful situation" that Henry regards as indicative of mental health.

Jahoda has translated this kind of emphasis on the positive, striving, aspects of behavior into a set of criteria amenable to empirical research. She proposes three basic features of mental health (31): (a) The person displays active adjustment, or attempts at mastery of his environment, in contrast to lack of adjustment or indiscriminate adjustment through passive acceptance of social conditions. (b) The person manifests unity of personality—the maintenance of a stable integration which remains intact in spite of the flexibility of behavior which derives from active adjustment. (c) The person perceives the world and himself correctly, independent of his personal needs.

Active mastery of the environment, according to Jahoda, presupposes a deliberate choice of what one does and does not conform to, and consists of the deliberate modification of environmental conditions. "In a society in which regimentation prevails, active adjustment will hardly be possible; in a society where overt regimentation is replaced by the invisible compulsiveness of conformity pressures, active adjustment will be equally rare. Only where there exists social recognition of alternative forms of behavior is there a chance for the individual to master his surroundings and attain mental health." (31, p. 563).

Such an approach is quite at odds with the subjective criterion of personal happiness, and with the conformity criterion referred to above as "adjustment." Attempted adjustment does not necessarily result in success, for success is dependent on the environment. The best mode of adjustment only maximizes the chances of success. It is mentally healthy behavior even if the environment does not permit a solution of the problem (33). Jahoda proposes that the criterion of happiness be replaced with some more "objective" definition of mental health, based on an explicit set of values.

In an unpublished community

study, Jahoda apparently attempted to assess only two of the aspects of mental health incorporated in her definition. Veridicality of perception (actually, of judgment) was determined by asking respondents to estimate certain characteristics of their communities concerning which objective data were available (e.g., proportion of people with only grade-school education), and at the same time inferring needs to distort reality from the respondent's evaluative statements about the problem (e.g., how important R believed education to be). This method of assessing need-free perception was regarded as something less than satisfactory (Jahoda, personal communication, August 1956), since the need was so difficult to determine, and it was difficult to establish unambiguously that distortion of judgment was due to the operation of a need rather than simply to lack of valid information.

The degree of attempted active adjustment was assessed by first asking a respondent to mention a particular problem in the community, then determining what he had done, or tried to do, about it, and how he felt about the problem at the time of interview (33). Three aspects of respondents' reactions were coded from their replies (32): (a) the stage of problem solution—mere consideration of the problem, consideration of solutions, or actual implementation; (b) the feeling tone associated with the problem—continued worry or improvement in feeling (either through partial solution or through passive acceptance); (c) the directness or indirectness of the approach—i.e., whether R went to the heart of the problem in his attempted solution or merely dealt temporarily with recurrent nuisances.

In her analysis Jahoda relates her measures of problem-solving and need-free perception to various characteristics of the respondents and of the communities in which they live. The relationships are interesting (e.g., in one of the communities the level of problem-solving was related to the degree of community participation of the respondent), but they appear to leave unanswered a basic question about the appropriateness of the criteria. If one accepts Jahoda's definition of mental health as involving the two components assessed in the study, then the results can be interpreted as showing what patterns of social interaction are associated with mental health. But if one is skeptical about the meaningfulness of the definition, then he is impelled to search for correlations between her two measures and other, more commonly accepted, criteria of mental health. These are not reported, although it would appear to be a fair question to ask about the relation of her concepts to those employed by other researchers.

If one is wedded to the happiness criterion of mental health, for example, one may speculate about the possibility of a negative relation between it and those provided by Jahoda. Unhappiness could conceivably lead to excessive coping behavior (attempted adjustment), or excessive coping behavior might elicit negative reactions from others which, in turn, would increase one's unhappiness. In like fashion, it could be that need-free perception would lead to increased unhappiness, since psychological defenses are not available to bolster one's self image. Though Jahoda might reject the suggestion that happiness is even relevant to her criteria, it would appear useful to explore, both conceptually and empirically, the interrelations among other measures of mental health and the novel one proposed by her.

Clausen (6) has maintained that researchers must ultimately face the task of relating mental health defined in positive terms to the individual's ability to resist mental illness under stress. At present it is not known whether they represent a common factor or are independent characteristics. Jahoda (personal communication, August 1956) suspects that positive mental health, as she defines it, may indeed represent a dimension orthogonal to that represented by the conventional psychological symptoms of mental illness. Thus, from a different approach than that employed by McQuitty•comes the suggestion that mental health and illness may be a multidimensional phenomenon.

In employing these particular criteria, especially that of active adaptation, Jahoda seems willing to defend the evaluative standards implicit in it. And it may well be that values relating to attempted mastery of problems are every bit as defensible as the values of conformity implied in the adjustment criteria discussed above. Nevertheless, the former appear to exemplify the application of the Protestant ethic to the mental health movement in a manner which might introduce culture and class biases into one's conclusions. Miller and Swanson (42) have hypothesized that lower-class children will show more defeatism than middle-class children, as a result of different interpersonal and environmental experiences. Would they thereby be less mentally healthy by any standards besides those of the middle class? Truly, the problems posed in setting up absolute values from which to judge mental health and illness are perplexing.

BASIC PROBLEMS IN THE DEFINI-NITION OF MENTAL HEALTH AND ILLNESS

Underlying the diversities in definition of mental illness one can discern certain basic differences of viewpoint concerning how the phenomena should be conceptualized. We may abstract certain foci of disagreement by posing the following four points of contention: (a) Does mental illness refer to a unitary concept or to an artificial grouping of basically different specific disorders? (b) Is mental illness an acute or chronic state of the organism? (c) Is maladjustment (or deviance from social norms) an essential concomitant of mental illness? (d) Should mental illness be explicitly defined according to values other than social conformity?

Each of the proposed definitions takes a stand, either explicitly or implicitly, on one or more of these issues. It is likely that resolution of disagreements will depend in part on the outcome of future empirical research. But at least some of the divergence inheres in the theoretical formulation of the problem, and is more a matter of conceptual predilection than of empirical fact. In either case, if one is to arrive at consistent theoretical and operational definitions of mental illness, it would be well to make explicit one's bias concerning each of these issues, and attempt to rationalize it in terms of his conception of the causes of disturbance.

THE UNITARY OR SPECIFIC NATURE OF MENTAL ILLNESS

The position that mental illness is manifest in some rather general form, regardless of the specific diagnostic category in which the patient is placed, would appear to be implicit in the subjective definition of the phenomenon. If the person's feeling of happiness or adequacy is regarded as the crucial indicator of his mental state, this would appear to imply that over-all health or illness can be assessed for a particular person, regardless of the area of functioning referred to. Likewise, the definition of mental health in terms of purposeful striving or active adjustment tends to ignore differences in the underlying bases for such striving or lack thereof. Such a position has been stated explicitly by Stieglitz: "The mensuration of health . . . closely parallels the measurement of biological age as contrasted to chronological age . . . . We are no longer seeking to discover specific disease entities, or even clinical syndromes, but attempting to measure biological effectiveness in adaptation" (51, p. 79). And such a unitary view of the phenomenon is implied in Schneider's comment: "The major 'cause' of mental disease is seen as some form of disorientation between the personality and society" (49, p. 31).

By contrast, the specific view of mental illness is taken by Gordon: "What we choose to call mental disease is an artificial grouping of many morbid processes. The first essential, in my opinion, is to separate the various entities, and in the approach to an epidemiology of mental diseases, to center attention on some one condition, or a few selected conditions, which have functions in common with other mass diseases well understood in their group relationships" (15, p. 107). McQuitty offers empirical evidence in favor of a specific view, in his isolation of two quite independent measures of mental illness (by psychological testing), both of which

correlate with external diagnostic criteria. And he further speculates that the number of areas in which the degree of personality integration varies rather independently is probably greater than the two which he has isolated. "One might expect that mental illness might develop within any one or more patterns. In order to understand the mental illness of a particular subject, we must isolate the pattern, or patterns, of characteristics to which his mental illness pertains" (40, p. 22).

While the weight of opinion and evidence appears to favor the multidimensional view, this may simply be a function of the operational definitions employed (e.g., mental health defined by responses to a battery of tests is bound to turn out multidimensional to the extent that intercorrelations among the test items are low). But there are yet insufficient empirical data collected from the unitary point of view to test whether its assumption is correct. Indeed, it seems quite plausible that both happiness and active adaptation may be partially a function of the situation, hence the concept of mental health implied by them must become multidimensional to the extent that they allow for intersituational variability.

THE ACUTE OR CHRONIC NATURE OF MENTAL ILLNESS

The psychologist's testing approach to assessing mental illness inclines him toward a view of the condition as chronic. That is, the predisposing conditions within the organism are generally presumed to be relatively enduring, though perhaps triggered off into an actual psychotic break by excessively stressful situations. The epidemiological approach, on the other hand, is usually concerned with the counting of actual hospitalized cases, and this may incline one toward a view of mental illness as predominantly acute. Felix has espoused this position explicitly: "Unless the kinds of mental illness are specified, I can't conceive that mental illness is a chronic disease. More mental illnesses by far are acute and even short term than there are mental illnesses which are chronic and long term." (15, p. 163). Of course, the epidemiological approach traditionally considers characteristics of the host, as well as characteristics of the agent and the environment. But the predisposing factors within the organism seem to be regarded, like "low resistance," not as a subliminal state of the disease, but rather as a general susceptibility to any acute attack precipitated by external factors.

It is easier to regard a psychosis as acute than it is similarly to regard a neurosis, since in the former disorder the break with normal behavior appears more precipitate. However, such a judgment, based on easily observable external behaviors, may be unduly superficial. Even in the case of such a discrete disturbance as suicide, at least one writer (21) recommends considering the biologic gradient of the disorder. He distinguishes varying degrees of suicide, with successful accomplishment as merely a possible end product. Where such continuity between morbid and non-morbid states can be discerned, the possibility of chronic disturbance might well be considered.

The Problem of Mental Health as Conformity to Social Norms

The criterion of mental health based on adjustment clearly implies that conformity to the social situation in which the individual is permanently imbedded is a healthy response. And such an assumption would appear to be lurking, in various shapes, behind nearly all of the other definitions considered (with the possible exception of some of the "positive striving" criteria, which stress conformity to a set of standards independent of the person's immediate social group). In fact, McQuitty's methods of scoring psychological inventories are all explicitly based on the assumption that conformity (either to the total community or to a significant subgroup) is healthy.

If the stability of the larger social system be regarded as the final good, or if human development be seen as demanding harmony in relation to that social system, then such an assumption would appear basic and defensible. But one is still impelled to consider the possibility that the social system, or even an entire society, may be sick, and conformity to its norms would constitute mental illness, in some more absolute sense. If any particular behavior pattern is considered both from the standpoint of its adaptability within the social structure to which the individual maintains primary allegiance and from the standpoint of its relation to certain external ideal standards imposed by the observer, perhaps a comparison of the two discrepancy measures would yield information about the degree to which the social system approaches the ideal. On the other hand, such a comparison might be interpreted as merely indicating the degree to which the researcher who sets the external standards is himself adapted to the social system which he is studying. The dilemma appears insoluble.

The Problem of Values in Criteria for Mental Health

The mental hygiene movement has traditionally been identified with one or another set of values—ideal standards from which behavior could be assessed as appropriate or inappropriate. The particular set of values adopted probably depends to a considerable degree on who is doing the judging. Such a diversity of evaluative judgments leads to chaos in the popular literature and to considerable confusion in the usage of the term "mental health" in scientific research. Kingsley Davis (8) presented a rather strong case for the proposition that mental hygiene, being a social movement and source of advice concerning personal conduct, has inevitably been influenced by the Protestant ethic inherent in our culture. The main features of this Protestant ethic, as seen by him, are its democratic, worldly, ascetic, individualistic, rationalistic, and utilitarian orientations.

To the extent that research on mental health is based on criteria devolved from such an ideology, it is middle-class-Protestant biased. To the extent that it is based on some other set of "absolute" norms for behavior, it is probably biased toward some other cultural configuration. At least one researcher, Jahoda (33), has clearly taken the position that mental health criteria must be based on an explicit set of values. There is some advantage in allowing the assumptions to come into full view, but in this case the resulting criteria appear to be rather specialized and not comparable with those used by other researchers. Perhaps the difficulty lies not so much in the existence of explicit assumptions as in their level of generality.' If a more basic set of assumptions could be found, from which the diverse criteria for mental health and illness can be derived, then comparability among researches might better be achieved. One would be in a better position to state when mental illness, as defined by psychological tests or by absence of active adjustment, is likely to be displayed in mental illness defined by psychiatric diagnosis or deviance from community standards.

SUMMARY

The various categories of definitions of mental illness discussed here have been distinguished primarily on the basis of their differing operational definitions: the dependent variables employed in empirical research on the phenomena are clearly different. Moreover the conceptualizations of mental illness explicit or implicit in the empirical criteria are often quite divergent—viz., the radically different viewpoints underlying the "maladjustment," "subjective unhappiness," and "lack of positive striving" definitions.

Certain conceptual and methodological difficulties in each of these types of definition have been noted: "Exposure to treatment" is deficient in that only a limited proportion of those diagnosable as mentally ill ever reach psychiatric treatment. "Social maladjustment" is open to question because of the varying requirements of different social systems and the diversity of criteria for adjustment employed by community members. "Psychiatric diagnosis" provides an expensive, and often unreliable, method of assessing the state of mental health. "Subjective unhappiness" can be criticized as a criterion since it may be a function of intolerable environmental conditions as well as the psychological state of the person, and is subject to distortion by defense mechanisms. The validity of "objective testing procedures" appears to depend considerably on the method by which they are scored, and there is strong evidence that a major component of their score may simply be the degree of conformity of the person to the community average. Finally, criteria included under the heading of "positive striving" are subject to question in that they are inevitably based on disputable value systems of their proponents.

While many of these difficulties would not be considered damaging from the point of view of certain of the definitions of mental illness, they run into conflict with others. Also they suggest certain basic incompatibilities among the various approaches to conceptualization of mental illness. Whether these incompatibilities should be reconciled by further theoretical and empirical exploration, or whether they should be regarded as valid indicators that mental health and illness constitute multidimensional phenomena is still a moot question. We can only note that various studies employing two or more of these different categories of criteria have tended to yield moderate, but not impressive, interrelations.

The criterion of "exposure to psychiatric treatment" has been related to "maladjustment," "psychiatric diagnosis," "subjective unhappiness," and "objective psychometrics." Also "maladjustment" has been related to "psychiatric diagnosis" and to certain "objective" measures; and "psychiatric diagnosis" has been related to both "subjective" and "objective" measures of mental illness. The areas of interrelationship for which no empirical studies have been found are between "subjective" measures and both "maladjustment" and "objective" assessment; also between the "positive striving" criteria and all of the other types of measures.

Two directions for future theory and research are indicated by these results. First, more investigations are needed of the extent of relationship among the various criteria, and of the conditions under which the magnitudes of the intercorrelations vary. Second, assuming absence of high intercorrelations under many conditions, it would be worthwhile to explore the implications of poor congruence between one measure and another—implications both for the person and for the social system in which he lives.

REFERENCES

1. BEILIN, H. The effects of social (occupational) role and age upon the criteria of mental health. *J. soc. Psychol.*, in press.
2. BEILIN, H. The prediction of adjustment over a four year interval. *J. clin. Psychol.*, 1957, 13, 270–274.
3. BELKNAP, I. V., & JACO, E. G. The epidemiology of mental disorders in a political-type city, 1946–1952. In *Interrelations between the social environment and psychiatric disorders*. N. Y.: Milbank Memorial Fund, 1953.
4. CHASE, P. Concepts of self and concepts of others in adjusted and maladjusted hospital patients. Unpublished doctor's dissertation, Univer. of Colorado, 1956.
5. CLARK, R. E. Psychoses, income and occupational prestige. *Amer. J. Sociol.*, 1949, 54, 433–440.
6. CLAUSEN, J. A. *Sociology and the field of mental health.* N. Y.: Russell Sage Foundation, 1956.
7. CLAUSEN, J. A., & KOHN, M. L. The ecological approach in social psychiatry. *Amer. J. Sociol.*, 1954, 60, 140–151.
8. DAVIS, K. Mental hygiene and the class structure. *Psychiatry*, 1938, 1, 55–65.
9. DOWNES, JEAN, & SIMON, KATHERINE. Characteristics of psychoneurotic patients and their families as revealed in a general morbidity study. *Milbank Memorial Fund Quarterly*, 1954, 32, 42–64.
10. DUNHAM, H. W. Current status of ecological research in mental disorder. *Social Forces*, 1947, 25, 321–326.

27

11. DUNHAM, H. W. Some persistent problems in the epidemiology of mental disorders. *Amer. J. Psychiat.*, 1953, 109, 567–575.

12. DURKHEIM, E. *Le suicide.* Paris: F. Alcan, 1897. (English translation, Glencoe, Ill.: Free Press, 1951.)

13. EATON, J. W. *Culture and mental disorders.* Glencoe, Ill.: Free Press, 1955.

14. EATON, J. W., & WEIL, R. J. The mental health of the Hutterites. In A. M. Rose (Ed.), *Mental health and mental disorder.* N. Y.: Norton, 1955.

15. *Epidemiology of mental disorder.* N. Y.: Milbank Memorial Fund, 1950.

16. FARIS, R. E. L., & DUNHAM, H. W. *Mental disorders in urban areas.* Chicago: Chicago Univer. Press, 1939.

17. FELIX, R. H., & BOWERS, R. V. Mental hygiene and socio-environmental factors. *Milbank Memorial Fund Quarterly*, 1948, 26, 125–147.

18. FRANK, L. K. The promotion of mental health. *Ann. Amer. Acad. of Pol. Soc. Sci.*, 1953, 286, 167–174.

19. FRUMKIN, R. M. Occupation and major mental disorders. In A. M. Rose (Ed.), *Mental health and mental disorder.* N. Y.: Norton, 1955.

20. GLIDEWELL, J. C., ET AL. Behavior symptoms in children and degree of sickness. *Amer. J. Psychiat.*, 1957, 114. 47–53.

21. GORDON, J. E., ET AL. An epidemiologic analysis of suicide. In *Epidemiology of mental disorder.* N. Y.: Milbank Memorial Fund, 1950.

22. GRUENBERG, E. M. Community conditions and psychoses of the elderly. *Amer. J. Psychiat.*, 1954, 110, 888–896.

23. GRUENBERG, E. M. Comment in *Interrelations between the social environment and psychiatric disorders.* N.Y.: Milbank Memorial Fund, 1953.

24. HALMOS, P. *Solitude and privacy.* London: Routledge and Kegan Paul, 1952.

25. HATHAWAY, S. R., & MONACHESI, E. D. The Minnesota Multiphasic Personality Inventory in the study of juvenile delinquents. In A. M. Rose (Ed.), *Mental health and mental disorder.* N. Y.: Norton, 1955.

26. HENRY, A. F., & SHORT, J. *Suicide and homicide.* Glencoe, Ill.: Free Press, 1954.

27. HENRY, W. E. Psychology. In *Interrelations between the social environment and psychiatric disorders.* N. Y. Milbank Memorial Fund, 1953.

28. HOLLINGSHEAD, A. B., & REDLICH, F. C. Social stratification and psychiatric disorders. *Amer. sociol. Rev.*, 1953, 18, 163–169.

29. HYDE, P. W., & KINGSLEY, L. V. Studies in medical sociology. I: The relation of mental disorders to the community socio-economic level. *New England J. Med.*, 1944, 231, 543–548.

30. JACO, E. G. The social isolation hypothesis and schizophrenia. *Amer. sociol. Rev.*, 1954, 19, 567–577.

31. JAHODA, MARIE. Toward a social psychology of mental health. In A. M. Rose (Ed.), *Mental health and mental disorder.* N. Y.: Norton, 1955.

32. JAHODA, MARIE. The meaning of psychological health. *Soc. Casewk*, 1953, 34, 349–354.

33. JAHODA, MARIE. Social psychology. In *Interrelations between the social environment and psychiatric disorders.* N. Y.: Milbank Memorial Fund, 1953.

34. KRAMER, M. Comment in *Interrelations between the social environment and psychiatric disorders.* N. Y.: Milbank Memorial Fund, 1953.

35. LEMERT, E. M. An exploratory study of mental disorders in a rural problem area. *Rural Sociol.*, 1948, 13, 48–64.

36. LEWIS, A. Social aspects of psychiatry. *Edinburgh med. J.*, 1951, 58, 241–247.

37. LINDEMANN, E., ET AL. Minor disorders. In *Epidemiology of mental disorders.* N. Y.: Milbank Memorial Fund, 1950.

38. LINDEMANN, E. Comment in *Interrelations between the social environment and psychiatric disorders.* N. Y.: Milbank Memorial Fund, 1953.

39. LOCKE, H. *Predicting adjustment in marriage: a comparison of a divorced and a happily married group.* N. Y.: Holt, 1951.

40. McQUITTY, L. L. Theories and methods in some objective assessments of psychological well-being. *Psychol. Monogr.*, 1954, 68, No. 14.

41. MALZBERG, B. *Social and biological aspects of mental disease.* Utica: State Hosp. Press, 1940.

42. MILLER, D. R., & SWANSON, G. E. A proposed study of the learning of techniques for resolving conflicts of impulses. In *Interrelations between the social environment and psychiatric disorders.* N. Y.: Milbank Memorial Fund, 1953.

43. POLLAK, O. Social adjustment in old age. *Soc. Sci. Res. Council Bull.* No. 59, 1948.

44. RENNIE, T. A. C. The Yorkville com-

28

munity mental health research study. In *Interrelations between the social environment and psychiatric disorders*. N. Y.: Milbank Memorial Fund, 1953.

45. ROGERS, C. *Client-centered therapy*. Boston: Houghton Mifflin, 1951.

46. ROGERS, C., & DYMOND, ROSALIND. *Psychotherapy and personality change*. Chicago: Univer. of Chicago Press, 1954.

47. ROSE, A. M., & STUB, H. R. Summary of studies on the incidence of mental disorders. In A. M. Rose (Ed.), *Mental health and mental disorder*. N. Y.: Norton, 1955.

48. ROTH, W. F., & LUTON, F. H. The mental health program in Tennessee. *Amer. J. Psychiat.*, 1943, 99, 662–675.

49. SCHNEIDER, E. V. Sociological concepts and psychiatric research. In *Interrelations between the social environment and psychiatric disorders*. N. Y.: Milbank Memorial Fund, 1953.

50. SCHROEDER, C. W. Mental disorders in cities. *Amer. J. Sociol.*, 1942, 48, 40–47.

51. STIEGLITZ, E. J. The integration of clinical and social medicine. In I. Galdston (Ed.), *Social medicine—its derivations and objectives*. N. Y. Acad. of Med., 1947. N. Y.: Commonwealth Fund, 1949.

52. TERMAN, L. M., ET AL. *Psychological factors in marital happiness*. N. Y.: McGraw-Hill, 1938.

53. TERMAN, L. M., & WALLIN, P. The validity of marriage prediction and marital adjustment tests. *Amer. sociol. Rev.*, 1949, 14, 497–505.

54. TIETZE, C., ET AL. Personal disorder and spatial mobility. *Amer. J. Sociol.*, 1942, 48, 29–39.

55. TIETZE, C., ET AL. A survey of statistical studies on the prevalence and incidence of mental disorders in sample populations. *Publ. Hlth Rep.*, 1943, 58, 1909–1927.

EMOTIONALLY DISTURBED CHILDREN:
A HISTORICAL REVIEW [1]

LEO KANNER

It is customary to begin a historical account with the search for the earliest observations, ideas, and practices pertaining to the topic under consideration. Ancient and medieval sources are consulted; discovered references are interpreted in the light of the over-all culture of the times and locale; eventually, an evolutionary pattern emerges which links the gradual steps from primitive origins to the facts and theories available when the quest is undertaken.

Similar efforts concerned with emotional disorders of children lead to the amazing disclosure of the total absence of an allusion, however casual, before the eighteenth century. Folklore, which seizes upon every conceivable aspect of human life, is peculiarly silent. Theologic, medical, and fictional writings have nothing to say. This does not warrant the assumption that infantile emotions always ran a smooth course in the past and that the occurrence of their disturbances is a relatively recent phenomenon. The truth is that, aside from occasional pious pleas for nondescript philanthropy, our ancestral lawgivers, physicians, and philosophers seem to have been indifferent toward the afflicted among many categories of the young and, for that matter, of the grown-ups as well. It was not until the decades immediately before and after the French and American revolutions that the new doctrine of the rights of the individual engendered an unprecedented spurt of humanitarian reforms. Vigorous spokesmen arose for the active alleviation of the plight of the slaves, the prison inmates, the insane, the blind, the deaf, and

---

[1] Presented in a symposium, "Research on Emotionally Disturbed Children," at the biennial meeting of the Society for Research in Child Development, Pennsylvania State University, March, 1961.

CHILD DEVELOPMENT, 1962, Vol. 33, pp. 97-102.

the mental defectives. For the first time, handicapped children were seen and heard. Young enthusiasts, mostly men in their twenties, undeterred by the skepticism of their renowned mentors, began to experiment with remedial and educational methods.

There was still no comprehension of the kind of children's difficulties which manifested themselves in disorganized feeling, thinking, and acting. Here and there sporadic sketches made their appearance, mostly with the implication of inherent evil. A few examples may suffice to give the flavor of these reports from the pens of outstanding alienists. I should like to precede them with the story of little Emerentia, as chronicled in a clergyman's diary which is cited in the masterful autobiographic novel, *Der grüne Heinrich* by Gottfried Keller (11), in whose native village the incident had taken place in 1713:

> This 7-year-old girl, the offspring of an aristocratic family, whose father remarried after an unhappy first matrimony, offended her "noble and god-fearing" stepmother by her peculiar behavior. Worst of all, she would not join in the prayers and was panic-stricken when taken to the black-robed preacher in the dark and gloomy chapel. She avoided contact with people by hiding in closets or running away from home. The local physician had nothing to offer beyond declaring that she might be insane. She was placed in the custody of a minister known for his rigid orthodoxy. The minister, who saw in her ways the machinations of a "baneful and infernal" power, used a number of would-be therapeutic devices. He laid her on a bench and beat her with a cat-o'nine-tails. He locked her in a dark pantry. He subjected her to a period of starvation. He clothed her in a frock of burlap. Under these circumstances, the child did not last long. She died after a few months, and everybody felt relieved. The minister was amply rewarded for his efforts by Emerentia's parents.

Such was the general milieu in which the alienists of those days came upon specimens of childhood psychosis. The great Esquirol (7, pp. 384-385) reported in 1838 the cases of three "little homicidal monomaniacs." Of an 11-year-old girl who pushed two infants into a well he had nothing more to say than that she "was known for her evil habits." An 8-year-old girl who threatened to kill her stepmother and her brother was returned to her grandparents who had violently disapproved of her father's remarriage. A 7½-year-old girl who had been tossed about among relatives refused to play, had temper tantrums, masturbated excessively, and expressed regret that her mother did not die; the neighbors, to teach her a lesson, put flour into a glass of wine, told her it was arsenic, and forced her to swallow it. On psychiatric advice, she was sent to a convent, where she promptly developed pediculosis. Eventually, she was apprenticed to a jewel cutter and was said to be submissive and to attend church services on Sundays.

In 1841, Descuret (4) told of a boy who lived with a nurse during the first two years of his life. When he was taken to his home, he grew pale, sad, and morose, refused to eat, and did not respond to his parents. The usual toys and diversions had no effect. On medical advice, the nurse was called back and, in the father's words, "from that moment on he began to live again." Eventually, he was separated from the nurse, first for a few hours, then for a whole day, then for a week, until finally the child was accustomed to her absence.

This last example indicates an emerging desire to look for possible explanations of deviant child behavior on other than pseudotheologic and pseudomoralistic grounds.

Around the middle of the nineteenth century, a growing number of such anecdotal bits was published, and a few psychiatrists were no longer satisfied with the mere mechanical recording of observed or quoted instances. In 1867, Maudsley included in his *Physiology and Pathology of Mind* a 34-page chapter on "Insanity of Early Life." In it, he tried to correlate symptomatology with the developmental status at the time of onset and suggested a classification of infantile psychoses. There was objection on the part of those who persisted in denying the existence of mental illness in children. In the 1880 revision of his book, Maudsley (16) felt compelled to counter such criticism with an introductory paragraph, which said, somewhat apologetically:

> How unnatural! is an exclamation of pained surprise which some of the more striking instances of insanity in young children are apt to provoke. However, to call a thing unnatural is not to take it out of the domain of natural law, notwithstanding that, when it has been so designated, it is sometimes thought that no more needs to be said. Anomalies, when rightly studied, yield rare instruction; they witness and attract attention to the operation of hidden laws or of known laws under new and unknown conditions; and so set the inquirer on new and fruitful paths of research. For this reason it will not be amiss to occupy a separate chapter with a consideration of the abnormal phenomena of mental derangement in children (p. 259).

In the last two decades of the nineteenth century, courageous attempts were made to collect and organize the existing material in monographs on "psychic disorders," "mental diseases," or "insanity" of children. These were the texts by Emminghaus (6) in Germany, Moreau de Tours (17) and Manheimer (15) in France, and Ireland (9) in Great Britain. There was a tendency toward fatalism which saw in the disorders the irreversible results of heredity, degeneracy, masturbation, overwork, religious preoccupation, intestinal parasites, or sudden changes of temperature.

Thus, around 1900, there was an assortment of publications, ranging all the way from single case reports to elaborate texts and announcing to an astonished world that children were known to display psychotic phenomena.

It was the year 1900 in which Ellen Key (12), the famous Swedish sociologist, made her much-quoted prophetic announcement that the twentieth century was destined to be "the century of the child." It is indeed remarkable that in the next few years many efforts converged on the interest in the doings and experiences of infants and children. The diaries of Preyer, Darwin, Pestalozzi, Tiedemann, and other writers, expanded by

Stanley Hall's questionnaires, had paved the way for the new science of developmental psychology and the monumental work of Binet, whose first draft of the psychometric scale was made public in 1905. This was the year in which Freud, on the basis of elicited adult patients' reminiscences, gave literary form to his theory of infantile sexuality. Three years later, Clifford Beers introduced the idea of the prevention of mental illness, focusing on the need to intercept behavioral deviations at the time of their earliest appearance. The establishment of juvenile courts, inaugurated in 1899 in Denver and in Chicago, led eventually to Healy's contributions in the teens of this century. Educators joined in by building into the school systems special instructional facilities for pupils with visual, auditory, neuro-orthopedic, and intellectual handicaps.

Yet it was not until the 1930's that consistent attempts were made to study children with severe emotional disturbances from the point of view of diagnosis, etiology, therapy, and prognosis. When the change did occur, it was centered around the concept of childhood schizophrenia. By that time, general agreement had been reached that children were not altogether immune against the illness described by Kraepelin as dementia praecox and referred to by Bleuler as the group of the schizophrenias. Ziehen (23) and Homburger (8) had given in their textbooks (both in 1926) ample space to a discussion of its incidence in preadolescence and adolescence. De Sanctis (3), at about the same time, had suggested the term "dementia praecocissima" for an assortment of marked disturbances appearing in preschool age. Increasing awareness of the looseness with which childhood schizophrenia was diagnosed or failed to be diagnosed caused Potter (18) in 1933 to delineate the concept so that there might be a consensus with regard to the nosologic assignment of any individual child. In the framework of this and similar definitions, the next step consisted of the search for a clear demarcation of existing variations in onset, symptoms, and course. Ssucharewa (21) in Russia, Lutz (13) in Switzerland, and Despert (5) in this country distinguished between cases with acute and insidious onset, with the implication that the peculiarities of the beginning determined the phenomenology and the progress of the illness.

In the 1940's, a period of controversy and confusion was inaugurated because of the parallel advocacy of two antithetical trends. On the one hand, there was a tendency to revert to pre-Kraepelinian indefiniteness. Beata Rank (19) introduced the notion of the "atypical child," with intended disregard of any distinctions between childhood psychosis, mental defect, and any other form of "severe disturbances of early development." Problems of mother-child relationship were declared to be a common causative denominator. Szurek proclaimed categorically: "We are beginning to consider it clinically fruitless, and even unnecessary, to draw any sharp dividing lines between a condition that one could consider psychoneurotic and another that one could call psychosis, autism, atypical development, or schizophrenia" (22, p. 522).

On the other hand, there was a decided disinclination to house an assortment of heterogeneous clinical entities under one supposedly common etiologic roof. Kanner (10), in 1943, outlined the syndrome of early infantile autism. Mahler (14), in 1949, described a form which she named symbiotic infantile psychosis. In the same year, Bergman and Escalona (2) called attention to what they called children with unusual sensitivity to sensory stimulation. In 1954, Robinson and Vitale (20) added the group of children with circumscribed interest patterns. Bender (1), seeing the origin of childhood schizophrenia in a maturation lag at the embryonic level, subdivided the condition into three clinical types: (a) the pseudodefective or autistic type; (b) the pseudoneurotic or phobic, obsessive, compulsive, hypochondriac type; (c) the pseudopsychopathic or paranoid, acting-out, aggressive, antisocial type.

It is strange, indeed, that a historical review of emotional disturbances of children should occupy itself predominantly, or almost exclusively, with psychoses and, more specifically, with schizophrenia. It is equally strange that, seek as one may, it is impossible to find anywhere a definition of the term "emotionally disturbed children" which had somehow crept into the literature some 30 years ago and has since then been used widely, sometimes as a generality with no terminologic boundaries whatever and sometimes with reference to certain psychotic and near-psychotic conditions. This is extremely important in the consideration and evaluation of past, ongoing, and planned research. It can be said that these studies do exclude such emotional disorders as occasional temper tantrums or night terrors of otherwise well-adjusted children; chronicity is apparently a paramount requirement. Also left out are emotional problems associated with, or secondary to, inherent mental deficiency or demonstrable organ pathology. But this still leaves a wide variety of heterogeneous conditions which, if thrown together indiscriminately, impart no greater meaning to a study than did the sixteenth century treatises on the fevers or the nineteenth century studies of the blood pressure of "the insane" or of the heredity of "feeblemindedness." It may perhaps be legitimate to link them together from the standpoint of practical epidemiology and the improvement of public health facilities but, beyond this, it would hardly do to claim scientific validity for any research which sets out to look for unitary features in disparate conditions.

A historical survey teaches us that progress has always consisted of a breaking down of diffuse generic concepts into specific categories. We no longer speculate about fevers generically; bacteriology knows of totally different varieties of febrile illness. We no longer speak about insanity generically; we recognize a variety of psychotic reaction types. We no longer speak about feeblemindedness generically; we know that there is a vast difference between mongolism, microcephaly, and phenylketonuria; it would not occur to anyone to lump them together in any meaningful investigation. I believe that the time has come to acknowledge the heterogeneity of the many conditions comprised under the generic term, "emotionally

34

disturbed children." We shall then be in a position to study each of these varieties with true precision. A symposium on the use of the term in scientific publications would, at this juncture, be a major contribution to clarity and mutual understanding.

References

1. BENDER, L. Current research in childhood schizophrenia. *Amer. J. Psychiat.*, 1954, 110, 855-856.
2. BERGMAN, P., & ESCALONA, S. Unusual sensitivities in very young children. *Psychoanal. Stud. Child*, 1949, 3-4, 333-352.
3. DE SANCTIS, S. *Neuropsichiatria infantile.* Rome: Stock, 1925.
4. DESCURET, J. B. F. *Médecine de passions.* Paris: Béchet et Labé, 1841.
5. DESPERT, J. L. Schizophrenia in children. *Psychiat. Quart.*, 1938, 12, 366-371.
6. EMMINGHAUS, H. *Die psychischen Störungen des Kindesalters.* Tübingen: Laupp, 1887.
7. ESQUIROL, J. E. D. *Maladies mentales.* Vol. I. Paris: Baillère, 1838.
8. HOMBURGER, A. *Vorlesungen über die Psychopathologie des Kindesalters.* Berlin: Springer, 1926.
9. IRELAND, W. W. *The mental affections of children.* Blakiston, 1898
10. KANNER, L. Problems of nosology and psychodynamics of early infantile autism. *Amer. J. Orthopsychiat.*, 1949, 19, 416-426.
11. KELLER, G. *Der grüne Heinrich.* Vol. I. Munich: Deutsch-Meister-Verlag, 1921.
12. KEY, E. *The century of the child.* (English Rev.) Putnam, 1909.
13. LUTZ, J. *Über die Schizophrenie im Kindesalter.* Zurich: Füssli, 1937.
14. MAHLER, M. S. On child psychosis and schizophrenia. *Psychoanal. Stud. Child,* 1952, 7, 286-305.
15. MANHEIMER, M. *Les troubles mentaux de l'enfance.* Paris: Société d'Editions Scientifiques, 1899.
16. MAUDSLEY, H. *The pathology of the mind.* Appleton, 1880.
17. MOREAU DE TOURS, P. *La folie chez les enfants.* Paris: Baillère, 1888.
18. POTTER, H. W. Schizophrenia in children. *Amer. J. Psychiat.*, 1933, 89, 1253-1270.
19. RANK, B. Adaptation of the psychoanalytic techniques for the treatment of young children with atypical development. *Amer. J. Orthopsychiat.*, 1949, 19, 130-139.
20. ROBINSON, F. J., & VITALE, L. J. Children with circumscribed interest patterns. *Amer. J. Orthopsychiat.*, 1954, 24, 755-766.
21. SSUCHAREWA, G. Über den Verlauf der Schizophrenien im Kindesalter. *Ztsch. f. d ges. Neurol. & Psychiat.*, 1932, 142, 309-321.
22. SZUREK, S. A. Psychotic episodes and psychic maldevelopment. *Amer. J. Orthopsychiat.*, 1956, 26, 519-543.
23. ZIEHEN, T. *Die Geisteskrankheiten des Kindesalters.* Berlin: Reuther & Reinhard, 1926.

The Epidemiology of Behavior Disorders in Children

REMA LAPOUSE, MD

A COMPARATIVE review of research into children's behavior disorders brings into sharp focus the major problems in such studies. Variability in the definitions and methods used by different investigators makes it difficult to select the more valid findings among the discrepant data reported.

An aspect of the dilemma is illustrated by Goldfarb's study [1] of the relative ability of school teachers and psychiatrists to identify psychiatric cases among school children. He found that these two professional groups disagreed on the identification of specific children with mental health problems and concluded that the teachers required further training to increase their sensitivity to psychiatric cases. The assumption that the correct definition of a psychiatric case is a secure part of the psychiatrist's armamentarium is open to question when psychiatric diagnosis still lacks the means for objective validation. Far more than in other medical fields, psychiatric diagnosis is known to vary with the theoretical system espoused by the diagnostician, which in turn influences his concept of normality and his diagnostic formulations.

The attachment of exaggerated psychopathologic significance to single behavior items such as nail biting, nose picking, and casual masturbation, says Kanner,[2] arises from the use of statistics contributed by selected groups of children from child guidance clinics and juvenile courts. He points out that, for the general population of children, neither the occurrence nor the ultimate psychiatric fate of the so-called symptoms is known, and he suggests that the unfavorable prognostic implications of these behaviors may be unwarranted.

How behavior disorders are defined is an issue crucial to their study. For the most part, psychiatrists, social workers, psychologists, and other workers in the field accept the assumption that some rather ordinary behaviors, like those mentioned by Kanner, have pathological import and predict future psychiatric casualty. As we have pointed out elsewhere,[3] this is as if observers, noting the presence of a cough in tuberculosis, interpreted all coughs as definitive evidence of this disease. Based solely on such an inclusive definition, prevalence studies will inevitably overreport the amount of tuberculosis in the population.

By the same token, an inclusive definition of behavior disorders overcounts the occurrence of this morbid state among children and creates a situation with dangerous implications. Among the dangers are: failure to distinguish between sick and nonsick children, with accompanying tendencies to treat the nonsick; invidious iatrogenic effects stemming from those tendencies which affect children, families, teachers, and other child-caring professions; consequent misapplication of existing psychiatric personnel and services and distortion of estimates for their need; and, finally, stimulation of misleading

AMERICAN JOURNAL OF DISEASES OF CHILDREN, 1966, Vol. 3, pp. 594-599.

hypotheses which affect the theoretical structure of child psychiatry.

To compound the confusion created by the diagnostic dilemma, the methods used by most investigators in studying children's behavior disorders suffer not only from the problem of selection already mentioned by Kanner, but additionally from the difficulty of establishing the validity and reliability of findings, and their comparability from one study to another. The common practice of placing reliance on the skill of the interviewer or observer in obtaining and interpreting information about children introduces subjective elements which defy verification.

Method

The study of children's behavior described in this paper was designed to overcome some of the more obvious shortcomings of previous investigations. The aims of this research were (1) to gain knowledge regarding the prevalence of a number of behavior characteristics of children in relation to sex, age, race, and socioeconomic status; (2) to determine the interrelationships of these behaviors; (3) to correlate these behaviors with adequacy of function in the individual child; and (4) ultimately, to devise an effective means of identifying the psychiatrically sick child in the community.

The methodologic features of the design were the selection of a representative sample of children, the use of a structured interview schedule for obtaining comparable information on all children, and the avoidance of a priori definitions of so-called symptomatic behavior. Such avoidance is an applicable procedure where the diagnosis or definition of a pathological entity is uncertain.

In this study we investigated the frequency, intensity, and duration of a wide variety of behaviors, and from these dimensions were derived criteria by which the definition of a behavior disorder may be formulated. By these criteria, a behavior is considered to be disordered when it deviates from the prevailing norms and when it is accompanied by impaired function as shown by maladjustment and poor performance.

The child behavior study was based on 482 children, aged 6 through 12 years, randomly selected from households which were systematically sampled in Buffalo. In 1½ hour sessions, trained interviewers administered more than 200 closed-ended questions to the mother of the selected children. Of the mothers approached, 94% consented to the interview. Mothers were selected as respondents because direct examination or observation of nearly 500 children would have been neither feasible nor

reliable, and because, as Luton Ackerson[4] remarked, "While the child's mother cannot be assumed to know the truth concerning the many aspects of his behavior, there is probably no other available class of informant which would know nearly as much." Also, evidence was available supporting the relative accuracy of mothers' observations.[5]

Subsequently, two substudies were undertaken to test the reliability and validity of the mothers' reports. In one instance, the interviews were exactly replicated on a 10% subsample of the mothers originally interviewed, and in the second, a new sample of children was selected, and both the mother and child were simultaneously interviewed by different interviewers using a part of the questionnaire.

The information obtained on the children was grouped to facilitate the analysis of the data. Several areas were identified, including behavior, adjustment, social relations, achievement, health, anxiety, and environment. The items comprised in these areas and the method used in classifying them have been discussed at length in previous papers.[3,6,7] Scores were established by assigning points reflecting the presence, frequency, intensity, and sometimes duration of the various items reported. For any given area, the points were accumulated to form a single area score. Each of these overall scores summarized the scores of the contributing items. The highest scores indicated that children with these scores had more of the behaviors studied, that these behaviors occurred more frequently and more intensely, and perhaps persisted longer in high-score children than in those with lower scores.

By selecting a proportion of children with the highest or most extreme scores for behavior, the first criterion defining abnormal behavior could be fulfilled, namely, deviation from the prevailing norm. The second criterion, malfunction, could be met by separating out a proportion of children with extremes scores for adjustment, social relations, and achievement. By this means it becomes possible to assess the extent to which deviant behavior and malfunction are associated, and to examine in greater detail the characteristics of the child whose aberrant behavior is coupled with impaired function.

Results

Of the 482 children comprising the sample, half were boys and half were girls: half were 6 through 8 years old and the other half were 9 through 12. Division into socioeconomic halves was predetermined by the sampling method. The proportion of nonwhites in the sample was 15%, which mirrored the proportion of nonwhites in Buffalo.

In the investigation of the prevalence of various behaviors, the first finding of significance was the surprisingly frequent occurrence of some characteristics commonly considered to be symptomatic of psychiatric disorder.[8] Over 40% of the children were reported as having seven or more fears and worries; about 30% were said to have nightmares, to be restless, and to bite their nails; and between 10% and 25% to engage in various other body manipulations. Mothers reported that almost 20% of the children wet the bed within the previous year and that over 10% lost their tempers once a day or more often.

With reports of such high prevalence of suspect behavior characteristics, it became very important to examine the possibility that these items were being inaccurately reported by mothers. In one substudy, the reliability of mothers' reports was tested by comparing the agreement between their first interviews and the reinterviews which took place on an average of six weeks later. It was found that for the more explicit and specific behaviors agreement occurred at a median of 91% of the paired answers. These behaviors are bedwetting, thumbsucking, stuttering, nail biting, temper loss, biting clothing, chewing lips, tics, picking sores, picking nose, grinding teeth, and similar behaviors. For the more implicit and nonspecific behaviors such as nightmares, fears and worries, restlessness, overactivity, and amount of food eaten, the median percentage agreement was 78. This finding indicates that the responses of mothers are fairly consistent over time, but that this consistency is greater when the reported behavior is more concrete and objectively observable. In a second substudy, the paired responses of mothers and children were examined. Their median agreement was lower than for the comparison of mothers with mothers, but the same phenomenon was observed of greater accord between mother and child on explicit-specific (68%) than on implicit-nonspecific behaviors (54%).[3,8]

The most striking finding in the mother-child comparison was that, contrary to expectation, mothers in general reported fewer positive items than did children. If the child's report is accepted as the criterion, the prevalence of so-called symptomatic behaviors appears to be even greater than reported above. This finding points to the need for reassessment of the serious implications which the presence of these behaviors connotes to many workers in the field. We have raised the question whether these characteristics are truly indicative of psychiatric disorder, or whether they occur as transient developmental phenomena in essentially normal children.

Further evidence bearing on this question comes from an examination of the occurrence of high-scoring (worst) behaviors as these are examined within subgroups of the sample divided by sex, age, race, socioeconomic status, and number of siblings in the family. The greatest difference was found in children aged 6 through 8 years as compared with 9 through 12-year-olds. A statistically significant excess of high scores in younger children was found for speech difficulties; for body manipulations, also called tension phenomena, including biting nails, grinding teeth, sucking thumb or fingers, chewing lips or tongue, sucking or chewing clothing, picking nose and picking sores; for wild behavior, bedwetting, nightmares, and masturbation; and for the overall area score for behavior. This finding is also consistent with the thesis that deviant behavior occurs as a transient developmental phenomenon in school-aged children.

Although marked differences in high-scoring behavior are commonly believed to exist between boys and girls, and were therefore anticipated, the only differences of any consequence were the excess of high scores among boys for bedwetting, masturbation, physical inactivity, and daydreaming. There was no sex difference in the overall behavior area score.

There were only minimal differences between white upper and lower social classes, possibly due to the dilution of the extremes in each half with intermediate socioeconomic groups. When Negro and white children were compared, however, the Negro children showed an excess of high scores for body management, including posture, gait, and coordination; for speech difficulties; and for thumb sucking, compulsive behavior, and daydreaming. No significant difference by race was observed in the overall behavior area scores.

When the sample is divided into only children and those with siblings, only one important difference appears: children from multiple child families seem more likely to suck their thumb or fingers. Since Negro families in this sample include fewer single-child families than do the white families, the excess in thumbsucking for Negro children may well be related to family size. Evidence is also very persuasive that Negro-white differences are due less to race than to socioeconomic disparity, since the Negro children in this sample, compared with the white lower class children, live under more adverse social and economic conditions. One third of the white lower class children have annual family incomes under $4,000, while this income level describes almost three quarters of the Negro children. Similarly, one third of the Negro children suffer the handicaps of poor housing and low status of the father's occupation in comparison with one eighth of the white lower class children.

In analyzing the interrelationships between various behaviors and the fears and worries of children, the evidence failed to support the thesis that fearful or anxious children (defined here as those with seven or more fears and worries) have more tension phenomena, nightmares, bedwetting, stuttering, temper loss, and tics than other children.[9] Because there is always the danger that mothers reported inaccurately, we repeated this analysis using data from interviews with children alone. The results showed an even lower correlation between a large number of fears and worries and these behaviors. Fearfulness, moreover, does not seem to be related to high scores for somatic complaints. Finally, the evidence also failed to support the expectation that the worrying mother would either *have* a worrying child or *report* a worrying child. The widespread occurrence of many fears and worries among children and the negative association between these fears and the various deviant behaviors tends to suggest that such anxieties, like many behaviors, may be a concomitant of the wide range of essentially normal developmental phenomena in children.

The search for the functional correlates of high-scoring or deviant behavior has been only partially completed. Analysis of the relationship between adjustment, as one aspect of function, and behavior has produced some interesting findings.[7] Adjustment was assessed from a series of so-called continua, described in previous papers.[3,7] Each continuum contains five statements delineating a range of adaptational possibilities among which the mother was asked to select the one which most nearly fitted her child. The statements chosen were scored according to whether they were extreme, intermediate, or middle, with the last being considered normal.

For the purpose of comparing behavior and adjustment in the subgroups, the distribution of high scores signifying maladjustment was examined.[7] It was interesting to find that, in contrast to high-scoring behavior, there was no difference in the occurrence of high scores denoting maladjustment between younger and older children. Nor, in fact, were there any notable differences between pairs of subgroups divided by sex or by number of siblings. The dramatic differences occurred among the social classes in a sharp stepwise ascent as socioeconomic status went down. The proportion of children who were judged to be maladjusted by their high scores was twice as high for the white lower class subgroup as for the white upper class; for the Negro subgroup, it was four times as high.

Although there was a significant correlation between overall scores for the behavior and adjustment areas, it was at a low level, and prediction of coexisting maladjustment from the presence of deviant behavior was quite insecure. However, some individual behaviors showed a significant relationship to scores for maladjustment. Without regard to age, the tension phenomena, restlessness, temper loss, eating habits, and eating behavior are so related. Younger children are more likely to be maladjusted in the presence of speech difficulties, tics, and physical inactivity. Older children have a greater likelihood of maladjustment when they display thumbsucking and nailbiting. No significant association with maladjustment was found in the total sample or in either age group for wild behavior, overactivity, bedwetting, disturbed sleep or bedtime behavior, and daydreaming.

For the foregoing analyses, the criterion for extreme or deviant scores for each item was arbitrarily chosen as the highest 25% of the distribution of scores in the total sample. Such a large percentage was selected because of the small sample size. As the criterion was progressively narrowed, the predictive accuracy of deviant behavior for coexisting maladjustment was increased. At the 25% level for each area, the risk of deviant adjustment is twice as great for children with, as it is for those without, deviant behavior. At the 5% level, this relative risk is increased to a ninefold difference. A definition of deviation limited to 5% of the distribution of scores would probably be optimal for the detection of children with behavior disorders.

Currently, possible associations are being looked for between behavior and adjustment on the one hand, and adequacy of function on the other. How well the sampled children function is judged by scores measuring their achievement at school and their success in family and community relationships. The finding of consistent and significant interrelationships among these modalities will increase the security of the criteria for the diagnosis and detection of behavior disorders in children.

The present child behavior study is most useful in demonstrating a method of collecting and analyzing information which reduces the subjective elements that plague most psychiatric studies related to children. Insofar as other data exist, some of the findings of this research, for example, those regarding the prevalence of enuresis and its relationship to adjustment, are borne out by other investigators. Most of the findings need confirmation. Further validation studies and tests of reliability need to be done. A much larger sample of children needs to be surveyed to permit adequate analysis of subgroups. A similar study replicating the present procedures on a larger population in other areas needs to be done to test independently both the prevalence data and the findings on interrelationships of the current work. The standardized instrument and methods developed in this study lend themselves to replication by other investigators.

Moreover, the same instrument and method used here for determining the prevalence of behavior and its correlates may also be applicable to other kinds of epidemiologic investigations. For example, comparison of findings in children with and without a particular condition is a technique which has numerous possibilities in the search for etiologic clues. The use of replicable methods described makes it possible to compare the characteristics of children of different ethnic or cultural backgrounds, of varying family origins, and of disparate health histories.

Finally, the instrument and methods can be adapted to serve as a detecting device for the early identification of children with disturbances of psychiatric import. The successful accomplishment of this objective will make it possible to find early or mild psychiatric cases, to distinguish specific subgroups of the population with the highest risk of mental disorder, and to base estimates of psychiatric need on a more realistic foundation than exists today.

Summary

Methods and findings are presented from a study of the prevalence of various behaviors and their correlates in 482 children aged 6 through 12, comprising a representative sample of children in Buffalo. Behavior disorders are defined as those which deviate from prevailing norms and are associated with functional impairment.

A major finding was that behavior deviations were much more frequent in younger than in older children, but expected differences in occurrence between boys and girls were not observed. In contrast, no age differences were seen for maladjustment, but the latter showed a stepwise increase as socioeconomic status decreased.

Fearlessness, as reported both by mothers and children, failed to demonstrate an association with various kinds of behaviors considered to have psychiatric significance. The correlation between such behaviors and adjustment was positive and significant but at a sufficiently low level that prediction of coexisting maladjustment from the presence of behavior deviations was not usually possible.

The strikingly high prevalence of so-called symptomatic behaviors, their excessive presence in younger as contrasted with older children, and the weak association between these behaviors and adjustment give rise to the question whether behavior deviations are truly indicative of psychiatric disorder or whether they occur as transient developmental phenomena in essentially normal children.

This study was supported in part by US Public Health Service grants M-1507 and M-3191, and the American Child Guidance Foundation.

REFERENCES

1. Goldfarb, A.: Teacher Ratings in Psychiatric Case Findings, *Amer J Public Health* 53:1919-1927, 1963.

2. Kanner, L.: Do Behavioral Symptoms Always Indicate Psychopathology? *J Child Psychol Psychiat* 1:17-25, 1960.

3. Lapouse, R.; Monk, M.A.; and Street, E.: A Method for Use in Epidemiologic Studies of Behavior Disorders in Children, *Amer J Public Health* 54:207-222, 1964.

4. Ackerson, L.: *Children's Behavior Problems*, Chicago: University of Chicago Press, 1954, vol 1.

5. Glidewell, J.C.; Mensch, I.N.; and Gildea, M.C.-L.: Behavior Symptoms in Children and Degree of Sickness. *Amer J Psychiat* 114:47-53, 1957.

6. Lapouse, R., and Monk, M.A.: Behavior Deviations in a Representative Sample of Children: Variation by Sex, Age, Race, Social Class and Family Size, *Amer J Orthopsychiat* 34:436-446, 1964.

7. Lapouse, R.: The Relationship of Behavior to Adjustment in a Representative Sample of Children, *Amer J Public Health* 55:1130-1141, 1965.

8. Lapouse, R., and Monk, M.A.: An Epidemiologic Study of Behavior Characteristics in Children, *Amer J Public Health* 48:1134-1144, 1958.

9. Lapouse, R., and Monk, M.A.: Fears and Worries in a Representative Sample of Children. *Amer J Orthopsychiat* 29:803-818, 1959.

DO BEHAVIOURAL SYMPTOMS ALWAYS INDICATE PSYCHOPATHOLOGY?

LEO KANNER

In 1931, shortly after the opening of the Children's Psychiatric Clinic in the pediatric department of the Johns Hopkins Hospital, I had in my office a distinguished visitor. He was one of the country's leading pediatricians, a man whose professional career was based on substantial scientific contributions and on sound judgement, a teacher whose word had great resonance among his colleagues. In the course of our conversation, he asked me what I thought of a person who had been enuretic until the age of 13 years. Did I, as a psychiatrist, think that he could be considered normal? I replied that normalcy or a departure from it cannot possibly be defined in terms of an isolated behaviour item. My visitor then disclosed smilingly that his reference to the enuretic boy was taken from a page out of his own unwritten autobiography. He grew up to be a sane, superbly adjusted, emotionally stable, highly respected and well-liked member of society.

As a matter of fact, is there anybody who has gone through the years of infancy, childhood and adolescence without ever experiencing any kind of emotional quandary and manifesting it in the form of one or another behaviour problem? Only those with a very poor memory, or those unnecessarily embarrassed, will deny that at some time in their early years they have had experiences and displayed modes of conduct which figure in an inventory of abnormal traits or in the index of a comprehensive textbook of child psychiatry. A period of capricious eating, an occasional temper outburst, or a number of more or less skilfully invented alibis has not greatly interfered with the satisfactory personality development of the great majority of the little perpetrators. The mere fact of their existence did not in itself indicate abnormality.

The standard dictionaries define "normal" as "conforming with or constituting an accepted standard, model or pattern; especially, corresponding to the median or average of a large group in type, appearance, achievement, function, development, etc." If such things as fear of the dark, rather ill-regulated motor activity, or vigorous expressions of anger could be shown to occur in "the median or average of a large group" of children, they would have to be included in the roster of "normal" phenomena. However, extremely few statistics of this nature are available. Those items which are not brought to professional attention remain unrecorded. In consequence, because they are often seen in clinics as a part manifestation of major psychopathological difficulties, there has been understandable puzzlement about the nosological significance of each behaviour item as such.

JOURNAL OF CHILD PSYCHOLOGY AND PSYCHIATRY, 1960, Vol. 1, pp. 17-25.

Nail-biting probably presents the best example of this puzzlement. Bérillon (1908) pondered over the question, at that time much discussed by French authors, whether or not "onychophagy" is a stigma of "degeneration". Cramer (1912) considered it as "an exquisitely psychopathic symptom". Wechsler (1931), noting that the fifth year of life is the earliest age of onset, inferred therefrom that nail-biting is "a symptom of the persistence of the unresolved oedipus situation". How "normal" or pathological is nail-biting then? Billig (1942) made an extensive study of its occurrence in elementary and secondary school children. Among tenth graders, 29 per cent bit their nails at that time, 37 per cent had been nail-biters, and 34 per cent had never indulged. This means that not fewer than 66 per cent of all pupils of an average high school classroom bit their fingernails at one time or another. It is hardly realistic to assume that two-thirds of our youth are degenerates, exquisitely psychopathic, or walking around with an unresolved oedipus complex. If this were true, then the future of the armed forces of the United States would be in serious jeopardy, indeed. Pennington (1945) found that approximately one-fourth of about 2500 naval recruits acknowledged indulgence in the habit.

The incidence of breath-holding may serve as another illustration. At the Well-Baby Clinic conducted in the Eastern Health District of the City of Baltimore, routine inquiry disclosed that 51 of 188 infants were said by their mothers to have breath-holding spells or to have had them. Cyanosis was observed in 18 per cent, unconsciousness in 2 per cent, and convulsions in 2 per cent. Anger was believed to be the "precipitating cause" in 90 per cent, fear and pain each in 5 per cent. Bridge *et al*, who tabulated these findings, compared them with 83 children brought to the Harriet Lane Home of the Johns Hopkins Hospital with the specific complaint of breath-holding spells. In this group, cyanosis was present in 93 per cent, unconsciousness in 60 per cent, and convulsions in 49 per cent. From this, it appears that mild and uncomplicated breath-holding spells are not uncommon in otherwise normal babies.

In most instances, statistics of symptoms, traits, habits or "behaviour problems" have of necessity been those of selected groups and not of the total population of children. Most numerical depositions depend unavoidably on the material of psychiatric and child-guidance clinics and juvenile courts. Ackerson (1931), the author of one of the most ambitious studies of the incidence and correlation of children's behavioural items, wrote: "Until parents can assume a more impersonal attitude toward the behaviour of their children and toward their own affairs, our only source of data for the scientific (that is, statistical) study of the more serious personality and conduct problems will be the somewhat selected group examined in behaviour and guidance clinics".

This selectiveness, in the absence of "normal controls", has often resulted in a tendency to attribute to single behaviour items an exaggerated seriousness with regard to their intrinsic psychopathologic implications. The high annoyance threshold of many fond and fondly resourceful parents keeps away from clinics and out of reach of statistics a multitude of early breath-holders, nail-biters, nose-pickers and casual masturbators who, largely because of this kind of parental attitude, develop into reasonably happy and efficient adults. But, in clinic statistics, these same symptoms, figuring among the "traits" found in the histories of "problem children", are apt to be given too prominent a place, far out of proportion to their role as everyday problems or near-problems of the everyday child.

An attempt to make up for this lack of normal controls has been made recently by Lapouse and Monk (1957). In November 1957, they presented an epidemiologic study of behaviour characteristics of children between 6 and 12 years of age. They interviewed the mothers who were chosen systematically from addresses in the 1955 Buffalo City Directory, every 75th address being designated as a sample. The sample was divided into four economic quartiles based on the median monthly rental of the census tract in which the address was located. At each place, the interviewer spoke to the mother if any children of the studied age-group lived in the house. Shortly before the field-work began, an article appeared in the local newspaper describing the purpose, method and sponsorship of the study. In addition, a letter was sent to the selected address just before the interview, explaining the reason for the survey and assuring the mothers of complete anonymity. Altogether 482 mothers of 733 children were included in the study.

The results are impressive. Overactivity was reported in 49·2 per cent, an assortment of fears and worries in 42·9 per cent, nail-biting in 27·4 per cent, nightmares in 27·7 per cent, problems of food intake in 35·3 per cent, temper loss once a month or more in 79·6 per cent, twice a week or more in 47 per cent, once a day or more in 10·9 per cent. Bedwetting within the year preceding the study was reported in 17·4 per cent. Nose-picking was present in as many as 25·8 per cent.

The authors sum up their paper by saying: "This preliminary study, designed as a testing device for a larger project, has presented two significant findings. The first is that for a representative sample of children, mothers report a high percentage of behaviour characteristics commonly thought of as pathological. The second is that mothers' reports (as checked by interviews with the children themselves) tend to err in the direction of under-enumeration, which suggests that the prevalence of the reported behaviour may be even higher than the data disclosed. This raises for serious consideration the question whether these characteristics are truly indicative of psychiatric disorder or whether they occur as transient developmental phenomena in essentially normal children."

This carefully conducted survey by Lapouse and Monk confirms an impression had by some for a long time. In 1928, Thom discussed a great many of the garden variety of more or less problematic behaviour items, in a book with the title *Everyday Problems of the Everyday Child*. The same year witnessed the publication of an important study which has not received the attention it deserves. Wickman (1928) asked the teachers in two large schools to list the behaviour problems which they encountered in their classroom experience, to check the frequency of occurrence of problems in each of their pupils, and to rate the total behaviour adjustment of each child. In the submitted reports, "there appeared a definite tendency on the part of the teachers to stress behavior disturbances that attack their standards of morality, obedience, orderliness, application to school work, and agreeable social conduct. On the other hand, there was a conspicuous paucity of items describing child behavior which does not directly disturb school routine but which is indicative of social and emotional problems."

44

The historical importance of Wickman's work lies in the fact that here, for the first time, a conscious effort was made to focus not only on the prevalence of emotional problems and their behavioural manifestations but also on the evaluation of children's conduct on the part of the observing adults. As a result of his investigations, Wickman wrote: "Behavior disorders arise out of a discrepancy between the child's capacity to behave and the requirements of behavior which are imposed upon him by parents, teachers, companions and social organization. The factor of adult attitudes which determines these requirements is an integral part in the production of the behavior problem as well as of the child's future behavior adjustment."

In other words, there is no absolute criterion for the normalcy of any of the common forms of behaviour problem of children. Their evaluation is bound up tightly with the general outlook of the evaluating agent. He who is determined to squeeze his children rigidly and prematurely into the straitjacket of suburban propriety will have a different measure of desired conduct from him who is able to step down from the pedestal of humourless perfectionism. A mother who is pre-occupied with calories, vitamins and the weight chart will have a different notion about her child's food intake from one who is wholesomely casual about the whole matter of eating: it is the latter's offspring who will eat reasonably well and present no feeding problem. In fact, the very term "feeding problem" implies that a child's ingestion of food is at least as much an issue of the feeder as of the eater.

Given a child who is not beset by cerebral, endocrine, metabolic or other major systemic disorders, and who is not markedly deficient in his intellectual endowment, it is safe to expect that he has the potentialities for adequate emotional development. It is also to be expected that in the course of his formative years there will be many occasions for trial and error in the task of adaptation to a socialized mode of living. The adult, with his settled performance pattern, often fails to realize the full weight of perplexities which crowd in on an infant during the rapid transition from biologically helpless passivity to volitional participation in the domestic routine. It is a transition from stationary sojourn in the crib or in the mother's arms to active locomotor exploration of the immediate environment; from being fed to self-feeding; from automatic urination and defecation to consciously regulated sphincter control; from a chance to yield indiscriminately to somnolence and wakefulness to set hours for naptime and bedtime; and generally from having things done to him by people to doing things for himself in his relations with people.

As a member of the human species, he has the centrifugal capacity for the acquisition of all these functions, which can be furthered or hindered by centripetal influences. Continuation of breast and bottle feeding long past the time when he is able to feed himself will delay the acquisition of this function. Impatient and forcible pushing ahead of a child's physiologic readiness may equally postpone the attainment of otherwise unimpaired efficiency.

It is obvious, then, that the smooth progress of domestication and socialization depends not only on the propensities existing within the child but also to a not inconsiderable extent on the manner in which these propensities are allowed to unfold with a minimum amount of impediment or coercive interference. Even under the most favourable circumstances, budding volition is put before alternatives which are not always chosen by the child in accordance with the supervising adult's preferences.

Every child is known to go through a phase when, having learned that he has a choice between compliance and defiance, he practises the novel experience of non-conformity. This period, usually between the second and fourth years of life, has been variously designated as the period of negativism, resistance or remonstrance. The manner with which this "normal" contrariness is met sets for a long time the pattern of relationship between the child and his family. It may lead to a friendly, democratic regime in which the youngster, regarded as a novice in this business of living with other people, is helped along peaceably in his moments of understandable confusion. On the other hand, submissive parental overprotection and over-indulgence may put the child on the throne of unchecked infantile autocracy, giving him the dreaded status of the *enfant terrible*. Thirdly, the punitive brand of harsh, intolerant discipline may turn the home into a field of combat, a tug-of-war situation between a small, forever noncomplying child at one end and two or more critical, nagging, agitated adults at the other end.

Modern parent education does not sufficiently stress the normalcy of the so-called period of resistance and its resulting behaviour. Much domestic unpleasantness could be prevented by a clearer recognition of the positive values of a child's quest for self-assertion. Gesell *et al.* (1940) stated: "The negativity of the 18-month-old child has had exaggerated emphasis because the adult has imputed contrariness to a type of behavior pattern which has developmental rather than emotional significance." Thom (1928) wrote: "The negativistic phase of a child's life is recognized as being a normal reaction occurring in the process of growing up. It is the period when the child begins to assert his own personality, when he resents domination by others. This is a natural and healthy reaction." Levy (1955), in his excellent study of oppositional behaviour, concluded: "We can see the oppositional behavior in the second year of life as a general movement toward the autonomy of the whole person, as the first flowering of self-determination, of which the budding had long been in evidence."

It is during this stage that most of the common emotional problems of young children make their appearance, and it is the management of the arising issues by the adults which determines whether the problems are ephemeral episodes or drag out into protracted discomfort. The management, in turn, is influenced by the pattern of the training adults' attitudes toward the child, toward themselves, and toward the particular behaviour item. These attitudes have their roots in the parents' own emotional needs, often reinforced by the impact of the cultural milieu.

There are group orientations which differ in various geographic areas, in various socio-economic settings, and at various periods of history. I should like to recall what has happened in the past half-century in the area of infant feeding. The early pediatricians, struggling for a standard of optimal nutrition, established rigid rules of four-hour intervals irrespective of the individual baby's demands, were painstakingly precise about what they decided were the required nutriments and quantities, and set up a so-called ideal weight chart as the essential criterion of nutritional success. All this was enjoined upon mothers as inflexible prescriptions to be carried out with ritual obsessiveness. What were the results? Anorexia became the dreaded crux paediatrica. Brennemann wrote (1932): "Anorexia is not an occasional occurrence, an isolated phenomenon in childhood; it is the rule in that very stratum in society in which mothers are lying awake nights planning a gospel diet and the most effective way of administering it. It has been stated that this condition exists only among the well-to-do—that a poor appetite is rare among the poor. This truly amazing phenomenon, the majority of the young of any animal refusing to eat a diet that is not only scientifically optimum but as appetizing as only culinary ingenuity can make it, can be explained only on a psychologic basis."

A gradual reorientation has led to a relaxation of the earlier rigidity about the medically recommended feeding schedules. In fact, a trend has developed which goes in the diametrically opposite direction. Self-demand feeding has become a modern slogan. One should think that this would remove all concern about an infant's nutrition. That it has not done so must be ascribed to the undeniable fact that the method is less important than the emotional involvement of him who uses the method. After all, not all of the children brought up in obedience to fixed schedules have fared too badly with regard to their physical and characterologic development. What is it, then, that spells the difference between the advantages or disadvantages of any method? The presence or absence of anxious preoccupation, of agitated fumbling, of plain common sense, of genuineness and naturalness, is the common denominator regardless of the mechanics of feeding. This is why obsessive enslavement has resulted in as much hardship with the self-demand procedure as with the scheduled routine.

Bruch (1952) summed this up by saying: "If rigidly adhered to and carried out by a literal-minded mother, the self-demand feeding may result in preposterous situations when the self-chosen schedules of a child's needs are completely at variance with the ordinary routine of the household. I have known of children who, by the age of 2 or 3, "demanded" their main meal late at night, would not fall asleep before midnight, demanded their snack at 5 or 6 in the morning, and breakfast at 10 or 11, with luncheon somewhere around 4 o'clock. The other members of the family had, of course, their regular mealtimes. Such procedure is unhealthy and undesirable for the whole family and interferes with their justified demands. It is also damaging from the child's point of view, for he is prevented from maturing and experiencing the satisfaction of being part of the family group."

I have dwelt at some length on the matter of infant nutrition because, more than any other feature involving the mutuality of parent–child relationship, it is an ever-present issue in which adult attitudes and the child's reactions to them are constantly interwoven. What happens at mealtime is a mirror of feeling tones and an unfailing barometer of fair or turbulent emotional weather. It is then that the parent, on the basis of her own personal outlook, adopts and modifies the methods current in the culture to satisfy her needs.

This holds true of every aspect in the life of the child. It is of course true that every youngster needs protection from dangers to his health which he himself has not as yet learned how to avoid. He must be kept from coming perilously close to the hot stove, from leaning too far out of the second-storey window, from darting out into a heavily trafficked road. He must be sheltered from atmospheric extremes and from known sources of infection. The great advances made in the area of prevention of illness have been adequately communicated to the public and have resulted in a substantial reduction of infant mortality, in increased longevity, and in the elimination of diseases that before then have been veritable scourges playing havoc with a large portion of the child population. But a mistaken notion of the beneficial concept of prophylaxis, founded on parental anxiety, has often tended to make a caricature of something that, practised with a reasonable degree of equanimity, has been a boon to mankind.

Most parents practise prevention by doing things calmly in a way which has been found to produce and maintain a satisfactory condition of well-being. They practise prevention by living with their children in a wholesome, sensible manner, by steering tranquilly between the Scylla of uninformed carelessness and the Charybdis of frantic oversolicitude. In so doing, they do not even know that they are preventing anything. The less they go out of their way to prevent, the more they are really preventing. But there are some parents to whom the idea of prophylaxis means an invitation to panic. Panic creates more problems than it prevents. Panic makes feeding problems of children who otherwise would be good eaters, constipates youngsters who, flooded with cathartics and enemas, lose their capacity for normal bowel routine, invalidizes children with healthy bodies because they are wrapped in heavy blankets of sickroom solicitude, and generally indulges in the frantic exercise of throwing inkwells at devils painted on the wall by the constant anticipation of disaster. Thus prevention, introduced into the culture as a beneficent preserver of life and health, is allowed by unwarranted anxiety to degenerate into a nightmarish bugaboo.

There can be no better example of this than the history of the evaluation of the habit of thumb-sucking. Parental apprehension about thumb-sucking is derived in a large measure from cultural attitudes. It has been caused by the warnings and admonitions of alarmists. Before such scares, the habit received but scant notice from parents, physicians or anyone else. Several famous artists depicted children with thumbs in their mouths to give them the expression of serene placidity. The notion that it is bad or harmful did not arise until the end of the nineteenth century. At that time, dentists and especially orthodontists asserted that thumb-sucking produces malformations of the jaws and palate. Parents were admonished to do everything within their power to curb a child's performance so injurious to his mastication and physiognomy. All sorts of mechanical devices were invented, publicized and marketed to keep the little thumb from reaching the mouth. Illustrated articles in dental and pediatric journals described ever new varieties of cuffs, muffs, Elizabethan collars and modified strait-jackets. People who refrained from hampering children's movements took refuge in ill-tasting substances which were smeared on the fingers in order to preclude sucking and subsequent damage to the configuration of the jaws. Later investigation tended to show that the shape of the palate does not become affected by early thumb-sucking. Temporary malocclusion may occur but does not become permanent.

Parents were also besought to beware of the germ danger. Said a famous psychologist who had become a widely read mentor for mothers: "From the standpoint of the child, the matter is serious. Physicians tell us that some 90 per cent of diseases due to germs find their way into the body through the mouth. The child with its mobile hands gathers germs everywhere. Next it puts the hands into the warm, moist mouth. The germs are thus given an ideal breeding place." And, as if this were not enough, he added: "The effect of thumb-sucking upon the child's personality is the most serious aspect of all". According to him, "millions of mothers who are almost criminally careless" use a pacifier to keep the child quiet and, if they let their offspring suck the thumb, they should be "condemned in progressive communities".

The finger-sucking of babies as such has, of course, no serious effect on personality development. The seriousness derives, instead, from the restraint and coerciveness to which the sucking child is subjected. It derives from the anxiety and from the disapproval which are implied in the parental countermeasures. Such tactics do not even "cure" the habit itself.

There are innumerable children who suck their thumbs at times when they are bored or frustrated. This means that there are innumerable children, as there are adults, who are at times bored or frustrated. There are many children who chew on their fingernails when they are tense. This means that there are many children, as there are adults, who are tense at times. There are many children who do not wish to finish their spinach, others who sob when they are unhappy, who throw themselves on the floor when they are driven into a corner, who insist on remaining before the television set past their decreed bedtime, who have nightmares after an exciting moving picture, or who stubbornly refuse to kiss visiting Aunt Ella, especially when they know that Aunt Ella has halitosis.

All these are everyday reactions of normal young children, who will remain normal unless parental overindulgence turns them into little tyrants, or unless parental perfectionistic disapproval and attempts to make them over cause them to surrender unconditionally and become guilt-laden, literal-minded stuffed shirts, or to remove themselves a bit too far from the unpleasant reality to the nebulous but more enjoyable land of phantasy, or angrily to defy all authority in unchannelled rebellion.

Ordinarily, the everyday reactions do not, and should not, come to psychiatric attention. Those children who are brought to child psychiatrists' offices and clinics have usually started already, at least part of the way, on the road to surrender, withdrawal, or rebellion. The job then is to return them to comfortable and smoothly functioning normalcy. But in the vast majority of instances, the management of normal early resistances, the handling of the little feeding, bedtime, elimination, truth-telling, thumb-sucking, fear, anger, jealousy and other issues should be a matter of parent education, most logically left in the hands of pediatricians. It is the pediatrician who can help parents to understand what is going on between themselves and the child. This is done neither by agitating the parents about the significance of these problems with the prescription of appetizers, tonics, sedatives and tranquillizers nor by using the phrase: "Pay no attention. He'll outgrow it." The overanxious parent needs help to see things in their proper perspective. The obsessive parent needs help to accept her or his child as he is and not as a model of non-existing perfection. I would be more apprehensive about the child who has surrendered to the degree of never showing a so-called problem than about a youngster who learns to assert his spontaneity and identity, if need be with the help of an occasional departure from infantile saintliness.

REFERENCES

ACKERSON, L. (1931) *Children's Behavior Problems* Vol. 1. Chicago University Press.

BERILLON, F. (1908) L'onychophagie est-elle un signe de degenerescence? *Rev. hypnot. psychol. physiol.* **23**, 27.

BILLIG, A. L. (1942) Fingernail biting: its incipiency, incidence and amelioration. *J. Abnorm. (Soc.) Psychol.* **37**, 406.

BRENNEMANN, J. (1932) Psychologic aspects of nutrition in childhood. *J. Pediat.* **1**, 145.

BRIDGE, E. M., LIVINGSTON, S. and TIETZE, C. (1943) Breath holding spells. *J. Pediat.* **23**, 539.

BRUCH, H. (1952) *Don't Be Afraid of Your Child* p. 177. Farrar, Straus & Young, New York.

CRAMER, A. (1912) Funktionelle Neurosen im Kindesalter. In: *Handbuch der Nervenkrankheiten im Kindesalter* p. 40. Karger, Berlin.

GESELL, A., et al. (1940) *The First Five Years of Life* p. 33. Harper, New York.

KANNER, L. (1957) Child Psychiatry (3rd Ed.). Charles C. Thomas, Springfield, Ill.

KANNER, L. (1957) *A Word to Parents About Mental Hygiene.* University of Wisconsin Press, Madison.

LAPOUSE, R. and MONK, M. A. (1957) *An Epidemiologic Study of Behavior Characteristics in Children.* Presented at the Annual Meeting of the American Public Health Association, Cleveland, Ohio, November 12.

LEVY, D. M. (1955) Oppositional syndromes and oppositional behavior. In: *Psychopathology of Childhood* (edited by HOCH and ZUBIN) pp. 204–206. Grune & Stratton, New York.

PENNINGTON, L. A. (1945) The incidence of nailbiting among adults. *American J. Psychiat.* **102**, 241.

THOM, D. A. (1928) *Everyday Problems of the Everyday Child.* Appleon, New York.

WECHSLER, D. (1921) The incidence and significance of fingernail biting in children. *Psychoanal. Rev.* **18**, 201.

WICKMAN, E. K. (1928) *Children's Behavior and Teacher's Attitudes.* Commonwealth Fund, New York.

Stability of deviant behavior through time

HARVEY CLARIZIO, Ed.D.

Most children experience problems in the course of development. The question arises, however, as to whether childhood problems are transient or permanent in nature. In other words, does a child grow out of his problems with increasing age, or does he become a mentally ill adult? The answer to this question is of interest to theoreticians as well as to practitioners. For the theorist, knowledge pertaining to the stability of deviant behavior furthers understanding of both normal personality development and of childhood psychopathology. For the clinician, such knowledge can mean being able not only to predict the outcome of various behavior problems better, but also to focus treatment on the cases most in need of professional intervention.

Clinicians and developmental psychologists have traditionally differed in their answers to this question of stability. The former are more inclined to view childhood problems as chronic in nature whereas the latter view them as transitory. The conflicting views may, in large measure, be a function of the populations studied. Studies based on fairly typical samples of children, for example, indicate that developmental problems are not particularly stable over time. Macfarlane and co-workers,[1] for instance, note that the magnitude of interage correlations of problems suggests a nonpersistence over a long age span. Lapouse and Monk[2] found age to be the variable most closely associated with the amount of behavior deviations, with young children surpassing older children. These authors conclude that behavior deviations in children are an age-bound phenomenon. In brief, studies based on non-psychiatric populations indicate that behavior problems do not tend to be chronic in nature.

The above evidence is based on a developmental approach using samples of normal children whose problems may have been less numerous and less severe than those of children typically referred to psychiatric clinics. How about the child whose problems are sufficiently visible to warrant referral to professional agencies? Does he grow up to be a mentally ill adult, or does he, too, tend to grow out of his problems? Investigations bearing on this issue have been of two kinds—retrospective studies and follow-up studies.

MENTAL HYGIENE, 1968, Vol. 52, pp. 288-293.

In retrospective studies, mentally ill adults are selected as subjects; and their childhood histories are reconstructed through the use of case studies, interviews with parents and teachers, inventories, and other means. Illustrative of this approach is the study by Kasanin and Veo [3] in which school histories were obtained through teacher interviews on 54 hospitalized adult psychotics. The subjects had a mean age of 20 years and were classified according to one of five categories on the basis of their earlier school histories. Of the 54 psychotics, half were placed in the three categories representing adequate adjustment (fairly well-adjusted, well-adjusted, and school leaders). Fifteen of the subjects were the "nobodies," that is, people whom the teachers could not remember. Only 15 of the 54 patients fell into the "peculiar and difficult" category. This latter finding is rather striking since, from the standpoint of rater bias, one would have expected the teacher's knowledge of the former student's hospitalization to have influenced her recall of the deviant aspects of his earlier behavior. Thus, even though the method should have facilitated the findings of a closer relationship between child and adult disorder, only moderate support was found to support such a hypothesis.

Bower and co-workers,[4] despite efforts to control teacher rater bias, found relatively similar results in their retrospective studies. Although teachers seemingly recognized the onset of schizophrenia among their former students, those who later became schizophrenic were not typically viewed by the teacher as being emotionally sick or as having major problems. The subjects did differ from control subjects with respect to teacher ratings; yet, on the basis of high school ratings, predictions regarding later adult pathology would not have been accurate.

A major methodologic difficulty with retrospective studies is that we do not know how many other children showed similar symptoms during the school years and yet grew up to be normal. This limitation is well exemplified in a study by Renaud and Estes,[5] who studied 100 mentally healthy adults and found that a significant proportion of them had had pathogenic childhoods. Traumatic and pathological events were so common that, had the subjects been plagued with psychosomatic or neurotic disorders, background factors could easily have been identified and have led to the erroneous conclusion that disturbed children become disturbed adults. Schofield and Balian,[6] in studying 150 normal adults, also found that nearly one-fourth of their subjects had histories of psychic trauma.

Another serious limitation in studies of this sort involves reliance on the memories of adults who knew the subject as a child. The memories of informants are, unfortunately, most likely influenced by knowledge of the psychiatric adult status. Informants may thus selectively forget certain incidents or tend to remember the unusual.

It would appear that, in the light of present findings and methodologic limitations, retrospective studies offer at best only moderate evidence to support the notion that the maladjusted child grows up to be the maladjusted adult.

The other major approach involves follow-up studies in which children seen by child guidance clinics are re-evaluated after a period of time has elapsed. The results of this approach vary appreciably with the criterion of mental health or illness used at the time of follow-up. When clinical judgment of the psychiatric interviewer is used as the criterion, the results suggest that subjects who show maladjustment as children will show maladjustment as adults.

In one of the best-known follow-up studies, Robbins [7] studied 525 children who had been referred to the same St. Louis Municipal Clinic between 1924 and 1929. Thirty years later the adult psychiatric and social status of these subjects was compared with that of 100 control subjects. In an evaluation of the adult psychiatric status of the subjects available for follow-up, only 20 per cent of the former patients fell into the "no disease" category, whereas 52 per cent of the control group were so classified. As adults, 34 per cent of the former child guidance patients were characterized by seriously disabling symptoms as compared with 8 per cent of the matched group of control subjects. Differences were markedly greater in the incidence of sociopathic personalities and somewhat greater for psychotic disorders and alcoholism. There was, however, little difference between the two groups in the rate of neurotic disturbances. Such behavior as shyness, nervousness, fears, tantrums, seclusiveness, hypersensitiveness, tics, irritability, and speech defects was not related to adult psychiatric outcomes. This finding suggests that neurotic symptoms in childhood are not predictive of adult neurosis. In fact, the control group subjects had a slightly higher rate of neurosis as adults than did the former patients. Interestingly enough, it was not withdrawn behavior that characterized the preschizophrenic group, but aggressive acting-out behavior of an antisocial nature.

In general, the findings of this study suggest that former childhood patients, especially those who engage in seriously antisocial behavior, contribute more than their share to adult mental disorders. The emphasis on clinic treatment of delinquency in the 1920's, differences among the groups with respect to socio-economic status, the question as to how representative the sample is of other populations, and possible contamination of psychiatric judgments through awareness of the subjects' past history illustrate some of the difficulties associated with this long-term follow-up study.

Another major follow-up study, which used a more demanding criterion of mental illness, namely, admission to a mental hospital, arrived at a somewhat different conclusion.[8] The subjects were 54 childhood patients who had been classified as "internal reactors" at the Dallas Guidance Clinic some 16 to 27 years earlier. Upon follow-up the majority of these subjects were found to have achieved a satisfactory adjustment. Just one-third of the group was seen as marginally adjusted, and only one subject had been hospitalized. Later analysis of data obtained from this same clinic suggests, as was true in the St. Louis follow-up study, that withdrawn and introverted youngsters have a low probability of developing schizophrenia. Schizophrenics were found more among the "ambiverts" than among the "introverts" and "extroverts." Former child patients at the Judge Baker Clinic who later became hospitalized as schizophrenics also had histories characterized by theft, truancy, running away, and antisocial sexual activity.[9]

What can we conclude in the light of the available evidence? It should be noted that conclusions must be tentative because there has been no study specifically designed to measure the stability of deviant behavior over time and because of the methodologic shortcomings of past studies. Bearing the above limitations in mind, the following tentative conclusions are advanced:

1. It appears that certain types of disturbed children do contribute more than their share to the population of adult psychiatric disability. The extent of overlap between childhood and adult disturbance remains uncertain, however. This is an area badly in need of additional extensive, longitudinal research, for it is neither judicious nor pragmatic, especially in view of the shortage of mental health specialists, to treat all disturbed children if, for example, only 25 per cent will become significantly maladjusted as adults.

2. Although it is commonly assumed that adult behavior and personality are established in early life experiences and although

there is a body of empirical research demonstrating the stability of personality over time, there is nonetheless a genuine danger in overgeneralization. The possibility of this type of error is well illustrated in Robbins' [7] finding that more than one-third of diagnosed sociopaths showed a marked decrease in antisocial behavior in later life. Though these improved sociopaths by no means became ideal citizens, the fact that more than one-third of this seriously antisocial population did improve noticeably challenges the notion of incorrigibility commonly associated with this diagnosis.

3. In large measure, the stability of the behavior deviation depends on the nature of the problem in question as well as the child's environment. Normal problem behavior that occurs as developmental phenomena seems to have a very high probability of being resolved with increasing age.

Clinical problems, though having a lower probability of improvement than those of a developmental nature, also seem to have a reasonably high probability of spontaneous remission.

Since it is obviously misleading to speak of clinical problems as a homogeneous entity, we have, in the following table, categorized specific clinical problems on the basis of follow-up studies as tending to be either chronic or transitory in nature.

We must not lose sight of the environment in which the individual must function as a major factor in his total adjustment. A dependent adult may, for instance, achieve an adequate adjustment if he has a supportive employer who will take time to give him the attention and direction he needs. Similarly, an individual with strong oppositional tendencies may not experience adjustment difficulties if he has a job in

Stability of clinically deviant behavior through time

Investigator	Relatively transitory	Relatively permanent
Robbins [7]	Tics Seclusiveness Nervousness Fears Tantrums Hypersensitiveness Speech defects	
Michael, Morris and Soroker [10]	Shyness	
Coolidge, Brodie and Feeney [11]	School phobia (47 of 49 returned to school)	
Balow [12]		Severe reading problems (needed continued supportive instruction)
Levitt, Beiser and Robertson [13]	Neurotic disorders (three-fourths improved)	
Berkowitz [14]	Predelinquent behavior (three-fourths had no record of delinquency)	
Robbins [7]	Sociopathic behavior (one-third showed moderate improvement)	Sociopathic behavior (two-thirds unimproved)
Eisenberg [15]	Autistic behavior (if useful speech was present by age 5)	Autistic behavior (if mute by age 5)
Eisenberg [16]	Childhood schizophrenia (one-fourth achieved a moderately good social adjustment)	Childhood schizophrenia (three-fourths either attained a marginal adjustment or required continuous institutional care)

which he is able to work under conditions of minimal supervision and has an easygoing, submissive wife. Thus, even if personality characteristics remain perfectly constant, we can expect some change in the individual's behavior as a consequence of environmental contingencies.

4. Somewhat contrary to prevailing clinical belief, it is aggressive, antisocial, acting-out behavior of a severe nature that is most predictive of later significant adult disturbance and most deserving of our treatment efforts. In addition to the evidence cited earlier, Roff [17] found that reliable group predictions of military adjustment could be made on the basis of earlier social adjustment in school. Children who were mean and disliked by their classmates commonly had bad conduct records in military service.

5. Although two of three unsocialized, aggressive youngsters continue in their antisocial ways, it must not be assumed that the majority of young norm violators become adult criminals. For, as Kvaraceus [18] points out, it is widely agreed that much juvenile delinquency does not inevitably terminate in adult criminal activity. There appears to be a curvilinear relationship between delinquent activity and age. After reaching a peak at age 16, the "delinquency curve" begins to level off. [19]

6. Shyness or withdrawn behavior tends to disappear with advancing age. Moreover, there is little evidence to suggest that shyness is predictive of later schizophrenia despite the fact that clinicians often view introverted behavior as having dire consequences for mental health. There is a vast difference between the child who can relate and does not, or who wants to relate and lacks the necessary social skills, and the child who cannot relate because of a severe basic incapacity. The best evidence to date suggests that the preschizophrenic child is characterized by both antisocial behavior and serious non-antisocial symptoms. [7]

7. Neurotic symptoms (fears, hypersensi-tiveness, tics, etc.) often presumed to be the precursors of adult neurotic disturbances have also been found lacking in prognostic power. The findings of current empirical research challenge the long-held assumptions that adult neurotic behavior results from disturbances in parent-child relations or from parental loss in childhood. [7]

8. The probabilities of remission as characteristic of childhood schizophrenia and infantile autism are indeed low. Yet, although these severe disabilities definitely tend to persist through time, about one in four of those so diagnosed apparently achieves a reasonably adequate adjustment. [16]

9. Generally speaking, it is very difficult to postulate any direct causal relationships between early childhood maladjustment and later specific psychiatric disability. We do know that a goodly number of disturbed children will grow up to attain a reasonably adequate adult adjustment. The truth of the matter is, however, that we still do not fully understand the role of later experiences on personality adjustment. Also, we must not overlook the possibility that some adult disturbances arise independently of childhood problems.

In our present state of knowledge, we can conclude that there is at best only mild or moderate evidence to support the notion that disturbed children turn into disturbed adults. Since the less noxious childhood disorders (e.g., shyness) are more common than the more severe disorders (e.g., childhood schizophrenia), it would seem that, all in all, change appears to characterize the course of behavior deviations in children as much as, or more than, chronicity or stability. The conception of emotional disturbance in children as a progressively deteriorating condition is thus called into question.

REFERENCES

1. Macfarlane, J., Allen, L., and Honzik, M.: A Developmental Study of the Behavior Problems of

Normal Children Between Twenty-one Months and Fourteen Years. Berkeley, Calif., University of California Press, 1954.

2. Lapouse, R., and Monk, M.: American Journal of Orthopsychiatry, 34:436, 1964.

3. Kasanin, J., and Veo, L.: American Journal of Orthopsychiatry, 2:212, 1932.

4. Bower, E., Shellhammer, T., Daily, J., and Bower, M.: High School Students Who Later Became Schizophrenic. Sacramento, Calif., State Department of Education, 1960.

5. Renaud, H., and Estes, F.: American Journal of Orthopsychiatry, 31:786, 1961.

6. Schofield, W., and Balian, L.: Journal of Abnormal and Social Psychology, 59:216, 1959.

7. Robbins, L.: Deviant Children Grown Up. Baltimore, Williams and Wilkins, 1966.

8. Morris, D., Soroker, E., and Burrus, G.: American Journal of Orthopsychiatry, 24:743, 1954.

9. Nameche, G., Waring, M., and Ricks, D.: Journal of Nervous and Mental Disease, 139:232, 1964.

10. Michael, C., Morris, D., and Soroker, E.: American Journal of Orthopsychiatry, 27:331, 1957.

11. Coolidge, J., Brodie, R., and Feeney, B.: American Journal of Orthopsychiatry, 34:675, 1964.

12. Balow, B.: The Reading Teacher, 18:581 (April), 1965.

13. Levitt, E., Beiser, H., and Robertson, R.: American Journal of Orthopsychiatry, 29:337, 1959.

14. Berkowitz, B.: The Nervous Child, 11:42, 1955.

15. Eisenberg, L.: American Journal of Psychiatry, 112:607, 1956.

16. Eisenberg, L.: A.M.A. Archives of Neurology and Psychiatry, 78:69, 1957.

17. Roff, M.: Journal of Abnormal and Social Psychology, 63:333, 1961.

18. Kvaraceus, W.: Early Identification and Prevention. In: Wattenberg, W. (ed.): Social Deviancy among Youth. Chicago, University of Chicago Press, 1966, pp. 189–220.

19. Miller, W.: Quoted by W. Kvaraceus (Reference 18).

Ordinal Position and Behavior Problems in Children

JACOB TUCKMAN AND RICHARD A. REGAN

SINCE antiquity, the general belief has been that there are unique and well defined risks and benefits connected with ordinal position of each child in the family. The first born has special status. Even apart from considerations of inheritance, he is the center of attention and his wants and needs are frequently attended to, to the point of indulgence. If continued over too long a period, the child runs the risk of developing dependency habits which ultimately interfere with personal and social adjustment. With the arrival of a brother or sister the older child's way of life is threatened, which may lead to feelings of anxiety, jealousy, and hostility. Unless handled properly by the parents these feelings lead to immature or excessive modes of adjustment in the older child.

Although the oldest child historically has enjoyed prestige in the family hierarchy, he is often confronted with a situation requiring a wide range of adjustments because the parents are more likely to be youthful and immature, to be stricter, and to be over-eager for accomplishments in the first born. For the youngest child, the situation in the family is less demanding but more protective. If continued over too long a time, this situation often makes it more difficult for him to establish independence. This would also apply to the middle child (children) in larger families when many years separate siblings. In most larger families, however, the middle child probably receives less parental attention and affection than those older or younger but he may also escape overdoses of the restrictions typically seen

for the oldest and of the over-protection for the youngest.

With the advent of more dynamic views of personality development, attempts were made to spell out the importance of each position for character development. Adler [1] defined, in perhaps greatest detail at the time, the special environmental pressures and opportunities to which each position was uniquely subjected. He saw danger for any child when infantile patterns of behavior become his life-style: the oldest child tends to become a leader in fear of authority as well as in fear of encroachments from below; the second child tends to be less concerned with authority, responsibility and absolute power but more with competition with his peers; the youngest tends toward an inflated self-esteem accompanied by uneasy consciousness of actual weaknesses.

More recently Bossard [2] emphasized the importance of birth order in role differentiation in the large family. Using such variables as "density of interaction," "availability of supplies," and "availability of roles," he summarized role specialization as follows: the oldest child is "responsible"; the second child is "sociable" or "popular"; and the youngest is "spoiled." Other roles are defined, but do not follow a definite birth order. Some children take on certain roles because other roles, e.g., "social

[1] A. Adler, *The Practice and Theory of Individual Psychology,* New York: Harcourt, Brace and Company, 1929.

[2] J. H. S. Bossard, "Personality Roles in the Large Family," *Child Development,* 26 (1955), pp. 71–78.

JOURNAL OF HEALTH AND SOCIAL BEHAVIOR, 1967, Vol. 8, pp. 32-39.

57

butterfly" have already been chosen by older children.

Early empirical investigations of birth order showed more mental retardation,[3] schizophrenia,[4] and alcoholism [5] among later-borns than among earlier-borns. In a number of these studies, the relationship disappeared when family size was controlled.[6] Schooler [7] suggested that the higher rate of schizophrenia for later-borns than for earlier-borns, even when controlled for family size, may be accounted for by age of the mother with accompanying changes in intrauterine environment; this suggestion may be even more relevant for mental retardation. Related to the studies referred to above were those by Terman [8] on the gifted child and by Cattell [9] on men of science, in which both found that the gifted were more likely to be first-borns or earlier-borns.

More recent investigations have focused on differences in personality and behavior among siblings. Among college students, Wrightsman [10] found that for first-borns more than for later-borns, situationally produced anxiety was reduced by the presence of other persons. Glass et al.[11] found later-borns reacted with greater annoyance to a frustrating agent. With younger children,

Krall [12] found a tendency for "accident prone" children to be late in the birth order.

The studies referred to so far have indicated better adjustment by first-borns. In contrast, from retrospectively written life histories and from interviews and family case records, Bossard and Boll [13] found that in families with six or more children, first-borns had the poorest adjustment record, middle children had the best, and the youngest had in-between adjustment; this was true for both males and females. Sears, Maccoby and Lewin,[14] and Henry [15] reported that the oldest child was more likely to be disciplined by the father and to show greater aggression toward authority. Lasko [16] reported that parental behavior toward the first child was less warm, more restrictive and coercive, and less consistent over the years.

In two-child families, Koch [17] found that the first-born tended more often than the second-born to view the mother as favoring the sibling and to see the father as more impartial; Vuyks [18] found that older siblings behaved more like the father, were less attached to the parents, were less spontaneous and vivacious, but more serious and calm than younger siblings. Implicit in the two studies is a differential adjustment depending upon the sex of the older child. It would be reasonable to suggest that identification with the father would facilitate

[3] E. Huntington, *Season of Birth; Its Relation to Human Abilities,* New York: Wiley, 1938.

[4] B. Malzberg, *Social and Biological Aspects of Mental Disease,* Utica, N.Y.: State Hospitals Press, 1940.

[5] D. Bakan, "The Relationship Between Alcoholism and Birth Rank," *Quarterly Journal of Studies on Alcohol,* 10 (1949), pp. 434–440.

[6] R. G. Smart, "Alcoholism, Birth Order and Family Size," *Journal of Abnormal and Social Psychology,* 66 (1963), pp. 17–23.

[7] C. Schooler, "Birth Order and Schizophrenia," *Archives of General Psychiatry,* 4 (1961), pp. 91–97.

[8] L. M. Terman, "The Gifted Child," in C. Murchison (Ed), *A Handbook on Child Psychology,* Worcester: Clark University Press, 1931.

[9] J. McK. Cattell, "Families of American Men of Science," *Scientific Monthly,* 4 (1917), pp. 248–262.

[10] L. S. Wrightsman, Jr., "Effects of Waiting with Others on Changes in Level of Felt Anxiety," *Journal of Abnormal and Social Psychology,* 61 (1960), pp. 216–222.

[11] D. C. Glass, M. Horwitz, I. Firestone and J. Grinker, "Birth Order and Relations to Frustration," *Journal of Abnormal and Social Psychology,* 66 (1963), pp. 192–194.

[12] V. Krall, "Personality Characteristics of Accident Repeating Children," *Journal of Abnormal and Social Psychology,* 48 (1953), pp. 99–108.

[13] J. H. S. Bossard and E. Boll, *The Large Family System,* Philadelphia: University of Pennsylvania Press, 1956.

[14] R. R. Sears, E. E. Maccoby, and H. Lewin, *Patterns of Child Living,* Evanston, Ill.: Row, Peterson, 1957.

[15] A. F. Henry, "Sibling Structure and Perception of the Disciplinary Roles of Parents," *Sociometry,* 20 (1957), pp. 67–74.

[16] J. K. Lasko, "Parent Behavior Toward First and Second Children," *Genetic Psychology Monographs,* 49 (1954), pp. 97–137.

[17] H. L. Koch, "Some Personality Correlates of Sex, Sibling Position, and Sex of Sibling Among Five- and Six-Year-Old Children," *Genetic Psychology Monographs,* 52 (1955), pp. 3–51.

[18] R. Vuyks, "Eltern Vergleichen Ihre Beiden Kinder" (Parents Compare Their Two Children). *Schweizerische Zeitschrift für Psychologie und ihre Anwendungen,* 20 (1961), pp. 224–237.

adjustment if the child were a male but would create problems if the child were a female.

The empirical studies referred to above do not provide a definitive answer to the problem regarding the relationship of position in the family to personal and social adjustment because of variation in criteria of adjustment, variation in or failure to control for size of family, failure to use actual position in the family, and differences in the composition of samples. The present study attempts to meet some of these limitations by looking at specific positions in two-child, three-child, and four-or more child families and by covering a broader range of behavioral problems in children admitted to outpatient psychiatric clinics.

SAMPLE AND PROCEDURE

From a broader study of children referred to outpatient psychiatric clinics in Philadelphia,[19] data on position of the child in the family, by race, sex, and age were available for 1,297 children of a total clinic population of 1,813. Three hundred and four "only" children were not included in the study, and information was not stated on age, race, size of family and position in family (or a combination of several of these) for 212 children. Of the 212, data on race, alone or in combination with other factors, were not available for 101 children. The percentage distribution of these race "not stated" cases fell about midway between the obtained percentages for whites and Negroes so far as family size was concerned. The absence of such data was probably a result of poor information collection in the clinics rather than any other biasing factor.

Of the 1,297 children in the present study, 67 percent were male and 33 percent female; 78 percent were white and 22 percent nonwhite; 15 percent were under 6 years of age, 51 percent from 6 to 11 years of age, and 34 percent from 12 to 17 years of age. Boys were overrepresented in the

clinic population, a typical finding.[20, 21, 22] Whites and nonwhites were represented to about the same extent as in the general population of Philadelphia based on the 1960 census.[23] Children under 6 years of age were greatly underrepresented in the clinic sample (15 percent in the clinic and 30 percent in the general population), those 6 to 11 were greatly overrepresented (51 percent in the clinic and 34 percent in the general population), and those from 12 to 17 were slightly overrepresented (34 percent and 27 percent, respectively).

Family size ranged from two to 11 children but the small number of larger families made it necessary to collapse the data into three categories: two-child, three-child, and four-or-more child families. For two-child and three-child families, the actual position was used; for four-or-more, three positions were used: the oldest child, the youngest child, and a middle group of children. Two-child, three-child, and four-or-more child families were represented approximately to the same extent in the clinic as in the general population[24] for Philadelphia (50 percent, 25 percent, and 25 percent, respectively, in the clinic, and 50 percent, 28 percent, and 22 percent, in the general population). The clinic figures assumed that each child represented a separate family, being based on estimates by the largest clinics that a maximum of 2 percent of the children came from the same families.

The referral problems were classified according to the 12 categories developed in the earlier study:

[19] J. Tuckman and M. Lavell, *A Study of Children Admitted to Philadelphia Outpatient Psychiatric Clinics in 1955*, Department of Public Health, City of Philadelphia, 1958.

[20] J. L. Roach, O. Gurrslin and R. G. Hunt, "Some Socio-Psychological Characteristics of a Child-Guidance Clinic Caseload," *Journal of Consulting Psychology*, 22 (1958), pp. 183–186.

[21] F. N. Anderson and H. C. Dean, "Some Aspects of Child Guidance Intake Policy and Practices," *Public Health Monograph No. 42*, U. S. Department of Health, Education and Welfare, U. S. Government Printing Office, Washington, D.C., 1956.

[22] G. M. Gilbert, "A Study of Referral Problems in Metropolitan Child Guidance Centers," *Journal of Clinical Psychology*, 13 (1957), pp. 37–42.

[23] Bureau of the Census, *U. S. Census of Population: 1960*, "Detailed Characteristics, Pennsylvania," Final Report PC(1)–40D, U. S. Government Printing Office, Washington, D.C., 1962.

[24] Bureau of the Census, 1962, *ibid.*

1. Anxiety and neurotic symptoms, e.g., fears, nail biting, depression, inferiority feelings, perfectionism, tendency to worry, nightmares.
2. Severe psychiatric symptoms, e.g., bizarre thinking or behavior, conversion symptoms, self-harm, ritualistic behavior.
3. Withdrawal behavior, e.g., daydreaming, passivity, seclusiveness, shyness.
4. School problems, e.g., poor school work, truancy, cheating, school phobia, tardiness.
5. Mental retardation.
6. Aggression, e.g., temper tantrums, disobedience, cruelty, running away from home.
7. Antisocial behavior, e.g., stealing, firesetting, delinquency.
8. Difficulties in interpersonal relationships, e.g., sibling rivalry, quarrelsome with playmates, "show-off."
9. Somatic symptoms, e.g., convulsions, asthma, overweight, diarrhea.
10. Problems of habit formation, e.g., enuresis, sleep problems, feeding problems.
11. Sexual problems.
12. Miscellaneous, e.g., emotional immaturity, slowness, inattentiveness.

Problem categories and not number of problems within the category were used. For example, a child referred to a clinic because of poor school work, truancy, and cheating in class was counted as one individual with one school problem. The number of problems (categories) ranged from one to eight: one reported in 28 percent of the cases; two, in 34 percent; three, in 24 percent; and four to eight, in 14 percent.

RESULTS

There was a significant difference between the clinic sample and general population of Philadelphia regarding the distribution of position by family size (Table 1).

In each of the three sized families the oldest child was overrepresented in the clinic sample while the youngest child was underrepresented. The middle child was overrepresented in the three-child but underrepresented in the four-or-more child family.

Table 2 shows that for children from two-child families, five of the problem categories were significantly related to position in the family. The older child was differentiated from the younger by a greater percent of referrals for anxiety and neurotic symptoms, severe psychiatric symptoms, aggressive behavior, and problems in interpersonal relations; the younger child was referred more often for problems involving mental retardation. Separate analyses for sex, race, and age, also shown in Table 2, indicated that the contribution to the differences between the older and younger child was greater for race than for sex and age. For the five referral problems significantly related to family position, whites contributed to all five; males to three and females to one; children under 6 years of age to one, 6–11 year-olds to two, and 12–17 year-olds to one problem. Other subfactors which were significant when the overall test was not significant can only be interpreted as random variations.

Table 3 shows that of the five problems that differentiated sibling position in the two-child family, only two, mental retardation and interpersonal relations, differentiated position in the three-child family but not as distinct positions. In problems of mental retardation, the middle child behaved like the oldest; in problems of interpersonal relations, like the younger. For mental retardation only the subfactor, children under 6 years of age, contributed sig-

TABLE 1. PERCENT OBSERVED AND PERCENT EXPECTED (IN PARENTHESES) OF DIFFERENT POSITIONS IN EACH SIZE FAMILY

Size of Family	Oldest	Middle	Youngest	Total
2-child	58 (50)	. . . .	42 (50)	100
3-child	39 (33)	41 (33)	20 (33)	100
4-or more *	28 (21)	53 (58)	18 (21)	100
Total	46 (39)	24 (23)	30 (39)	100

* Based on the U. S. Census of Population for Philadelphia for 1960, the average or expected number of children in families with four or more children was 4.754.
Overall $\chi^2 = 55.5$; df=3; p < .001.

Factor	Position[b]	N	Anxiety	Severe Psychiatric	School Problems	Aggression	Antisocial	Withdrawal	Somatic	Habit Formation	Sex Problems	Mental Retardation	Interpersonal Relations	Miscellaneous
Total	O	374	53	11	39	52	6	15	14	25	3	2	25	12
	Y	270	44 *	6 *	41	42 **	8	13	13	28	6	6 *	15 **	11
Male	O	257	48	11	43	54	7	15	14	21	2	1	28	13
	Y	174	44	5 *	48	44 *	10	14	12	31 *	2	3	14 **	14
Female	O	117	64	12	31	48	4	15	13	35	3	5	18	9
	Y	96	45 *	7	28	38	5	11	17	24	1	9	17	5
White	O	322	57	11	38	50	7	16	14	26	3	1	26	12
	Y	238	46 *	6 *	40	39 **	7	14	13	29	2	5 **	16 **	12
Nonwhite	O	52	37	13	50	65	4	12	10	21	(4)	12	17	(10)
	Y	32	31	(3)	44	63	(16)	(6)	(13)	22	(3)	(6)	(9)	(6)
<6 Yrs.	O	73	53	(7)	(3)	55	—	12	15	32	—	7	21	15
	Y	48	35	(4)	(4)	44	— N.T.	(2) *	13	54 *	— N.T.	(15)	(4) *	13
6–11 Yrs.	O	191	53	8	43	56	7	16	13	22	2	2	26	13
	Y	144	46	6	52	38 **	10	15	14	33 *	1	3	15 *	13
12–17 Yrs.	O	110	53	19	57	45	10	15	14	19	5	(1)	25	7
	Y	78	47	8 *	42 *	46	10	18	13	7 *	(5)	(5)	22	8

[a] Percents in parenthesis indicate expected frequency less than 5; N.T.: no test made.
[b] O—oldest child; Y—youngest child.
* χ^2 significant at 5 percent level.
** χ^2 significant at 1 percent level.

nificantly to positional differences; for problems of interpersonal relations, whites, children 6 to 11 years, and those 12 to 17 contributed. Again, other subfactors which were significant when the overall test was not, can only be ascribed to random variation.

For three-child families, miscellaneous problems also differentiated position but the meaningfulness of this finding is difficult to evaluate.

Table 4 shows that for children from 4- to 11-child families, none of the problems differentiated position in the family, categorized as oldest, youngest, and all in-between children.

DISCUSSION AND CONCLUSIONS

The findings that older children coming from two-child families were more likely than younger children to be referred to an outpatient psychiatric clinic for anxiety and neurotic symptoms, severe psychiatric symptoms, aggressive behavior and for difficulties in interpersonal relations suggest that these problems are reactions to threat of loss of position or actual displacement as the center of attention with the birth of a younger sibling. These findings are in agreement with the prevalent theory and observation about the adverse effects of sibling rivalry on the older child, and are also supported when the "only" child is compared with the older child from two-child families.[25] The "only" child showed less anxiety than the older child (42 percent compared with 53 percent), fewer severe

[25] J. Tuckman and R. A. Regan, "Size of Family and Behavioral Problems in Children," *Journal of Genetic Psychology* (in press).

psychiatric symptoms (7 percent compared with 11 percent), less aggressive behavior (47 percent compared with 52 percent), and less difficulty in interpersonal relations (18 percent compared with 25 percent). This strongly indicated that the birth of a younger sibling aggravates or disturbs the existing situation. In the two-child family, the older child was referred less frequently for problems involving mental retardation but it seems to be more reasonable to in-terpret this finding on physical and physio-logical grounds, i.e., declining capacity for childbearing for reasons of age and poor health, rather than as a behavioral reaction to threat with the birth of a sibling.

The subfactors of age, sex, and race con-tributed differentially to the observed dif-ferences in referral problems between older and younger children but there are other factors not covered in this study which may have equal or even greater relevance. One

TABLE 3. THREE-CHILD FAMILY: RELATION OF SIBLING POSITION TO REFERRAL PROBLEMS (IN PERCENTAGES [a])

Factor	Position [b]	N	Anxiety	Severe Psychiatric	School Problems	Aggression	Antisocial	Withdrawal	Somatic	Habit Formation	Sex Problems	Mental Retardation	Interpersonal Relations	Miscellaneous
Total	O	129	41	5	47	46	11	19	20	16	4	5	26	32
	M	136	39	3	46	40	8	17	16	22	5	5	12	13
	Y	65	31	(8)	46	46	3	6	17	20	(3)	17	15	9
												**	*	**
Male	O	88	32	(5)	50	51	15	18	11	15	(3)	6	25	34
	M	99	41	—	50	42	7	16	18	20	(3)	6	12	15
	Y	35	34	(6)	63	51	(6)	3	9	26	(3)	(9)	17	11
				N.T.			*				N.T.			**
Female	O	41	61	(5)	39	34	(2)	20	39	20	(5)	(2)	27	27
	M	37	32	(11)	35	32	(11)	19	11	27	(11)	(3)	11	8
	Y	30	27	(10)	27	40	—	10	27	13	(3)	(27)	13	(7)
			*				N.T.		*		N.T.			**
White	O	95	40	(4)	46	47	13	21	20	18	(3)	3	27	34
	M	108	41	3	45	37	7	19	18	25	(4)	5	12	12
	Y	56	27	(9)	46	43	(4)	7	14	23	(4)	(18)	16	9
													*	**
Nonwhite	O	34	44	(6)	47	41	(6)	(12)	21	(12)	(6)	(9)	21	27
	M	28	32	(4)	46	50	(14)	(7)	11	(11)	(11)	(7)	(11)	18
	Y	9	(44)	—	(44)	(67)	—	—	(33)	—	—	(11)	(11)	(11)
				N.T.			N.T.	N.T.		N.T.	N.T.	N.T.		
<6 Yrs.	O	11	(55)	(18)	(9)	36	—	(9)	(18)	(27)	—	(18)	—	(36)
	M	22	32	—	(5)	55	5	(5)	(23)	41	5	14	18	(14)
	Y	18	17	(6)	(22)	39	—	(6)	(22)	33	—	56	—	(6)
				N.T.	N.T.		N.T.	N.T.			N.T.	**	N.T.	
6–11 Yrs.	O	85	42	(2)	45	49	13	15	22	20	(1)	(5)	25	29
	M	73	37	(3)	51	40	4	19	15	23	(4)	(4)	10	15
	Y	31	39	(10)	52	58	—	10	16	16	—	(3)	23	10
							**				N.T.	N.T.	*	*
12–17 Yrs.	O	33	33	(6)	64	39	(9)	30	15	(3)	(12)	—	36	36
	M	41	46	(5)	59	32	17	20	35	(10)	(7)	2	12	10
	Y	16	31	(6)	63	31	(13)	—	(13)	(13)	(13)	—	(19)	(13)
				N.T.								N.T.	*	**

[a] Percents in parenthesis indicate expected frequency less than 5; where deemed necessary, groups were combined; where not feasible, no test was made (N.T.).

[b] O—oldest child; M—middle child; Y—youngest child.

* χ^2 significant at 5 percent level.

** χ^2 significant at 1 percent level.

TABLE 4. FOUR TO 11 CHILD FAMILY: RELATION OF SIBLING POSITION TO REFERRAL PROBLEMS (IN PERCENTAGES [a])

Factor	Position[b]	N	Anxiety	Severe Psychiatric	School Problems	Aggression	Antisocial	Withdrawal	Somatic	Habit Formation	Sex Problems	Mental Retardation	Interpersonal Relations	Miscellaneous
Total	O	92	34	2	58	48	21	15	8	18	(9)	(2)	16	8
	M	172	31	6	48	46	19	11	13	17	3	2	11	5
	Y	59	32	(15)	44	31	7	10	19	19	(3)	(10)	15	(7)
Male	O	62	29	—	61	45	19	16	8	19	(10)	(2)	15	(6)
	M	119	27	6	53	50	21	10	10	13	4	(2)	11	6
	Y	33	21	(9)	39	33	9	(9)	(9)	18	(3)	(12)	(15)	(9)
											*	N.T.		
Female	O	30	43	(7)	50	53	(23)	(13)	7	20	(3)	(3)	(20)	(10)
	M	53	40	6	38	38	15	13	21	25	—	(4)	11	(4)
	Y	26	46	(23)	50	27	(4)	(12)	31	19	(4)	(8)	(15)	(4)
											N.T.	N.T.		N.T.
White	O	55	38	(2)	45	42	20	18	11	24	(7)	(2)	16	(11)
	M	96	29	4	49	49	19	10	12	20	(4)	(1)	11	6
	Y	39	36	(15)	41	36	8	(5)	18	21	(3)	(13)	13	(10)
											N.T.	N.T.		
Nonwhite	O	37	27	(3)	76	57	22	11	3	11	(11)	(3)	16	(3)
	M	76	33	8	47	42	20	12	16	13	(1)	(4)	11	(4)
	Y	20	25	(15)	50	20	(5)	(20)	(20)	(15)	(5)	(5)	(20)	—
						*			*		N.T.	N.T.		N.T.
<6 Yrs.	O	0	—	—	—	—	—	—	—	—	—	—	—	—
	M	14	(29)	7	7	(29)	—	14	7	50	—	(14)	7	—
	Y	8	(13)	—	—	(25)	—	—	—	(50)	—	(63)	—	—
			N.T.	N.T.	N.T.	N.T.	N.T.	N.T.	N.T.		N.T.	N.T.	N.T.	N.T.
6–11 Yrs.	O	45	33	(4)	60	47	13	18	9	22	7	4	18	(9)
	M	76	30	(1)	50	49	20	10	15	18	—	—	8	11
	Y	21	33	(14)	62	43	(10)	(10)	(14)	(29)	—	—	(19)	(10)
				N.T.							N.T.	N.T.		
12–17 Yrs.	O	47	34	—	55	49	28	13	6	15	(11)	—	15	(6)
	M	82	32	10	54	46	22	13	13	10	6	(2)	15	(1)
	Y	30	37	(20)	43	23	7	(13)	(27)	(3)	(7)	(3)	(17)	(7)
				*								N.T.		N.T.

[a] Percents in parenthesis indicate expected frequency less than 5; where deemed necessary, groups were combined; where not feasible, no test was made (N.T.).
[b] O—oldest child; M—middle child; Y—youngest child.
* χ^2 significant at 5 percent level.
** χ^2 significant at 1 percent level.

may be the sexes of the children in the two-child family. Presumably the interaction between the children and with the parents would be quite different if the offspring were of the same sex than if they were cross-sex siblings. Another factor may be the spacing of the siblings. Here too, the effect on the older child would be quite different if the age differences between the two siblings were one or two years than if they were five, 10, or 15.

Although in two-child families there were differences between older and younger, as family size increased, the differentiation among positions in the family tended to disappear. In three-child families, excluding mental retardation and miscellaneous problems which are not relevant to our discussion at this point, the only problem showing a significant difference by family position was interpersonal relations, but here the differentiation was between the oldest and the two younger children and not among the three positions. In four-or-more child families, none of the problems showed a significant positional difference. The finding of lack of differentiation in position as family size increased may be accounted for by a number of factors including changes in parental attitudes and behavior, greater experience in dealing with children, increasing importance of influences outside the home, and increasing ability on the part of the older child in dealing with anxiety, aggression, and interpersonal relations.

Although positional differences for individual problems tended to disappear as family size increased, the data regarding the overrepresentation in the clinic population of the oldest child in all sized families suggests that there were residual effects despite factors operating to minimize specific adjustment difficulties. By contrast, the underrepresentation in the clinic population of the youngest child in all sized families suggests that he was in a more advantageous position, receiving more attention, care and protection. The overrepresentation of the middle child in three-child, but underrepresentation in four-or more child, families suggests that his adjustment was somewhere between the oldest and the youngest. This inconsistency may be due to the fact that he did not consistently receive the kind of attention accorded the youngest but this displacement from the center of attention was not as critical as for the oldest child.

Size of Family and Adjustment of Children*

GLENN R. HAWKES, LEE BURCHINAL, AND BRUCE GARDNER

THERE is common agreement among social scientists that various family influences constitute important determiners of an individual's personality development. The interaction of the child with his parents is generally thought to be particularly important for the development of the child's personality. Hawkes has suggested that in addition to measuring various parent-child psychological relationships we need to consider certain family structural variables in relation to children's adjustment.[1] One of the obvious and important family structural variables which might condition the interaction patterns between parents and their children is the size of the family. There seems to be a popular belief that children and parents of large families in our society are different in certain respects from parents and children of small or medium sized families, but the direction of the differences is still largely a matter of conjecture. Therefore, the purpose of this paper is to present some additional data on size of family and adjustment of children and to compare these results with findings of several previous studies.

OTHER STUDIES

Bossard and Boll report that persons raised in large families agree that desirable influences for personality development are found in the large family. They report that their informants, ninety children reared in large families, presented a majority view that, "there is something in the atmosphere of the large family that tends to promote emotional security even in the face of economic, and other, difficulties.[2] Support for this point of view can be found in a study by Ellis and Beechley in which the case records of one thousand child guidance patients were examined. They found that children from large families (seven or more children) were significantly less emotionally disturbed than children from small (one child) or medium (two to six children) families. When sex, age, and intelligence were controlled, significant differences among children coming from large and small families still remained.[3] However, Nye has found that adolescents from small families show much better relations with their parents than those from larger families. Differences in parent-adolescent adjustment relations for children from different sized families still remained when socio-economic level was held constant.[4]

SAMPLE AND METHODOLOGY

In order to study the relationship between family size and adjustment of children, the Rogers test of personality adjustment was used to estimate adjustment characteristics of the 256 children included in the sample.[5] Definitions of the four subscores and the total score derived from the Rogers test, reliability and va-

* Published as Journal Paper No. J-2992 of the Iowa Agricultural Experiment Station, Ames, Iowa, Project No. 1171, Home Economics Research. Acknowledgment is due Mrs. Leone Kell of the Kansas Agricultural Experiment Station, Ruth Hoeflin of the Ohio Agricultural Experiment Station, and Helen Dawe of the Wisconsin Agricultural Experiment Station for their collaboration in this regional research project.

[1] Glenn R. Hawkes, "Family Influences on Personality," *Journal of Home Economics*, 44 (December, 1952), pp. 768-769.

[2] James H. S. Bossard and Eleanor S. Boll, "Security in the Large Family," *Mental Hygiene*, 38 (October, 1954), p. 531.

[3] Albert Ellis and Robert M. Beechley, "A Comparison of Child Guidance Clinic Patients Coming from Large, Medium and Small Families," *Journal of Genetic Psychology*, 79 (September, 1951), pp. 137-138.

[4] Ivan Nye, "Adolescent-Parent Adjustment: Age, Sex, Sibling Number, Broken Homes and Employed Mothers as Variables," *Marriage and Family Living*, 14 (November, 1952), p. 328.

[5] Carl Rogers, *Measuring Personality Adjustment in Children Nine to Thirteen Years of Age*, Teachers Coll. Contr. to Educ. No. 458, New York: Teachers College, Columbia University, 1931. A discussion of the Rogers test may be also found in H. H. Remmers and N. L. Gage, *Educational Measurement and Evaluation*, New York: Harpers, 1943, pp. 354-356.

JOURNAL OF MARRIAGE AND THE FAMILY, 1958, Vol. 20, pp. 65-68.

65

TABLE I. ROGERS MEAN SCORES BY NUMBER OF SIBLINGS

Number of Siblings	Number	Personal Inferiority	Social Mal-adjustment	Family Relations	Day Dreaming	Total Scores
1	65	11.45	14.31	8.09	2.83	36.68
2	61	11.54	14.59	8.34	3.10	37.57
3	59	11.85	14.54	9.76	3.08	39.07
4	28	11.39	14.18	9.61	3.68	38.89
5	16	11.81	15.63	10.50	4.12	41.06
Over 5	27	11.78	17.15	9.00	4.11	40.67
Total*	256	11.61	14.80	8.95	3.09	38.38

* Total mean scores are based on the data from the 256 children, not the average of the mean scores. Standard deviations for the five total mean scores were 4.57, 4.43, 3.84, 2.55, and 8.23, respectively.

lidity data for the test based on the original report and the use of the test in the present investigation, and some of the unique characteristics of this test were reported previously.[6]

Fifth-grade children living in rural areas and towns with populations under ten thousand (1950 census) in Ohio, Kansas, Iowa, and Wisconsin were defined as the study population. Descriptions of the stratified probability sample design used in this investigation to select the 256 children included in the sample have been reported elsewhere.[7]

The children completed the Rogers test in their classrooms under the direction of one researcher who did all the field work. Field work was begun in Iowa in October, 1954, and completed in Ohio, 1955.

THE FINDINGS

The 256 children who completed the Rogers test were classified into one of six categories according to the number of brothers and sisters they had. Only families in which both parents were living together and in which there were at least two children, one of whom was in the fifth grade, were included in the universe of interest for this study. Therefore, all the fifth

grade children tested had at least one brother or sister.[8] Family sizes ranged from two to eleven children. For the purposes of analysis, the children have been classified as having one, two, three, four, five, or more than five siblings. In Table I the number of children in each classification and their mean adjustment scores are given. In the last category, more than five siblings, there were eight families in which there were six children, nine families in which there were seven children, eight families in which there were nine children, and two families in which there were eleven children.

Each set of mean scores was tested by analysis of variance to determine if the differences among the means were significant, but for brevity, the calculation tables have been omitted. Amazing similarity was found for the mean personal inferiority scores. The mean of the total sample was 11.61 and the greatest difference among any two means was only .46 points. The F ratio for these means was not significant ($F_{(5,250)} = .08$, P>.05). The F value for the social maladjustment means was also non-significant ($F_{(5,250)} = 1.99$, P>.05), but higher mean scores were observed for the children who had five or more siblings. Children with five siblings had a mean of 15.63, children with more than five siblings had a mean of 17.15, while children with four or less siblings had

[6] Lee Burchinal, Glenn R. Hawkes, and Bruce Gardner, "Marriage Adjustment, Personality Characteristics of Parents and the Personality Adjustment of Their Children," *Marriage and Family Living*, 19 (November, 1957), pp. 366-372.

[7] Lee Burchinal, Glenn R. Hawkes, and Bruce Gardner, "The Relationship Between Parental Acceptance and Adjustment of Children," *Child Development*, 28 (March, 1957), pp. 65-77. Also Lee Burchinal, "The Relations of Parental Acceptance to Adjustment of Children," Unpublished Ph.D. dissertation, The Ohio State University, 1956; see Chapter III, "Methodology," for a complete description of the rationale and mechanics of selection for this sample.

[8] Since all the children had at least one brother or sister, the child's ordinal position appeared to be another logical variable to investigate in relation to the child's adjustment characteristics. The children were classified as oldest, middle, or youngest. Mean score differences for each subscore and total score for these three categories were tested by variance analysis. None of the F values yielded significant probabilities. Hence, it appears that for these children, ordinal position and adjustment as measured by the Rogers test are unrelated.

means which ranged from 14.18 to 14.59.

When the family relations means were tested, the differences among the mean scores for the six family size categories were significant ($F_{(5, 250)} = 2.56$, $P < .05$). Children with only one brother or sister had the lowest mean, 8.09. The next lowest mean was found for children with two siblings, 8.34. Children with more than five siblings came next with a mean of 9.00. The children with four siblings had a mean of 9.61 while the children with three siblings followed closely with a mean of 9.76. The highest mean, 10.50, was found for the children with five siblings.

Non-significant differences were found for the variance analysis for daydreaming and for total scores. For the former the F ratio taken at five and 250 degrees of freedom was equal to .43 and for the latter ratio with the same degrees of freedom the F value was equal to 1.55 and both had a probability greater than .05. It should be noted for both of these sets of means, however, that children from smaller families had lower scores than children from medium sized and larger families.

DISCUSSION

At first glance, these findings are at variance with the results reported by Bossard and Boll and by Ellis and Beechley and tend to agree with the findings of Nye. Nye investigated adolescents' reports of their relations with their parents, not, as he was careful to point out, all the relations of the adolescent. He found that adolescents in smaller families, one or two children, showed much better adjustments to their parents than children from larger families. The Rogers family relations scores refer to more than children's relations with their parents; they also refer to children's relations with their brothers and sisters. In this study, it was found that children from smaller families had more favorable relations with parents and siblings than children from larger families.

The present data gave little support to the hypothesis that a large family generates an atmosphere favorable to personality adjustment. If the findings of either Bossard and Boll or

Ellis and Beechley could be generalized to this investigation, lower scores should have been expected for children coming from families of six or more children. Except for the personality inferiority mean scores which showed virtually no variation, the children from larger families had mean scores which were higher than the mean score for the total sample of children.

What can be said concerning these differences in results? First, it should be recognized that the two studies cited above differ considerably from one another in purpose, samples used, and methods of analysis employed. Furthermore, the present investigation differs from either of these two studies. It seems that the survey by Bossard and Boll offers the least defensible basis for demonstrating the hygienic influence of the large family for personality development. They relied upon the informant's answer to the question, "Do you think a large family makes for a sense of security among its members? (a) economic security; and (b) emotional security?" They state that informants were encouraged to write out their thoughts on this question, and that the question was discussed with those who were interviewed. They do not mention how many persons were interviewed, but they do state that adequate responses were obtained from ninety sibling informants. Of this ninety, 81.1 per cent agreed that the large family produced feelings of security with emotional security rated more highly than economic security. They go on to list the reasons why the informant felt that the large family produced feelings of emotional security, but really all that is known is that members of larger families "feel" that the families produced feelings of security; whether the children were better adjusted personally or socially is not known. Further, can an informant who has experienced only a large family adequately compare the "atmosphere" in his own family with that of other, or perhaps, smaller families?

Ellis and Beechley obtained data from children who were patients at a child guidance clinic. The children's emotional disturbance was described as none or little, moderate, or severe. The authors, however, do not describe the manner in which the children were rated in relation to their emotional disturbance. Neither do we know the reasons for which the children were referred or taken to the clinic. Without this information, the fact that the child guidance clinic patients who came from larger families showed less emotional disturbance cannot be readily interpreted.

The present study, in contrast to the study of Ellis and Beechley, was based on a sample of "normal" fifth grade children from Midwestern schools. Respondents' recall or ideas concerning the security engendering functions of their families was not used as was the case in the Bossard-Boll study, but an "objective" personality measure was employed. Analysis of personality adjustment scores for these children indicated that small family size may be conducive to better adjustment although the differences were not statistically significant. It was clear that children from smaller families reported more satisfactory family relations than children from larger families.

It seems clear from the data obtained in this investigation that the large family does not necessarily provide the child with a more favorable environment for personality development as compared with the family in which there are only two or three children. The advantages of the large family in providing the child with a play group, thus aiding in his socialization process, may be offset by feelings of rivalry and jealousy which may develop in the large family. Certain economic problems may be generated in the large family which create threatening situations for the child. This would be particularly important in the child's peer culture where conformity in dress, ability to have things, et cetera, are strongly stressed and where the child from a large family might not be able to successfully "keep up" financially with children from smaller families. In our urban-industrial society, a large family presents economic limitations if not difficulties for many parents. Of course, these points run counter to the ideal description of the large, usually rural, American family. However, they may be more relevant for present day American family living in an industrialized and urbanized setting.

The other side of the argument, the possible detrimental effect of the small family, usually hinges about the arguments of over-protection or indulgence of the child. It is possible that jealousies among children are more likely where there are just two children seeking recognition and attention from their parents than where there are more children present.

The invocation for further research on this problem might appear trite, but may have real value in light of the tendency today toward larger families, especially among younger and more well educated couples. Perhaps paper and pencil tests are not adequate for measuring the relation between family size and children's adjustment. Certainly studies employing a larger sample or ones in which important variables such as socio-economic status and perhaps age differences among the children have been controlled need to be initiated.

On the basis of the findings of this investigation, it appears that a small family environment does not have a detrimental effect on the children's personality development. Predictive differences in favor of children from larger families were absent, but there was a suggestion that children from smaller families might fare better psychologically than children from larger families.

FACTORS IN THE RELATIONSHIP BETWEEN SOCIAL STATUS AND THE PERSONALITY ADJUSTMENT OF THE CHILD *

William H. Sewell   A. O. Haller

IN an earlier paper the writers demonstrated the existence of a significant relationship between social status and measured personality adjustment of school children when other variables known to be related either to social status or personality adjustment were controlled.[1] This confirmed the findings of a number of less rigorously designed studies which had shown that children of lower social status tend to rank somewhat below middle- and upper-status children on personality tests.[2] The present

* Revision of a paper read at the annual meeting of the American Sociological Society, August, 1957. The writers gratefully acknowledge the help of Chester W. Harris on technical aspects of the factor analysis and the computational assistance of Masako I. Yamada and the staff of the Numerical Analysis Laboratory of the University of Wisconsin. The research reported in this paper is part of a larger project under the direction of William H. Sewell which is supported by the Agricultural Experiment Station and the Research Committee of the University of Wisconsin.

Other published papers reporting research on the larger project include: William H. Sewell, "Field Techniques in Social Psychological Study in a Rural Community," *American Sociological Review*, 14 (December, 1949), pp. 718–726; Sewell, "Infant Training and the Personality of the Child," *American Journal of Sociology*, 58 (September, 1952), pp. 150–159; Sewell and P. H. Mussen, "The Effects of Feeding, Weaning and Scheduling Pro-

cedures on Childhood Adjustment and the Formation of Oral Symptoms," *Child Development*, 13 (September, 1952), pp. 185–191; Sewell and B. F. Ellenbogen, "Social Status and the Measured Intelligence of Small City and Rural Children," *American Sociological Review*, 17 (October, 1952), pp. 612–616; Sewell, P. H. Mussen, and C. W. Harris, "Relationships Among Child Training Practices," *American Sociological Review*, 20 (April, 1955), pp. 137–148; Sewell and A. O. Haller, "Social Status and the Personality Adjustment of the Child," *Sociometry*, 19 (June, 1956), pp. 114–125; and Sewell, "Some Observations on Theory Testing," *Rural Sociology*, 21 (March, 1956), pp. 1–12.

[1] Sewell and Haller, *op. cit.*

[2] An extensive bibliography appears in the review

paper explores the nature of this relationship through further examination and analysis of personality test items which were found to be most highly associated with the social status of the children in the original sample.

The research reported here is exploratory in that it starts with no fixed notions to account for the relationship between status and personality. Its purpose is to re-examine the data already at hand in an attempt to learn which of the items in the personality test employed in the original study are most highly associated with social status, the extent to which such items are intercorrelated, whether or not any pattern can be found among intercorrelated items, the manifest content of any such constellations of items, the extent to which any factors discovered may be related to each other and to social status, and finally, to relate the results to current views regarding social structure and personality. It is believed that such analysis will help to indicate some possible directions for research on status and personality, and perhaps, may suggest a pattern for the examination of the bearing of other social structure variables on personality.

RESEARCH PROCEDURE

The sample upon which the research is based has been discussed elsewhere; in brief, it consists of 1462 children in grades 4–8 who live in a typical midwestern *rurban* community characterized by a fairly wide range of social status levels.[3] The social status of the child was determined by an index consisting of a linear combination of father's occupational level, parental educational attainment, and the prestige of the child's family in the local community. These status indicators are among those most widely accepted in the sociological literature.[4] The information on parents' education

and occupation was taken from school records; the prestige ratings were obtained from local informants. The California Test of Personality—Elementary Form A (hereafter referred to as the CTP) was administered to the children as a part of the testing program of the schools, under the direct supervision of persons with considerable experience and training in testing techniques.[5] The CTP consists of 144 questions which the child reads and answers "yes" or "no." These questions deal with a broad range of behavior and appear to be quite similar in content to those found in numerous other paper-and-pencil tests of personality. Thus they provide a wide range of test response data for the analysis attempted in this study. Each child's answers to these questions, along with his status index score, were punched on IBM cards so as to facilitate statistical analysis.

The analysis included the following steps: (1) The association of each of the personality test items with social status was determined by simple chi-square analysis, in which the social status scores were separated into three equal-sized categories and responses to the test items were dichotomized into favorable and unfavorable responses. The thirty test items most highly associated with social status were selected for further analysis. For the thirty items, all of the relationships appeared to be approximately linear and in all instances lower-status children were more likely than those of higher status to give test responses indicating less favorable adjustment.[6] The retained items or questions, numbered and stated exactly as on the printed form of the test, are given in Table 1. (2) These items were then intercorrelated using phi-coefficients.[7] The result-

Rural Society," *Rural Sociology*, 18 (March, 1953), pp. 12–24.

[5] *The California Test of Personality—Elementary Form A, No. 1*, Los Angeles: The California Test Bureau, 5916 Hollywood Blvd., 1942.

[6] This particular technique for selecting the test items was used because of ease of computation, although it may not be strictly applicable to these data. If one wished to apply a level of significance criterion, all of the retained items surpass the .001 level. An additional fifty items, not included in this analysis because of practical and computational considerations, are between the .05 and .001 levels.

[7] G. U. Yule and M. G. Kendall, *An Introduction to the Theory of Statistics*, London: Griffin, 1948, pp. 252–253.

article by B. F. Auld, Jr., "Influence of Social Class on Personality Test Response," *Psychological Bulletin*, 49 (July, 1952), pp. 318–332. Additional references are given in Sewell and Haller, *op. cit.*, pp. 121–125.

[3] A brief description of the community and information about the social status background of the children is given in Sewell and Haller, *op. cit.*, pp. 115–117.

[4] See H. F. Kauffman, N. Gross, O. D. Duncan and William H. Sewell, "Problems of Theory and Method in the Study of Social Stratification in

TABLE 1. CTP ITEMS MOST HIGHLY ASSOCIATED WITH SOCIAL STATUS

CTP Item No.	CTP Item	Unfavorable Response	CTP Item No.	CTP Item	Unfavorable Response
14.	Do most of your friends and classmates think you are bright?	No	71.	Do you often have dizzy spells?	Yes
			72.	Do your eyes hurt you often?	Yes
16.	Do you wish that your father (or mother) had a better job?	Yes	88.	Does it make you feel angry when you lose in games at parties?	Yes
21.	Do your folks seem to think that you are doing well?	No			
			93.	Do you usually forget the names of people you meet?	Yes
25.	May you usually choose your own friends?	No	104.	Is it hard to make people remember how well you can do things?	Yes
30.	Do you have a chance to see many new things?	No			
			109.	Do you have a hard time because it seems that your folks hardly ever have enough money?	Yes
39.	Do your classmates think you cannot do well in school?	Yes			
45.	Do you have just a few friends?	Yes	111.	Are you unhappy because your folks do not care about the things you like?	Yes
46.	Do you often wish you had some other parents?	Yes			
47.	Are you sorry you live in the place you do?	Yes	114.	Do you like both of your parents about the same?	No
48.	Do your friends have better times at home than you do?	Yes	115.	Does someone at home pick on you much of the time?	Yes
57.	Do people often try to cheat you or do mean things to you?	Yes	117.	Do you try to keep boys and girls away from your home because it isn't as nice as theirs?	Yes
61.	Do you often have sneezing spells?	Yes			
62.	Do you often have bad dreams?	Yes	120.	Have you often felt that your folks thought you would not amount to anything?	Yes
63.	Do you bite your fingernails often?	Yes			
66.	Do you often find you are not hungry at meal time?	Yes	124.	Is school work so hard that you are afraid you will fail?	Yes
68.	Do you often feel tired in the forenoon?	Yes	144.	Do you dislike many of the people who live near your home?	Yes
70.	Do you often feel sick at your stomach?	Yes			

ing matrix of intercorrelations is shown in Table 2. (3) This matrix was then factor analyzed according to Rao's canonical factor method.[8] Nine orthogonal factors were required to reduce the significant residual variation to zero, as indicated by Lawley's maximum likelihood criterion.[9] Only the first four of these factors were judged to have any meaningful content; since these four accounted for approximately 90 per cent of the common variance among the items, the remaining factors were dropped from the analysis. The four retained factors were then rotated obliquely to yield Thurstone's simple structure.[10] The resulting oblique rotated factor matrix is shown in Table 3. (4) The interrelationships among the factors were determined by intercorrelating the factors. The resulting correlations are shown in Table

[8] C. R. Rao, "Estimations and Tests of Significance in Factor Analysis," *Psychometrica*, 20 (June, 1955), pp. 99–111.

[9] D. N. Lawley, "The Maximum Likelihood Method of Estimating Factor Loadings," in G. H. Thomson, *The Factorial Analysis of Human Ability*, New York: Houghton Mifflin, 1948, pp. 324–326.

[10] L. L. Thurstone, *Multiple Factor Analysis*, Chicago: University of Chicago Press, 1946, pp. 319–348.

TABLE 2. INTERCORRELATIONS OF THE STATUS RELATED PERSONALITY TEST ITEMS*

Item No.**	14	16	21	25	30	39	45	46	47	48	57	61	62	63	66	68	70	71	72	88	93	104	109	111	114	115	117	120	124	144
14	**140**																													
16	233	**093**																												
21	113	072	**117**																											
25	141	192	106	**052**																										
30	247	167	229	068	**164**																									
39	166	140	140	104	177	**254**																								
45	037	049	127	058	077	075	**051**																							
46	127	193	120	057	167	170	181	**182**																						
47	197	214	156	100	242	212	195	154	**216**																					
48	225	191	098	060	166	195	229	078	190	**249**																				
57	082	109	032	066	118	097	047	105	063	187	**202**																			
61	142	063	046	031	108	054	128	068	053	165	259	**342**																		
62	092	072	050	036	097	094	093	028	053	097	127	127	**131**																	
63	140	085	051	026	072	068	077	062	078	128	179	210	258	**112**																
66	094	165	062	068	097	096	096	062	116	201	206	255	254	121	**257**															
68	139	127	070	065	120	148	112	059	141	183	199	177	270	129	257	**337**														
70	082	116	059	035	053	128	046	114	150	199	177	105	093	171	214	294	**294**													
71	084	126	093	066	050	152	092	094	125	162	156	105	171	184	252	244		**244**												
72	105	084	114	074	055	119	114	112	092	146	113	085	076	053	060	126	134	063	**096**											
88	176	114	123	101	107	118	079	089	082	183	211	199	231	139	166	196	190	144	107	**112**										
93	177	112	112	052	106	146	175	077	082	213	235	114	128	050	114	155	136	122	074	169	**186**									
104	159	159	125	082	175	147	107	135	144	319	226	115	113	046	055	126	136	090	101	125	136	**188**								
109	163	303	149	088	254	162	137	149	181	272	182	134	128	050	136	175	172	179	138	132	127	244	**271**							
111	156	191	145	102	135	120	150	133	144	214	096	134	037	020	009	052	110	081	104	061	115	085	170	**170**						
114	093	145	123	069	120	146	119	075	127	124	100	062	072	070	059	114	089	052	104	091	105	115	233	170	**115**					
115	162	119	123	099	108	166	118	098	131	181	090	141	047	047	096	150	144	110	081	138	128	227	241	211	217	**110**				
117	085	113	122	156	145	152	177	113	152	273	153	180	141	111	150	144	133	083	104	160	161	231	160	260	102	211	**152**			
120	131	123	208	094	108	177	118	098	152	252	186	090	072	070	096	150	089	082	088	091	128	171	171	203	083	226	113	**224**		
124	253	164	227	145	097	206	172	113	131	252	095	215	069	111	140	216	189	129	146	160	161	193	172	203	083	226	110	224	**134**	
144	100	095	111	027	088	199	111	095	135	156	095	062	069	040	078	095	075	102	101	105	113	095	050	152	117	110	127	084	134	**134**

* Decimal properly preceding each entry have been omitted.

** Items numbered as in CTP. For item descriptions see table 1.

TABLE 3. OBLIQUE ROTATED FACTOR MATRIX *

Item No.	Item **	I	II	III	IV
			Factors		
14	Do most of your friends and classmates think that you are bright?	000	373	000	000
16	Do you wish that your father (or mother) had a better job?	388	−010	005	023
21	Do your folks seem to think that you are doing well?	−087	331	212	−098
25	May you usually choose your own friends?	−004	139	134	−042
30	Do you have a chance to see many new things?	365	049	−070	−020
39	Do your classmates think you cannot do well in school?	019	297	149	−010
45	Do you have just a few friends?	100	273	021	−039
46	Do you often wish you had some other parents?	050	−038	295	053
47	Are you sorry you live in the place you do?	264	−108	346	017
48	Do your friends have better times at home than you do?	255	100	135	089
57	Do people often try to cheat you or do mean things to you?	149	160	−052	232
61	Do you often have sneezing spells?	043	−049	−009	481
62	Do you often have bad dreams?	−006	038	−081	504
63	Do you bite your fingernails often?	106	010	−116	221
66	Do you often find you are not hungry at meal time?	−042	030	−013	410
68	Do you often feel tired in the forenoon?	003	−005	069	459
70	Do you often feel sick at your stomach?	002	−014	035	506
71	Do you often have dizzy spells?	−034	−069	176	422
72	Do your eyes hurt you often?	−039	−045	208	327
88	Does it make you feel angry when you lose in games at parties?	−021	148	161	064
93	Do you usually forget the names of people you meet?	053	164	−010	257
104	Is it hard to make people remember how well you can do things?	104	223	000	094
109	Do you have a hard time because it seems that your folks hardly ever have enough money?	445	−039	065	−003
111	Are you unhappy because your folks do not care about the things you like?	145	083	213	101
114	Do you like both of your parents about the same?	000	000	380	000
115	Does someone at home pick on you much of the time?	069	146	058	234
117	Do you try to keep boys and girls away from your home because it isn't as nice as theirs?	229	−139	395	−001
120	Have you often felt that your folks thought you would not amount to anything?	044	178	195	072
124	Is school work so hard that you are afraid you will fail?	−027	284	095	142
144	Do you dislike many of the people who live near your home?	−038	124	235	033

* Decimals properly preceding each entry have been omitted.
** Unfavorable.

4. (5) Finally, each of the four factors was then correlated with the social status index to determine the direction and extent of any relationship which might obtain between the derived factors and social status. These correlation coefficients are presented at appropriate points in the following discussion.

The factorial matrix in Table 3 may be examined by columns in order to interpret the meaningful content of the factors. For purposes of this analysis any item with a factor loading of .200 or greater was arbitrarily considered to make a sufficient contribution to the factor to be retained. To clarify the meaning of the factors, all of the items meeting this criterion were transformed from questions into positive, first-person statements indicating the supposedly unfavorable response in terms of personality adjustment. Thus, for example, item 14—"Do most of your friends and classmates think you are bright?"—to which the unfavorable response is "no," became "Most of my friends and classmates do not think I am bright."

Factor 1. The six items which comprise the first factor in order of magnitude of the loadings are:

Loading	CTP Items	Content
.445	109	I often have a hard time because it seems that my folks hardly ever have enough money.
.388	16	I wish my father (or mother) had a better job.
.365	30	I don't have a chance to see many new things.
.264	47	I am sorry I live in the place I do.
.255	48	My friends have better times at home than I do.
.229	117	I try to keep boys and girls away from my home because it isn't as nice as theirs.

These six items seem to reflect the concern of the child with his family's social status. An examination of all 144 items in the test reveals no others which directly refer to the child's perception of his family's social status. In its negative form the factor manifests itself in the child's concern over the social status of his family; its more favorable manifestation indicates his freedom from such concern. In the present context it may be called *concern over social status.* That the child's perception and concern with his social status, as measured by this factor, are associated with social status is revealed by its correlation (−.312) with the social status index used in this study. This indicates that children from lower-status families tend to show more concern about their social status than children from higher-status families. Thus one of the elements in the correlation of social status and personality adjustment test scores, namely concern over social status, has been tentatively isolated and identified.

Factor 2. The following items have the greatest loading on this factor:

Loading	CTP Items	Content
.373	14	Most of my friends and classmates do not think I'm bright.
.331	21	My folks do not seem to think I'm doing well.
.297	39	My classmates think I cannot do well in school.
.284	124	School work is so hard I am afraid I will fail.
.273	45	I have just a few friends.
.223	104	It is hard to make people remember how well I can do things.

The six items most heavily saturated with this factor seem to deal with the child's concern with how others rate his ability and achievements. Three of the items (14, 39, and 124) have specific reference to the school situation. Two (21 and 104) have no specific reference, but in the context of the child's usual tasks may well be seen by him to refer to school work. One item (45) has no direct reference to the child's perception of how others view his ability or performance. Again, examination of the CTP reveals no other items which appear to relate directly to the child's concern about his ability and achievements. Since the child who is concerned over the negative way in which others evaluate his abilities and achievements scores high on this factor, the factor may be simply labeled *concern over achievement.* In its more favorable manifestation it takes the form of freedom from concern over the way others evaluate one's ability and performance. This factor has a low negative correlation (−.178) with social status. This means that children of lower status are somewhat more likely than those of higher status to manifest concern over their ability to perform up to the levels expected of them. The isolation and identification of this factor provides another element in the association between social status and personality test performance.

Factor 3. The third factor is made up of the following eight items:

Loading	CTP Items	Content
.395	117	I try to keep boys and girls away from my home because it is not as nice as theirs.
.380	114	I like one of my parents more than the other.
.346	47	I am sorry I live in the place I do.
.295	46	I often wish I had some other parents.
.235	144	I dislike many of the people near my home.
.213	111	I am unhappy because my folks do not care about the things I like.
.212	21	My folks do not seem to think I am doing well.
.208	72	My eyes hurt me often.

The five items (117, 114, 47, 46, and 144) which have the greatest projection on this factor all seem quite clearly to deal with the child's rejection of his home and parents. Two of the remaining items (111 and 21) may well be interpreted as representing essentially a complementary reaction to the child's rejection of his family, namely his conviction that they in turn reject him. However, the remaining item (72) does not fit the general pattern of family rejection manifest in the other variables which comprise this factor. The factor may be called *rejection of family,* as it appears in its negative form. The children who score high on this factor tend to express attitudes of rejection of their families, while those with low

scores are relatively free from these negative attitudes. The correlation between social status and this factor is −.117, indicating some tendency for lower-status children to reject their parents and their homes. This factor may also be considered tentatively as another element in the relationship between status and personality, at least with respect to the children under study.

Factor 4. Eleven of the 30 items included in the analysis have loadings of .200 or higher on the fourth factor, as follows:

Loading	CTP Items	Content
.506	70	I often feel sick at my stomach.
.504	62	I often have bad dreams.
.481	61	I often have sneezing spells.
.459	68	I often feel tired in the forenoon.
.422	71	I often have dizzy spells.
.410	66	I often find I am not hungry at meal time.
.327	72	My eyes hurt often.
.257	93	I usually forget the names of people I meet.
.234	115	Someone at home picks on me much of the time.
.232	57	People often try to cheat me or do mean things to me.
.221	63	I bite my fingernails often.

All of the items, but particularly the seven with the heaviest loadings on the factor (70, 62, 61, 68, 71, 66, and 72), clearly deal with what are commonly termed neurotic symptoms in the clinical literature. Sick stomach, bad dreams, sneezing spells, tired feeling, dizzy spells, lack of appetite, sore eyes, nail biting, and feeling "picked on" are widely interpreted as psychosomatic symptoms associated with underlying personal anxieties. Consequently, this factor may be termed *nervous symptoms.* Those scoring high on this factor tend to display symptoms of nervousness, while those scoring low are relatively free from such symptoms. The correlation between scores on this factor and social status is −.236, indicating that lower-status children tend to exhibit more nervous symptoms than those of higher status. The isolation of this rather clear-cut factor pro-

TABLE 4. INTERCORRELATION OF FACTORS

	I	II	III	IV
I. Concern over social status	1.000			
II. Concern over achievement	.587	1.000		
III. Rejection of family	.383	.391	1.000	
IV. Nervous symptoms	.401	.447	.249	1.000

vides still another element in the correlation between social status and the measured personality of the children studied.

Intercorrelation of factors. The interrelationships among the factors are shown in Table 4. Each of the factors is moderately and positively correlated with each of the other factors. The correlations range from +.249 (factor 3 with factor 4) to +.587 (factor 1 with factor 2). There is thus a consistent tendency for those children in the sample who are concerned about the social status of their family to be worried also about their own achievements, to reject their families, and to display nervous symptoms.

DISCUSSION

The isolation of four interrelated factors which seem to account for most of the relationship between social status and personality test scores in this sample of grade school children has several implications for theory and research in the general area of social structure and personality.

An examination of the content of the factors and of their correlations with social status indicates that much of the behavior represented by the items can be interpreted as expressions of anxiety on the part of lower-status children. The items included in the first factor appear to deal with the concern that the child has over the status of his family in the community. Such concern is most commonly expressed by children of lower status. The variables comprising the second factor seem to indicate the child's concern about his ability to perform up to acceptable standards, particularly in the school situation. Again, the lower-status child is most likely to manifest this concern. The variables in the third factor indicate the extent to which the child rejects his family and home environment and may be interpreted as a sign of anxiety on the part

of the child. Certainly the norms of our society require that the child, especially the young child, accept and defend rather than reject his family. This rejection is likely to be fraught with considerable anxiety. Its correlation with the other factors lends further support to this interpretation. The lower-status child, once more, is most likely to reject his family. The various nervous symptoms making up the fourth factor may be thought of as behavior patterns which are at least in part products of the anxieties of the child. The intercorrelation among the factors and their correlations with social status permit the tentative inference that it is generally the lower-status child in the supposedly middle-class environment of the school who is most likely to be concerned about the social status of his family in the community, to be anxious about his ability to perform up to expectations—particularly in school, to reject his family and home environment, and to display nervous behavior.

These findings do not square with the conclusion reached by some sociologists and anthropologists, based upon their observations of and views concerning the socialization of children in our society, to the effect that middle-class children are subjected to more frustrations in learning and are more anxious as a result of these pressures than are lower-class children.[11] Yet there is con-

[11] See, e.g., A. W. Green, "The Middle-Class Male Child and Neurosis," *American Sociological Review,* 11 (February, 1946), pp. 31–41; M. C. Ericson, "Child Rearing and Social Status," *American Journal of Sociology,* 52 (November, 1946), pp. 190–193; A. Davis and R. J. Havighurst, *Father of the Man,* Boston: Houghton Mifflin, 1947. Chapter 5; and A. Davis and R. J. Havighurst, *Father of the Man,* Color Differences in Child-Rearing," *American Sociological Review,* 11 (December, 1946), pp. 698–710.

It should be noted that recent studies have presented evidence which contradicts the earlier conclusions; their findings indicate that middleclass parents are more permissive than lower class parents in their child rearing practices. See E. E. Maccoby and P. K. Gibbs, "Methods of Child Rearing in Two Social Classes" in W. E. Martin and C. B. Stendler, editors, *Readings in Child Development,* New York: Harcourt, Brace, 1954; R. R. Sears, E. E. Maccoby, and H. Levin, *Patterns of Child Rearing,* Evanston, Ill.: Row, Peterson, 1957; R. A. Littman, R. C. A. Moore, and J. Pierce-Jones, "Social Class Differences in Child Rearing: A Third Community for Comparison with Chicago and Newton," *American Sociological Review,* 22 (December,

siderable evidence from other studies which in general supports the results of the present research. Most of the investigations which have attempted directly to relate the child's social status to his personality adjustment, rather than to infer personality effects from observed status-related patterns of socialization, have clearly shown that lower-status children are less well adjusted than those from middle- and high-status families.[12] Moreover, a study by Gough, of particular significance because it includes correlations between social status and certain MMPI scales which are similar to the factors isolated in this study, reports results in agreement with the present findings.[13]

Finally, there seems to be good reason on theoretical as well as empirical grounds to expect the results obtained. A general explanatory formulation for the findings of this study might well take the following form: (1) The early socialization of the lower-status child results in the internalization of values and the development of behaviors characteristic of the lower-status family and neighborhood in which he is reared. (2) When the lower-status child extends his activities into the larger social environment of the school and the community, he encounters many values and behavior expectations that are quite different from those of his family and neighborhood. (3) He is made to feel that some of these values and behaviors are superior to those of his

own family and neighborhood, so he tries to adopt them. (4) Since these values and behaviors are in conflict with those of his family and neighborhood and since the low status position of his family in many ways inhibits the behavior dictated by them, he experiences tension states which may be manifested in (a) concern about the social status of his family; (b) concern over his ability to perform up to expected levels, particularly in school; (c) rejection of his family, since its members are perceived by him as responsible for his inability to behave according to his higher status values; and finally, (d) a syndrome of nervous behaviors indicative of general anxiety. Further field research is required to test this general formulation. But at least it offers a plausible explanation for the pattern of results found in this study and is consistent with current social psychological theory and research.

Another plausible and more specific explanation of the results of the present study is that the relatively low negative association between social status and the isolated factors may be due to the presence of some children among the lower-status group who are striving hard for upward social mobility, encountering a great deal of frustration, and consequently are showing significantly greater anxieties than their status peers or their peers from middle and higher status levels who are not experiencing as serious frustrations in attaining their goals. This possibility cannot be tested with the limited data at hand but should be carefully examined in future studies of status and personality.

Of course, status-related anxieties are not necessarily dysfunctional for the lower-status child.[14] From other evidence it appears that the lower-status children in this sample did not generally suffer from serious personality problems. Moreover, if he is to be spurred on to the achievements that upward social mobility demands, it is probably necessary for the lower-status child to experience a

---

1957), pp. 694–704; and M. S. White, "Social Class, Child Rearing Practices, and Child Behavior," *American Sociological Review,* 22 (December, 1958), pp. 704–712.

[12] See Auld, *op. cit.,* p. 330; and Sewell and Haller, *op. cit.,* p. 119.

[13] Gough constructed a status scale from items included in the MMPI which differentiated significantly between students of different status levels as measured by other status scales. H. G. Gough, "A New Dimension of Status: I. Development of a Personality Scale," *American Sociological Review,* 13 (August, 1948), pp. 401–409. He subsequently correlated the status measurements produced by the scale with the scales of the MMPI and found that students of higher status when compared with those of lower status show less tendency toward serious personality disturbances, less insecurity, less social introversion, fewer somatic complaints, and more satisfactory over-all adjustment. Gough, "A New Dimension of Status: II. Relationship of the St. Scale to other Variables," *American Sociological Review,* 13 (October, 1948), pp. 534–537.

[14] For an excellent discussion of the function of social anxiety in upward social mobility, see A. Davis, "Socialization and Adolescent Personality, *Forty-third Yearbook of the National Society for the Study of Education,* Chicago: National Society for the Study of Education, 1944, Part I, Chapter 11.

77

certain amount of anxiety regarding his social status and his present performance levels, and even to reject the standards of his parents. The question of the extent to which socially derived anxieties may be functionally effective in stimulating achievement-striving, without concomitantly creating pathological personality patterns, is one of the most important and intriguing problems of theory and research in the field of social structure and personality. The data of this study do not bear directly on this problem and additional research will be necessary to approximate an answer to this question. An equally important problem to students of social structure—and again one with which this research is not adequate to cope—is the question of how open the channels of social mobility must remain in order to provide lower-status persons with sufficient incentive to struggle for higher positions in the social structure; what will be the consequences for society if the anxieties here assumed to be necessary for upward social mobility are generated in lower-status persons without some good chance of its attainment? This is a problem of great practical as well as sociological significance.

From the methodological point of view, the writers believe that the general design used in this research could be employed fruitfully in the examination of the relationship between other structural variables and personality. Data on such variables as age, sex, religious affiliation, race, ethnic origins, and rural-urban backgrounds are usually obtained in personality studies. Application of the model developed for this research, with appropriate variations depending on the available data and the specific problem, might provide a means of further analysis of

the nature of the relationship between these variables and personality. This could result in verification and extensions of existing theories and in the formulation of new theoretic leads for further development of knowledge and research on social structure and personality.

A last word of caution is in order concerning the results of the present study. First, it should be remembered that practical considerations precluded a complete factor analysis of all of the personality test items related to social status or to extract completely all of the possible factors from the more limited matrix that was analyzed. Therefore, it may be that additional status-related factors of importance would be found in a more complete factor analysis of the personality test items used in this study. Secondly, it should be clear that the results of the type of analysis undertaken here are necessarily conditioned by the content of the personality test employed. Another test with a different set of items might produce different factors from those isolated in this study. It might be suggestive to determine the factor content of the status-related items of other commonly used personality tests and, particularly, to determine whether or not factors with similar manifest content can be isolated and identified. In this case, theoretical and research effort could be directed quite profitably to further examination of the functional relationship between social status and anxiety. Finally, it should be pointed out that, because of the exploratory nature of this study and the limitations of the sample, the data, and the analysis, the usual cautions regarding the tentative nature of empirically derived conclusions should be especially observed.

SOME EFFECTS OF PATERNAL ABSENCE ON MALE CHILDREN [1]

JOAN McCORD, WILLIAM McCORD, AND EMILY THURBER

"That children are best reared in a home with two loving and understanding parents is so obvious as to need no statement" Dorothy Barclay (1959) has commented, typifying current opinion. This viewpoint is so prevalent that it comes close to heresy to question it. Although William Goode (1956), in his comprehensive study of divorce, points to the almost total lack of research on the effects of divorce on children, he concludes:

At every developmental phase of childhood, the child needs the father (who is usually the absent parent) as an object of love, security, or identification, or even as a figure against whom to rebel safely. . . . It would be surprising if the absence of the father had no effect on the child.

The same view prevails throughout social science. Few empirical studies of child development fail to include the words "intact homes" as a criterion of sample selection. It has long been the tradition to view anxiety as a primary outcome of father absence (Fenichel, 1945; Freud, 1953; Gardner, 1959). Such disorders as alcoholism, homosexuality, and totalitarian tendencies have been attributed to paternal absence (Meerloo, 1956). The high incidence of broken homes among the delinquent population has led to theories which might account for the apparent causative relationship (Burton & Whiting, 1960; Whiting, Kluckhon, & Anthony, 1958).

In research comparing united homes with those in which the father is permanently or temporarily absent, and in psychological and psychoanalytic theory concerning paternal absence, attention has been particularly centered on three areas of personality development:

the extent to which the child develops a feminine as opposed to a masculine self-image, the intensity and type of anxiety which he experiences, and the probability of his engaging in antisocial behavior. In the following pages, we will examine various hypotheses in these areas as they relate to a (primarily) lower-class sample of boys. In the analyses, comparisons are made between boys raised in permanently broken homes and those in united homes. By varying the subgroups compared, the dynamic relationship between family disorder and abnormal behavior is assessed.

METHOD

Design of the Research

During the 1930s, Richard Clark Cabot initiated the project, from which the subjects for this study of broken homes were taken, as an adjunct of an experimental program aimed at the prevention of delinquency in Cambridge and Somerville, Massachusetts (Powers & Witmer, 1951).

For an average period of 5 years, between the ages of 10 and 15, 255 boys [2] were observed at home, at school, and at play. Trained social workers, who

[2] Originally 325 boys had been included. Because of heavy case load, 65 boys were retired from the project in 1941, 5 additional boys were dropped because of their death or moving out of Massachusetts. The original sample was selected as follows: Teachers, police, and other officials recommended boys whom they believed showed signs of incipient delinquency. The Cambridge-Somerville Youth Study staff gathered information about them for the matching procedure (one boy to receive treatment and the other to be placed in a control group) so that the criteria of selection consisted in a willingness to participate and ability to find two boys with similar backgrounds in family structure, age, and "general personality." To avoid stigmatizing the boys in the project, an approximately equal number were added who were considered "normal" by the same authorities (again, equally divided between the treatment and the control groups).

[1] This research has been generously supported by the Ella Lyman Cabot Foundation, the Harvard Laboratory of Social Relations, and the National Institute of Mental Health (Grant M-2647).

JOURNAL OF ABNORMAL AND SOCIAL PSYCHOLOGY, 1962, Vol. 64, pp. 361-369.

visited the families approximately every other week, noted the behavior of the parents as well as the child. The counselors would appear unannounced, with a frequency which made it possible to observe the families at meals, during their leisure, in the midst of crises, and during their ordinary daily routines. They recorded their observations after each visit. Thus, running records were kept for 255 subjects between 1939 and 1945.[3]

In 1956 and 1957, trained researchers read each case record and rated the boy and his parents on a number of variables ranging from occupation and religion to affectional interaction. Interrater agreement, tested on a random sample, was high[4] and several factors point to the validity of the information obtained in this manner. Expected relationships which might have indicated a middle-class bias or operation of a halo effect were not found (e.g., the lower-class boys were not pictured as more aggressive and the brighter boy were not pictured as leaders). Most importantly, the categorized ratings of the case records yielded strong relationships to completely independent measures of social deviance among the subjects when they had become adults (McCord & McCord, 1960).

Sample Characteristics

Among the 255 boys[5] in the study, 105 had lost one or both parents. Because we wished to focus on the effects of paternal absence, we dropped boys who were not living with their natural mothers (12 had lost both parents and 20 had lost their mothers) and the 18 who had step- or foster fathers. The remaining 55 boys from broken homes were living with their natural mothers; these were children whose fathers had died (24), deserted (8), been placed in mental hospitals (4), were serving long prison terms (3), or whose parents had been divorced or legally separated (16). The 150 boys whose natural parents were living together were used for the control group.

A number of studies have indicated that broken homes are associated with low socioeconomic status (Burgess, 1950; Hollingshead, 1950; Weeks, 1943). To the extent that social class affects personality development, this relationship between social class and family stability may lead to false conclusions regarding the effects of broken homes. Since the Cambridge-Somerville Youth Study centered upon the congested areas of these two cities, the entire sample

[3] Between 1955 and 1957, these subjects and a matched control group who had received no direct attention from the project were traced through the Massachusetts Board of Probation, mental hospitals, and various agencies dealing with alcoholism. It was found that the treatment program had no discernible effect upon criminality or alcoholism (McCord & McCord, 1959, 1960).

[4] The reliability of each of the ratings is fully discussed in *Origins of Alcoholism* (McCord & McCord, 1960).

[5] From 237 families.

TABLE 1

PARENTAL DEVIANCE

Condition	Broken homes ($N = 55$)	United homes ($N = 150$)
Father deviant	30%	31%
Mother deviant	1	4
Both deviant	24	5
Neither deviant	45	60

had a strong lower-class representation. A comparison of fathers' occupations between broken and united homes within the sample showed slight (not statistically significant)[6] differences between the groups.

Various studies have indicated that Catholic families may be slightly more stable, although they seem to contribute more than their share of desertion cases (Bell, 1938; Monahan & Kephart, 1954). In our sample, records of the mother's religion showed that 65% of the boys raised in united homes and 64% of the boys in broken homes had been raised by Catholic mothers.

Theorists have also suggested that the wife may alter her behavior to compensate for her husband's absence. P. O. Tiller (1958) reports that Norwegian sailors' wives whose husbands were absent for extended periods of time exceeded matched mothers whose husbands were not absent in being overprotective and stressing obedience and politeness (in contrast to happiness and self-realization). In our sample, we did not find a significantly greater incidence of either maternal overprotection (31%/29%) or punitiveness (49%/44%) in the broken homes than in the united homes. Nor did we find significant differences between the mothers' attitudes toward their sons[7] in united homes and broken homes.

Two potentially important variables, however, strongly differentiated broken home boys from boys in united homes. William Goode (1956) reported that about a third of his sample of divorced women cited sexual or alcoholic deviance of their husbands as the primary cause of divorce. We found a significantly higher proportion of deviant (i.e., alcoholic, criminal, or promiscuous) fathers ($p < .001$) and deviant mothers ($p < .025$) among the boys from broken homes than among the boys whose parents were living together (see Table 1).

In addition, a significantly lower proportion of the boys in broken homes had immigrant fathers

[6] Throughout the research, the chi square test, two-tailed, was used when $N > 30$ and the Fisher test, two-tailed, was used when $N < 30$. Differences were considered significant if $p < .05$.

[7] "Warm" mothers openly expressed their affection; "cold" mothers showed passive concern, but seldom demonstrated affection; "ambivalent" mothers displayed extreme variation between overt affection and overt rejection; and "rejecting" mothers cared little for their children or their welfare.

TABLE 2
DISTRIBUTION OF BROKEN HOMES

Father	Mother	Age of boy at time of break		
		0–5	6–12	Over 12
Dead	Normal[a]	4	6	4
Living	Normal[a]	4	6	1
Dead	Abnormal[b]	3	3	4
Living	Abnormal[b]	7	11	2

[a] Warm, nondeviant.
[b] Deviant, cold, ambivalent, or rejecting.

($p < .001$). Fifty-eight percent of the fathers in united homes, compared to 29% in broken homes, were immigrants.

To insure that the effects of these differences were not attributed to paternal absence, we matched each boy from a broken home to a boy similar in background whose parents were living together. Besides parental deviance and father's birthplace, the mother's attitude toward the boy, her disciplinary technique, her degree of control over her son, and the consistency of her discipline 'were used as criteria for matching.

We anticipated that paternal absence might have different effects under various conditions. Therefore, we divided the broken home boys on three dimensions:

1. The reason for the father's absence. The father's death might be presumed to have a different effect on the child than would his disappearance from the home after preliminary quarrels.

2. The age of the boy at the time when his father left. The child's age at the time of the break was divided roughly into preschool, preadolescent (or middle childhood), and adolescent.

3. The affectional relationship and stability (nondeviance) of the mother. Warm, nondeviant mothers were considered "normal." The distribution of the boys in broken homes on these three dimensions is shown in Table 2.

Since overt conflict probably precedes divorce and separation, and may have preceded desertion or death, the putative effects of broken homes may actually be the result of parental conflict. Ratings from direct observation of parental interaction were used to divide the boys whose parents were living together into two groups: the 30 whose parents quarreled constantly and were in overt conflict, and the 120 whose homes were relatively tranquil.

RESULTS

Feminine Identification

One of the most widely held beliefs about the effects of paternal absence is that male children will develop unusually strong feminine components in their personalities. Three

sets of ratings on the 205 boys in our study were used to test feminization in the father-absent group: homosexual tendencies, dependency, and lack of aggressiveness.[8] Although the trend of past evidence would suggest that father-absent boys would be relatively more feminine (Burton & Whiting, 1960; Leichty, 1960; Lynn & Sawrey, 1959; Winch, 1949), more dependent (Stolz, 1954), and less aggressive (Bach, 1946; Sears, Pintler, & Sears, 1946), we found that neither homosexuality nor dependency differentiated significantly between the boys whose fathers were absent and those whose fathers were present and that the aggression scale was significantly related—but in the opposite direction from that predicted. (Eighty-seven percent of the broken home boys, as opposed to 67% of those from tranquil homes, were moderately or strongly aggressive.)

Since aggressive behavior may be considered as an exhibition of "masculinity," it seemed probable that those who were both aggressive and showed signs of feminine identification [9] were expressing an instability in sex role identification or defending against feminine identification. This combination of feminine-aggressive behavior (as compared to feminine-nonaggressive behavior) was found significantly more frequently among boys in broken homes than among boys in tranquil homes ($p < .001$).

Since both parental conflict and paternal absence were related to feminine-aggressive behavior, it seemed likely that either parental

[8] Boys were considered to have strong homosexual tendencies if they played with dolls, sometimes wore dresses, frequently expressed the wish to be a girl, or were overtly homosexual. They were considered to be dependent if they showed an unusually strong desire for adult approval. Femininity and dependency were not significantly related to each other. A three-point scale of behavioral aggression, ranging from little to unrestrained, was used.

[9] Boys who evidenced high dependency or strong homosexual tendencies were classified as showing feminine identification. We hypothesized that feminine identification (with or without aggression) would arise from the "teasing" effect of an ambivalent nondeviant mother or from the combination of rejection from a stable father and affection from a stable mother; among the 22 boys whose parents were of these types, 77% evidenced feminine identification.

81

TABLE 3
Sex Role Behavior

Sex role	Broken home (N = 55)	Conflictful home (N = 30)	Tranquil home (N = 120)
Masculine[a]	49%	43%	58%
Feminine-nonaggressive	4	14	20
Feminine-aggressive	47	43	22

[a] Nine percent of the broken home boys, none of those in conflictful homes, and 13% of those in tranquil homes showed masculine role behavior but were not aggressive.

conflict or parental deviance (found in almost equal proportions among broken and conflictful homes)[10] might fully account for the difference. Neither of these explanations, however, fit the data. We reasoned that parental conflict would have been less among homes severed by death of the father; yet a higher proportion (58%) of the sons in these homes showed feminine-aggressive behavior (see Table 3).

To check whether the home milieu rather than paternal absence itself was responsible for the high rate of feminine-aggressive behavior, we used the group of boys with similar backgrounds in united homes.

Because the comparison with matched controls (see Table 4) showed higher feminine-aggressive behavior among broken home boys ($p < .005$), the difference in sex role behavior could not be attributed simply to conditions which might have precipitated the family break.

Analysis of the father-absent boys provided a clue to their reasons for sex role conflict. We contrasted sons whose mothers were normal (affectionate and nondeviant) with those having mothers rated abnormal. In these two groups of boys, the age at which

[10] Immigrant families, too, were found in almost equal proportions among broken and conflictful homes, i.e., they were less likely to be either conflictful or severed.

TABLE 4
Sex Role Behavior

Sex role	Father absent	Matched controls
Masculine	49%	45%
Feminine-nonaggressive	4	24
Feminine-aggressive	47	31

paternal absence began and the reason for such absence had different relationships to sex role behavior. These differences suggest that feminine-aggressive behavior has different origins in broken homes in which a normal, as opposed to an abnormal, mother had remained.

Whereas the child's age when his father left was of great importance among boys whose mothers were warm and nondeviant, it had slight relationship to feminine-aggressive behavior for boys raised by abnormal mothers (see Table 5).

Boys reared by normal mothers showed feminine-aggressive behavior only if their fathers left when the boys were between the ages of 6 and 12 ($p < .01$). Since only 25% of their matched controls indicated sex role

TABLE 5
Percentage Who Exhibited Feminine–Aggressive Behavior

	Boy's age when father left		
	0–5	6–12	Over 12
Normal mother	(N = 8) 0	(N = 12)75[a]	(N = 5) 0***
Abnormal mother	(N = 10)70	(N = 14)50	(N = 6)50

[a] Twenty-five percent of matched group exhibited feminine-aggressive behavior ($p < .05$).
*** $p < .01$.

conflict of this type, the home milieu of these boys were apparently not responsible for their high rate. Studies of children's sex differentiated behavior give reason to believe that the years of middle childhood may be critical ones in the development of sex identification. In an early study, P. H. Furfey (1927) noted little sex differentiation in the play of 6–8 year olds, with increasing separation and differentiation after that age. Observations of recreational clubs at the Merrill-Palmer School in Detroit indicated that 5- and 6-year-olds seem to ignore sex as a basis for choosing play groups, but that sex segregation is almost complete for 10- and 11-year-olds (Campbell, 1939). Studies of friendship choices point to the same phenomenon (Moreno, 1934).

Previous research with father-separated samples whose mothers were probably "nor-

82

mal" by our criteria tend to point also to the importance of age at the time of separation. A study by Sears et al. (1946) found that early differences in sex role behavior between father-absent and father-present boys had begun to disappear by age 5. Bach (1946), however, reported evidence of femininization among 6–10 year olds whose fathers had been absent 1–3 years.

Early separation, as Sears et al. (1946) suggested, may result in sex typing delay—but both theirs and our evidence indicates that this effect is of relatively short duration: probably because the boy is able to find substitute role models during the period of sex identification. During the critical years of sex identification, perhaps because memory of the father interferes with adoption of a substitute model, loss of the father seems to have a more permanent affect on sex role identification. By age 12, the process of sex role identification is probably fairly complete, thus, explaining the absence of feminine-aggressive behavior among the older boys raised by normal mothers.

Among boys raised by abnormal mothers, age at the time of separation was of relatively minor importance in relation to feminine-aggressive behavior; death of the father (see Table 6), however, seemed to be highly productive of this type of confused sex role behavior ($p < .05$).

One can argue that death of the father raises a conflict in the male child between his desire to replace the father and his denial of this desire; yet this theory does not explain the *lower* proportion among those whose mothers were affectionate ($p < .05$) who showed feminine-aggressive behavior.

It seems reasonable to explain this type of sex role instability among boys exposed to cold or rejecting mothers in terms of dependency needs and their satisfactions: When resources for satisfaction of dependency needs are limited (as they would be in broken homes of this type), the child becomes both more dependent on this limited source and also more resentful of his dependency because it fails to bring satisfaction.[11] Thus, such children re-

[11] It seems likely that a relationship between maternal rejection and parental separation or divorce (see Newell, 1936) leads to disproportionate repre-

TABLE 6

PERCENTAGE WHO EXHIBITED FEMININE-AGGRESSIVE BEHAVIOR

	Reason for father's absence	
	Death	Other
Normal mother	($N=14$) 36	($N=11$) 36
Abnormal mother	($N=10$) 90[a]	($N=20$) 40*

[a] Ten percent of matched group exhibited feminine-aggressive behavior ($p < .01$).
* $p < .05$.

sponded to the conflict by being relatively dependent and feminine, and simultaneouly behaving aggressively, in a compensatory masculine fashion.

Anxiety

Although it has received less research attention, the belief that paternal absence results in anxiety is widespread. Specific research relating anxiety to paternal absence has yielded conflicting results. A number of studies have linked such various manifestations of anxiety as feelings of inferiority, poor school performance, immaturity, and tensions to paternal absence (Hardy, 1937; Lynn & Sawrey, 1959; Rouman, 1956; Stolz, 1954). Other studies have found no evidence of increased anxiety (Leichty, 1960; Rowntree, 1955; Russell, 1957). In an attempt to clarify this confusion in the literature, we tested three hypotheses derived from clinical theories.

Hypothesis 1. Father-separated boys should manifest many or intense fears because their heightened Oedipal desires cannot be brought to gratification (Freud, 1953), or because the child fears that his mother will desert him (Gardner, 1959). We found no confirmation of this hypothesis that loss of the father results in abnormal fears. Forty percent of the

sentation of this type of home in some studies of the effects of broken homes on sex role identification. Whiting (1961) suggested that cultures in which there are exclusive mother-child sleeping arrangements also tend to define the maternal role in terms which would be considered abnormal in our society (i.e., maternal rejection and promiscuity are common among them). It seems possible that the cross-cultural relationship found between father separation in infancy and evidence of sex role conflict is dependent upon the limited resources for satisfaction of dependency needs in these cultures.

83

TABLE 7

PERCENTAGE WHO EXHIBITED SEX ANXIETY

Condition	Percentage
Broken home ($N = 55$)	47[a]
Conflictful home ($N = 30$)	57
Tranquil home ($N = 120$)	27

[a] Forty-nine percent of the matched group exhibited sex anxiety.

broken home boys and 40% of those raised in tranquil homes gave evidence of abnormal fears (e.g., fear of the dark or excessive fear of bodily injury). Among boys reared in conflictful homes, 50% had abnormal fears. These negative results relating paternal absence to abnormal fears tend to confirm the findings of Rowntree (1955) for matched pairs of preschool children in Britain and Russell (1957) for matched pairs of school age children in America.

Hypothesis 2. Father-separated boys should have anxiety about sex; this should be particularly strong for those whose fathers have died (Fenichel, 1945). A number of boys expressed to their counselors their concern over achieving normal sexual relations or about their sexual adequacy; others publicly masturbated during periods of tension.[12] These boys were considered to be sexually anxious. Although a significantly higher proportion of those whose fathers were absent than of those whose homes were tranquil evidenced sex anxiety ($p < .02$), roughly the same proportion of those whose parents were in open conflict were sexually anxious (see Table 7).

There was little variation within the father-absent group in the proportions who showed sex anxiety: 45% of those whose fathers were

[12] The two measures were significantly related in the sample ($p < .01$).

TABLE 8

ORAL TENDENCIES

	Broken home ($N = 55$)	Conflictful home ($N = 30$)	Tranquil home ($N = 120$)
Oral regression	22%[a]	13%	10%
Oral and anxious	15	23	16
Neither	63	64	74

[a] Thirteen percent of the matched group exhibited oral regression.

living, compared to 50% of those whose fathers had died; 54% of those whose mothers were rejecting and 41% of those whose mothers were affectionate evidenced sex anxiety. None of the four boys with affectionate deviant mothers evidenced sex anxiety. Although sex anxiety was prominent among boys raised without their fathers, the fact that 49% of the matched controls (compared to 47%) exhibited sex anxiety suggests that high sex anxiety may not be specifically related to paternal absence.

Hypothesis 3. Father-separated boys should show signs of regression (Fenichel, 1945). Thumb sucking, nail biting, excessive smoking, and constant playing with the mouth were used as behavioral signs of oral tendencies. Since these forms of behavior may also indicate general anxiety, only those who did not exhibit abnormal fears were classified

TABLE 9

PERCENTAGE WHO SHOWED SIGNS OF ORAL REGRESSION

	Father absent	Matched controls
Normal mother	($N = 25$) 8%	($N = 25$) 20%
Abnormal mother	($N = 30$) 33	($N = 30$) 7[**]

[**] $p < .025$.

as showing oral regression. Oral regression, though not oral anxiety, was found most frequently among the father-absent group. The relationship was not, however, strong enough to reject the possibility that it had occurred by chance (see Table 8).

As a further check, we examined oral regression in relation to normal and abnormal mothers among the father-absent boys. Although the proportion showing oral regression was not higher among the normal mother group than among those raised in tranquil homes (8%/10%), the comparison revealed a significantly higher proportion (see Table 9) showing signs of oral regression (33%) among those whose mothers were rejecting or deviant ($p < .005$).

Rejection or deviance, with or without paternal absence, might have explained oral regression. Comparison with the matched group led to rejection of this hypothesis.

84

Reasoning that death of the father would most fully realize the Oedipal wish, we hypothesized greater regression among boys whose fathers had died. This hypothesis, too, was not supported. These comparisons indicate that paternal absence, probably following conflict, *in combination with* maternal deviance or rejection result in oral regression.

Antisocial Behavior

The lay public as well as professional criminologists have linked broken homes to antisocial behavior. There seems to be general agreement that the proportion of broken homes among criminals is greater than that of the general population (Shulman, 1959). It was possible to use two measures of antisocial behavior for our sample. The counselors' reports of direct observations permitted ratings of primary reference groups during adolescence. Boys whose primary reference groups were delinquent gangs participated in behavior disapproved by the majority in their community. In 1955, court records for each of the subjects were obtained as an additional independent record of criminality; these traced the boys into adulthood. Those who had been convicted for a felony (or for a crime which would be a felony if the boy were an adult) were considered criminals.

There was little support for the theory that paternal absence led to delinquent gang activities. A significantly higher proportion of those boys whose parents continued to live together despite considerable overt conflict than *either* those whose parents were in little conflict ($p < .01$) or those whose fathers were absent ($p < .05$) were gang delinquents (see Table 10).

That parental conflict rather than paternal absence tends to result in gang delinquency is given further support by the fact that the

TABLE 10

PERCENTAGE WHO HAD DELINQUENT REFERENCE GROUPS

Condition	Percentage
Broken home ($N = 55$)	20
Conflictful home ($N = 30$)	43
Tranquil home ($N = 120$)	18

TABLE 11

PERCENTAGE WHO BECAME CRIMINALS

Condition	Percentage
Broken home ($N = 55$)	36
Conflictful home ($N = 30$)	40
Tranquil home ($N = 120$)	22

older the boy at the time of the break, the more likely he was to become a gang delinquent. It should further be noted that a significantly higher proportion of those who had parent substitutes (34%) than of those who lived in tranquil homes had become gang delinquents. This latter group, it appears, is responsible for the apparently high rate of juvenile delinquency among the broken home population of the lower class—a correlation which has been erroneously attributed to the absence of a paternal model.[13]

Using convictions for felonies as a measure of antisocial behavior, the expected relatively high rate of criminality was found among the father-absent group (see Table 11). Tranquil homes produced a significantly lower proportion of criminals than did the father-absent homes and the conflictful homes ($p < .025$).

Several findings point to the fact that the absence of a generally stable home environment, rather than the specific absence of the father, is related to criminality: (*a*) boys reared by parents who were in overt conflict were as likely to become criminals as boys from father-absent families; (*b*) the criminal rate among boys who had parent substitutes was identical (i.e., 36% became criminals) to that of the father-absent boys; (*c*) the criminal rate increased with an increase in the age of the boy at the time of the family break;

[13] With this theory in mind, we recomputed the Glueck (Glueck & Glueck, 1950) figures reported in *Unraveling Juvenile Delinquency*, breaking down the broken home boys into those who did and those who did not have parent substitutes. Recomputed, the Glueck figures no longer support the theory that broken homes as such are causally related to delinquency: Among their 500 delinquents, 72 were from broken homes without parent substitutes; among their 500 nondelinquents, 111 were from broken homes without parent substitutes. In contrast, 230 of the delinquents, compared to 60 of the nondelinquents, had substitute parents.

and (d) none of the 13 father-absent boys cared for by warm nondeviant mothers whose fathers had not been deviant became criminals.[14]

SUMMARY

Repeated direct observations of 205 boys and their families during a period of approximately 5 years of their early adolescence and court records for convictions for felonies were used to assess the effects of paternal absence upon boys. The sample, drawn from former members of the Cambridge-Somerville experiment, came from a lower-class, relatively deprived environment. The results of this study suggest the following conclusions:

1. Although feminine-nonaggressive behavior was negatively related to paternal absence, feminine-aggressive behavior appeared to be produced by paternal absence if the boy was between 6 and 12 when his father left, or the mother was deviant or rejecting (especially if the father had died).

2. No support was found for the theory that paternal absence leads to abnormal fears.

3. Intense sexual anxiety was found among almost half of the boys who had lost their fathers. Yet this anxiety seemed to be a response to a generally unstable environment rather than to paternal absence per se.

4. Oral regression was related to father-absence only among those whose mothers were deviant or rejecting.

5. Gang delinquency was found to be unrelated to paternal absence, although it did occur more frequently in broken homes in which the father or mother had been replaced by substitutes. In fact, the proportion of gang delinquents among boys whose parents quarreled but remained together was significantly higher than among those whose fathers were absent.

6. The relationship between criminality and paternal absence appears to be largely a result of the general instability of broken homes rather than of paternal absence in itself.

The evidence drawn from this sample indicates that many of the effects often presumed to result from paternal absence can, largely, be attributed to certain parental characteristics—intense conflict, rejection, and deviance —which occur more commonly in broken families.

---

[14] Nine of the 10 father-absent boys whose mothers were both rejecting and deviant had been convicted for felonies.

REFERENCES

BACH, G. R. Father-fantasies and father typing in father-separated children. *Child Develpm.*, 1946, 17, 63–79.

BARCLAY, DOROTHY. When one parent plays the double role. *N. Y. Times Mag.*, 69, April 5, 1959.

BELL, H. *Youth tell their story.* Washington, D. C.: American Council on Education, 1938.

BURGESS, E. W. Predictive methods and family stability. *Ann. Amer. Acad. Pol. Soc. Sci.*, 1950, 272, 47–52.

BURTON, R. V., & WHITING, J. W. M. The absent father: Effects on the developing child. (Rev.) Paper read at American Psychological Association Convention, Chicago, 1960.

CAMPBELL, E. H. The social-sex development of children. *Genet. psychol. Monogr.*, 1939, 21, 461–552.

FENICHEL, O. *The psychoanalytic theory of neurosis.* New York: Norton, 1945.

FREUD, S. Three essays on sexuality. In, *Standard edition.* Vol. VII. (Originally published 1905) London: Hogarth, 1953.

FURFEY, P. H. Some factors influencing the selection of boys' chums. *J. appl. Psychol.*, 1927, 11, 47–51.

GARDNER, G. E. Separation of the parents and the emotional life of the child. In S. Glueck (Ed.), *The problems of delinquency.* Boston: Houghton Mifflin, 1959. Pp. 138–143.

GLUECK, S., & GLUECK, ELEANOR T. *Unraveling juvenile delinquency.* Cambridge, Mass.: Harvard Univer. Press, 1950.

GOODE, W. J. *After divorce.* Glencoe, Ill.: Free Press, 1956.

HARDY, M. C. Aspects of home environment in relation to behavior at the elementary school age. *J. juv. Res.*, 1937, 21, 206–225.

HOLLINGSHEAD, A. B. Class differences in family stability. *Ann. Amer. Acad. Pol. Soc. Sci.*, 1950, 272, 39–46.

LEICHTY, MARY. The absence of the father during early childhood and its effect upon the Oedipal situation as reflected in young adults. *Merrill-Palmer Quart.*, 1960, 6, 212–217.

LYNN, D. B., & SAWREY, W. L. The effects of father-absence on Norwegian boys and girls. *J. abnorm. soc. Psychol.*, 1959, 59, 258–262.

MCCORD, W., & MCCORD, JOAN. *Origins of crime.* New York: Columbia Univer. Press, 1959.

MCCORD, W., & MCCORD, JOAN. *Origins of alcoholism.* Stanford, Calif.: Stanford Univer. Press, 1960.

MEERLOO, J. A. M. The father cuts the cord: The role of the father as initial transference figure. *Amer. J. Psychother.*, 1956, 10, 471–480.

MONAHAN, T. P., & KEPHART, W. M. Divorce and desertion by religious and mixed-religious groups. *Amer. J. Sociol.,* 1954, **59,** 454–465.

MORENO, J. L. *Who shall survive?* Washington, D. C.: Nervous and Mental Disease Publishing Co., 1934.

NEWELL, H. W. The psycho-dynamics of maternal rejection. *Amer. J. Orthopsychiat.,* 1936, **6,** 576–588.

POWERS, E., & WITMER, HELEN. *An experiment in the prevention of delinquency.* New York: Columbia Univer. Press, 1951.

ROUMAN, J. School children's problems as related to parental factors. *J. educ. Res.,* 1956, **50,** 105–112.

ROWNTREE, GRISELDA. Early childhood in broken families. *Popul. Stud.,* 1955, **8,** 247–263.

RUSSELL, I. L. Behavior problems of children from broken and intact homes. *J. educ. Sociol.,* 1957, **31,** 124–129.

SEARS, R. R., PINTLER, M. H., & SEARS, PAULINE S. Effects of father-separation on preschool children's doll play aggression. *Child Develpm.,* 1946, **17,** 219–243.

SHULMAN, H. M. The family and juvenile delinquency. In S. Glueck (Ed.), *The problems of delinquency.* Boston: Houghton Mifflin, 1959. Pp. 128–136.

STOLZ, LOIS M., ET AL. *Father relations of war-born children.* Stanford, Calif.: Stanford Univer. Press, 1954.

TILLER, P. O. Father-absence and personality development of children in sailor families: A preliminary research report. *Nord. Psykol.,* 1958, Monogr. No. 9.

WEEKS, A. H. Differential divorce rates by occupations. *Soc. Forces,* 1943, **22,** 334–337.

WHITING, J. W. M. Paper read to Graduate Colloquium in Psychology, Stanford University, January 19, 1961.

WHITING, J. W. M., KLUCKHON, R., & ANTHONY, A. The function of male initiation ceremonies. In Eleanor E. Maccoby, T. M. Newcomb, & E. L. Hartley (Eds.), *Readings in social psychology.* (3rd ed.) New York: Holt, 1958. Pp. 359–370.

WINCH, R. F. The relation between the loss of a parent and progress in courtship. *J. soc. Psychol.,* 1949, **29,** 51–56.

EFFECTS OF MATERNAL EMPLOYMENT
ON THE CHILD [1]

Lois Wladis Hoffman

Empirical studies of the effects of maternal employment have long suffered from a paucity of adequate controls. It was the lack of controls, for example, which led to the long-standing belief that maternal employment was strongly associated with juvenile delinquency. In fact, both maternal employment and delinquency were associated with social class and with broken homes; and, when the latter variables were controlled the relationship disappeared, suggesting it had been a spurious one (3).

Yet, the new studies on maternal employment, despite their more adequate controls, have often produced more confusion than clarification. Maternal employment has been associated with *less* delinquency, *more* delinquency, withdrawal behavior, dominance behavior, and nothing at all (1, 4, 9, 10, 11). Furthermore, there are existing theories to account for each of these findings. Thus, delinquent and hostile-assertive behavior might result from parental neglect and lack of sufficient discipline due to the mother's absence from the home; from hostility on the part of the child at being deserted; or, in conjunction with Henry's notion (5) that father discipline leads to the expression of hostility outward whereas mother discipline leads to intrapunitiveness, from father discipline replacing mother discipline.

Withdrawal and dependency responses by the child might also be expected. Loss of mother through death or hospitalization has been associated

[1] This paper was presented at the National Council on Family Relations, Ames, Iowa, 1959. The research was supported by the National Institute of Mental Health.

CHILD DEVELOPMENT, 1961, Vol. 32, pp. 187-197.

with overdependency—the young child perhaps seeking in this crisis a return of the maternal relationship he had in the past. Something similar might occur as the result of the mother's spending a great deal of time outside the home working. Still another reason for withdrawal and dependency might be that the working mother feels guilty about working outside the home and responds with a pattern of "smother love" or overprotection. Such a pattern could alleviate the mother's guilt. In addition, if it is true that working mothers have greater power needs than nonworking mothers, it would also be an appropriate pattern for expressing power over the child in a way that appears to be benign and admirable.

Some, such as Cyrus (2), would expect working mothers to be less frustrated and more capable of warm interaction. Others would say that the energy output required by trying to fill two jobs would make the mothers more irritable with their children.

Instead of speculating as to which of these theories is correct, the present paper will suggest and illustrate an approach in which the question is: *When does one pattern operate and when does another?*

Each theory assumes something about the working situation that is sometimes, but not always, correct; and, when certain assumptions hold, different mother-child interactions will result and the child will be affected accordingly. One important factor implicit in several of the theories involves the question of whether or not the mother enjoys her employment. It is this difference that the present study has selected for focus. It was expected that the effects of employment on the mother-child relationship, and consequently on the child, would be different when the working mother enjoyed work than when she did not.

Two of the theories mentioned above, the "guilt-overprotection" theory and the "neglect" theory, lead to very different predictions about the mother's behavior toward the child, and, although both theories predict that the working mother's child will be disturbed, the pattern of disturbance predicted by each is very different. Both these theories served as guides in the present investigation. The "guilt-overprotection" theory was expected to operate for the working women who enjoyed work, and the "neglect" theory for the working women who did not enjoy work.

Only the working woman who enjoys her employment should be guilty about it, and as such it was predicted that such a woman would try to compensate for her employment by showing a great deal of affection toward the child, disciplining the child adequately to leniently, and being careful that the child should not be inconvenienced by the fact that she works, e.g., by having to help with household tasks. The child correspondingly should be relatively nonhostile, nonassertive, and, if this parental pattern were carried to the point of overprotection, somewhat withdrawn and passive. The working woman who dislikes her work should, on the other hand, be quite guiltless. As such, she was expected to show more of a withdrawal from the maternal role—showing less positive affect and less disciplining. She should feel freer to inconvenience the child—specifically to expect the child to help with household tasks. The child, feeling somewhat resentful and lacking sufficient discipline, was expected to be assertive and hostile. The predictions were, then, that both groups would show different patterns than when the mother was not employed, but that these differences would not be the same.

PROCEDURE

The sample included 176 white, *intact* families with at least one child in the third through sixth grades of three elementary schools in Detroit. There were 88 working-mother families and 88 nonworking-mother families matched on occupation of father, sex of child, and ordinal position, including the important status of being an only child. Except for sex of child, all matched variables were selected because they were known to be related to maternal employment (7) and because it was believed they might be related to the dependent variables. Pairs of families were matched by sex of child so that it might be possible to examine the relationship between maternal employment and the dependent variables separately for boys and girls, to be certain that combining was legitimate. All statistical comparisons are between working and nonworking populations, and with a few exceptions which will be pointed out later, *all comparisons are for matched pairs.*

The data reported here are based on questionnaires filled out by the children, interviews with the mothers, teacher ratings, and a classroom sociometric. Each of these measures will be taken up in turn when the findings are presented.

In the interview with the mothers, the working mothers were asked, "How do you feel about working?" These answers were coded as to the predominance of positive or negative attitudes toward work. Responses to this question were on the positive side for most respondents. Sixty-five respondents were classified as liking work, and 23 as disliking it.

All hypotheses were tested separately for the two groups, i.e., by comparing the 65 mothers who liked work with their 65 matched nonworking counterparts and the 23 mothers who disliked work with their 23 matched nonworking counterparts. Significance tests for differences included the *t* test for correlated means where the data were quantitative, sign tests where the data were qualitative, and the *t* test for proportions where the data could not be analyzed by pairs.

RESULTS

Table 1 summarizes the results dealing with the mother's affect and behavior toward the child. The first comparison deals with the child's perception of the mother as a source of positive affect. The child had been asked to indicate the persons who, from his own experience, best fitted each of a series of verbs, such as "praises" and "smiles," and to indicate the

TABLE I

MOTHER'S AFFECT AND BEHAVIOR TOWARD CHILD:
WORKING-NONWORKING COMPARISONS BY ATTITUDE TOWARD WORK

Variable	Working mothers with positive attitude toward work	Working mothers with negative attitude toward work
Child's report		
positive affect from mother	more than nonworking*	less than nonworking
coerciveness from mother	less than nonworking	less than nonworking*
Mother's report		
severity of discipline†	less than nonworking*	no difference
power assertion by the mother† ..	less than nonworking	less than nonworking*
mother's feelings of sympathy† ..	more than nonworking*	no difference
mother's feelings of hostility† ...	less than nonworking*	less than nonworking

NOTE.—Findings reported in all tables are based on the *t* test for significance of difference between correlated means except where indicated.

* Significant at the .05 level, one-tailed test.

† Comparisons not possible between matched pairs. Each working group therefore compared to pooled sample of nonworking mothers and the *t* test for significance of difference between proportions used.

degree of fitness of person to verb. The perception of positive affect in the mother-child relationship was measured by the extent to which the child associated "mother" with the following words: "praises," "smiles," "listens," "helps," "explains." As can be seen in Table 1, where the working mother indicates a positive attitude toward her work, the child associates more positive affect with the mother than do children in the matched group of nonworking women. This difference is significant. When we compare the children of working mothers who have negative attitudes toward their work to the nonworking group, we find the opposite relation although it is not a significant one.[2]

The second set of findings deals with the child's perception of coerciveness on the part of the mother. This variable was similarly measured using the words, "threatens," "punishes," and "hits." The table shows that the working mother is less likely than the nonworking mother to be associated with coerciveness in both groups and that the relation is significant for the working mothers who dislike work.

The remaining findings in this table are based on the mother's report. In the interview, mothers were asked to give detailed accounts of two recent occasions when they wanted the child to do something that the child did not want to do. These descriptive accounts were coded for degree of severity

[2] The direction of the relation is reported even where differences are small; so, except for the significant relations, differences can be due to chance variations.

of discipline, degree of power assertion over the child, sympathy, and hostility. Unfortunately, these descriptions were not available on all of the matched nonworking respondents. To have a large enough N, it was therefore necessary to pool the nonworking respondents and compare the two groups of working women separately with this pooled group. These are not, then, matched comparisons, although the working and nonworking groups are, on the whole, comparable with respect to the matching variables. The findings show that where the mother has positive attitudes toward employment she is less severe in her discipline, uses less power-assertive influence techniques, and feels more sympathy and less hostility during the interaction than is the case with the nonworking group. For the working mothers with negative attitudes toward employment there is less power assertion and somewhat less hostility.

Taking the findings in Table 1 as a whole, they tend to support the hypothesis that the working woman who gains pleasure from her work shows the child more affection and uses milder discipline. Although she is emotionally involved in the discipline situation, the involvement is to a great extent one of sympathy for the child. The working mother who does not enjoy her work, and whom we would expect to be relatively guilt-free thereby, also shows a tendency toward mild discipline. However, here it is not part of a larger pattern which includes affection and sympathy toward the child. Instead it seems to be part of a general pattern of less involvement with the child. This suggests that the dislike-work group tends to withdraw from the maternal role.

Table 2 deals with the child's participation in tasks. This was measured by the child's responses to a form of the "Doing Things" questionnaire

TABLE 2

CHILD'S PARTICIPATION IN HOUSEHOLD TASKS:
WORKING-NONWORKING COMPARISONS BY ATTITUDE TOWARD WORK

Variable	Working mothers with positive attitude toward work	Working mothers with negative attitude toward work
Child's report		
regular participation in household tasks	less than nonworking	more than nonworking*

* Significant at the .05 level, one-tailed test.

developed by Herbst (6), in which the child is asked to report the extent of his participation in several household tasks (20 tasks in this case). As expected, the children of the working mothers who do not enjoy their work participate more in household tasks than do the children of the nonworking mothers; the children of the working mothers who enjoy work participate

92

TABLE 3

CHILD'S BEHAVIOR:
WORKING-NONWORKING COMPARISONS BY ATTITUDE TOWARD WORK

Variable	Working mothers with positive attitude toward work	Working mothers with negative attitude toward work
Mother's report		
child's assertiveness toward mother‡	no difference	more than nonworking*
child's playing with younger children rather than own age or older§	more than nonworking*	no difference
Teacher's report		
initiation of friendships	less than nonworking*	less than nonworking
influence attempts made to peers	less than nonworking	more than nonworking
influence success with peers	less than nonworking*	no difference
teacher dependency (girls)	no difference	no difference
teacher dependency (boys)	more than nonworking	more than nonworking†
aggressiveness	no difference	more than nonworking
use of physical force	less than nonworking	more than nonworking*
impulse control	no difference	less than nonworking*

* Significant at the .05 level, one-tailed test.

† Significant at the .05 level, two-tailed test, difference not predicted.

‡ Comparisons not possible between matched pairs. Each working group therefore compared to pooled sample of nonworking mothers and the *t* test for significance of difference between proportions used.

§ Sign test used for this variable.

less. This is in keeping with the notion that the mothers who enjoy work go out of their way to avoid inconveniencing their children because of their employment.

Table 3 deals with the child's behavior. The child's assertiveness toward the mother is based on the mother's account of the conflict situations in which she wanted the child to do something that the child did not want to do. The child's behavior was considered assertive when he directly indicated that he did not wish to comply and that he did not expect to do so. These behaviors included requests such as "Is it all right to stay up until the end of this program?"—as well as statements of intention such as "No. I am not going to bed until the end of this program."—where the context made it clear that the child was not "just talking." Pleading, crying, complying with complaints or silent anger, and devious attempts to obtain ends ("I have a stomach ache.") were all considered less assertive. The child's tendency to play with younger children is based on the mother's report that his playmates were "mostly older," "mostly younger," or "the same age."

The remaining variables reported in Table 3 are based on teacher ratings. These ratings are described more fully elsewhere (8).

It was hypothesized that the children of working mothers who have positive attitudes toward employment would be nonhostile, nonassertive, and possibly withdrawn and passive as compared with their nonworking counterparts, but that the children of working women who do not like work would be assertive and hostile. The data seem to bear this out. The children whose mothers like work differ in their general lack of initiative-taking and tend to play with children younger than themselves. The children whose mothers do not like work, on the other hand, show assertive behavior toward their mothers and toward their peers. This assertiveness toward peers includes aggressiveness, use of physical force, and less impulse control in general. Only teacher dependency does not operate as expected, the boys in both groups showing more dependency, significantly more in the dislike-work group.

Both the "guilt-overprotection" theory and the "neglect" theory lead to the prediction that the children of working mothers will be more disturbed in general than the children of nonworking mothers. This was tested by comparing the matched pairs on the use of nonadaptive responses to frustration, intellectual performance, and sociometric ratings by classmates. The results of these tests are reported in Table 4. The first measure was based on a teacher rating of how the child typically reacts to frustration. "Realistic

TABLE 4

CHILD'S ADJUSTMENT:
WORKING-NONWORKING COMPARISONS BY ATTITUDE TOWARD WORK

Variable	Working mothers with positive attitude toward work	Working mothers with negative attitude toward work
Teacher's report		
nonadaptive response to frustration†	more than nonworking	more than nonworking*
intellectual performance	less than nonworking*	less than nonworking*
Classroom sociometric		
liking by others	less than nonworking	less than nonworking

* Significant at the .05 level, one-tailed test.
† Sign test used for this variable.

acceptance of insolvable problem" and "attacks problem directly" were considered adaptive responses, while responses such as "cries," "goes to pieces," "blames others," and "becomes overcritical of self" were considered nonadaptive. Both groups of working-mother children were more likely to use nonadaptive responses to frustration. They also showed lower intellectual performance and were somewhat less liked by the other children in the class.

The lower intellectual performance of children whose mothers work is a particularly interesting finding. Being low on performance may be a function of low ability or low motivation. If it is true that the working mothers who like work are guilty about their employment and consequently over-protect their children, then the intellectual *ability* of their children may be impaired. Mothers who solve their children's problems for them may hamper their intellectual development by depriving them of valuable problem-solving experience. Thus, these children would be expected to be low on ability as well as performance. The low performance of the dislike-work children, on the other hand, might be part of the rebellious pattern that seems to characterize this group; here we would not necessarily expect low ability. Scores on the Primary Learning Aptitude Test for third graders and the Detroit Alpha Intelligence Test for fourth, fifth, and sixth graders were available. The expectations were borne out. Only the children whose mothers were positive about their work obtained lower scores on these tests than their nonworking counterparts, and this difference was significant. The others showed no such difference.

Summary and Conclusions

The over-all pattern of findings suggests that the working mother who likes working is relatively high on positive affect toward the child, uses mild discipline, and tends to avoid inconveniencing the child with household tasks; the child is relative nonassertive and ineffective. The working mother who dislikes working, on the other hand, seems less involved with the child altogether and obtains the child's help with tasks; the child is assertive and hostile.

The data do not show conclusively that the reason for these different patterns is the presence or absence of guilt in the mother, but they are consistent with such an interpretation. If one were to argue that the causality is reversed, that the attitude toward work is a function of the effect of employment on the child or that happier women produce happier children, it would not be consistent with the fact that both groups of working-mother children show indications of maladjustment. It is only that they show different *syndromes* of maladjustment. Furthermore, in Table 5 it can be seen that the attitude toward employment is in large part a function of the particular job the woman holds.[3]

It is interesting to note in Table 5 that, while attitude toward employment is not purely a function of social class, there is somewhat of a tendency for higher status jobs to be well liked. Because middle-class women,

---

[3] The data presented in Table 5 are consistent with the data reported by Weiss and Samelson (12). Their data also show, for example, a positive attitude toward employment on the part of domestic workers.

TABLE 5

OCCUPATION AND ATTITUDE TOWARD WORK

Occupation	Working mothers with positive attitude toward work	Working mothers with negative attitude toward work
Professional and semiprofessional, e.g., teacher, social worker, registered nurse ..	14	1
Skilled, e.g., secretary, bookkeeper	11	7
Sales	14	0
Waitress	1	4
Semiskilled or unskilled factory and clerical	20	10
Domestic	5	1
Total	65	23

compared to lower-class, can obtain higher status jobs, because their employment is likely to be choice rather than necessity, and because there is probably greater anxiety about childrearing in the middle class, it is likely that guilt and overprotection are more a middle-class response to maternal employment while neglect is more a lower-class response.

The real purpose of this paper, however, is not so much to elaborate on any particular theory as to suggest an approach to the study of the effects of maternal employment. The need to control on spurious variables has been established. The problem now is to differentiate the all-inclusive variable of maternal employment into more highly specified categories. Only in this way can we come to understand the processes by means of which employment affects the child. If one wants to know whether or not the sheer absence of the mother from the home is the important variable, then one should subdivide the working women according to the number of hours they are away from home while the child is there. If one wants to know the importance of the adequacy of supervision, then one should subdivide the women according to whether or not the substitute supervision provided is adequate. One might feel that the important variable is the father's reaction to the mother's employment. In this case, the working women can be subdivided according to some measure of the father's attitudinal or behavioral response to his wife's employment. In short, by selecting a particular aspect of mother's employment, differentiating the working mothers according to this variable, and examining the differences between working and nonworking groups separately, one can make a more formidable step toward understanding the crucial aspects of maternal employment in relation to the child.

There are still other advantages of this kind of approach. When the working-mother group is not differentiated, it includes a heterogeneous group and, as such, the working-nonworking comparisons will obscure differences due to counteracting subgroup relations. For example, in the data reported here, since one group of working-mother children was less assertive and the other group was more assertive, the two tendencies canceled one another out. Thus, when the total group of working-mother children was compared with the matched nonworking group, there appeared to be no differences in child assertiveness. The same is true for the participation of children in household tasks.

Another kind of error that can result from failure to differentiate the working mothers is when what seems to be a single pattern of findings actually includes two or more distinct patterns. For example, when the total groups were compared, working mothers' children were found to play more with younger children and also to show less impulse control. Doing separate analyses for the two groups of working mothers, however, revealed that these results did not come from the same subjects. Although it was not true of the present data to any great extent, it would be possible for a pattern to emerge from the general working-nonworking comparisons which actually characterized neither the total group nor any single subgroup, but was entirely a coincidence of findings contributed by different clusters of subjects.

One final point should be made. In most working-mother studies, relations are examined between maternal employment and some aspect of the child's behavior *directly,* without considering intervening variables such as the effect of maternal employment on parent-child relations, family structure, or other aspects of family life. The jump between maternal employment and child behavior is too broad to be covered in one leap. One must first understand the various steps that intervene.

In summary, this paper suggests that maternal employment has a different effect on the mother-child relationship and on the child's behavior depending on whether or not the mother enjoys working. The purpose in doing this analysis was to show that greater understanding of the effects of maternal employment will come about when working mothers are differentiated along some theoretically relevant dimension and when the effects on family life, as well as on the child, are examined.

References

1. BANDURA, A., & WALTERS, R. H. *Adolescent aggression.* Ronald Press, 1959.
2. CYRUS, D. Problems of the modern homemaker-mother. In J. T. Landis and M. G. Landis (Eds.) *Readings in marriage and the family.* Prentice-Hall, 1952. Pp. 392-402.
3. GLUECK, S., & GLUECK, E. Working mothers and delinquency. *Ment. Hyg.,* 1957, 327-352.
4. HAND, H. B. Working mothers and maladjusted children. *J. educ. Sociol.,* 1957, 30, 245-246.

5. HENRY, A. F. Sibling structure and perception of the disciplinary roles of parents. *Sociometry*, 1957, 20, 67-74.

6. HERBST, P. G. Analysis and measurement of a situation: The child in the family. *Hum. Rel.*, 1953, 6, 113-140.

7. HOFFMAN, L. W. Effects of the employment of mothers on parental power relations and the division of household tasks. *Marriage Fam. Living*, 1960, 22, 27-35.

8. HOFFMAN, L. W., ROSEN, S., & LIPPITT, R. Parental coerciveness, child autonomy and child's role at school. *Sociometry*, 1960, 23, 15-22.

9. NYE, F. *Family relationships and delinquent behavior.* Wiley, 1958.

10. ROUMAN, J. School children's problems as related to parental factors. *J. educ. Res.*, 1956, 50, 105-112.

11. SIEGEL, A. E., STOLZ, L. M., HITCHCOCK, E. A., & ADAMSON, J. Dependence and independence in the children of working mothers. *Child Develpm.*, 1959, 30, 533-547.

12. WEISS, R. S., & SAMELSON, N. M. Social roles of American women: their contribution to a sense of usefulness and importance. *Marriage Fam. Living*, 1958, 20, 358-366.

CHILDREN'S EMOTIONAL PROBLEMS AGGRAVATED BY FAMILY MOVES

ROBERT L. STUBBLEFIELD, M.D.

APPROXIMATELY 20 per cent of the people in the United States move to a new location in each calendar year. The reasons for such moves are multiple—economic, military, social, emotional, etc. These moves affect the mental health of individuals in a variety of ways (5, 9). The effect of these moves on the mental health adjustment of children is frequently minimized and poorly understood by parents and by professional personnel (10). The observations of behavior problems of children who were seen in diagnostic and treatment interviews may lead to further exploration and study of these events, their effects, and the possible development of positive approaches of a preventive nature.

An examination of current census reports on the mobility of the population for the United States reveals several significant facts (11). From April 1950 to April 1951, 13.9 per cent (20,694,000) of the people moved within their same county. In the same time, 3.6 per cent (5,276,000) moved to a different county within their state, and 3.5 per cent (5,188,000) moved to another state. The growth and population have been concentrated more heavily in the urban centers so that approximately 60 per cent of the population now resides in urban centers. Young men in their twenties were more mobile than any other age group, since about 35 per cent of them changed their residence during the above-mentioned period of one year. Mobility also varies with occupation; for example, professional and technical groups have a much higher mobility rate than farmers and farm managers. Migratory laborers and their families create many education and health problems and have required the special attention of social agencies for some time (12). It should be noted that fewer people moved in the large urban areas than in smaller cities of 50,000 or less.

Each family's concept of the significance of the move to their children is unique and different. This concept is a production of the individual and group psychodynamics of the family. Where options exist, one might assume that certain practices could be considered more thoughtfully. For example, in view of the work of Spitz (8), Bowlby (3), and others on the importance of early mother-child relationships, preserving these relationships would seem indicated even if the parents are inconvenienced by the presence of the

AMERICAN JOURNAL OF ORTHOPSYCHIATRY, 1955, Vol. 25, pp. 120-124.

younger child in a major family move. I have had occasion to note rather casual placements of infants in a nursery or with a grandparent for several weeks while "mother gets the home in shape." Later these children were seen in pediatric clinics with feeding difficulties and sleep disturbances. In one such instance the pediatrician noted a five-month-old boy who was quite apathetic and withdrawn. The child had not gained weight during the previous month. On inquiry it was learned that the mother had followed her husband to a nearby city where she was establishing their new home. She had planned the child's nursery with great care and had rather casually returned to her mother's home on week ends to be with her young son. With some supporting uncritical comments from the pediatrician, the mother returned to a more intense relationship with the child and the symptoms gradually disappeared.

In school-age children, it would seem indicated to consider the relative importance of the relationships with peers. An eight-year-old girl was transferred in mid-school year, was poorly placed and initially ignored by her classmates and her teacher. In this situation, she reacted with marked aggression, negativism, and regressed to an extremely ambivalent relationship with a younger sibling. This girl had many daydreams about her former playmate, a girl her own age. Her hostility toward her brother was strengthened by his acceptance in his peer group and she attacked him verbally and physically. In a second case, a nine-year-old boy reacted with defiance, aggression, grandiose behavior, and effectively alienated himself from his classmates. He had many fantasies about his early school experiences and developed phobic attitudes about school. One particular fantasy was the recollection of an idealized relationship with a boy his own age. They had roamed the neighborhood together, planned short hikes, and apparently mutually supported each other in the repression of oedipal strivings. As the boy revealed the true nature of his depressed feelings that followed the separation from his playmate, the aggressive behavior subsided. Both his dreams and his spontaneous comments revealed the significance of the loss of his peer group and the return of a strong attachment to his mother. In both of these children, there was good evidence for satisfactory social relationships outside the immediate family group. They reacted to the proposed family moves with intense hostility, which was focused on the parent of the same sex, and developed many magical notions of how they might delay or prevent the family plan. In both of these situations, the family moves were optional and could have been delayed until summer. It is suggested that these children could have established new peer relationships in a more comfortable manner without the concurrent tension of a new school situation.

Problems of adolescents deserve special attention (6). The importance of social groups and clubs to them has been clearly shown by several observers.

Two case examples revealed quite clearly the aggressive nature of the reactions seen in adolescents when they are removed from a satisfactory group and placed in a new, hostilely indifferent group. One girl developed mild obesity, hostility to her environment in fantasy, and other evidences of mild depression. She than resolved a part of her problem by intense preoccupation with her future career, college plans, etc. One 13-year-old boy reacted to the family move with openly aggressive behavior and was expelled from school. Later he made direct sexual attacks on his mother and ran away from home. In this situation, the parents planned their move to a different city but "didn't tell him until the last minute because we didn't want to hurt the poor little fellow's feelings."

How does one evaluate the child's understanding of the family move? It requires some observation of the child's attitude about exploring the outside world, of the type of ego defenses, and his relative security and comfort within the family group. There is an additional dynamic factor to be considered—the emotional attitude of the parents and siblings about the move. If the father's transfer by the company means a better way of life for the family, the child will be more likely to respond to the general enthusiasm about the new venture. If the mother feels that she will lose her dependent position with her own mother, she will convey her own anxiety and resentment in a traumatic way to the child.

It seems to me that children should be aware of proposed family moves a reasonable period of time in advance of the event. There is probably little value in the common practice of "consulting with the child about the advisability of a move to a new location," since this is likely to have little realistic influence on the family's ultimate decision. It seems advisable that parents should be the source of information on the matter—not the casual comment of a family friend or acquaintance. In view of the probable ambivalence in the child who is old enough to grasp the meaning of the occurrence, some attention should be paid to the timing of the discussion. Preferably the child should have an ample opportunity to react to the discovery, to express some of his emotions about it, and to begin the exploration of the reasons for the move and its probable impact on him and on his relationships with his peers.

What are the stabilizing factors that make it easier for a child to make a major family move without a crippling regressive reaction? Proper discussion of this point would involve a broad discussion of the general problems of mental hygiene which are beyond the scope of this paper. Dr. Ridenour indicated in a recent paper (7) that there are multiple kinds of mental health activities in our country and that the purpose of mental health education is to change behavior in certain specified ways. The thesis that behavior can be changed is often belittled by clinicians, either openly or in more subtle ways. In the history of science, we have many examples of careful observations which have led to newer, briefer, and sometimes more effective treatment measures. We are making observations about the significance of inner fantasy life in the development of personality, and most of us, whether correctly or not, are making efforts to apply certain principles derived from play therapy and psychotherapy techniques to pertinent social problems. Naturally, I feel that healthy family relationships are the most significant, stabilizing factor for the child (2, 4). The presence of mutual friends, the friendly understanding and acceptance of teachers, the acceptance and security within church organizations, and the counsel of a competent family physician can make valuable contributions to the well-being of the child (4). Sociologists have studied the mobility in our population in great detail (1). Psychiatry and its related disciplines need to become more familiar with the contributions from sociology in order to develop better methods of dealing with children who are faced with a dramatic change in their environment.

I am not suggesting that the fundamental psychodynamic problems in the individual members of the family are unimportant. I am suggesting that we need to pay more attention to the methods that are used by parents and other persons who come in contact with children, if they attempt to give psychological support to children at the time of a major family move.

In summary: 1) Family moves occur very frequently in our American society. 2) Family moves can significantly distort existing family adjustments. 3) Behavior, dreams and daydreams of children reveal the ambivalence and regression which frequently develop in the children. 4) Methods can be developed which will minimize the traumatic effect of these family moves and which will permit the development of positive attitudes about new friends, new experiences, etc.

REFERENCES

1. ALBIG, W. *A Method of Recording Trends in Urban Residential Mobility.* Sociol. and Soc. Res., 21: 36, 1937.

2. BEACH, A. W. and W. G. *Family Migratoriness and Child Behavior.* Sociol. and Soc. Res., 21: July 1937.

3. BOWLBY, J. *Maternal Care and Mental Health.* World Health Organization, Geneva, 1951.

4. LANGTON, GRACE, and IRVING W. STOUT. *These Well Adjusted Children.* John Day, New York, 1951.

5. LUYKX, H. M. C. *Family Studies in the Eastern Health District.* Hum. Biol., 19: 91–132, 1947.

6. MANGUS, A. R., and R. H. WOODWARD. *Analysis of the Mental Health of High School Students.* A report based on studies conducted jointly by the Division of Mental Hygiene of the Ohio State Department of Public Welfare and Other Agencies, July 1949.

7. RIDENOUR, NINA. *Criteria of Effectiveness in Mental Health Education.* Am. J. Orthopsychiatry, 23: 271–279, 1953.

8. Spitz, R. A. "The Psychogenic Diseases in Infancy," in *The Psychoanalytic Study of the Child*, Vol. 6, p. 255. Internat. Univ. Press, New York, 1951.

9. Tietze, T., P. Lemkau, and M. Cooper. *Personality Disorder and Spatial Mobility.* Am. J. Sociol., 48: 29, 1943.

10. Wattenberg, W. *Mobile Children Need Help.* Educ. Forum, 12: 335–342, 1948.

11. *Current Population Reports.* U. S. Dept. of Commerce, July 14, 1952, Series F-20, No. 39.

12. *Postwar Problems of Migration.* Milbank Memorial Fund, New York, 1947.

INTERVIEWS OF PARENTS OF HIGH ANXIOUS
AND LOW ANXIOUS CHILDREN [1]

KENNETH S. DAVIDSON

An important part of an ongoing project concerned with anxiety in children was a series of interviews with the parents of a selected group of high anxious (HA) and low anxious (LA) children. Descriptions (5) have been presented of the test anxiety (TA) and general anxiety (GA) scales[2] which were used to determine placement of children in the LA and HA groups in the present study. In other reports dealing with these same subjects results were presented of their Rorschach (4), Draw-a-Person (2), and learning task[3] (6) performances, of observations of their classroom behavior (3), and of their parents' ratings (1) of them on a personality check list.

The previous studies provided evidence bearing on the validity of the two anxiety scales. The interviews of the parents were done to assess the validity of the scales further. However, an additional purpose was to obtain information about the children and their environments that would aid in understanding the development of anxiety in children and in deciding on

---

[1] The project of which this study is a part is being supported by a grant from the U. S. Public Health Service, (M-712).

[2] Copies of these two scales are available for research purposes only.

[3] In the study involving the experimental learning task, 24 of the 32 matched pairs of children were used for reasons cited in that publication.

the most fruitful approaches in future investigations. Therefore, for exploratory purposes, many items were formulated and integrated into two standardized interviews without specific predictions about the nature of results or differences between the HA and LA subjects. In a general way, it was predicted that the interview data would describe the LA children more favorably and with fewer and less severe stresses, emotional disturbances, conflicts, and anxieties than the HA children.

Two standardized interviews were developed to provide relevant information with respect to the two anxiety scales. The first interview was focused primarily on the child's school experiences and was more related to the TA scale. The second interview inquired about the subject's personality and emotional development so that information pertaining more to the GA scale was obtained.

METHOD

Subjects

The 64 subjects of this study were chosen from 747 pupils in grades 2 through 5 who had been administered the TA and GA scales the year before. All had taken the Otis Alpha Intelligence Scale and children were excluded who were regarded as serious arithmetic, reading, or behavior problems by their teachers. Additionally, only children whose parents were living and not divorced or separated were selected. Subjects were placed in the HA group if their TA and GA scores fell in the upper quartiles of both distributions; those whose scores were in the lower quartiles were regarded as LA. By matching LA with HA on grade, sex, and Otis Alpha T scores, 32 matched pairs of children were obtained. For each grade-sex group, there were four matched pairs, and in a 2 (anxiety) by 2 (sex) by 4 (grade) arrangement there were four children in each of 16 cells in the design.

Procedure

The parents of each of the 64 subjects were interviewed twice in their homes at their convenience by the author who did not know whether they were parents of a LA or HA subject. In most instances, only the mother was interviewed, although 21 of the fathers were present for all or part of either or both interviews. After all parents had been seen for the first interview, the second interviews were begun. An interval of about two months lapsed before the second interview in each case. After the first interview the mothers completed an attitude scale on child rearing, and in the second interview they rated their children on a personality check list (1). Fathers who were not present completed these rating scales which were left for them. The cooperation of the parents generally can be characterized by the fact that no parent refused to answer any question in either interview.

The analysis of the interview data fell into four categories: biographical data of the children, biographical data of the parents, the childrens' school experiences, and their personality development and emotional adjustment. However, in considering the results in these categories, it was felt that a fifth set of analyses—on the parents' interview behavior—might have important implications. The reason for this was the previous finding (1) that, on the personality check list, fathers of LA rated them significantly more favorably than fathers of HA rated their children while the ratings by the mothers did not differentiate in this respect between the LA and HA subjects. Since the interview data came almost exclusively from mothers, significant differences might be masked, presumably as a result of the mothers of the HA children giving more favorable descriptions of them than the fathers of those children might report. For these reasons the interview behavior of the parents was analyzed and the results will be presented and discussed. Following that, the findings will be presented for the four categories of analyses indicated above. In all the categories the analyses utilized a one-tail test of significance whenever the direction of the results were predicted.

Parental Interview Behavior

The problem that parents' evaluations might mask differences between the LA and HA subjects came to our attention only after the data were collected. As a result, there was no carefully planned attention to, or measurement of, defensiveness during the interviewing. However, after each interview, the interviewer had written his spontaneous reactions—approximately one and a half typed pages—to the mother and the interview. It was decided to evaluate these reports for possible differences between mothers of LA and HA in the tendency to distort or be defensive in answering questions. Such distortions by mothers can be of at least two kinds: conscious withholding or falsification and unconscious defense against recognition both of the mother's and the child's "unacceptable" covert and overt behavior. Of these two kinds of distortions, it was likely that it was the conscious type which may have been noted by the interviewer. Therefore, six judges independently read the two write-ups for each parent with the instructions to rate a parent as "defensive" if the interviewer said something in his report to indicate the parent was consciously censoring the information she was revealing. The judgment was whether *the interviewer had concluded* the parent was defensive, not whether the judge so concluded. Parents not noted as defensive automatically were rated as nondefensive. Judges were unaware of the anxiety group to which a subject belonged. For three of the judges, there was a significant tendency for more mothers of HA boys than mothers of LA boys to be rated as defensive ($p < .10$). For two of the other judges there was a nonsignificant tendency in the same direction while the relationship for the sixth judge was of the chance variety. The ratings of "defensive" were added across judges for each subject and the mothers of the matched pairs of LA and HA boys were compared on this "defensive" score by a dependent t test. The difference between the LA and HA "defensive" scores yielded a t value of 1.745 which indicates a tendency, significant almost at the 5 per cent level, for the HA boys' mothers to get higher "defensive" scores than mothers of the LA boys. The ratings on defensiveness, though in the same direction, did not differentiate significantly between the mothers of the LA and HA girls. Thus, even though the interviewer's write-ups were not as focused on defensiveness as would have been the case if the distortion of the HA mothers had been anticipated, these findings present evidence that the mothers of HA boys were more defensive than the LA boys' mothers.

The implication of this finding is twofold. First, it definitely points to the possibility that the mothers of the HA boys consciously withheld information or distorted the picture in describing their children. For example, the mothers of the HA boys said their children had no more of the anxieties on a check list than the mothers of LA said their boys had, despite the fact that the HA children have admitted to more fears and anxieties. Clearly the suggestion is that the findings for the boys in the categories to be discussed later can be regarded as slanted more favorably toward the HA subjects than would have been the case if their mothers had not been more defensive. Secondly, this finding can be interpreted to mean that HA boys' mothers had more "unacceptable" behaviors to cover up in themselves and in their children, thus lending further evidence to the validity of the anxiety scales. Seeking corroboration of this finding, several objective analyses of the mothers' responses to questions of the interviews were done. All utilized chi square analyses and can be summarized as follows:

1. In a free description of their child's first day of school in the first interview, parents of LA boys used more words (actual count) than parents of HA boys ($p < .01$).

2. To begin the second interview, the examiner said, "Last time we talked about how S felt about school. This time we would like to get a clear picture of what S is like as a person. How would you describe S so that a person like myself who doesn't know S would get an idea of the kind of child S is?" In giving their descriptions, more parents of HA children asked the interviewer a question than parents of the LA subjects ($p < .05$). This finding was more significant for girls ($p < .10$) than boys ($p < .20$).

3. In that free description of their child, parents of HA children said less (word count) before asking the interviewer a question than parents of the LA children ($p < .025$), and they said less in total than LA parents on the same question ($p < .05$).

Thus, it would seem that the LA parents were more spontaneous, told more, and were less dependent on the interviewer than the HA parents in discussing their children's experiences and personalities. Twice as many parents of HA girls as parents of LA girls failed to mention any affect in telling about their child's first day in school ($p < .10$). This offers slight evidence that the LA girls' mothers tended to deal more freely with emotional factors than the mothers of HA girls. More important, these findings indicate further that HA mothers were more defensive in the interviews than LA mothers. As a result the findings below can be regarded as presenting the HA subjects in a better light than if the HA mother had been less defensive. With these considerations in mind, the remaining analyses will be presented and discussed.

Biographical Data of the Children

The results of the analyses of this data are summarized as follows:

1. HA children had more brothers than sisters, while the LA subjects had more sisters than brothers ($p < .02$). This relationship was more significant for boys ($p < .05$) than for girls.[4]

2. Related to that, more HA than LA subjects did not have any sister ($p < .02$), and this finding was stronger for boys ($p < .10$) than for girls.[4]

3. HA boys had more illnesses than the LA boys ($p < .01$).

Additionally, the LA children tended to be followed by sisters or to be the youngest child, while HA subjects were followed by brothers or are themselves "only" children ($p < .10$). The four only children—three boys and one girl—were all in the HA group. These findings suggest that having sisters was less anxiety inducing, especially for boys, than having brothers.

Biographical Data of the Parents

Several items in the first interview concerned the background of the parents. Of these analyses, the results of those attaining significance are listed here:

1. One question asked whether the parents had ever been away for any reason from S for more than a day. The fathers of LA subjects were away from their children overnight more frequently than the fathers of the HA subjects ($p < .05$). This finding was stronger for boys ($p < .10$) than for girls.[4]

2. The mean level of education of the LA fathers was significantly higher than that of the fathers of the HA children ($p < .01$). This difference, too, was significant for the boys ($p < .01$) but not the girls. The same result is expressed in the finding that more LA fathers graduated from high school than fathers of the HA subjects ($p < .025$), with greater significance again for boys ($p < .05$) than for girls.[4]

3. Then, more mothers of the HA boys worked since the subjects were born than did the mothers of the LA boys ($p < .05$).

---

[4] A two-tail test of significance was utilized in obtaining the p values given.

Children's School Experiences and Adjustment

This area was of prime importance in view of the focus of this research on "test anxiety." Analyses of interview data yielded the following significant results:

1. Parents said HA children worry more about missing school for illness than LA children do ($p < .02$). This finding was more significant for girls ($p < .025$) than for boys.

2. Another question was "The first day of school is certainly an important one for a child. But it is also an important one for parents. What were your thoughts and feelings about S starting school?" Parents of HA children felt more conflict and uncertainty when their children first entered school than the parents of LA subjects ($p < .025$). This finding was also more significant for the boys ($p < .025$) than the girls.

3. HA boys tended to start Sunday School at an older age than LA boys ($p = .055$).[4]

4. The last question of the first interview was "Do you think S has learned: (a) *more than* you expected of him, (b) *as much as* you expected of him, (c) *less than* you expected of him?" Parents of LA boys said they learned *as much as* expected while HA boys were described by their parents as learning either *more* or *less* than expected ($p < .05$). In this respect LA girls were said to learn *more* than their parents expected while the parents of HA girls said they learned either *less* than or *as much as* expected of them ($p < .10$).[4]

5. The LA felt more positive than the HA children about starting school this year ($p < .10$) and this was truer for the boys ($p < .05$) than for the girls.

Some trends which approached significance in this category involved communication about school. The LA children found more to tell about school when at home ($p < .10$), and LA boys said more about school before they first entered than HA boys ($p < .10$). The latter subjects had more trouble learning to read than the LA boys ($p < .10$).

In respect to the subjects' school experiences and adjustment, the subjects' actual grades were regarded as important, so they are reported here incidentally, although the data were obtained from school records rather than the interview. The grades were given one full year after the anxiety questionnaires were administered, and matched subjects were compared over-all by dependent t tests and in individual marks by sign tests. The following significant findings, using one-tail tests, were found between the final school marks of the two groups of subjects:

1. LA got higher marks than HA children ($t = 1.900$, $p < .03$).

2. LA got higher marks than HA children as follows: social studies ($p = .095$); work habits ($p = .039$).

3. LA boys got higher marks than HA boys ($t = 2.331$, $p < .025$).

4. LA boys got higher marks than HA boys as follows: social behavior $(p = .073)$; language arts $(p = .011)$; social studies $(p = .090)$; science $(p = .090)$; music $(p = .035)$; and work habits $(p = .055)$.

5. LA girls got higher marks than HA girls $(t = .571, p < .30)$.

Clearly, the LA boys functioned more effectively than their HA mates who were matched on IQ with them. In nine of the 16 matched pairs of LA and HA boys, the LA had better marks, while the HA boys had higher marks in only three. On the other hand, for the girls the results were chance. In half of the pairs the HA had higher grades while the LA girl received higher marks in the other half of the pairs. An interesting point is that whichever girl of a pair did better, tended to do so significantly.

Children's Emotional Adjustment and Development

The major analysis in this category involved the interviewer's write-ups of the first interview. In this, the interviewer rated each sentence of a write-up as to the presence or absence of positive and negative qualities and factors in the environment that pertain to or affect the subjects' emotional adjustment. A positive rating for a sentence would indicate adequate or successful adjustment by the child or an environmental factor promoting such an adjustment. A negative rating of a sentence would indicate difficulties in the child's efforts to cope with his problems. In the event positive and negative aspects were both present and about equal in a sentence, a rating of "both" was given. Sentences which had no bearing on the child's adjustment were rated "neither." To provide a clearer understanding of these ratings, the following are examples of sentences and the judge's evaluations of them.

+   The inner peace and outward quiet is easy to see—they are not demanding or pressing but take what comes and give their children lots of love and affection.

+   Both Mr. and Mrs. ⸺ seem basically in agreement in basic things, but differences can be tolerated and I feel that whatever problems they have between them—they have few, I would guess—would not be saddled on the children.

+   *S* is seen as an able, independent child who goes out to meet the world and the experiences it offers.

−   *S* is sensitive and cries easily if reprimanded, punished, frustrated or has difficulties with playmates *S* can't solve.

−   *S* is a child with phobias and anxieties, some masked, others blatant.

−   Mrs. ⸺ is a nervous woman, expecting danger and trouble everywhere and wants to solve her child's problems before they come up.

+ −   But still one gets a feeling of immaturity in many things as well as maturity in many others.

+ −   *S*'s feelings can be hurt easily but *S* is much more resilient than before.

+ − She describes S as generally meeting situations effectively and eagerly, though she says S is slow in school and that S worries quite a bit about S's difficulty in keeping up with the class.

As a reliability check, the interviewer's ratings of the sentences were compared with those by an independent judge on the write-ups of the first interviews for eight pairs of LA and HA children. There were four pairs each of boys and girls chosen at random. Each judge independently rated each sentence of 16 reports. When the ratings were completed and compared, it was found that total agreement was present on 263, or 78 per cent, of the 338 ratings each judge had made. Of the 75 disagreements, only four involved completely opposite ratings, plus by one and minus by the other rater. For each of these 16 cases, the number of minus ratings was subtracted from that of the positive ratings and the direction, plus or minus, indicated by sign. In the reliability check this procedure gave two "favorable-unfavorable" scores (one from each judge's ratings) for each subject. The interjudge correlation of these scores was $+.94$, indicating a high degree of agreement as to over-all favorableness of their ratings for these subjects. Finally, when the dependent t test was applied to the differences in "favorable-unfavorable" scores of the eight matched pairs, the results were significant beyond the 1 per cent level for both judges. That is, both judges rated the LA reports significantly more favorably than those written for the HA subjects.

Then, for each of the 64 subjects the number of plus and minus ratings by the interviewer were added algebraically to obtain a "favorable-unfavorable" score for each child. The differences in these scores for the 32 matched pairs were then subjected to the dependent t test. For all 64 subjects the LA subject write-ups were rated more favorably than those of the HA children ($p < .01$), and the results were significant for both boys ($p < .01$) and girls ($p < .01$). Of all the results obtained from comparisons of LA with HA, this is certainly one of the most striking. Additionally, HA children tended to have more negative than positive statements written whereas the LA tended to have more positive than negative statements written in the reports of the interviews ($p < .025$). That finding was more significant for the boys ($p < .05$) than for the girls ($p < .15$). The interviewer not only did not know at any time which children were HA and which were LA but all through the interviewing had the impression that the write-ups would not predict which were the HA and LA subjects. While these findings are not based on ratings of anxiety, they clearly indicate that the interviewer and an independent judge evaluated the LA children as better adjusted and having more favorable environments in general mental health terms than the HA subjects.

Finally, it was found that LA children tended to have more modes of expressing anger than their HA mates ($p < .025$). For both the girls and the boys separately the findings tended toward significance ($p < .10$). Parents indicated whether or not S, when angry, (a) gets sulky and silent,

111

(b) hits people, (c) throws things, (d) talks angrily, or used any other methods of expressing anger. The suggestion here is that the LA were freer to express aggression, at least in choosing how to vent their feelings and impulses. The HA, more concerned about the consequences of their actions in regard to anger, tended to find one "safe" way of releasing their tensions and to rely on it rather exclusively. Thus, they were more blocked in selecting appropriate modes of expression of anger depending on the situation.

Discussion

There are three outstanding features of the results. The first is that not one of the findings obtained presented a more favorable picture for the HA children. Each result described the LA as more effective, having fewer and less intense conflicts and better preparation and ability to face and solve the problems of emotional development. Actually many questions did not yield significant results—this for a variety of reasons, such as parental defensiveness, phrasing of questions, and inclusion of many exploratory questions, which were not based on specific predictions or hypotheses. It might be maintained that the fathers of the LA being away overnight more could be regarded as favoring the HA subjects. It is true that the LA children experienced more departures of their fathers which could evoke greater anxiety in those children. However, in all cases these subjects experienced the "safe return" of their fathers, and it is easily conceivable that this was the crucial aspect of the fathers' being away overnight. From that viewpoint the LA children would have had greater opportunity to develop a feeling of security that the departing fathers would return safely.

The second noteworthy feature of these results is not only did the findings favor the LA but the evidence that the mothers of the HA were more defensive, less verbal, and more dependent on the interviewer suggests that further significant findings favoring the LA children were masked or covered up as a result of the greater defensiveness of the HA mothers. Without the differential tendency to censor, the near-significant findings presented might have attained more reliable levels of significance and other analyses of the interview data might have yielded meaningful differences.

The third feature of the findings presented here is that only two of the results were significant only for girls, while significant results were obtained repeatedly for the boys but not for the girls. This is even more striking when it is noted that the difference in anxiety score was greater for the girls than for the boys. The HA girls had higher anxiety scores than HA boys, while LA boys' anxiety scores were only slightly lower than those of the LA girls. In spite of this, more significant differences were found between LA and HA boys than were found for the girls. This could suggest that the anxiety scales are actually "boys' scales" or sex-biased in that they measure the anxieties which can be interfering in boys. This is supported by the finding that the HA boys' school marks were significantly lower than those of the LA boys, whereas the finding for the girls in this respect was one of chance difference. On the other hand, there was the finding, equally significant for girls as well as boys, that the interviewer's write-ups were rated favorably for the LA and unfavorably for the HA children. This finding indicates that the LA girls and boys were seen by the interviewer and an independent judge as more effective and having more favorable experiences in their emotional growth and interpersonal relationships. This result suggests that the TA and GA scales are valid measures of anxiety for both boys and girls.

In evaluating the differential results for boys and girls, perhaps it should be mentioned that there is often a tendency to regard children as a homogeneous group and to disregard the sex differences because similarities *are* found and broader generalizations *may seem* more desirable than more specific ones. Certainly, there is simple cultural evidence indicating that boys and girls receive different evaluations, treatment, and training. With regard to anxiety girls are permitted to express anxiety and in fact in many respects are rewarded if they are or behave as if they were anxious. On the other hand, boys are rewarded if they are brave little men without fears. Such a view aids in understanding why girls' anxiety scores are higher than boys' and helps explain why admission of anxiety by girls is not necessarily related to interference with their effectiveness, while significant results are found for the boys. Among girls, for example, admitting the fearing of animals may be acceptable and ego-syntonic, and such fears need not reflect an interfering factor on performance or adjustment. But in boys the same fears are unacceptable or ego-alien, and fear is related to conflicts which interfere with the HA boys' successful adjustment.

Some attention, we feel, should be given to the finding that HA and LA girls, as in the case of boys, were significantly differentiated by the evaluation of the interview write-ups, the LA girls being evaluated more favorably. This is one of the very few times that we have obtained the same findings for boys *and* girls. Before attempting to interpret this finding it is necessary to recall that on the basis of teacher grades the LA girls *as a group* did no better than the HA girls. However, in approximately half the cases the LA girl tended to do significantly better than her paired mate while in the remaining cases the HA girl tended to do significantly better than her paired mate. It is possible that among girls an HA score can reflect a high degree of motivation, or the strength of interfering factors, or a combination of both. While an HA score among boys may reflect the same possibilities, it more often than not reflects the strength of interfering factors. Our observations (3) of these same subjects in the classroom fits in well with this interpretation. In that study we found that more HA than LA girls were described as having a high need for achievement, while the observational picture of the HA boys emphasized their inadequacies rather than their strength of motivation. If these spsculations have merit, they suggest as an important problem for future investigation why two girls, both of whom admit to many anxieties, apparently differ in how they are affected by such anxieties. Or to put it another way: It appears necessary to determine whether girls' admission of much anxiety on a questionnaire is experienced as ego-syntonic or ego-alien. From our various studies it appears that among boys such admissions are most frequently experienced as ego-alien.

REFERENCES

1. DAVIDSON, K. S., SARASON, S. B., LIGHTHALL, F. F., WAITE, R. R., & SARNOFF, I. Differences between mothers' and fathers' ratings of low anxious and high anxious children. *Child Develpm.,* 1958, 29, 155-160.

2. FOX, CYNTHIA, DAVIDSON, K. S., LIGHTHALL, F. F., WAITE, R. R., & SARASON, S. B. Human figure drawings of high and low anxious children. *Child Develpm.,* 1958, 29, 297-301.

3. SARASON, S. B., DAVIDSON, K. S., LIGHTHALL, F. F., & WAITE, R. R. Classroom observations of high and low anxious children. *Child Develpm.,* 1958, 29, 287-295.

4. SARASON, S. B., DAVIDSON, K. S., LIGHTHALL, F. F., & WAITE, R. R. Rorschach behavior and performance of high and low anxious children. *Child Develpm.,* 1958, 29, 277-285.

5. SARASON, S. B., DAVIDSON, K. S., LIGHTHALL, F. F., & WAITE, R. R. A test anxiety scale for children. *Child Develpm.,* 1958, 29, 105-113.

6. WAITE, R. R., SARASON, S. B., LIGHTHALL, F. F., & DAVIDSON, K. S. A study of anxiety and learning in children. *J. abnorm. soc. Psychol.,* 1958, 57, 267-270.

COMPARISON OF DATA OBTAINED FROM MOTHERS AND FATHERS ON CHILDREARING PRACTICES AND THEIR RELATION TO CHILD AGGRESSION [1]

LEONARD D. ERON,[*] THOMAS J BANTA,[2]
LEOPOLD O. WALDER, *and* JEROME H. LAULICHT[3]

Rip Van Winkle Foundation

In reviewing the literature having to do with behavior of children as it is related to behavior and attitudes of parents, one is struck by two methodological biases which do not permit a clear-cut evaluation of the substantive findings of a majority of these studies. The first has to do with the disregard of the father both as an important socializing influence and as an informant. A search of the literature between 1929 and 1956 revealed 160 publications dealing with mother-child relationships but only 11 with father-child relationships (10). Since that time there have been a few more studies which have considered the importance of father-centered variables, e.g., Bronfenbrenner (2), Miller and Swanson (9), Sears, Maccoby, and Levin (11), Sears, Pintler, and Sears (12), but information about fathers in these studies usually has been obtained second-hand, either from the mother or from the child himself. This introduces the second methodological bias which is the contamination that is likely when assessments of both parental and child behavior (presumed antecedent and consequent) are made by the same individual. A study in identification by Levin and Sears (8), as well as the earlier Sears' studies (12, 13), are not subject to this error, although they are to the first. When both the predictor and criterion are obtained from the same subject, then response set cannot be eliminated from the possible interpretations of the results. In addition to contributing important information which has usually been lacking in childrearing studies, the use of both mother and father as informants could serve as one check on this source of error. The optimal procedure, of course, is to have completely

[*] Mental Health Research Center, Rip Van Winkle Foundation, 886 Columbia Street, Hudson, New York.

[1] This is a revised version of a paper delivered at the Eastern Psychological Association meetings, New York City, April 16, 1960. The research has been supported by grant M-1726 from the United States Public Health Service. Thanks for cooperation and support are due to W. Richards Bonneau, Principal, Ockawamick Central School; Robert Cullen, Principal, Claverack Union Free School; George Pike, Elementary Supervisor, Hudson Public Schools; Jack Roosa, Principal, Greenport School; and the following third-grade teachers: Mrs. Kathelyn Caswell, Mrs. Grace Clapp, Mrs. Rose Healy, Mrs. Catherine McNamara, Mrs. Patricia McNamara, and Mrs. Winifred Rockefeller. We should also like to thank all the children and their parents, who of course must remain anonymous, for their excellent cooperation.

[2] Now at University of Wisconsin.

[3] Now at Berkshire Industrial Farm, Canaan, New York.

CHILD DEVELOPMENT, 1961, Vol. 32, pp. 457-472.

independent observations of the child and individual measures obtained from both parents. A few recent studies have approximated this goal. Davidson *et al.* (5) administered anxiety questionnaires to a group of children; they then interviewed the mothers *vis a vis,* but merely left a check list of personality characteristics of the child to be completed by the father. Both parents were interviewed by Peterson *et al.* (10), but they did not have independent observations of the child's behavior; although they partially overcame this type of contamination by comparing the attitudes of one parent with judgments of the child's behaviors based on reports of the other parent. Despite these limitations on clear-cut interpretation, both of these studies showed differential results when predicting to child behavior from either mother or father interviews. In the study here reported it has been possible to interview fathers and mothers separately and to obtain independent measures of the children from other informants. It is with the relations among items from these three sources of information that this paper is concerned.

SUBJECTS AND PROCEDURES

A group of 158 children, the total population of six third-grade classes from divergent socioeconomic areas in a semirural county, served as a pool of subjects. Sixty children were drawn from this group on the basis of their scores on an aggression sociometric (described below) administered in the classroom. Thus, the subjects included the 10 most aggressive boys in this sample, the 10 least aggressive boys, 10 boys in the middle range, and three similar groups of girls. Both parents (where available) of each of these children were contacted for personal, individual interviews. The families of only three of these preselected children refused to participate, and they were replaced by subjects with very comparable scores. It was thus possible to interview all of the mothers and 50 of the 58 available fathers. The interviews were conducted by six experienced interviewers[4] either in the subject's home or the Foundation offices. At the time of the interview, the interviewers had no knowledge of the aggression classification of the subject.

MEASURES

Aggression Index

This is a Guess-Who technique in which every child in a class rates everybody else on a selected series of 22 specific aggression and four aggression anxiety items. These 26 items were what remained after a process of "sifting and winnowing" from an original pool of 1000 short behavioral descriptions which had originally been collected from the literature and by interviewing experts:

---

[4] Thanks are due to Dr. Marjorie Collins and Mrs. Madeline Eron, psychologists, and Miss Mary Lawrence, psychiatric social worker, who assisted three of the authors (LE, JL, and LW) in obtaining these interviews.

(The labels in parentheses refer to type of aggression.)

Cluster 1
1. Who is a pest? (Indirect)
2. Who does not obey the teacher? (Unclassified)
3. Who takes the teacher's things without permission? (Acquisitive)
4. Who is always getting into trouble? (Unclassified)
5. Who tattles to the teacher? (Indirect)
6. Who is rude to the teacher? (Verbal)

Cluster 2
7. Who starts a fight over nothing? (Physical)
8. Who says mean things? (Verbal)
9. Who makes it hard for children to get things done? (Indirect)
10. Who pushes or shoves children? (Physical)
11. Who does things that bother others? (Indirect)

Cluster 3
12. Who forgets to return borrowed things? (Acquisitive)
13. Who often says "Give me that"? (Acquisitive)
14. Who makes marks on the desk? (Physical, against property)
15. Who takes other children's things without asking? (Acquisitive)

Individual Aggression Items
16. Who will always fight back if someone else hits them first? (Physical)
17. Who gives dirty looks or sticks out their tongue at other children? (Verbal)
18. Who complains to the teacher when she tells them what to do? (Verbal)
19. Who grabs things from other. children? (Acquisitive)
20. Who uses bad words when another child bothers them? (Verbal)
21. Who gets very, very mad at times? (Unclassified)
22. Who makes up stories and lies to get other children into trouble? (Indirect)

Anxiety about Aggression Items
23. Who is always polite? (Unclassified)
24. Who will never fight even when picked on? (Physical)
25. Who will never argue even when they are right? (Verbal)
26. Who says, "Excuse me," even when they have not done anything bad? (Unclassified)

Rejection by Peers
27. Who are the children that you wish were not in your class at all?

Popularity with Peers
28. Who are the children that you would like to have for your best friends?
29. Who do you know best of all?
30. Who would you like to sit next to in class?
31. Who would you like to play with?

They represented the final distillation of a long series of preliminary studies including armchair judgments by experts as to type of aggression involved, pilot studies with groups of 8-year-olds, and an extended tryout of two alternate forms on 974 third graders, with subsequent cluster and item analyses. The purpose was to find items on which the children, as judges, could agree with each other as to who of their classmates did what. Also included in this sociometric were one rejection and four popularity items. The procedure involved giving each child a booklet containing one page for each question. The names of all children in the class were listed on each page, and subjects were instructed to cross out the names of those children who acted in the way described by the particular question for that page which was read aloud to them by the examiner. The score for each child was based on the number of judges choosing him as someone who fitted a particular behavioral description. Thus, if 10 members of a class crossed out Johnny Jones' name as someone who said mean things, Johnny's raw score was 10 for that item. The raw scores were converted into percentages to correct for differences in class size.

The reliability of this instrument, based on interjudge agreement, had been shown to be excellent, with minimum shrinkage on cross-validation. A cluster analysis isolated three sets of items, one concerned with aggression against teacher, one with aggression against peer, and one having to do with a particular type of aggression which was called acquisitive (*see* Table 1). Also included in this measure which was derived from the two alternate forms were a number of individual items, each with good reliability (at least .70). These had been retained in order to tap different types of aggression, different objects, and different provocation levels.

TABLE 1

CLUSTER RELIABILITIES

	Cluster	Median Reliability*	Cross Validation
Teacher as object	1	.92	.86
Peer as object	2	.87	.77
Acquisitive	3	.85	.80

* The median reliability is based on 12 different groups (six classes, each divided by sex into two groups). Typically, the mean is higher than the median.

There was no relation between score on the aggression measure and amount of interpersonal activity the child engages in as rated by the teacher (r ranged from $+.22$ to $-.38$ in six classes with median r of .00) nor with the position of a child's name on the list (r ranged from $+.19$ to $-.15$ with median r of .00). As for the distribution of the aggression scores among the subjects, it was found that very few children were highly aggressive; however, the vast majority were moderately aggressive and girls had lower scores than boys. The more popular children were less aggressive, but even the most popular children were rated as aggressive in some ways. On the cluster having to do with aggression towards the teacher, identically shaped distributions of scores (J curves) were obtained for boys and girls. This type of distribution would be expected in most kinds of nonconforming behavior, of which aggression towards teachers is certainly an example.

In addition, Cureton's r_{rb} (4) of .84, uncorrected for attenuation, was obtained between teacher's and peers' rating on this cluster. It is reasonable to assume that the high reliability coefficients themselves indicated validity because the raters were probably basing their judgments on observations of the same specific behaviors (3, 6). The shape of the distribution curves and its consistency from class to class and between boys and girls were further evidence of validity, as were the predicted relations into which the aggression and aggression anxiety items entered with the other classroom measures: popularity-rejection, IQ, and teacher's ratings of aggression (see Table 2). There was also some clinical evidence of validity since a few of the subjects had been referred to the Clinic Guidance Service prior or subsequent to the administration, and in each case, the children who were shown to be overly aggressive scored high on the sociometric.

TABLE 2

INTERCORRELATIONS AMONG CLASSROOM MEASURES*

Other Measure	Aggression Measure	Aggression Anxiety
Rejection	.73	—.46
Popularity	—.38	.48
Teacher rating on all items	.63	—.34
IQ	—.17	.20

* A correlation of .23 is significant at the .01 level of confidence.

Parent Interview

This is an objective, almost entirely precoded interview which takes about 1½ hours to administer. Its purpose is to get at the sociocultural and psychological antecedents of aggression as they are mediated by child-parent interaction. Included in this interview, which was pretested on 200 mothers and fathers, are a number of variables suggested as important by both general behavior theory and clinical hunches. It was felt that a profitable way to look at the differential distribution of behaviors which exist in varying degree in different segments of society was through the learning environments provided by these subcultures. Thus, the pertinent variables had to do with rewards and punishments for aggressive behavior, standards of aggressive behavior, role models, identification, and presumed frustrating antecedents to such behavior. These variables are listed below, with definitions and examples of items to tap them:

PARENT INTERVIEW VARIABLES

1. *Approval of Aggression*—Evaluative standards for aggressive behavior stated in terms of approval or disapproval of specific items of aggressive behavior which appear in the school aggression measure. Example: Suppose

NAME said mean things to another child. Would you: 0. strongly disapprove, 1. mildly disapprove, 2. not care (and don't know), 3. mildly approve, 4. strongly approve.

2. *Confessing by Child*—Extent to which a child behaves as if he were monitoring his own behavior in a way he thinks a socializing agent would. These items are closed-end versions of two questions by Sears, Maccoby, and Levin (11). Example: When NAME has done something naughty and you haven't seen him do it, does he come and tell you about it without your having to ask him? 4. all the time, 3. most of the time, 2. some of the time, 1. almost never, 0. never.

3. *Dependence Avoidance of Child*—Inability or unwillingness of the child to accept help or rely on others. Example: Does NAME seem embarrassed when you take his part? 0. no, 1. sometimes (and don't know), 2. yes.

4. *Ethnicity* (generational level)—Number of generations in which parents' forebears have lived in the United States.

5, 6. *Father's and Mother's Aggression*—Tendency of the parent to display aggressive behavior in situations which often elicit aggressive responses. Each parent rates himself and is rated by the other parent on each of these situations. Example: Suppose you are driving a new car and get into an accident which is clearly the other driver's fault. Would you show your anger if: 1. he says, "What's the matter, can't you drive?" 2. he apologizes? 3. he says, "I'm not going to say anything until I see a lawyer"? 4. he laughs it off?

7. *Home Aggression of Child*—Frequency of acts whose goal response is injury to another object. Example: How often does NAME say mean things to another child? 0. never, 1. rarely, 2. occasionally, 3. pretty often, 4. frequently, 5. daily. These alternatives were specifically defined in terms of frequency in time and typed on cards which were handed to the respondent.

8. *Lack of Social Participation*—Degree of participation of respondent in formal and informal social relationships. Example: About how many times in the past year have you attended meetings or affairs of any *local* organizations, societies or clubs? 0. 13+, 1. 7-12, 2. 4-6, 3. 1-3, 4. none.

9. *Nonrecognition of Child's Needs*—An aspect of nonnurturant behavior. (For other aspect of nonnurturant behavior see *Punishment for Nurturance Signals* below.) Example: Do you usually have time so that NAME can talk to you about things that interest him? 0. yes, 1. no (and don't know).

10. *Parental Aspirations for Child*—Level of education parent hopes child will attain. Example: How much education do you expect NAME to get? 1. high school + specialized training or college, 2. high school graduate or less.

11. *Parental Aspirations for Self*—Example: When you left school what particular kind of occupation or life work was it your ambition to reach some day? Aspirations for: 1. professional status, 2. minor profession, small business or farm owner, 3. skilled worker trades, 4. semiskilled or unskilled occupations.

12. *Parental Disharmony*—The extent of disharmony in the home as measured by disagreement about various specific matters of importance in a family; items dealing with arguments between husband and wife, and presumptive evidence such as separation, divorce, amount of time spent together, etc. Example: Are you satisfied with how your SPOUSE handles money? 0. yes, 1. sometimes (and don't know), 2. no.

13. *Parental Rejection*—The number of changes in the child's behavior (aggression excluded) and characteristics desired by the socializing agent. The parent is considered to be accepting when he indicates that his needs are

satisfied by the child: "I like you the way you are." Example: Do you think NAME wastes too much time? 2. yes, 1. sometimes (and don't know), 0. no.

14. *Parental Restrictiveness*—Extent to which the child defines behaviors which are proper for him to perform rather than the agent defining proper behaviors for the child. Restrictiveness refers to the amount of control exercised by the agent over the child. Example: Do you make NAME finish up everything he is served as mealtime? 2. yes, 1. sometimes (and don't know), 0. no.

15. *Punishment for Aggression*—Rewards and punishments of various *intensities* administered by socializing agents contingent upon the child's aggressive behavior. Example: What do you usually do when NAME is rude to you? (Verbatim response and probes recorded, subsequently rated by three judges on a scale from 1 to 7.) 1. rewarding aggression, 2. don't do anything, 3-7. mild to severe punishment for aggression.

16. *Punishment for Dependency*—Rewards and punishments of various intensities administered by socializing agent when child asks for help. Example: What do you usually do when NAME asks for help? (Each response was rated by three judges on a scale from 1 to 4): 1. giving help, to 4. pun--ishing the child.

17. *Punishment for Nurturance Signals*—Rewards and punishment of various intensities administered to child by socializing agent in situations which might tend to lead to nurturant behavior on part of agent. Example: What do you usually do when NAME is afraid? (Each response was rated by three judges on a scale from 1 to 4): 1 giving nurturance, to 4. punishing the child.

18. *Residential Mobility*—A measure of the number of times the child changed residence and thereby had to change schools and/or find new friends. Example: How often has moving meant that NAME had to find new friends? 0. none, 1. once, 2. 2-3 times, 3. 4+.

19. *Rural Background*—Population size of geographic area in which respondent was born and grew up. Example: Where did the family live when you were born—on a farm, or in a village, town, small city, medium-sized city, or big city? 1. big city (500,000+), 2. medium-sized city (100,000-500,000), 3. small city (10,000-100,000), 4. town (1,000-10,000), 5. village (under 1,000), 6. farm.

20, 21. *Shame, at home and out of home*—Tendency to punish in public assessed by items involving different kinds of punishments and different publics. Example: Suppose NAME was naughty and you felt he deserved a scolding. Would you do it when: (1) your SPOUSE and other children could hear it? (2) one of NAME's friends could hear? (3) one of your close friends or relatives could hear? (4) a neighbor or acquaintance could hear? (5) you were in public and someone else might hear? 0. no. 1. sometimes (and don't know), 2. yes. The first item constitutes a separate measure, punishing the child in front of his family which defines home shame.

22. *Social Isolation of Child*—Frequency and type of contacts with peers outside of school. Example: About how many children of NAME's age live in the neighborhood? Would you say about one or two, three to five, or more than five? 3. none, 2. 1-2, 1. 3-5, 0. 5+.

No definition was accepted for these variables until items could be written which were judged by a number of experts to fit the definition. Emphasis was placed on the necessity for distinctive definitions and measures of each concept in order that hypotheses about how they relate to overt aggression in school could be tested both singly and in combination. The median number of items for each variable was 10, with a range from 1 to 20.

Before the relations of mother and father interview variables to each other and to the independently obtained criterion measure were tested, the homogeneity of the variables was increased by eliminating all items which correlated less than .30 with the total scale score of which it was a part. These item-total correlations were done separately for mothers and fathers since it was felt that there would be some questions more appropriately asked of fathers and others of mothers. For 14 of the 22 variables under consideration, overlap of questions between mother and father was complete. Of the remaining eight, subsequent analyses on six of them showed there was little difference in results whether or not items completely overlapped (1). It turns out that it makes little difference in this report whether scores are calculated on the basis of the refined scales with incomplete overlap between mother and father· questions or on scales with identical questions for both groups.

RESULTS AND DISCUSSION

Once homogeneous sets of items had been derived, a number of correlational analyses were done. First, scores on each variable from mother's interview were correlated with scores on similar variables in the father's interview. As is shown in Table 3, of 22 correlations, only 10 were significantly better than zero ($p < .05$). It is obvious that mothers' and fathers' responses cannot be substituted for one another, at least in this childrearing questionnaire.

An examination of Table 3 reveals that the higher correlations generally are for those variables which have to do with the respondent himself, his

TABLE 3

CORRELATIONS BETWEEN MOTHERS AND FATHERS ON
INTERVIEW VARIABLES*

Variable	r	Variable	r
Residential Mobility	.91	Confessing by Child	.25
Parental Rejection	.64	Ethnicity (Generational Level)	.21
Lack of Social Participation	.63	Nonrecognition of Child's Needs	.20
Parental Aspirations for Child	.52	Shame Out of Home	.16
Parental Disharmony	.46	Mother's Aggression	.15
Social Isolation of Child	.42	Punishment for Nurturance Signals	.13
Punishment for Aggression	.42	Approval of Home Aggression	.09
Parental Restrictiveness	.38	Parental Aspirations for Self	.07
Father's Aggression	.35	Shame at Home	—.06
Rural Background	.32	Child's Dependence Avoidance	—.05
Home Aggression of Child	.25	Punishment for Dependency	—.04

*$r_{.05} = .28$.

own attitudes and feelings; the lower correlations, for the most part, are for those variables having to do with the child's behavior or the parent's interaction with the child. This reveals something about marital choice perhaps (likes attract), but it also shows that mother and father cannot agree in reporting their perceptions of their own child's behavior. However, on the one really objective item that both parents rated, residential mobility, the correlation was .91. Thus, it is not that the parents cannot render reliable information, but perhaps mother and father each observe and react to children differently, and the observations and reactions of each must be taken into account to get a complete picture of parental socialization influences on child behavior.

The same conclusion can be drawn from the next analysis which was the intercorrelation of each interview variable with the other, as well as with the independently obtained classroom measures, done separately for mothers and fathers. For any one variable, all correlations significant at or beyond the .05 level for either mother or father are reported. These appear in Table 4. Although the correlation between mothers' and fathers' scores on any one variable may be better than zero, their scores on that particular variable do not relate to those on other variables in the same way. Thus, for example, the correlation between mother's and father's rating of rejection is .64; however, while mother's rejection score relates significantly to all the classroom measures, father's rejection relates to only one of them. On the other hand, father's rejection relates to a number of other variables in his interview while mother's rejection relates to none of these.

The opposite is true for ethnicity or generational level, a classification of parents on how long ago their ancestors came to this country (on which

TABLE 4

SOME CORRELATIONS AMONG SCALES

Variable	Mother $N=59$ $r_{.05}=.26$		Father $N=50$ $r_{.05}=.28$
A. *Parental Rejection* (*r* mother-father = .64)			
School Aggression	.40		.31
Aggression Anxiety	—.37		—.17
Popularity with Peers	—.29		—.12
Peer Rejection	.35		.20
Home Aggression of Child	.11	*	.49
Confessing by Child	—.07	**	—.58
Parental Disharmony	.10	*	.42
Parent's Aggression	—.03	*	.32
Rural Background	—.12		—.37
Punishment for Dependency	.07		.36
Punishment for Aggression	.20		.44

(continued on next page)

Table 4 (*continued*)

SOME CORRELATIONS AMONG SCALES

Variable	Mother N=59 r.₀₅=.26		Father N=50 r.₀₅=.28
B. *Ethnicity* (generational level) (*r* mother-father = .21)			
School Aggression	.00		.26
Popularity with Peers	.08	*	—.30
Peer Rejection	—.03	**	.41
Home Aggression of Child	.11	**	—.29
Lack of Social Participation	.06		.28
C. *Parent's Aggression* (*r* for mother's aggression = .15; *r* for father's aggression = .35)			
Home Aggression of Child	—.05	**	.36
Parental Rejection	—.03	*	.32
Spouse's Aggression	.24		.29
Punishment for Dependency	—.10	**	.33
Nonrecognition of Child's Needs	—.37	*	—.02
D. *Punishment for Aggression* (*r* mother-father = .42)			
School Aggression	.0?		.31
Home Aggression of Child	.4?		.46
Confessing by Child	—.17		—.35
Parental Disharmony	.28		.18
Parental Rejection	.20		.44
Parental Restrictiveness	.42		.28
Approval of Home Aggression	.00		—.28
Rural Background	—.26		—.16
Shame at Home	.16		.32
Child's Dependence Avoidance	.00	*	.38
Nonrecognition of Child's Needs	—.35		—.14
E. *Confessing by Child* (*r* mother-father = .25)			
School Aggression	—.21		—.31
Peer Rejection	—.10		—.29
Home Aggression of Child	—.28		—.07
Residential Mobility	.04	*	—.32
Parental Rejection	—.07	**	—.58
Approval of Home Aggression	—.32		—.14
Rural Background	.12		.28
Lack of Social Participation	.04	*	—.34
Punishment for Dependency	.10	*	—.28
Punishment for Aggression	—.17		—.35
Punishment for Nurturance	—.04		—.28

* Difference between *r* for mother and father significant at .10 level.
** Difference between *r* for mother and father significant at .05 level.

there is no significant relation between mother and father). Here it is the father's score that is discriminating. Whereas mother's ethnicity was not significantly related to any other variable, father's ethnicity was significantly related to rejection by peers and home aggression of child, among other things. The relation between father's ethnicity and child's behavior is especially significant when fathers and sons are paired. For example, father's ethnicity related $+.53$ ($p < .001$) to son's school aggression and $-.53$ to his home aggression. One possible interpretation would be that ethnic fathers do not tolerate aggression in the home, and thus the tendency on the part of the son to aggress is displaced to the school context. Another possibility is that ethnic fathers may provide a more aggressive role model by their punitive behavior at home. At any rate, it would seem that father's ethnicity has a more important influence on the child's behavior and the reaction of others to him than does mother's ethnicity, at least for boys (correlation between father's ethnicity and daughter's aggression fails to reach significance at the .05 level; indeed, the only significant correlations for ethnicity of girls' fathers are with social participation [$-.40$] and sanctions for nurturance [$-.42$]).

The likelihood of contaminated data which is present when both predictor and criterion measures are obtained from the same informant, as is often done in childrearing studies, is seen in the relation of the parent's self-rating of aggression to other variables. This measure is not related to school aggression or any other independently obtained measures but is related, at least for fathers, to ratings of the child's home aggression, as well as spouse's aggression and rejection. The relation of parent's aggression to rejection is especially marked for father-daughter pairs (.52). Furthermore, those fathers who score high on rejection of their daughters also tend to rate their wives as aggressive (.49). Thus, those respondents who are willing to admit that they themselves are aggressive will also tend to say that wife and daughter are aggressive and that daughter does not measure up to their standards. Since father's self-rating of aggression related only to his own rating of child's aggression and not at all to the independently obtained rating, response set is certainly a compelling consideration.

Again, although both mother's and father's punishments for aggressive behavior are related to the frequency of aggression at home, in each case both these sets of items are reported by the same informant, and response set must also be considered as a reason for this relation. Only father's punishment is significantly related to the independently obtained measure of school aggression. This relation holds especially for father-son pairs ($r = .46$). Thus, it seems that what the father does in response to the child's home aggression is more likely to influence aggressive behavior of the son than what the mother does. The same results obtained when each of the 13 items of aggressive behavior in school which comprised the aggression score from the parent's interview were considered separately. It was still the more punitive father who had the more aggressive child in school. The results for mother were in the same direction, but none of the correlations between punishment by the mother for a specific behavior and the appearance of that behavior in school was significant. The importance of the father as a role model for aggressive behavior is here strongly suggested. Levin and Sears (8) have stressed the importance of the father as a model. In a study of fantasy aggression they found that boys (attending nursery school) who were punished by their fathers and who were also identified with their fathers tended to be more aggressive in the doll play situation than those not so identified or punished. Their measure of identification was a rating of superego formation based on four open-ended questions having to do with confessing and denying by the child of proscribed acts he was known to have committed. These questions were asked of mothers only.

In the present study two of these four questions were adapted to a closed-end version, thus forming the scale of confessing. They were asked of both mothers and fathers with differing results. It was found that indeed, confessing behavior of the child as rated by the father was related to the independently obtained measure of school aggression, but in the opposite direction from the Levin and Sears results and with these results holding for both boys and girls ($-.39$ for girls; $-.37$ for boys). However, the relation between confessing and school aggression was not significant either for mother-son or mother-daughter pairs. The same holds true for the relation between confessing and punishment for aggression. There is a significant relation for fathers but not for mothers, especially for father-son pairs ($-.53$). The important feature in the aggression-confessing-punishment relation may indeed be the punitiveness which would lend support to the role model hypothesis. At any rate, these results are similar to those of Levin and Sears in stressing the importance of the father, especially for boys. The difference in direction of the results is likely a function of the difference in the nature of the criterion, in one case real-life aggression as rated by the child's peers, and in the second case, fantasy aggression, as observed in doll play by the experimenters. In the latter case, the child, who is rated by the experimenter, is actually playing the role of the "daddy" doll; in the former he is rated by his peers as he, the child himself, behaves in the natural setting. Also accounting for the variation may be the difference in age level, preschool vs. third grade, as well as the different operations used in measuring the variable, confessing.[5]

Discussion thus far has dealt with correlations between measures obtained from the same informant. When cross-over correlations are considered, e.g., the correlation of each mother score with all other father scores, there is considerable shrinkage in size of correlation. For example, the correlation between father's rating of rejection and father's rating of frequency of aggression is .46, but the correlation between father's rating of rejection and mother's rating of frequency of aggression is only .15.[6] A separate analysis was also done in this manner for each of the 13 individual items of aggres-

---

[5] Levin (7) has stated that the use of superego development as an index to identification, "assumption of adult role models by the child," may be valid for young children but that by the age of 8 years role modeling and superego functioning quite likely have differentiated into separate behavior patterns.

[6] For an extended discussion of the results of this cross-over analysis, see paper by Banta *et al.* (1).

sive behavior which go to make up the composite child's home aggression score. A significant relation between mother's punishment and mother's rating of child's home aggression was found on five items, between mother's punishment and father's rating of child's home aggression on only two. In the same way, father's rating of punishment correlates with father's rating of child's home aggression significantly on four of the 13 items and with mother's rating of child's home aggression on none of them. This consistent drop, when going from correlations between predictor and criterion obtained from the same individual to correlations between predictor and criterion each independently obtained, reinforces suspicions of contamination in those studies which use only the mother as informant about both child-rearing practices and child behavior.

In general, it would seem that mothers and fathers observe, sanction, and report their children's behavior from different vantage points. Which one should we accept, and which ignore? Traditionally, childrearing studies have utilized information obtained only from the mother. Our results show that indeed mothers may be more discriminating observers in some areas; however, in others, fathers give us more consistent results. As noted above, mother's rejection related to all the classroom measures and none of the interview measures, while the reverse was true for fathers. Father's punishment for aggression and father's ethnicity, on the other hand, related to school aggression, while neither mother's punishment nor ethnicity did. Father's ethnicity was also related to rejection by peers as well as to a number of variables within the interview, while mother's ethnicity was related to no other variable. Moreover, these relations were more marked for father-son than for father-daughter.

It seemed obvious that both fathers' and mothers' reports had to be taken into account. Therefore, an attempt was made to predict from combined mother and father scores on various interview variables to the classroom aggression scores, and indeed it was found that variables which did not relate when predictions were made from the scores of only one parent did show a relation to the criterion when scores of both parents were considered. On each variable the mothers and fathers were split into high and low groups at the median score for their respective samples. The median classroom aggression scores for the four cells containing subjects classified according to whether mother and father were each or both high or low on the specific variable appear in Table 5.

This combination of mothers' and fathers' scores clarifies the relation between father's ethnicity and child's school aggression. If it is only when there is a high ethnic father and low ethnic mother that the aggression score is very much elevated. When both mother and father are ethnics or both are nonethnics, the aggression score is near the median for the entire group. On the other hand, when the mother is high ethnic and the father is low ethnic, the median school aggression score is noticeably low. This suggests that there may indeed be a conflict of cultural values behind the obtained

TABLE 5

MEDIAN SCHOOL AGGRESSION SCORES OF SUBJECTS BY COMBINED PARENT
POSITION ABOVE AND BELOW MEDIAN ON SOME INTERVIEW VARIABLES

	Hi Father		Lo Father	
Variable	Hi Mother	Lo Mother	Hi Mother	Lo Mother
Ethnicity	15.5 (14)	69 (8)	6 (9)	16 (19)
Confessing by Child	5 (15)	22.5 (8)	16 (13)	25.5 (14)
Parental Disharmony	15.5 (16)	14 (8)	45 (8)	8.5 (18)
Parental Rejection	36 (17)	3.5 (8)	13 (9)	4.5 (16)
Punishment for Aggression	21.5 (16)	34 (9)	7.5 (10)	4 (15)
Punishment for Dependency	19 (12)	22 (11)	10 (13)	8 (14)
Parent's Aggression	16 (13)	22 (11)	18 (11)	4 (15)
Lack of Social Participation	16 (19)	15.5 (6)	22.5 (6)	5 (19)
Shame at Home	12 (25)	18 (12)	18 (11)	2 (2)
Shame Out of Home	22 (14)	10.5 (12)	25 (10)	10 (14)

NOTE.—Number in parenthesis refers to frequency of subjects in cells (total $N = 50$).
Median school aggression score for entire group of 50 children $= 15$.

ethnicity-aggression relationship. The high ethnic woman, married either
to a low or high ethnic man, perhaps brings Old World values into her
relationship with him, deferring to him as the decision-maker, authoritarian,
etc. Their roles are well defined. On the other hand, the low ethnic woman,
married to the high ethnic man, has a different conception of the marital
relationship which then conflicts with what is expected by the husband,
value conflicts ensue, role definitions are not agreed upon, and the children
are deviant, at least as far as peer rating of aggression is concerned.

The importance of getting evaluations from both mother and father is
again seen in the relation of confessing to aggression. It is only for those
children whose mother and father agree that the child does not deny his
guilt that the aggression score tends to be low. When both agree he does
deny, the aggression score tends to be high. When there is disagreement
between mother and father on this variable, the result is closer to the median
for the entire group.

Parental disharmony operates differently. When both mother and father
agree that parental disharmony is low, the child's aggression score tends
to be low. When both agree parental disharmony is high or when father
says it is high and mother says it is low, the child's aggression score tends
to be around the median for the whole group. However, when the mother
says disharmony is high and father says it is low, the child's aggression
score tends to be very high. Thus, the mother's rating seems to be the crucial
one here as it does in some aspects of the rejection-aggression relationship.
But the father's role in the latter relationship is also important. Both mother
and father must be high on rejection for the child's aggression score to
be elevated, but only a low score for mother is needed for the child's aggression score to be low. When father is low and mother high, the aggression

score is at the median for the whole group. In other words, there must be two rejecting parents to make for a high aggressive child, but only the mother's lack of rejection results in a low aggressive child. Quite the opposite is true for punishment for aggression. Here it is just when the father is high that the child's aggression score tends to be high. This is especially true when the father is high and the mother is low. When father is low in punishment for aggression, regardless of mother's score, the child tends to be low on aggression. With punishment for dependency, only low punishment by the father is associated with low aggression. When the father is a high punisher for dependency, regardless of whether mother is high or low, the child's aggression score tends to be moderately elevated.

The results with parent's aggression, when data from mother and father are considered jointly, indicate that an erroneous interpretation can be drawn if only one parent is taken into account. The father's importance as a role model for aggression was suggested in the results mentioned above; however, it is only when both mother and father rate themselves as low on aggressive behavior that the child's aggression score tends to be low. When either or both rates himself as high, the child's score tends to be at the median or slightly higher. The same is true for lack of social participation and shame at home; however, for shame out of home it is the low mother only who tends to have the low aggressive child. It is interesting that there are only two families in which both mother and father rate themselves as low on shame at home. In general, however, it should be apparent from this rudimentary analysis that, for a more complete picture of the effect of socialization practices and attitudes on child behavior, the contribution of both mother and father to this effect must be taken into account.

SUMMARY

Sixty subjects were selected out of a pool of 158 children on the basis of scores on an aggression sociometric administered in their classrooms. All of the mothers and 50 of the 58 available fathers of these children were then independently interviewed to gain information on a number of presumed psychological and social antecedents to aggressive behavior. It was found that mothers and fathers did not agree to an appreciable degree in rating either their children's behavior or their interactions with their children. Even on those variables where agreement between mother and father was moderately high, the relation to other variables was not the same for the two groups of parents. There was a consistent shrinkage in size of coefficient when proceeding from correlations between predictor and criterion which were both obtained from the same parent to correlations when the predictor was obtained from one and the criterion from the other. When an outside, independently obtained criterion was used, very often the father's scores related more adequately than did the mother's scores. The most meaningful and theoretically interesting relations were found when predicting from a combined mother and father score to the independent criterion. Only recently have studies emphasizing the importance of the father in socialization of the child begun to appear. These results are further evidence of his importance both as a new method and a new dimension in child-rearing research.

REFERENCES

1. BANTA, T. J, WALDER, L. O., & ERON, L. D. Convergent and discriminant validation of a childrearing survey questionnaire. Paper read at East. Psychol. Ass., New York City, April, 1960.

2. BRONFENBRENNER, U. Family structure and development. Presidential address, Div. 7, Amer. Psychol. Ass., Washington, D.C., September, 1958.

3. CHAMPNEY, H. Measurement of parent behavior. *Child Develpm.*, 1941, 12, 131-166.

4. CURETON, E. E. Rank-biserial correlation. *Psychometrika,* 1956, 21, 287-290.

5. DAVIDSON, K. S., SARASON, S. B., LIGHTHALL, F. F., WAITE, R. R., & SARNOFF, I. Differences between mothers and fathers of low anxious and high anxious children. *Child Develpm.,* 1958, 29, 155-160.

6. GUILFORD, J. P. *Psychometric methods.* (2nd Ed.) McGraw-Hill, 1954.

7. LEVIN, H. Discussion of symposium: some methodological considerations in childrearing research. Paper read at East. Psychol. Ass., New York City, April, 1960.

8. LEVIN, H., & SEARS, R. R. Identification with parents as a determinant of doll play aggression. *Child Develpm.,* 1956, 27, 135-153.

9. MILLER, D. R., & SWANSON, G. E. *The changing American parent.* Wiley, 1958.

10. PETERSON, D. R., BECKER, W. C., HELMER, L. A., SHOEMAKER, D. J., & QUAY, H. C. Parental attitudes and child adjustment. *Child Develpm.,* 1959, 30, 119-130.

11. SEARS, R. R., MACCOBY, E. E., & LEVIN, H. *Patterns of child rearing.* Row, Peterson, 1957.

12. SEARS, R. R., PINTLER, M. H., & SEARS, P. S. Effects of father separation on preschool children's doll play aggression. *Child Develpm.,* 1946, 17, 219-243.

13. SEARS, R. R., WHITING, J. W. M., NOWLIS, V., & SEARS, P. S. Some childrearing antecedents of aggression and dependency in young children. *Genet. Psychol. Monogr.,* 1953, 47, 135-234.

MATERNAL OVERPROTECTION AND REJECTION

DR. DAVID M. LEVY

An analysis of maternal overprotection was made by selecting from large numbers of overprotected children,. twenty cases in which the overprotection was obvious — pointed out both by lay observers and professional workers — and in which the patient was clearly a wanted child. The object was to select cases of this human relationship in its simplest and most complete form; then, to think through all the significant facts known about the parents and children involved in the relationship in the terms of this study. In contrast with other cases of maternal overprotection, the twenty selected for this special investigation were referred to as "pure" forms.

The term "maternal overprotection" was accepted as synonymous with excessive maternal care of children. It connotes such terms as babying, oversolicitude, too much mothering, overindulging and a host of similar expressions indicating that the mother exceeds the "normal" in her care of the child. According to our clinical observations, the excess may be formulated in terms of: (1) excessive contact, e.g., a mother sleeping with her son, aged 14; (2) prolongation of infantile care, e.g., breast feeding to the age of 4 years; (3) prevention of the development of independent behavior, including such descriptive terms about the mother-child relationship as, "she won't take any risks," "she always fights his battles," and (4) lack or excess of maternal control, shown in overindulgence of the child in regard to privileges or possessions, and by the child's disregard of eating and sleeping time — in general, by his doing what he pleases undeterred by the mother's commands or pleadings. This is in contrast with excessive maternal control in which a relative overmodification of infantile traits is manifested in undue obedience on the part of the child.

ARCHIVES OF NEUROLOGICAL PSYCHIATRY, 1931, Vol. 25, pp. 886-889.

All factual data on maternal overprotection, when formulated by this plan, show much dovetailing; nevertheless, the stress is often found greater in one group than in another. It appears so far that overindulgent overprotection yields aggressive-egocentric behavior of varying degrees in the offspring, whereas dominating overprotection yields submissive and effeminate behavior. Since in our cases the patterns of the mother-child relationship appear to have been well established in infancy and by a series of factors operating in the mother before the birth of the child, the mother-child relationship is considered primary; all other factors (the patient's relationship with other adults and children, physical and intellectual factors, and special abilities and disabilities) as secondary modifying influences, exaggerating or diminishing the influence of the primary relationship. For example, consider the case of a child who is treated by his mother more like a baby, is held closer to her and is more dependent on her for aid in his school work and in social contacts than are other boys. At 7½ years, he is referred to the Institute for Child Guidance for symptoms of irresponsible, dependent and immature behavior in keeping with the overprotective relationship. He presents a series of submissive and aggressive traits, though largely the former. His teachers note his docility. He accepts the lead of his brother, aged 4, in play, and likes to indulge in baby talk. This docility is in contrast with his wish to dominate the group, yet he runs to the mother for protection from other boys. Although in the primary relationship such observations are easily discerned and anticipated, yet they are influenced considerably by the following factors in this patient: developmental delay and inadequacy of muscular strength, coordination and intelligence. Besides these factors, there are an interfering, indulgent grandmother, a father who favors the younger brother and a great deal of rivalry between the brothers. In this case, as in all others of "pure" form, the events following infancy affect, as in this case they intensified, an overprotective relationship previously established.

After classifying the symptoms of overprotection as they are objectively manifested in the mother-child relationship and through the behavior pattern of the child as its direct outgrowth, all factors in our social-psychiatric investigation are evaluated in terms of the primary relationship in the following order:

1. Period of anticipation during pregnancy and childbirth of patient. All conditions that delay the coming of a wanted child in the form of relative sterility, miscarriages or stillbirths obviously compel the mother to go through periods of anticipation and frustration. The maternal attitude toward the child, following such experiences, will be more apprehensive and protective than if the child's birth occurred in the usual time. Such experiences occurred in our series eight times.

2. Extra hazard. The illnesses of infancy and childhood were evaluated in terms not of their actual seriousness but of the maternal response. It was found that frightening illnesses or accidents in which the child "looked dead," as in fainting and convulsions, from whatever cause, stimulated more overprotective response than familiarly known though serious diseases. Protective and infantilizing care and prevention of the usual training of children may be occasioned, for example, by frequent "colds" and operative procedures, as well as by actual deformity. An only child or a first child, who, however long, is an only child, represents a greater risk than a child who is one of a large family. If it is known or assumed by the parents that an only child represents, or is, an only pregnancy, the hazard is presumably increased. A combination of events such as a relative sterility or a succession of miscarriages, followed by a viable child, after which pregnancy is considered impossible, is a frequent pattern in our series.

3. Maternal factors. Satisfactory sexual and social life with the husband sets up a number of conditions that operate against a mother-child monopoly. On the other hand, sexual incompatibility and lack of social interests in common with the husband intensify the mother-child relationship. The child must then bear the brunt of the unsatisfied love life of the overprotective mother and absorb

all her social activities. Such observations are especially frequent in our group. Sexual incompatibility occurs in every case.

In the early life of the overprotective mothers, two factors stand out clearly: inadequate affection and early responsibility. The responsibility is shown in early self-support or contribution to family earnings, and also in occupying an authoritative position over other siblings. It appears plausible that mothers in our group, affection-hungry since early years, try to satisfy their incomplete lives almost exclusively in their maternal relations. Attaining that state, they intrench themselves in a mother-child monopoly through an aggressive offensive against all intruders, including the husband, who, frequently submissive to the wife, may not interfere at all in matters pertaining to the child and who frequently is not consulted. The wife is competent, takes responsibility readily and is often derogatory of her husband. Such observations apply to fourteen mothers in our series. In the remaining six, the overprotection is of the submissive, dependent type — mothers who, divested of other social relationships, cling to the child as though in a hostile environment. Such mothers are in contrast with the larger group of aggressively overprotective mothers. The picture of the latter group is that of mothers, independent and competent, who, attaining their love-object in an offspring, push away everyone in the effort to create a mother-child monopoly. In the case of the dependent, overprotective mother, the situation is reversed, though with a similar result. She is in a passive relationship with the social environment — the mother-child monopoly is created for her.

4. Paternal factors. The following characterization of the fathers is consistent in our series: responsible, steady workers, submissive to their wives, dependent on them for family decisions, who exert little influence on the patient or add to the overprotection. The fathers in our series do not exert authority in the family, are not looked up to by the wife for family decisions, or do not aid in disciplining the child; hence, they do not help in mitigating the effects of the maternal overprotection. When the paternal role is weak or negligent, the maternal rôle is unmodified. Given an inadequate or indifferent father, it is assumed that, out of necessity, the mother plays a more important rôle with her child. This holds true especially in cases in which no paternal influence exists, as in the case of widows or divorcees.

5. Other factors modifying overprotection. Of these factors, relatives chiefly were considered. Some cases, as in our series, are complicated by a grandmother who lives in the home and whose rivalry with the mother is manifested in an overprotective attitude toward the grandchild.

6. Problems of the patient. General attitudes of our patients may be classified according to behavior manifestations, as aggressive, submissive or indifferent. All of these forms may be represented in any given case. Aggressive behavior, however, is the most frequent of all of the forms, and also most readily understood as an expression of the dynamics of the mother-child relationship. The child's attempt to dominate every situation, and its corollary, his refusal to yield to other persons, results in a series of complaints from teachers and parents that are well comprehended under the heading, "rebellion against authority." This includes various forms of disobedience, impudence, temper tantrums, bullying and general undisciplined behavior. The freedom of action and speech which parents allow these children is often extreme. In a number of cases the point of tolerance of the parents toward the child is reached. The typical attitude of the mother toward such a child is that, as a reward for all her devotion, she has reared a monster who makes life intolerable for herself and her husband.

The irresponsible behavior of both the submissive and aggressive child is explained on the basis of unmodified and overmodified infantile experiences. In the aggressive child, it is understood as a throwing off of responsibility, a refusal to do one's share; in the submissive child, as an immaturity, an infantile expectation of help from others.

Consistent for all of these patients is the difficulty in making friends. The most frequent reason for this is the attempt on the patient's part always to be

133

leader, to boss the game, to give orders, to quarrel and to fight. A small number keep away from friends because of timidity or refusal to join in rough sports. A number of patients have been entirely restricted to adult society until school age; a number have not been allowed to play with other children in the neighborhood.

Difficulty in making friends is understood as a carry-over of the mother-child monopoly. The inability to make friends reenforces maternal overprotection. It compels the mother to bear the brunt of the child's unpopularity. With the absence of friends, an important mitigating influence of maternal overprotection is lost. The group of boys, so far as it puts a value on independence and courage, is an antidote to infantilization. It strikes out against mother dependency. For our patients, the value of the group in developing freedom from maternal overprotection is lost.

When difficulties occur in the classroom they follow closely the overprotective pattern, mostly in the form of attention-getting behavior. Our patients for the most part, however, are good students, a few of them excellent. School work, as well as secondary interests (evaluated in terms of maternal overprotection), are seen as helpful agents in the development of "independent" success on the part of the child. Failure in school throws a further burden on the mother-child relationship. The excellent adaptation to the classroom on the part of some of our patients is explained in terms of satisfaction through achievement, made easy by natural abilities; in some cases, when it is consistent, it is response to the authority of the school teacher, and for the most part, it is an identification with the educational values of the mother. It has been shown that for certain objectives, overprotective mothers sacrifice all their indulgences and become stern, unyielding and effective. The child then learns to surrender when all the artifices, used successfully in eluding most responsibilities, fail.

Of the "vegetative" adaptations, our patients show more frequent bladder control than the general group, though more feeding problems. This is consistent with the careful bladder training by the overprotective mother, in contrast with that by the negligent mother who has a correspondingly greater number of problems in this regard. The acts of eating and sleeping become socialized through excessive contact with the mother, and hence, more frequently a difficulty.

Developmental data show nothing significant in regard to motor or speech development that is not consistent with the intelligence of the children.

Overprotected children in this series average nine months on the breast, in contrast with children of rejecting mothers, who average four months on the breast.

Check groups for this study have been made on 200 other cases at the Institute, taken seriatim from the records, weeding out the overprotective cases. The frequency of sexual incompatibility was compared with normal samplings and with other groups.

134

DOMINANCE ATTITUDES IN PARENTS AND ADULT
AVOIDANCE BEHAVIOR IN YOUNG CHILDREN [1]

E. Philip Trapp *and* Donald H. Kausler

The fruitfulness of predicting child behavior from family variables is indicated by the trend of research in this direction (1, 4). In most of these studies, however, the effort has been to relate children's behavior to parental practices rather than to parental attitudes, mainly because of the general unreliability of attitude measurements in this area. The advantage of being able to predict children's behavior from measures of parental attitudes is obvious in terms of convenience and simplicity of data gathering.

Read (12) attempted to relate parents' expressed attitudes to nursery school children's ratings on a behavior inventory and found some relationship between attitudes of parental control and ratings on the inventory. Children of parents favoring strong control were rated with more undesirable behavioral characteristics than children of parents expressing a more liberal attitude. The ratings were the pooled judgments of the nursery school teachers.

The present study is a further investigation into the effects of parental attitudes of dominance on child behavior. Shoben (15) has developed a parent attitude scale which shows promise of being a reliable and sensitive instrument, although a recent validity study (7) indicates a limitation in its

[1] Special thanks are reserved for the nursery school staff at the University of Arkansas for their kind assistance throughout the study, and for Miss Peggy Wall, who made the observations on the children.

CHILD DEVELOPMENT, 1958, Vol. 29, pp. 507-513.

clinical use. The three major attitudes it purports to measure fall under the subscale headings of Dominant, Possessive, and Ignoring. Thus far, the sensitivity of the scale has been demonstrated in differentiating mothers of problem children from mothers of nonproblem children. The usefulness of the scale in differentiating less extreme cases, that is, parents of children not undergoing psychiatric reatment, is tested in the present study. More specifically, the focus of this study is on the relationship between parental dominance attitudes and adult avoidance behavior in young children.

Children of parents reflecting strong dominance attitudes are likely to develop more than the average amount of negativistic feelings toward their parents. These feelings should reinforce parent avoidance responses and generalize to other adult relationships. It is also logical to propose that parents with weak dominance attitudes might increase negativistic feelings in their children. In such cases, the child, because of insufficient guidance, is likely to experience more than the ordinary amount of frustrations and project his frustration on his parents. One manifestation of this process would be in increased parent avoidance behavior which would generalize to other adult relationships.

This proposed curvilinear relationship between parents' dominance attitudes and children's adult avoidance behavior is predicted to be in evidence only with children displaying normal personality development. In the more extreme cases of problem children, the higher anxiety drives would probably generate more variable response patterns, reflected in either excessively dependent behaviors or extreme forms of withdrawal behaviors. The net result would obscure the specific effects hypothesized here.

As a second and related problem, the present study investigated the relationship between differences in expressed parental dominance attitudes and children's behavior. It is proposed that parents with large differences in dominance attitudes between themselves would create a conflict situation for the child. Therefore, the parent-child relationships within these families are likely to be less positive than parent-child relationships within families where there is more agreement on dominance attitudes. Evidence of this less positive relationship should be indicated by increased adult avoidance behavior in their children.

These two predictions regarding the relationship between parental dominance attitudes and children's adult avoidance behavior may be stated more precisely in the following two hypotheses: (a) Nursery school children of parents scoring either relatively high or low on a dominance attitude scale will avoid adult contacts in a free-activity setting to a greater degree than nursery school children of parents scoring in the intermediate range on a dominance attitude scale. (b) Nursery school children of parents reflecting large differences in scores on a dominance attitude scale will avoid contacts in a free-activity setting to a greater degree than nursery school children of parents reflecting small differences in scores on a dominance attitude scale.

136

Subjects

At the outset of the study, 20 children attending the University of Arkansas Nursery School served as *S*s. By the end of the study, the normal process of attrition left completed data on 16 children. Eight *S*s were males, ranging in age from 3-4 to 5-0, with a mean age of 4-2 (computed in years and months). The eight female *S*s also had an age range from 3-4 to 5-0, with a mean age of 4-4. The educational and socioeconomic backgrounds of the parents were fairly homogeneous, most of them of professional middle class.

Procedure

Each parent was given the USC Parent Attitude Survey (13). The Dominant subscale served as the predictor measure. The parents were informed that the survey was part of a nation-wide study to investigate sectional differences in child-training attitudes. They seemed satisfied with the explanation and cooperated fully with the project. Anonymity was assured them by the use of coded numbers in place of their signatures. The survey was administered and collected by the director of the nursery school, who had known each parent for at least six months.

Each child was observed individually at five-minute time intervals, approximately once every 10 days through a period of 15 weeks, resulting in a total of 50 minutes of observation per child. The children were observed in the mornings between 11:00 and 11:50, the free-activity period in the nursery school program. The observations followed a prearranged schedule to insure that each child was observed throughout the entire period and never more than once at the same time of the period.

The observer was equipped with two concealed stop watches. One ran continuously for the five-minute time interval and the other watch ran only at the time the child was in contact with an adult. At the end of a day's observation, the observer made notations on the nature of the adult contacts and other qualitative remarks on the children's behavior. Since the children were accustomed to adults about them (the nursery school provides training facilities for University students), they did not show any unusual curiosity toward the observer, and, in fact, gave no indication that they were aware of being under any special form of observation. To assist in achieving this desired end, the observer spent a few days in the play area before beginning the formal observations.

Regarding the first hypothesis investigated, the two dominance scores for each set of parents were added together and a combined single dominance score determined. These combined scores ranged from 233 to 304.

The parents were divided into quartiles based on their combined scores. The first and fourth quartiles represent extreme dominance attitudes; the second and third quartiles represent intermediate dominance attitudes.

Children with parents in the extreme quartiles constituted one group of Ss (Extreme Group, $N = 8$); children with parents in the intermediate quartiles constituted a second group (Intermediate Group, $N = 8$). The two groups were found to be nearly identical in average age and average length of attendance in the nursery school. To test the related hypothesis, the mean time (in minutes) spent in adult contact was determined for each group, and the difference between group means was tested for significance by the t test. Summary data for this analysis appear in Table 1.

TABLE 1

SUMMARY OF CHILDREN'S AVOIDANCE BEHAVIOR: GROUPS DETERMINED
BY COMBINED PARENTAL DOMINANCE SCORES

Group	Mean (min.)	SD	t
I Children of parents with extreme attitudes ($N=8$)	5.7	4.6	
			2.3*
II Children of parents with intermediate attitudes ($N=8$)	12.5	6.3	

* $p < .05$ (two-tailed test).

The results support the hypothesis ($t = 2.3$, $p < .05$, two-tailed test). Children with parents scoring either high or low on a dominance attitude scale displayed more adult avoidance behavior than children with parents in the intermediate range on the scale. A clearer pattern of this curvilinear relationship may be seen in a further breakdown of the data in Table 1 in terms of the quartile means. The means of the quartiles from top to bottom were 6.5, 8.6, 16.4, and 4.9, respectively.

Regarding the second hypothesis investigated, a difference score on dominance attitude for each set of parents was obtained in the following manner. For each of the 34 items on the USC Parent Attitude Survey measuring dominance, a score was recorded indicating the discrepancy between the two parents on that item. The 34 discrepancy scores were added to produce the total score for each set of parents. The parents were again divided into quartiles, this time on the basis of their difference score. The difference scores ranged from 18 to 33.

Children with parents in the first quartile (large difference between parents on dominance attitude) constituted one group of Ss; children with parents in the fourth quartile (small difference between parents on dominance attitude) constituted the second group of Ss. These two groups were likewise nearly identical in average age and average length of attendance in the nursery school. To test the related hypothesis, the mean time (in minutes) spent in adult contact was determined for each group, and the difference between group means was tested for significance by the *t* test. Summary data for this analysis appear in Table 2.

The results support the second hypothesis ($t = 3.2$, $p < .05$, two-tailed test). Children with parents reflecting large differences on a dominance attitude scale displayed more adult avoidance behavior than children with parents reflecting small differences on a dominance attitude scale.

TABLE 2

SUMMARY OF CHILDREN'S AVOIDANCE BEHAVIOR: GROUPS DETERMINED BY DIFFERENCES BETWEEN PARENTAL DOMINANCE SCORES

Group	Mean (min.)	SD	t
I Children of parents with large differences ($N = 4$)	5.8	1.1	3.2*
II Children of parents with small differences ($N = 4$)	15.0	4.9	

* $p < .05$ (two-tailed test).

DISCUSSION

Two pertinent questions may be raised concerning the first hypothesis. The first question regards the sex of the parents. Are the dominance attitudes of mothers better predictors of their children's avoidance behavior than the dominance attitudes of fathers? The second question regards the sex pairing of parent and child. For example, are the dominance attitudes of mothers better predictors of avoidance behavior for daughters than for sons? These questions are discussed below.

An analysis of the data revealed no difference in predictive value between mothers' dominance attitudes and fathers' dominance attitudes. In both cases, the difference in avoidance scores between children with parents in the first and fourth quartiles and children with parents in the second and third quartiles was in the predicted direction and significant at the .10 level (two-tailed test). As indicated in the results section, the difference is significant at the .05 level when the dominance attitude scores are combined for parents. A further analysis also failed to disclose a closer parent attitude - child behavior relationship when parent and child are paired by sex. The dominance attitudes of both mother and father apparently affected the child about the same irrespective of the sex of the child.

A similar breakdown was made on the second hypothesis. Again the predictive value of dominance attitude scores was not enhanced either when the sex of the parents was considered separately or when pairings were made between parent and like-sex child.

The data were inspected to determine if children of parents reflecting highest difference scores on the attitude scale (Group I of Table 2) tended also to be children of parents scoring at the extremes on the scale (Group I of Table 1). The inspection revealed that only one of the four children of parents in the high difference group also had parents in the extremes group. This relative lack of overlap suggests that our two hypotheses have been fairly independently confirmed by our data.

The present study supports the usefulness of the USC Parent Attitude Survey in differentiating between parents of normal children. In spite of the relatively small sample size, and the relatively homogeneous character of the sample, the scale was sufficiently sensitive to discriminate between groups at the .05 level of confidence on the two-tailed test.

SUMMARY

Two hypotheses were tested regarding the relationship between parental attitudes and children's behavior. The first hypothesis stated that nursery school children of parents scoring either high or low on dominance attitude will avoid adult contacts in a free-activity setting to a greater degree than nursery school children of parents scoring in the intermediate range on dominance attitude. The second hypothesis stated that nursery school children of parents reflecting large differences in dominance attitudes will avoid adult contacts in a free-activity setting to a greater degree than nursery school children of parents reflecting small differences in dominance attitudes.

The sample consisted of 16 children, of equal sex proportion, with an average age of four years, three months, and their parents. The USC Parent Attitude Survey was administered to the parents, and the Dominance subscale served as the predictor variable. Five-minute time samples, totalling 50 minutes of observation in all, were made on each child. The time spent by a child in adult contact during the observation period served as the dependent variable.

The results supported the curvilinear relationship predicted in the first hypothesis at the .05 level (two-tailed test). The results also supported the second hypothesis at the .05 level. Further breakdowns of the data in terms of the sex of the parent or pairing the child to the like-sex parent did not increase the predictive power of the dominance scale. The combined attitudes for both parents were more discriminating than the attitudes for either parent considered separately.

REFERENCES

1. ANDERSON, H., HANLEY, C., & HURLEY, J. Personality development in infancy and the preschool years. *Rev. educ. Res.*, 1955, 25, 453-468.
2. AUSUBEL, D. P., BALTHAZAR, E. E., *et al.* Perceived parent attitudes as determiners of children's ego structure. *Child Develpm.*, 1954, 25, 173-184.

3. AYER, M. E., & BERNREUTER, R. G.   A study of the relationship between discipline and personality traits in little children.   *J. genet. Psychol.*, 1937, 50, 165-170.

4. BALDWIN, A. L.   Child psychology.   In P. R. Farnsworth (Ed.), *Annual review of psychology*.   Stanford, Calif.: Annual Reviews, 1956.   Pp. 259-283.

5. BORNSTON, F., & COLEMAN, J.   The relationship between certain parents' attitudes toward child rearing and the direction of aggression of their young adult offspring.   *J. clin Psychol.*, 1956, 12, 41-44.

6. CHAMPNEY, H.   The variables of parent behavior.   *J. abnorm. soc. Psychol.*, 1941, 36, 525-542.

7. GORDON, J.   The validity of Shoben's Parent Attitude Survey.   *J. clin. Psychol.*, 1957, 13, 154-156.

8. KOCH, H. L.,   The relation of certain family constellation characteristics and attitudes of children toward adults.   *Child Develpm.*, 1955, 26, 13-40.

9. LORR, M., & JENKINS, R.   Three factors in parent behavior.   *J. consult. Psychol.*, 1953, 17, 306-308.

10. MUMMERY, D. V.   Family backgrounds of assertive and non-assertive children.   *Child Develpm.*, 1954, 25, 63-80.

11. RADKE, M. J.   The relation of parental authority to children's behavior and attitudes.   *Univer. Minn. Child Welf. Monogr.*, 1946, No. 22.

12. READ, K. H.   Parents' expressed attitudes and children's behavior.   *J. consult. Psychol.*, 1945, 9, 95-100.

13. SEARS, R., *et al*.   Some child-rearing antecedents of aggression and dependency in young children.   *Genet. Psychol. Monogr.*, 1953, 47, 135-236.

14. SEWELL, W. H., MUSSEN, P. H., & HARRIS, C. W.   Relationship among child training practices.   *Amer. sociol. Rev.*, 1955, 20, 137-148.

15. SHOBEN, E. J.   The assessment of parental attitudes in relation to child adjustment.   *Genet. Psychol. Monogr.*, 1949, 39, 101-148.

EMOTIONAL DEPENDENCE AND INDEPENDENCE IN A PHYSICAL THREAT SITUATION

GLEN HEATHERS[1]

This paper reports an approach to measuring emotional dependence and independence in grade school children responding to a novel situation involving the threat of physical injury. One way in which people depend on others is by seeking reassurance in situations they perceive as threatening to themselves. We assume that a child develops the tendency to look to others for reassurance in threatening situations because others protect him from injury. Thus he learns to associate their presence, their encouraging remarks, or their help with being safe from harm. Thereafter, when he becomes anxious in anticipation of injury, the child may seek reassurance as a means of relieving his anxiety. In a study of children's fears of the dark and of high places, Holmes (2) demonstrated how children may utilize the reassuring presence of an adult as an emotional support in facing feared situations.

A child exhibits independence when physically threatened if he copes with the situation without requiring reassurance or help. It is assumed that he will tend to rely on himself if he expects that he can avoid injury or that he can tolerate whatever injury he may suffer. Also, the child may show independence as a way of winning approval from others, or as a way of avoiding their disapproval. Finally, he may express independence in order to experience the self-approval which comes from knowing that he has mastered a difficult or threatening situation.

METHOD AND SUBJECTS

In selecting a task for measuring dependence and independence under physical threat, six criteria were employed: (*a*) the task should involve the possibility of physical injury which all subjects will perceive; (*b*) it should not be so threatening that any grade school children will refuse to perform it; (*c*) it should be a task which children in the 6-1. ·ge range are capable of performing independently; (*d*) it should be novel in order to minimize differences in the children's experience with similar tasks; (*e*) it should allow a clear choice between dependent and independent modes of coping with it; and (*f*) it should provide a series of trials to permit adjustive changes to be measured.

[1] The writer is grateful to Mrs. Ruth Bean, Edna Small and Suzanne Hamberger for assistance in conducting this study.

CHILD DEVELOPMENT, 1953, Vol. 24, pp. 169-179.

The physical threat situation devised for this exploratory study was the Walk-the-Plank Test, a task which meets the six requirements relatively well. In this test, the subject was blindfolded and instructed to walk the length of a plank balanced on springs and raised eight inches off the floor. The plank was six feet long and 12 inches wide, with sideboards rising two inches above the level of the plank to prevent stepping off the side. It was pivoted at the center like a teeter-totter, and was attached at either end to a baseboard by two springs. It required a weight of about sixty pounds applied to the end of the plank to tip it downward until it touched the floor. To add to the instability of the plank, the cross-board on which it was pivoted was an inch higher at the center of the plank than at either side so that the plank tipped sidewise as well as endwise. One foot from the exit end of the plank, a small strip of wood was nailed across it so that the subject, when his foot bumped against the strip, would know he was near the end.

The subject was led into the testing room past the apparatus and seated at a desk facing away from the apparatus. When he went by the apparatus, he was not permitted to inspect it or test it in any way. After he was interviewed for about fifteen minutes in connection with another study, the subject was administered the Walk-the-Plank Test. For this, he was blindfolded with rubber goggles adapted for the purpose, then given the instructions which follow.

"This is a game where you walk along a wiggly board and step down to the floor when you get to the end. (E leads S to starting end of plank.) Step up. (E holds S's arm while S gets into position.) Turn this way. (E exerts pressure to turn S facing toward exit end of plank.) Feel the sides. (If necessary, E helps S bring his feet against both edge boards.) You will know when you get to the end because your toe will bump against a board stretched across the end. Walk between the sides till your toe bumps against the board, then step down to the floor."

"O.K. Do you want me to walk along with you this time?" (E touches back of S's hand and waits for him to accept or reject the help offered. If S takes the hand, E walks beside him to the end of the plank. If he ignores or rejects the hand, E walks silently behind him to catch him if he loses his balance.)

Five trials were given in immediate succession, with the subject led back to the starting end and helped into the starting position after each trial. At the beginning of each trial, the helping hand was offered in the same way and with the same statement as on the first trial. A record was kept of acceptance or rejection of the offer and of the subject's remarks. The reason for limiting the test to five trials was that previous exploratory work with the test indicated that a fair proportion of children become resistant if the number of trials exceeded five or so.

The subjects were 56 children, 31 boys and 25 girls, between six and 12 years of age. All were members of the Fels Research Institute's longitudinal research population which draws almost exclusively from the middle socio-economic class. The writer served as experimenter.

RESULTS

General Reactions to the Test

We may infer that a high proportion of the subjects perceived the task as physically threatening from the fact that two-thirds of them accepted the helping hand on the first trial while, of the remaining one-third, most were obviously tense and cautious while walking the plank. Subjects' spontaneous remarks, such as "It's scary," "I'm afraid I'll fall," and "It feels funny," verbalized the anxiety which they felt while performing the task. A small proportion of the subjects (about one in ten) behaved from the start with calm assurance, walking quickly and confidently along the plank and offering remarks such as "I like it" and "It's fun." Although nearly all of the subjects perceived the task as threatening, none of them refused to perform any of the five trials.

Concerning the novelty of the task, all 56 children reported, when interviewed at the end of the task ,that they had rarely been blindfolded before and never before had walked a springy board when blindfolded. Their experiences with blindfolds had been limited to occasional games of pin-the-tail-on-the-donkey, blind-man's buff, or the like.

The need for reassurance in coping with the situation was shown not only by taking the helping hand but, with several subjects, by leaning toward the experimenter while walking the plank. Some subjects rejected the hand but asked the experimenter to walk along beside them.

In interpreting the independence most subjects showed on the first or later trials, it is important to note that they were never instructed to walk the plank alone. The fact that most did so indicates their own tendencies toward independence, either because they assumed this was expected of them or because they desired to master the task. Typical remarks indicating their desire to perform the task alone were, "I'll try it by myself," "I believe I can," and "I'll do it alone."

Sex Differences

A popular notion is that girls are more fearful than boys in physical threat situations, and more inclined to be dependent on others for protection against injury. The present test offers the opportunity to check this notion in a situation which was highly novel for both the boys and girls who served as subjects.

For the sex comparison, twenty boys and twenty girls were selected from the 56 children on the basis of closest possible age matching. The means

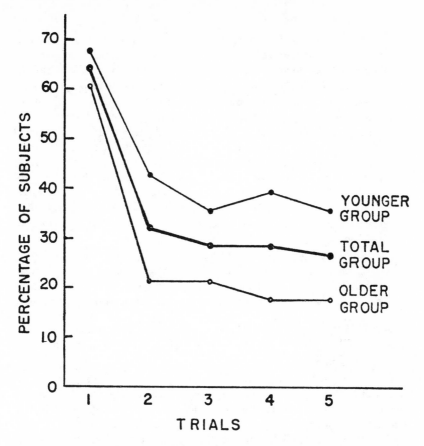

FIGURE 1—Percentages of subjects who accepted the helping hand on each of five trials in the Walk-the-Plank Test. The curves give results for 28 younger and 28 older children and for the total group of 56 children.

of both groups were 121.4 months. The median age of the boys' group was 129 months; of the girls' group, 130 months. Both groups had a semi-interquartile range of 17 months. On the first trial of the test, 12 of the boys and 14 of the girls accepted the helping hand. On all five trials taken together, the twenty boys accepted the helping hand a total of 32 times, the twenty girls also 32 times. The evidence of this study thus failed to support the view that girls are more fearful or less self-reliant than boys in physical threat situations when the factor of experience with the situation is controlled. If the boys did have more experience than the girls in facing physical threats, or if they were generally under more social pressure to exhibit courage, these differences did not generalize to this task.

Trial-to-Trial Differences

The Walk-the-Plank Test confronted the subjects with a situation which was novel in that it required them to walk an unstable platform without visual cues to direct them and to help them keep their balance. While almost all of the subjects were capable of doing the task without help, on Trial 1 they could not be sure of the hazards ahead or of their ability to cope with them. This meant that on Trial 1, anxiety and the associated need for reassurance should have been at a relatively high level, and a higher proportion of subjects would be expected to accept the helping hand on this trial than on later trials. After Trial 1, all the subjects had a more realistic basis for knowing the requirements of the task and for estimating their ability to perform it without aid. From this, it was reasonable to predict a greater decline in the number of subjects accepting the hand on Trial 2 (as compared with Trial 1) than would occur on Trials 3, 4 or 5 as compared to Trials 2, 3 or 4, respectively.

The results strongly supported this prediction. Thirty-six of the 56 subjects accepted the helping hand on Trial 1, 18 on Trial 2, 16 on Trial 3, 16 on Trial 4, and 15 on Trial 5. Figure 1 presents graphically the percentages of the 56 subjects who accepted the hand on each trial (note curve marked "Total Group"). The decline in the proportion of subjects who accepted the hand on Trial 2 as compared with Trial 1 was significant beyond the .01 level.[2] The further declines which occurred on Trials 3 and 5 were not significant.

Ten of the 56 children (six boys and four girls) accepted the hand on all five trials. Their failure to learn to walk without help raises significant questions for independence training in threatening situations. Five of the ten not only held the experimenter's hand but leaned on him as they walked the plank. This meant they were giving themselves no chance to learn to balance themselves and it is not surprising they remained dependent throughout the task. The conditions under which a person "throws away his crutches" in a threat situation is an important research problem.

The fact that nine subjects "regressed" by accepting the helping hand after walking without help on one or more trials indicates a conflict between dependent and independent tendencies. The most likely explanation is that, with these subjects, the experience of walking the plank by themselves increased their anxiety in anticipation of injury to the point where they resorted to help as a way of lessening their anxiety. The Walk-the-Plank Test evidently provides a good situation for further research on dependence-independence conflict directed to the question, "What situational variables

---

[2] The proportion of subjects accepting the hand in Trial 1 was .643. Using the formula $\sigma_p = \sqrt{pq/N}$, the fiducial limits of $\pm 3\sigma_p$ for the population sampled in Trial 1 are .829 and .457. The proportion of subjects accepting the hand in Trial 2 was .321 which is outside these limits.

determine the choice of dependent or independent responses in a physical threat situation?"

Age Differences

In this study it was assumed that dependent responses (taking the helping hand) indicated relatively high anxiety in anticipation of injury and/or relatively low tendencies to assert independence. By and large, older children were expected to have less anxiety than younger children in a given physical threat situation as a result of their greater capacities. Also, it was assumed that, in this culture, older children would have stronger needs to behave independently than younger children as a reflection of stronger social expectations that they handle situations on their own. These assumptions led to the prediction that older children would be less dependent(or more independent) than younger children in the Walk-the-Plank Test.

Considering that the test was a highly novel situation for the subjects and that none of them could know what to expect until after the first trial, it was predicted that on this trial the older children would express more nearly the same amount of dependence as younger children than would be true on later trials. In other words, it was assumed that the older subjects would be unable to utilize fully the advantages their greater capacities and experience gave them until they knew what the task required of them.

The age differences obtained support the analysis given above. The 56 children were divided into younger and older groups of 28 each. The younger group ranged from 80 to 114 months of age with a median age of 98 months, the older group from 114 to 150 months with a median age of 134 months. On trial 1, 19 of the younger and 17 of the older children accepted the helping hand. Thus, on the initial trial, age differences were at a minimum. On later trials, age differences were larger. On Trials 2, 3, 4 and 5, respectively, the numbers of younger children accepting the helping hand were 12, 10, 11 and 10. Corresponding numbers of older children were 6, 6, 5 and 5. These results are presented graphically in Figure 1. Another indication of age differences in the task was the fact that, of the ten children who accepted help on all five trials, eight were in the younger group.

While the age-differences found in this study were consistent with theoretical expectations, the data were insufficient to yield statistically significant differences.

Mothers' Behavior in Relation to Dependence-Independence

It is generally assumed that a child's parents play critical roles in determining his ways of dealing with problem situations. At the Fels Research Institute, data on the mothers' ways of relating to their children are available in the form of periodic ratings using the Fels Parent Behavior

Rating Scales. These thirty scales deal with various aspects of mothers' behavior toward their children. The ratings are made following a visit to the home by the Fels Home Visitor who observes the mothers' interaction with her children. These ratings offer the basis for an exploratory test of the relationships between certain aspects of mothers' behavior and the dependence-independence behavior of their children in the Walk-the-Plank Test.

Five of the 30 aspects of mothers' behavior rated in the Scales were selected on theoretical grounds as having particular relevance for learning to express dependent or independent tendencies in physical threat situations. These are Child-centeredness of Home, General Babying, Protectiveness, Accelerational Attempt, and Democracy of Policy. These scales have been described in detail by Baldwin, Kalhorn and Breese (1). They are characterized in briefest terms in this report.

High child-centeredness of the home means that the household revolves around the children, with major sacrifices made for the children's trivial comforts. Low child-centeredness means that the children's welfare is subordinated to that of other family members, with the children being left largely to fend for themselves. It was predicted that high child-centeredness would be associated with high dependence in the Walk-the-Plank Test on the assumption that it encourages the child to lean on others rather than taking care of himself in problem situations.

High babying means that the child is continually helped, even when he is fully capable of doing things by himself. Low babying means the child is left alone to solve his problems, and is often refused aid when he asks for it. It was predicted that high babying would be associated with high dependence in the Walk-the-Plank Test.

High protectiveness means that the child is sheltered from discomforts and difficulties, while low protectiveness means he is deliberately exposed to hazards or dangers. It was predicted that high protectiveness would be associated with high dependence on the Walk-the-Plank Test.

High acceleration means that the child is deliberately trained to develop skills, while low acceleration means he is held back from "growing up." It was predicted that high acceleration would be associated with high independence on the Walk-the-Plank Test on the assumption that acceleration involves training for mastery of situations.

High democracy of policy means that a child is given a definite share in deciding policies which concern him, while low democracy means that he is dictated to without regard to his own wishes. It was predicted that high democracy would be associated with high independence, assuming that it fosters self-reliance and discourages passive dependence.

To test the predictions, only the results for Trial 1 of the Walk-the-Plank Test were used. On later trials, too few subjects accepted the helping hand to permit adequate statistical analysis of differences between those subjects who accepted and those who rejected the helping hand. On Trial 1, thirty-six subjects accepted help and twenty rejected it. From the thirty-six who accepted help, twenty were selected strictly on the basis of choosing the group which most closely matched, in terms of sex and age, the group of twenty subjects who rejected help. Both groups contained 11 boys and nine girls. The Dependent Group (composed of subjects who accepted help) had a mean age of 119.9 months, the Independent Group (composed of subjects who rejected help) a mean age of 119.6 months. As further evidence that the groups were satisfactorily matched in terms of age, the Dependent Group had a median age of 124.5 months and a semi-interquartile range of 17.2 months, while the Independent Group had a median age of 127.0 months and a semi-interquartile range of 19.3 months.

In selecting ratings for use in this study, those made following the last home visit prior to the time the child was given the Walk-the-Plank Test were used. Since home visits are not conducted with children past the age of (approximately) ten years, the interval between the time the ratings were made and the time the data of this study were obtained was almost three years for some of the older subjects. The mean interval for the forty subjects involved in this part of the study was 18.3 months. With 63 per cent of the subjects, the interval was between 11 and 15 months; with eight per cent, between 16 and 24 months; and with 29 per cent, between 25 and 34 months. If one makes the plausible assumption that there is marked consistency from year to year in a mother's way of relating to her children, the time discrepancy should not render the home visit ratings selected inapplicable to the purpose of exploring relationships between mothers' behavior and the subjects' performance of the Walk-the-Plank Test.

The home visit ratings used were in the form of T-Scores, which place the individual in relation to other children in the Fels research population. A rating of 50 thus places the child at the mean of the norming group, a rating of 40 places him one sigma below the mean, while a rating of 60 places him one sigma above the mean. In comparing the parent-behavior ratings given children in the Dependent and Independent Groups, the mean T-Scores were computed for each group for each of the five mother-behavior variables. The reliabilities of differences in means of the Dependent and the Independent Groups were determined using Wilcoxon's non-parametric test for unpaired replicates (3).

Table 1 summarizes the results obtained with each of the five variables. It was predicted that high child-centeredness, high babying and high protectiveness would be associated with dependence rather than independence in the Walk-the-Plank Test. The results for child-centeredness and babying were in the predicted direction, though babying did not yield a significant difference. With protectiveness, a slight and insignificant difference was found in the opposite direction from that predicted. This finding may reflect unreliability of the measures employed, or it may indicate that the prediction made with respect to the protectiveness variable was incorrect.

It was predicted that high acceleration and high democracy would be associated with independence in the Walk-the-Plank Test. The results with both variables were in the predicted direction, though the difference in means was not significant with respect to democracy.

The results of this analysis support the view that a child's behavior in a physical threat situation is related to certain aspects of his mother's behavior toward him. Further research is needed to establish the nature and

TABLE I

MEAN RATINGS ON FIVE MOTHER-BEHAVIOR VARIABLES FOR 20 SUBJECTS
WHO ACCEPTED THE HELPING HAND (DEPENDENT GROUP) AND
20 SUBJECTS WHO REJECTED THE HELPING HAND (INDEPENDENT
GROUP) ON TRIAL 1 OF THE WALK-THE-PLANK TEST

Mother-Behavior Variable	Mean of Dependent Group	Mean of Independent Group	Difference	Predicted Direction?	Reliability
Child-centeredness ...	51.8	44.6	+7.2	Yes	<.02
Babying	47.6	44.0	+3.6	Yes	Non-signif.
Protectiveness	48.7	49.8	−1.1	No	Non-signif.
Acceleration	48.4	54.0	−5.6	Yes	<.05
Democracy	47.6	51.3	−3.4	Yes	Non-signif.

degrees of such relationships because of several limitations of this exploratory analysis. The results presented here involved too few subjects to be conclusive with some of the variables employed. The ratings of mothers' behavior used may be unrepresentative because they were based on a single home visit and because they were made from one to three years prior to the subjects' performance of the Walk-the-Plank Test. Also, no measure of the reliability of the Walk-the-Plank Test was available.

It should be noted that differences in mothers' behavior toward the children in the Dependent and the Independent Groups may reasonably be interpreted in two ways. It may be that a mother influences her child's performance in threat situations by indulging him or coaching him, or it may be that the child's behavior in problem situations influences the way his mother treats him. For example, a child may be fearful and dependent because his mother babies him, or his mother may baby him because he is fearful and dependent. Thus the data of this study do not permit determining whether the mother's behavior or the child's behavior was the independent variable.

The Walk-the-Plank Test is a promising technique for investigating dependent and independent responses to physical threat in grade school children. The task is threatening enough to arouse marked anxiety and to induce a high percentage of children to seek reassurance, particularly on the initial trial. At the same time it is not so threatening or so difficult that children as young as six years of age cannot perform it independently. The blindfold, in combination with the raised and unstable platform, offers a highly novel situation for children in the age range studied. Acceptance or rejection of the helping hand offers a clear differentiation of dependent and independent modes of coping with the task. The task as designed for this study is not well suited for studying individual adjustment to threats because, with most subjects, adjustment occurs within a trial or two. Also, the all-or-none measurement of dependent and independent responses does not permit ranking individuals in terms of fine differences in their adjustive responses to the situation. For these reasons, the task is primarily of value in differentiating groups of subjects in terms of dependent and independent behavior.

A major limitation of the task as employed in this study is that no measure was obtained of the amount of threat the subject perceived in the situation, or the amount of tension or anxiety it aroused. If measures of autonomic arousal or verbal reports of anxiety were obtained on each trial, dependent and independent modes of response could be interpreted more meaningfully. The task would probably be improved by blindfolding the subjects before they saw the apparatus. Also, it would probably be an improvement to reduce the instability of the plank since this would place less emphasis on differences in the subjects' skills in maintaining balance.

In considering further studies for which the Walk-the-Plank Test is suited, the investigation of factors which affect the shift from dependent to independent modes of coping with the situation seems particularly promising. Thus different techniques of offering reassurance might be employed with comparable groups of subjects. A comparison of the groups on, say, the fifth trial of the test would indicate the relative effects of the different techniques employed. Similarly, one group of subjects might be offered reassurance and help on each trial and another group required to perform the task on a "sink-or-swim" basis without any form of support. Also, the test lends itself to study of the effects of social factors such as the presence of one's parents or one's peers on performance of the task.

SUMMARY

1. This paper reports an exploratory study of emotional dependence and independence in the Walk-the-Plank Test which required the subject while blindfolded to walk the length of a six-foot plank balanced by springs

and raised eight inches off the floor. Fifty-six children, 31 boys and 25 girls, between six and 12 years of age individually performed five trials on the apparatus. On each trial, the subject might exhibit dependence by holding the experimenter's hand while he walked the plank, or he might exhibit independence by walking the plank without help.

2. Evidence was presented to indicate that almost all of the subjects perceived the task as threatening. However, the task was not so threatening that any of the subjects refused to perform any of the five trials.

3. No sex differences were found in the subjects' performance of the Walk-the-Plank Test.

4. Two-thirds of the subjects accepted the helping hand on the first trial of the test and approximately one-third on each of the succeeding four trials. The difference in the proportion of subjects accepting the helping hand on Trials 1 and 2 was significant. The fact that a very high proportion of the shifts from dependence to independence occurred on the second trial was interpreted as related to the novelty of the task on the first trial.

5. Almost the same proportion of younger and older children accepted the helping hand on the first trial of the test. However, on later trials, the younger children accepted the helping hand twice as often as the older children. The lack of evidence for age differences on Trial 1 was interpreted as related to the novelty of the task on that trial.

6. There was evidence that the amount of dependence or independence children showed in the Walk-the-Plank Test was related to certain aspects of their mothers' behavior toward them at home as rated with the Fels Parent Behavior Rating Scales.

7. The Walk-the-Plank Test was discussed in relation to its suitability for use with further studies of dependence and independence.

REFERENCES

1. BALDWIN, A. L., KALHORN, J. and BREESE, F. H. The appraisal of parent behavior. *Psychol. Monogr.*, 1949, 63, No. 4.

2. HOLMES, F. B. An experimental investigation of a method of overcoming children's fears. *Child Develpm.*, 1936, 7, 6-30.

3. WILCOXON, FRANK. *Some rapid approximate statistical procedures.* (Rev. July 1949.) American Cyanamid Co., 30 Rockefeller Plaza, New York City.

Children Who Set Fires

Thornton A. Vandersall, MD, and
Jerry M. Wiener, MD

FIRESETTING in children is a serious symptom, and is considered by many to be a valid reason for emergency consultation. While there is uniformity of opinion about its consequences, there is less agreement about its causes and meaning. This study reviews the literature on firesetting in children, reports 20 cases in which firesetting was a symptom, and attempts to draw some conclusions from the cases presented regarding the circumstances, ego integration, and psychopathology involved in children who set fires. It will be demonstrated that firesetting occurs in many different situations and personality constellations, may have a variety of dynamic meanings, and that the consistent factors in firesetting have to do with ego integration and impulse control.

Review of the Literature

The literature on firesetting includes the classic psychoanalytic formulations by Freud[1] and Simmel,[2] the well-known study of firesetters by Lewis and Yarnell,[3] and the clinical impressions of others gathered from their patient populations.[4-7]

Freud[1] made some early comments on firesetting in his case report on Dora. Regarding the first dream, which began with the statement, "A house was on fire," Freud noted that children are warned not to play with fire for fear that if they do they will wet their beds. Later in the same study Freud stated that the resumption of bed wetting in a child was most frequently due to masturbation prohibitions. Thus, fires and enuresis were linked to sexual drives.

For many years psychoanalytic thinking viewed firesetting as a result of uretheral-phallic fixated drives, especially in association with masturbatory impulses. A half century after Freud's initial comments, Simmel[2] reported a case of firesetting in a 21-year-old man in which the dynamics essentially coincided with those described by Freud. Simmel concluded that the firesetting was "an unconscious compulsive attempt to find a substitute gratification for . . . the infantile masturbatory impulses." The presentation is essentially a study of drives inexorably working out their fate on a static background.

Helen Yarnell[4] reported 60 cases of firesetting in children, and a chapter in the Lewis and Yarnell[3] monograph on firesetting is devoted to child and preadolescent firesetters. The adolescent group differed from the latency group in several ways. The adolescents tended to set fires in pairs, often planned their escapades, and seemed to enjoy the excitement associated with firesetting. They revealed little guilt about their acts. The latency children were average or below average in intelligence, enuresis was present in nine of the 60 children for a prevalence of 15%, antisocial acts other than firesetting were frequent in the histories, and firesetting was not the reason for referral in most cases. All of the children showed "some evidence of sexual conflict," and many told of experience with masturbation, sodomy, and fellatio. Most of the chil-

ARCHIVES OF GENERAL PSYCHIATRY, 1970, Vol. 22, pp. 63-71.

dren had experienced a real deprivation of love and security. Many of the children revealed a fantasy life containing destructive, retaliatory, hostile impulses directed at a family member which were displaced to the school and expressed in behavior there. In the latency children Yarnell viewed the firesetting as an aggressive act directed at some member of the family, to accomplish some desired end. The symbolic meaning of the fire was not felt to be as important as the result of the fire.

The 1951 monograph by Lewis and Yarnell[3] contains many more observations and speculations regarding the adolescent firesetter. These boys were often noncompetitive, sexually immature, and ineffective. Lewis and Yarnell believed the adolescent set fires when he felt a pressure of things closing in on him, and the act represented a drastic attempt to avoid personality distintegration. The fires were then seen as possessing many varied meanings and uses. The fire could give sexual satisfaction, symbolize sexual activity, or serve as a revenge against the parents. In an attempt to simplify the obviously overdetermined symptom, Lewis and Yarnell commented that the desire to use fire for revenge was more predominant in their cases than the desire to use fire as a sexual substitute.

While the work of Lewis and Yarnell still devotes much attention to firesetting as a manifestation of drives, their focus is clearly on the vicissitudes of the aggressive drives rather than the libidinal drives, and more consideration is given to ego functioning. They make notations regarding the immature personality of the firesetters and their difficulty in control of inner conflicts—clearly an ego function rather than a direct drive manifestation. While attention is paid to the reasons for choosing firesetting as a symptom—noting its powerful, magical, sensual qualities—there is no consideration of the more difficult problem of why firesetting is chosen instead of some other act or symptom. The bulk of Lewis and Yarnell's theoretic discussion is an effort to elaborate the dynamics and unconscious meanings of firesetting to the firesetter.

Kanner[6] stressed the disturbed family relationships in the cases of firesetting he had seen. He noted that, "The combination of unhappiness over maternal perfectionism or outright rejection and disappointment in the father, augmented sometimes by sibling rivalry, recurs in our cases with surprising regularity."

Kaufman et al[7] reported on 30 boys who set fires. Ten of the boys were drawn from outpatients at a child guidance clinic, ten from a residential center for delinquents, and ten from a state hospital. Of the 14, 30 were enuretic, a prevalence of 47%. They diagnosed eight of their patients as primary conduct disorder, 11 were considered borderline personality disorders, and 11 were considered psychotic. The family histories ". . . revealed a relatively large number of deserting, alcoholic abusive, and psychotic parents." The level of instinctual development in the children studied was thought to be primarily oral, rather than phallic-urethral. The libidinal and aggressive drives were described as fused and undifferentiated. The children feared that they would be destroyed by the potentially overwhelming force of their own inner tensions—an observation strikingly similar to that made by Lewis and Yarnell.[3] In spite of the primary emphasis on instinctual drives in Kaufman's study, many comments on the ego mechanisms in the firesetting child were made. In an attempt to cope with inner tensions of a primitive, oral nature, the child first uses denial and flight. Later he attempts to externalize his inner turmoil in firesetting. The fire was then a restitutive act, combining denial, externalization, identification with the aggressor, and active mastery.

In a report on four adolescent firesetters, Macht and Mach[5] make a strong plea for consideration of firesetting as a "highly determined behavioral complex or syndrome," having many important instinctual, dynamic, and adaptive aspects. The fathers, or surrogate fathers, of each of the patients had a specific, long-standing association with fire through occupation. None of these fathers were associated with the adolescent when the fire was set and one determinant of the fire was felt to be desire for reunion with the father during a difficult period of intensified closeness with the mother.

In summary, firesetting was first described in terms of drive vicissitudes, particularly sexual drives. Lewis and Yarnell began to note aggressive drive manifestations and introduced ego considerations, commenting on the immature personality and attempts to maintain control of inner tensions. Kaufman's work supports and repeats most of the Lewis and Yarnell formulations regarding the act as multidetermined, influenced by both aggressive and sexual drives, and undertaken by the ego in an attempt to control inner conflicts. However, Kaufman's major thrust is to emphasize the oral fixation of the firesetter and the consequently more primitive and disorganizing nature of the anxiety, as opposed to the previously described phallic-urethral fixation. The Macht and Mach study emphasizes the act of firesetting as multidetermined and urges consideration of it as a symptom complex.

Simmel, Lewis and Yarnell, Kanner, and Kaufman all note the deprived family background of the firesetter, but with varying degrees of emphasis. The Macht and Mach study provides the only information available about fathers, and this indicated a strong association of the fathers with occupations involving fire.

Study Group

Twenty cases of firesetting were seen out of 860 consecutive evaluations, giving an overall incidence of 2.3%. Fourteen came from 660 evaluations done in the outpatient child psychiatry clinic of a large voluntary hospital, and six from 200 evaluations in a suburban private practice. The age range of the firesetters in this population was from 4 to 11 years old, and all but one were boys. The age range of the total patient population in which these cases appeared was early childhood to age 18, boys outnumbering girls about three to one.

Home Setting.—*Fathers.*—A mature, effective, and consistently available father was not present in the home of *any* of these children. In ten cases, or 50%, the father had been totally absent for many years, and the child had been raised entirely by women. In three cases the fathers were absent from the home most of the time, and when home they were demanding, complaining, and critical. In two homes there were frequently shifting male figures. Five of the boys had fathers who were reasonably re-

sponsible providers, but these men were away from home most of the entire waking hours of the child; and when they were with the child they were, to varying degrees, uninvolved and distant, often taking the position that it was a woman's job to raise children.

Case Example

The character of one father is illustrated by his decision to buy an expensive car and leave his wife and four children after a promotion significantly increased his income. He acquired a mistress and announced to his wife that while he had formerly felt he wanted and needed a family, he no longer believed he did.

Mothers.—The mothers of these children, were, to varying degrees, affectively distant, rejecting, ineffective, and in some cases overprotective. While many of the traits overlapped and not all were present in any one mother, several patterns of relatedness to their children emerged.

Six of the mothers showed little feeling and warmth for the child. The child seemed to be viewed from afar with a flat and detached quality. Almost any explanation or plan presented for the children seemed equally acceptable.

Case Example

One mother in this group was the one whose husband left her for a new car and woman. His wife was a distant, unemotional, bland woman. Her affect never varied, she was passively cooperative but essentially disinterested. By missing appointments and minimizing issues she drifted away from any effective involvement.

COMMENT.—Seven of the mothers could be characterized as rejecting and indifferent. They showed varying degrees of rage over their children's behavior, and their main response was a wish to rid themselves of the child. All mothers in this group felt their children had been a problem since birth. One mother told of wishing her son would be born dead.

Case Example

This mother chronically complained about her son and wanted to know what the doctor was going to do about him. All suggestions for change were rejected. This boy's appointments were often "forgotten" or cancelled for minor illness. A younger brother, who the mother felt was a "good egg," was in therapy during the same interval and his appointments were never missed.

COMMENT.—Four of the mothers were ineffective as caretaking individuals. One of these women showed severe disorganization. Another was very superstitious, sought the help of mediums and soothsayers for advice, and was quite anxious and insecure. One mother was very concerned and affectively involved with her children, but was overwhelmed by caring unaided and without paternal support for three young children.

Case Example

This latter mother was solicitous and overly anxious to meet her childrens' needs. She was capable of warmth but not of setting limits. She lamented the "loss" of her husband who worked long hours. There was a suspicion that she may have been ineffective in discipline as a way of pulling her husband into more involvement with the children and, indirectly, with her. Her own needs for approval and acceptance also made corrective or critical behavior with the children difficult.

COMMENT.—Three mothers were overprotective as their predominant mode of relating to the child. These mothers infantilized their children, indulged in excessive closeness, discouraged socialization, and had difficulty in controlling their children appropriately. The third mother was overprotective in a way that indicated reaction formation to her own hostile impulses.

Case Example

One overprotective mother slept with her son, fed and dressed him at the age of six, walked him to and from school, observed him at recess and met him at lunch.

The reactively overprotective mother was quite tense and seemed to be sitting on a "tinder-box" of anger, while professing pleasant cooperation. She had overreacted in degree and duration to the death of a brother and the illness of her parents. She was unable to tolerate criticism of her son and left therapy as soon as the slightest directness was used in delineat-

ing mechanims of behavior in her son and herself.

Enuresis

Enuresis, a symptom long associated with firesetting, was present in 4 of our 20 cases, a prevalence of 20%. One of these was a severely retarded and eventually institutionalized girl. One was only 4 years old, another was 6 and still sleeping with the mother. He stopped wetting by age 7. By comparison, Yarnell[4] found enuresis in 15% of the sixty firesetters she reported, and Kaufman et al[7] found enuresis in almost 50% of their cases.

Intellectual and Organic Factors

Psychological examination was done in ten of our 20 cases. The intelligence quotient (IQ) range was 62 to 112 with an average of 87. IQ testing was done selectively, usually in those patients suspected of having intellectual deficits. The average IQ of 87 is therefore not representative of the entire group and is probably a low rating for the group as a whole. Of our total group, 12 had experienced academic difficulty.

On reproducing Bender drawings, three of the children demonstrated rotations, perseverations, separations of contiguous figures, and angulation difficulties; findings associated with organic brain damage. These same three children also had such symptoms as hyperactivity, short attention span, immature speech, poor coordination, and difficulties in conceptual and abstract thinking. While organic factors certainly added another insult to the ego of these children, they could not be used to characterize the group.

Fires

With one exception, the fires did not progress to any serious damage. All the fires were quickly discovered, although in a few cases it seemed that the discovery was accidental. The one fire that progressed to serious damage was set by a 7-year-old boy under the crib of his 9-month-old sister. His mother was warming a bottle for the infant at the time and came into the room when she smelled smoke. In a panic, she picked the infant up and fled from the apartment. Although the apartment was severely damaged, this could have been avoided had the mother acted more effectively. All the patients living in the city set fires in buildings. One of these was in the school, but the rest were in their own apartments. Five were in the parental bedroom, three in the living room, and one in a closet. All the apartment fires were set when the mother was in a nearby or adjoining room. (However, newspaper reports of children burned to death after being left alone by their mothers are not infrequent, and many of these are the presumed result of playing with fire by the children.)

Four of the six suburban patients set fires in fields. It was these fires that were "accidentally" discovered, and the parents usually related something such as "if we hadn't happened to go by then, the entire field would have gone up." The two suburban boys who set fires in their homes did so in the cellar in what was described as an "experiment."

Personality and Ego Structure

These children demonstrate a wide range in levels of ego and drive development, with varying degrees of manifest neurotic symptomatology and character pathology. As an aid to discussion, differentiation, and planning for treatment they can be divided into three roughly defined groups.

One group of nine children could be described as infantile, impulsive, and clearly deviant. A second group of eight children was more controlled and compulsive in their behavior, presenting as more organized, compliant and eager to please. The third group of only three children seemed the most sophisticated in that they appeared more independent, assertive, and successful in coping, albeit in combination with deviant behavior. Each of the groups will be described further with illustrative case material.

Within the group of nine described as infantile, impulsive, and clearly deviant, a range of behavior was seen. Some of the children demonstrated severe retardations

and deviations in development, and one was clearly psychotic. As a group they were characterized by immature speech patterns, hyperactivity, disruptive school behavior, learning problems, tendencies toward isolation from peers, and more dependent behavior in the family. While this group contained the two children with IQ results below 75, it also contained children with normal IQs. No significant concentration of truancy, school failure, enuresis, or stealing was found in this group in comparison with the other groups.

Case Examples

CASE 1.—This 11-year-old boy had been hyperactive during infancy, had seizures with fever, and frequently had accidents. He truanted often and did no work when in school. He stole, and often threatened to kill himself. This threat at times was a way of coercing his mother. He had eaten glass and frequently run in front of cars. There was no father in the home and the mother was strikingly disinterested in the boy. An infant had been born to the mother a month prior to referral, and it appeared that the loss of what little attention and supervision he had, together with his consequent resentment, were the main precipitants of further decompensation in an already vulnerable ego. This boy set fire to a string in the kitchen that was used to pull on a light. He did this repeatedly during one day in an announced attempt to "burn the apartment down or blow it up." There was a clear disorder present in his thinking and he was hospitalized.

CASE 2.—This 6-year-old boy was seen because of hyperactivity and tantrums in school. He was the youngest of four children, cared for by an older mother. There was no father in the home. All the older children were, by history, to some degree independent and caused the mother little concern. This was striking in view of her very close attachment to our patient. He slept in his mother's bed and was her constant companion. He had little useful speech except in conversation with his mother. In the presence of strangers he was silent and smiling, nodding and shrugging in response to questions with a silly, coy manner. After suspension from school he began to have tantrums at home and destroy furniture when frustrated. He seemed more and more demanding and his mother devoted herself almost exclusively to him. He set several small fires when he was out visiting with his mother. He required hospitalization at this point and was able to demonstrate moderately good control over his behavior in the hospital on low phenothiazine dosage. Psychometrics yielded an IQ of 85 with results suggestive of central nervous system damage. Neurological exam also noted "soft signs" consistent with minimal brain dysfunction.

COMMENT.—The second group of eight children tended to present as neat, compliant, and ingratiating. They were also relatively friendless and in several instances quite isolated. Depression was frequently manifest in this group and a fearful and hesitant quality was noted in many of them. As a whole, this group demonstrated more organized ego function and more sophisticated adaptive development than the first group. No easily apparent significant difference in parenting, age range, IQ, or school failure differentiated this group from the others. While stealing was a prominent symptom in this group none of these boys was truant or enuretic.

Case Examples

CASE 1.—This boy was referred by his school because he was restless, inattentive, detached, and isolated. Although his mother brought him to the clinic at the school's suggestion, she seemed more interested in correction of a mild pigeon-breast deformity than with his other problems. It was only in the course of obtaining a routine history that we found he had set a fire in a closet with paper towels so he could "see what would happen." He seemed little aware of the danger or the consequences of his act. The lack of emotional rapport contrasted with the physical care she bestowed upon this complaining and quietly manipulative boy. The mother continued to dress, wash, and assist this 8-year-old boy at the toilet. There were somatic concerns along with fears of damage and injury expressed by both the boy and his mother. His detachment and apparent aloofness, coupled with an impression of effete frailness, led to teasing by other boys which increased his alienation. While we remained concerned about his constricted ego development, we were unable to interest the mother in further contacts after his chest wall surgery was completed.

CASE 2.—This quiet, affable 9-year-old boy openly discussed his struggles with "evil thoughts" about whether to build a fire. When he did set a match book on fire his mother saw this as the culmination of defiant behavior that could not be controlled by her and she sought psychiatric hospitalization for him. He was not hospitalized and no serious behavior problems were noted during a brief period of out-patient observation.

He was a compulsive and uncertain boy who had been reared by several mother surrogates primarily because of his mother's inability, for reasons having to do with her own problems, to care for him consistently. There was no father in the home and the firesetting took place after the mother and the patient had been reunited and were living with friends. This was the first time this boy had lived with his mother for five years, and signaled the end of a period of relative stability with his grandmother. A definite depressive element was present during the initial interviews, but this later subsided and was replaced by angry feelings about his current situation. Stealing and killing of goldfish were reported by his mother. His main defenses against such thoughts and behavior appeared to be obsessive. He tried to be a "good" boy, neat in appearance, and compliant to adult requests. These controls were not able to function effectively for him while with this mother, and she impulsively returned him to his grandmother in a characteristic riddance reaction. It was clear that the move from grandmother to mother had aroused not only a sense of loss, rage, and depression with wishes both for restitution and revenge, but also placed him in a more intimate relationship with his young mother. Although he did not elaborate fantasies about the fire, it clearly could represent an expression of both destructive and libidinal impulses.

COMMENT.—We have commented that a third group seemed most resilient in ego adaptation. The three boys in this group could be characterized as having a "plucky" or "cocky" quality, with a good natured defiance, and a facade of bravado, and control. Much of their behavior was passive-aggressive and resourcefully manipulative.

Case Examples

CASE 1.—This 9-year-old, wiry, active boy was a "crewcut" with an everready, engaging smile. From the beginning of each interview he led things, with careful attention to the responses of the interviewer. In addition to firesetting he was chronically truant, had vandalized the school, and had set off a fire alarm in school. Speaking about the alarm, he noted, "this kid dared me to do it and I didn't think it was hooked up." In the clinic waiting room he got two boys to fight by informing one that the other was saying things about him, and then

158

quickly assumed the role of peacemaker when an adult appeared. He spoke of his love for "little kids," and conspicuously held his baby sister in the waiting room, although his mother was unencumbered beside him. In the playroom he chose the activities and frequently seemed to have a program for what he wanted to do that day. This boy was enuretic. His main wish was for "a gang—for protection."

CASE 2.—A 10-year-old boy was referred by his school because of short attention span, talking, clowning in class to the point of disruption, and academic underachievement. His mother was animated and defensive about him. He was the second of three boys, a fact the mother delighted in, since she strongly preferred boys to girls. It appeared that he was chosen by his mother to be especially close to her because he was born during the terminal illness of her brother. She had been particularly close to this brother and mourned his death for almost two years. The father worked long hours and was a quiet and detached man who was concerned about, but not involved with, his children.

The school had urged the mother to seek counselling for herself so that she might be firmer in controlling this boy, yet she sought consultation about the boy. He was somewhat mercurial in manner, at times engaging and verbal and other times quiet and depressed. While his mother described him in rapturous terms as a boy "full of joy about life and it's beauty," he presented to the school and psychiatrist as a person who "didn't care" what he did. He seemed well aware of the sense of frustration his attitude created in the teacher and therapist.

He set fire to a pile of leaves next to a barn, almost burning the barn down. He did not reveal any fantasies about the fire and spoke about it only in descriptive, unemotional terms. While his mother was concerned about the danger inherent in such acts, she spent much time in pleasurable identification with his boisterous, unruly, and dangerous acts.

Comment

It was expected that most firesetters would be boys. Our one female patient was a mentally retarded girl who had to be institutionalized.

We have commented on the age range of the children (4 to 11 years of age), and the fact that firesetting was not a symptom in the numerous adolescents we had seen. Cases from other sources, such as were available to Lewis and Yarnell (1951), document that adolescents do set fires. It may well be that adolescent firesetters are more likely to come to the attention of the courts rather than psychiatrists.

It is striking that firesetting represented the main reason for referral in only 3 of our 20 cases. Other behavior problems tended to be focus of parental or, more often, school concern. Firesetting most often emerged as only another symptom among other indications of poor impulse control and a more generalized behavior disturbance.

As previously noted, 20% of these patients were enuretic. We were unable to attach any specific meaning to or relationship of enuresis to firesetting. In addition, the 20% incidence of enuresis is actually misleading. The sample is small, one of the cases was nonrepresentative in being a severely retarded girl, another was still only 4 years old, and a third had stopped wetting by age 7. Obviously, these cases represent widely differing kinds of problems.

Ten of our patients had experienced significant school failure and had either been held back in school or were described as "failing in everything." The failure could not always be related to the results of IQ testing, where that was available, nor could it be related to any personality type. Stealing was described in six of the patients. The incidents usually involved taking things from mother's purse or candy from stores rather than larger thefts.

No characteristic personality type or disorder was found. We have attempted to describe the range of personality developments by defining three groups among our patients, since it was not possible to find or present a "typical" patient. The children were as a rule unproductive in discussing their reasons for setting the fire or their feelings about or during the fire. Many did report a sense of curiosity and impatience. Some wanted to see what the fire would do and said they "couldn't wait" in order to start it at some other time or place. One boy, eg, ignited "smoke bombs" in his room on the day before Halloween because he "wanted to see how they were going to work" the following evening. The oldest child in our series was 11. Accounts of fantasies associated with firesetting and good reporting about affective states associated with firesetting, summoning firemen, and then aiding in extinguishing the fire all seem to be associated with older children or adolescents. From sources separate than those used in the collection of these cases, we know of two children (one 7 and one 12 years of age) who set fires and were able to give some account of their fantasies, purposes, and affective states surrounding the firesetting episode. Both of these children were very intelligent, the older one was borderline psychotic and the younger one was essentially a healthy child reacting to the divorce and impending remarriage of his mother. However, our experience is that information directly from the children about their firesetting is chiefly descriptive. Very few of these children spontaneously referred to their firesetting, and fewer still could reveal fantasy, dream or other directly dynamic material during the course of their diagnostic evaluation. Very few of the boys gave any material directly suggestive of predominant conflict around sexual issues. Their most demonstrable difficulty seemed more centered about issues of aggression and impulse control. A sense of exclusion, inadequacy and loneliness was conveyed by many of the boys, originating from a real or a perceived lack of dependency gratification and low self-esteem. The presence of a new sibling, in several instances, appeared to have quite a direct relation to the firesetting. We have already noted the boy who set a fire under his 9-month-old sister's crib. In other cases the arrival of another sibling was perceived as a further loss of attention and support, and the resultant resentment was often compounded when the mothers expected our patients to aid in the care of the younger sibling. Where the siblings were closer in age to our patient, an intense rivalry was often found.

None of our patients had adequate, age-appropriate relationships with other children. They frequently were teased, seemed isolated, and did not participate in any group activity. Many of them felt they were "not good in sports" or were "picked last all the time."

All these findings and observations occur in a select group of firesetters, since they are those who came to psychiatric attention and usually for reasons other than firesetting.

There is certainly another and probably larger group of boys who have set fires who do not come to psychiatric attention. This latter group would include instances of firesetting which represent episodic or transient self-limited behavior, and the more circumscribed symptom formation of neurotic conflict around sexual or aggressive impulses or both. These cases (by and large) would be expected to have healthier ego development and better adaptive functioning than the group of boys being discussed in this study.

In the study group firesetting is only one manifestation of a more generalized disturbance in ego development. We found a diagnostic range from personality disorder to childhood psychosis. In some cases the firesetting represented evidence that further disorganization, regression, and loosening of controls were occurring in response to either an identifiable environmental stress (object loss, birth of a sibling) or during a time of developmental crisis, or a combination of the two. In other cases no immediate personality disorganization or precipitating stress could be identified, and here the firesetting seemed imbedded in a more generalized personality disorder.

The literature has stressed the erotic-libidinal wishes and impulses expressed in acts of firesetting. In our study cases, these underlying fantasies usually could not be specified. The expression of primitive destructive-aggressive drives was clinically clear and consistent. The ego development and adaptive functioning of these boys were seriously influenced by combinations of deprivation, parental loss, inappropriate stimulation, inconsistency in setting limits, rejection and overprotection. The consistency with which the fathers were either completely absent or affectively unavailable was striking. Likewise, the degrees of disturbance in the mothers and consistency of pathologic mother-son relationships were equally impressive. The environmental matrix for disturbances in identification, self-esteem, mood, object relations, frustration tolerance and impulse control is certainly present in each of these cases. Such disturbances are demonstrable to varying degrees and in different combinations in each of the

160

boys. One group of boys was strikingly infantile, regressed, and impulse dominated; another group functioned better by being more constricted, compulsive, ingratiating, and controlled but with more manifest depression and social isolation; and a third group was defined as pseudomature, with an illusory self-sufficiency and superficial charm, but also had shallow interpersonal relationships combined with denial of any dependency needs or vulnerabilities at all. Where oedipal conflict played a part, it was considered secondary rather than primary for an understanding of the pathology and planning of appropriate intervention.

Summary

Twenty children who set fires have been reported. They came from homes that had a significant amount of parental psychopathology. Firesetting was usually only one of several behavioral problems in these children. There were no consistent precipitating stresses, no one personality type was found, and we were unable to delineate specific sexual conflicts. A sense of exclusion, loneliness, and unfulfilled dependency needs were prominent. While there were certainly unconscious conflicts around specific issues, the one consistent factor represented in all the fires was an at least temporary breakdown of controls in the child.

While we wish to stress that the underlying conflict may be variable, we would not minimize its importance. Surely a dynamic consideration of conflict, tied to the developmental level, is essential in planning any rational intervention. The elaboration and understanding of the inner conflict in the child firesetters we studied was seen as an ultimate goal of therapy. Immediate intervention demanded not so much insight by the child, but support and the reinstitution of appropriate controls Sometimes this had to be provided directly by a more restrictive environment. In other cases dependency or self-esteem needs could be recognized and met, thereby decreasing vulnerability. In all cases, ego considerations appeared most crucial in planning intervention.

If one is to predict who is going to set fires, it would seem more profitable to look for the child with tenuous control over impulses rather than a child with specific sexual conflicts. A thorough evaluation of ego strengths and weakness is called for in any firesetter as the only practical approach to an understanding of the determinants of the act and a guide to rational intervention and planning.

References

1. Freud, S.: *Fragment of an Analysis of a Case of Hysteria (1905)*, London: Hogarth Press, 1953.

2. Simmel, E.: "Incediarism", in *Searchlights on Delinquency*, New York: International Universities Press, 1949.

3. Lewis, N.D.C., and Yarnell, H.: *Pathological Firesetting (Pyromania)* Nervous and Mental Disease Monographs, No. 82, 1951.

4. Yarnell, H.: Firesetting in Children, *Amer J Orthopsychiat* 10:262-286 (April) 1940.

5. Macht, L.B., and Mach, J.E.: The Firesetter Syndrome, *Psychiatry* 31:277-288 (Aug) 1968.

6. Kanner, L.: *Child Psychiatry*, Springfield, Ill: Charles C Thomas, Publisher, 1957.

7. Kaufman, I.; Heims, L.W.; and Reiser, D.E.: A Re-evaluation of the Psychodynamics of Firesetting, *Amer J Orthopsychiat* 31:123-137 (Jan) 1961.

ENCOPRESIS IN CHILDREN

Hale F. Shirley, M.D.

ENCOPRESIS is defined by Kanner[1] as "the act of involuntary defecation which is not directly due to organic illness." The term was suggested in 1926 by Weissenberg,[2] who considered the condition to be analogous to enuresis. The term fecal incontinence is now reserved for soiling which is caused by organic lesions such as abnormalities of the rectum or anal sphincter, cerebral or spinal diseases or injuries, and infectious or toxic conditions in which there is general weakness, delirium, or stupor. A diagnosis of encopresis is not made, therefore, until organic causes are, as far as possible, ruled out.

HISTORICAL

It has long been known that involuntary defecation for which no organic cause can be found occasionally occurs in children. Fowler[3] reported 2 cases in 1882. One, a seven-year-old boy "of mushroom growth and hothouse culture," because of excessive study under pressure, "developed into a sort of loaded phonograph, capable of starting automatic expressions which afforded much entertainment to visitors, and gave the ambitious father great hope and comfort. Under such conditions," the author stated, "it is not to be wondered at that something gave way, and fortunately for the brain, it was the sphincter ani." Cessation of punishment and relief from study resulted in discontinuance of the almost daily involuntary discharges in about three weeks. The other case was that of a thirteen-year-old girl who had "befouled herself" nearly every day since infancy. Ergot, strychnine, and tonics were followed by recovery. Fowler considered ergot to be a specific cure in these cases, as in enuresis, because of its "contractile effects upon the vessels of the cord" and "its established value as a restorative of contractile power to muscle."

In 1905 Ostheimer,[4] having seen 3 boys with soiling in a period of six months, reviewed the literature and was able to find only 12 cases. Five of these children, however, had either general or local organic conditions. In 3 cases the soiling was associated with severe constipation. In one of Ostheimer's cases there was a vesicle calculus.

Goodhart and Still[5] stated in 1905 that this condition "is nearly always associated with peculiarities of mental action, which indicate that the treatment should be moral rather than physical. For instance, al-

JOURNAL OF PEDIATRICS, 1938, Vol. 12, pp. 367-380.

though these children are quite sane, one may be subject to outbursts of passion, another will be unduly timid, another will be quite insensible to pain, another may be sullen; in all, in fact, if inquiry be carefully made as to home behavior, there is some unnatural mental trait which shows that we are dealing with some of the milder forms of mental instability. Our experience has not led us to think highly of local treatment in these cases; they do well under kind but firm moral control; it is best to send them away from home to a small school, and in most cases the condition disappears.''

In 1923 Morichau-Beauchant[6] described a number of cases with what he called "paragenital autoerotism." It was his opinion that the "pseudo-incontinence" is a survival of the autoerotism of the infant, and that children hold back their stools because of the pleasurable sensation from the excitation of the mucous membrane of the anus until the imperious demands of nature intervene.

According to Pearson,[7] "training methods may be unsuccessful for much longer than the usual time because the child is of the constitutional type which gets much pleasure from bowel activities." "In many cases," he further stated, "there is definite evidence of lack of parental love for the child," and "the soiling becomes a method of attracting the parents' attention and of spiting them."

Hendrick,[8] an exponent of the Freudian viewpoint, stated that after the oralerotic stage of the "pregenital psychosexuality," the child's "anus supplants the mouth as the chief source of sensual pleasure. Its use, however, is soon much limited by toilet training, and his resentment of this frustration of his pleasure is expressed in phantasies in which defecation represents definite aggression and destruction of the hated one."

Pototzky[9] reported an eleven-year-old boy whose trousers were found filled with feces about an hour after each scolding by his parents. He delighted in their embarrassment and disgust which was caused by their handling of his soiled clothing.

Thom[10] mentioned a seven-year-old girl who reacted to a jealousy situation not only by encopresis but also by smearing with her feces the walls of her room, her clean linen, and her dishes and food. He stated that "one can only say that these cases call for a careful psychiatric examination by the best qualified person available. And it will often test all of his skill and ingenuity to understand the mental processes at work that result in such conduct."

REVIEW OF 70 CASES

Because of the scant attention which is given in the pediatric literature to this condition, it seemed worthwhile to review the cases of encopresis which have been seen in the Psychiatric Clinic of the Harriet

Lane Home for Invalid Children. From Nov. 1, 1930 to March 11, 1937, 2,406 children under fifteen years of age were examined; of these 70 were encopretic. This is an incidence of 2.91 per cent or 1 to every 34.36 patients. In this group encopresis was about one-tenth as frequent as enuresis. It is interesting to compare this frequency with that found in the Maryland State Mental Hygiene Clinics where in 1936 soiling was a complaint in only 5 of 469 cases, 373 of whom were under fifteen years of age. All of the 70 encopretic children, before being seen in the psychiatric clinic, were given physical examinations in the pediatric department, and the diagnosis of encopresis was not made if the child was under two years of age or if any physical finding could be logically considered to be the direct cause of the soiling.

ENCOPRESIS IN THE MENTALLY RETARDED CHILDREN

Twenty-six of the 70 encopretic children were feebleminded. Twenty-one had intelligence quotients below 50 (idiots and imbeciles) and 5 had I.Q.'s between 50 and 70 (morons). Approximately 4.8 per cent of all the feebleminded children, about 14 per cent of the idiots and imbeciles, and about 1.3 per cent of the morons seen in the clinic were encopretic. Their ages varied from two years, three months to ten years. In 16, however, the mental age was less than two years; in the other 10 it ranged from two years to five years. Twenty-one were boys, 7 were colored, and all but 4 were enuretic.

Ten of the 70 encopretic children were of borderline intelligence (I.Q. 70 to 80). This is about 2.6 per cent of the children of this intellectual level seen in this clinic. Nine were boys, 5 were colored, and all were enuretic. Their ages ranged from three to eleven years.

There was one child in the group whose I.Q. was not determined. This was a six-year-old colored girl with a history of masturbation, enuresis, and encopresis, who at the time she was seen at the clinic had a toxic delirium following a skin graft for a large burn. She later received her first adequate training from the nurses on the ward, resented it, and reacted to it with a good deal of trickery.

ENCOPRESIS IN THE CHILDREN WHOSE I.Q. WAS 80 OR ABOVE

Thirty-three of the 70 encopretic children had I.Q.'s of 80 or above. This was about 2.2 per cent of all the children seen in the clinic with dull normal, normal, or superior intelligence. The I.Q.'s were as follows:

I.Q.	NUMBER OF CHILDREN	I.Q.	NUMBER OF CHILDREN
80-85	4	105-110	2
85-90	4	110-115	1
90-95	7	115-120	0
95-100	8	120-125	0
100-105	5	125-130	2

164

Twenty-nine were male; 4 were female. Thirty-one were white; 2 were colored. Their ages were:

AGE	NUMBER OF CHILDREN	AGE	NUMBER OF CHILDREN
2 years 5 months	1	8 years	5
2 years 9 months	2	9 years	4
3 years	1	10 years	1
4 years	2	11 years	1
5 years	2	12 years	0
6 years	7	13 years	0
7 years	6	14 years	1

THE COMPLAINT

It should be emphasized that in most of these patients encopresis was one of a number of complaints. It was the only complaint in 3 of the 33 intellectually adequate children. It was the chief reason for reference in 3 others. In 17 it was one of several complaints (6 or less) and in 10 it was one of many (more than 6). One accusing mother glibly elaborated on 16 complaints. Associated complaints which occurred more than once were as follows:

ASSOCIATED COMPLAINTS	NUMBER OF CHILDREN
Enuresis	20
Temper tantrums	11
Feeding difficulties	10
Poor school work	10
Fighting	7
Stealing	6
Disobedience	6
Nervousness	5
Stubbornness	5
Constipation	4
Misconduct in school	4
Lying	4
Fears (one each of father, storms, dogs, autos)	4
Running away from home	4
Pains	4
Crying easily	4
Restless sleep	4
Nailbiting	3
Destructiveness	3
Fear of dark	3
Fingersucking	3
Masturbation	2
Stuttering	2

Indistinct speech	2
Cough	2
Restlessness	2
Vomiting	2

Additional complaints which occurred once were: "fellatio, head-shaking, head-banging, night terrors, sleepwalking, hollers out in sleep, cruel, high-strung, talks to self, fidgety, inattentive, can't sit still, grouchy, cranky, excitable, negativistic, doesn't answer when spoken to, talks you dumb, setting a fire upstairs, truancy from school, doesn't want to use the toilet, left-handed, teases younger brother, picks on sister, can't talk (deaf mute), doesn't seem to hear (deaf mute)."

The length of time in which the encopresis had been present when the children were first seen in the clinic varied greatly. In 7 cases it had persisted from infancy; in 2 of these to the age of eight years. It had been present a year or more in 6 (the longest duration being six years) and less than a year (one to ten months) in 9. In one case it was said to have been present "a long time," in another "for some time," and in 9 the duration was not recorded.

There was a great variation also in the frequency of the soiling episodes:

FREQUENCY	NUMBER OF CHILDREN
Occasional	8
Daily	4
2 or 3 times a week	3
2 or 3 times a month	2
7 times a day	1
2 or 3 times a day	1
Every day at times	1
Once a week	1
Twice a week	1
4 or 5 times a week	1
Once a month	1
5 times in 7 months	1
3 times in 1 month	1
Irregular (2 or 3 times a day for about 2 days a month)	1
3 times	1
Not stated	4

The encopresis began in 2 cases when the child started to school, in 1 when the child was kept by the Salvation Army when the mother was ill, and in 1 it followed acute diarrhea. In 2 cases it occurred only at school, in 1 after scoldings, in 4 when the children were outdoors playing, in 1 at night in bed, and in 1 it was associated with wetting the clothes.

The parents' complaint was recorded as nearly as possible verbatim. This, in many cases, gives considerable insight as to the parents' attitude not only towards the problem but towards the child himself. Several typical complaints in regard to the encopresis were as follows:

Mother (of a three-and-one-half-year-old colored boy of average intelligence): "He would hide to have a movement in his pants and would get constipated if I tried to make him sit on the pot. I did this the same time each day but it did not work. Each time he would promise next time to ask for the pot, but would always hide under the table or behind the door, and then tell me about it after it was over. I would spank him and put him to bed for it. These would just make him nervous and jumpy, and he would stop having a bowel movement for a day or two and become constipated even though I would sit him on the potty for one and one-half hours and give him books to read and toys to play with."

Mother (of a nine-year-old white boy, I.Q. 89): "He used to soil his clothes until he was six years old. He said he was afraid to sit on the toilet. He was afraid he'd go down in the ground."

Mother (of a six-year-old white boy, I.Q. 83): "He has soiled himself 2 or 3 times a week the past year. For three months he has messed himself with feces when in the toilet alone. Recently he smeared feces on his shoes and hands. When I saw him he said, 'Smell, mamma, smell.'"

Boarding home mother (of a seven-year-old white boy, I. Q. 97): "He has soiled himself three times since I've had him when he didn't go to the toilet in time. The second time I didn't have any clean clothes and I put a diaper on him to shame him. That day at school he had plenty of time and I paddled him when he got home."

Mother (of an eight-year-old white boy, I.Q. 92): "About twice a week when playing, he comes home with his clothes soiled. He claims that he does not know it, but I think that is because he does not want to lose his playmates. He's too lazy to come inside."

Mother (of an eight-year-old white boy, I.Q. 90): "Then he had the bad habit of doing something in his clothes and I whipped him and rubbed his nose in it and made him wash them, and the next day he'd do it again."

Mother (of a six-year-old white boy, I.Q. 94): "The first time he had a bowel movement in his clothes was about a month ago. When I was undressing him to go to bed. I noticed a terrible odor in his pants. I said, 'What's the matter, are you too tired to wipe yourself clean?' Then I saw what he had done. I've spanked him for it several times. I've told him if he didn't quit it I'd rub it in his face, just to scare him, see. I've put him on the commode and he says, 'I don't have to,' and I say, 'You've got to sit there until you do,' and he cries and carries on. Then later I smell him and I spank him and tell him he is too big a boy for that. What are you going to do? He never did that when he was younger."

Mother (of a fourteen-year-old white girl, I.Q. 97): "The specific difficulty is that she is unable to control her bowels at various intervals. Just when these times appear I cannot say specifically because I feel she is afraid of telling me or permitting me to know. However, at different times I have found her soiled underwear hidden in various parts of the room, and when I have asked her about the reason or the cause, she remained silent and sullen and passed it off nonchalantly."

167

From investigation of the causes of the encopresis in the 33 children with adequate intelligence, it becomes evident that the condition, in most cases, cannot be considered to be due to any one specific factor. There is usually a combination of such factors as make-up, unhappy home environment, interpersonal conflicts, lack of training, social difficulties, school difficulties, and fears. A clean-cut classification as to etiology is therefore not possible. Each case must be considered individually, and even then, from the information available, a clear explanation of the difficulty is not always obvious.

Outstanding, however, is the fact that many of these children came from unhappy homes. At least 12 of the homes could be considered to be highly undesirable environments for the rearing of children. In 4 cases the parents were separated. Four fathers were alcoholic; 1 was epileptic. Three fathers and 6 mothers were mentally deficient. One mother was an irresponsible vagrant and prostitute. Two fathers and 1 mother were paranoid. Such homes, obviously, were characterized by emotional tension, personal friction, and lack of effective training.

An example of such a home was that of F. K., a healthy six-year-old white boy of dull normal intelligence, who was referred because of stealing, lying, running away from home, bad temper, cruelty to animals and children, destructiveness, and encopresis of one year's duration. The child was reared in an atmosphere of tension and discord and never had any sympathetic or consistent training. The father, alcoholic and lazy, frequently accused the mother of infidelity and on one occasion chased her with a butcher knife. The mother, who divorced her first husband, was feebleminded, hypochondriacal, and once attempted suicide. After several temporary separations, the parents decided to separate permanently; the mother went to work, and the patient was placed in an orphanage at the age of four years. There his conduct became so bad that the orphanage refused to keep him. His behavior gradually became more serious. He ran away, shut himself up in a gas oven and was dazed when found, jumped from box cars, turned on gas, set fire to his mother's bed, fried dog's dung and ate it with mustard, carelessly fell out of a second story window, sustaining a skull fracture; at school he ate crayons, tried to choke a girl, and drank out of the toilet bowl. Institutionalization was recommended but it was eighteen months before he was placed in the State Training School for Feebleminded. Two years later, because he was not feebleminded, he was transferred to a boy's training school where, about two months later, the only complaints made about him were that he was inattentive, restless, and tore his clothes, supposedly unintentionally. His encopresis persisted fourteen months after he was first seen in the clinic.

Occasionally one finds a home in which there is actual parental hostility towards the child. C. A., a seven-year-old white boy of average intelligence, whose physical examination revealed hypertrophied and chronically infected tonsils, dental caries, eczema behind the ear, and vasomotor instability, was brought by his stepmother who accused him of fellatio, lying, stealing, enuresis, and encopresis two or three times a week. His parents separated when he was two years old. The father said that the mother ran around with other men and deserted him. The mother said that the father drank excessively, went with a fifteen-year-old girl and other women, and that when she left him she took the child with her. She later obtained a divorce and the court gave the child to the father because she had no means of support. The boy then, for a period of three years, lived with relatives who had no complaints to make concerning his behavior. Two years before the child was seen in the clinic, the father remarried and the patient went to live with his father and stepmother. As investigation of the home proceeded, it became increasingly evident that the stepmother, and probably the father, wanted to get rid of the child. The stepmother exaggerated the boy's misconduct in order to convince the neighbors that he was a terrible child and that she was justified in her attempt to have him placed in an institution. Social workers, feeling that the home was not a good one, tried to place him in a boarding home, but the father, when he discovered that he would have to contribute to the boy's support, suddenly became very fond of the child and told the stepmother if the boy were taken from the home, he would leave. The stepmother, not relishing the thought of losing a source of support, also expressed her fondness for the boy. The domestic difficulties were thrashed out in court and a better understanding was brought about. Six months later the child's encopresis had ceased and the stepmother defended him as ardently as she formerly had accused him. His teacher reported that his school conduct was much better.

In one case unhappiness in a boarding home was the essential etiologic factor. J. H., a white boy, seven years, ten months old, of average intelligence, physically healthy, and of good parentage, was referred because of misconduct and lack of application at school, frequent soiling of his clothes, lying, stealing, and fighting. The encopresis began while he was at summer camp. He was sly about it, hid soiled garments, but was detected and punished by being made to wash his clothes. This child was a well-behaved boy until two years before he was first seen in the clinic, when he was placed in a boarding home because it was suspected that his brother had tuberculosis and his parents did not want him to be exposed. The boarding mother, a former school teacher, was strict with him and left much of his care to her 3 daughters, the youngest of whom (ten years old) the patient did not like. The situation became such that he was in constant disgrace and very unhappy. He was therefore returned to his home. The encopresis stopped promptly, his conduct and school marks rapidly improved, and four years later he was found to be a well-adjusted boy.

In 7 cases an important etiologic factor was an oversolicitous, overprotective attitude on the part of the mother. Not only were these children spoiled, inadequately trained, and not allowed to grow up emotionally, but some were made miserable by a strange mixture of indulgence, anxious hovering and nagging.

An example of the effect of spoiling was M. B., a healthy four-and-one-half-year-old boy of superior intelligence (I.Q. 126), who was brought to the clinic by his mother at the suggestion of his nursery teacher because he was nervous and had soiled his clothes five times in school. The child's mother separated from the father because he was alcoholic and failed to support her. The mother had only a fourth grade education, was emotionally childish, and was overindulgent towards the patient. At home there was played a "family game": the mother was supposed to be the father, the eight-year-old sister the mother, and the patient the baby. The mother and sister had the habit of carrying the child around like a baby, and in their presence he was very babyish. A more sensible home atmosphere resulted in immediate cessation of the encopresis, and four years later it was reported that the child was doing well in school and was well adjusted at home.

In addition to the spoiling, in 2 cases there was a home atmosphere permeated with preoccupation with body sensations, fear of disease, concern over heredity, and superstitious medical notions. C. E., a healthy four-year-old white boy, of average intelligence, was referred because he had a dry cough and "stiff knees" for which no organic cause could be found, was nervous, bit his nails, ate poorly, vomited, and slept poorly at times. There was a history of finger-sucking, earpulling, breathholding spells, temper tantrums, fear reactions, and occasional encopresis. The child had an anxious, oversolicitous mother who was upset by "every little thing." The father was thought to have a "gastric condition," was on a diet, and the mother feared that the child had inherited it. The spoiling of the child was helped along by an overindulgent grandmother and two fond maiden aunts who lived in the same house. It was advised that the father submit to a physical examination, that the mother give up her notions of heredity and her oversolicitous attitude, and that the domination by the child of a group of enslaved females come to an end. The mother later expressed her gratitude for her relief from worry about the boy's physical condition. The father, with the encouragement of a physician, gradually resumed taking a normal diet. For about three and one-half years the child continued to soil occasionally when he was outdoors playing. Four years after the first visit to the clinic the mother reported that he had not soiled for six months and, except for poor appetite and occasional temper outburst, was getting along well at home and at school.

In the case of J. W. the bowel trouble resulted from the mother's constant preoccupation with bowel activity and her prevention of normal bowel function by the daily use of enemas and cathartics, until the child rebelled at the mistreatment. This child was a white girl, five years, four months old, in good physical health and of superior intelligence (I.Q. 128), who was brought by her mother because of chronic constipation and refusal to go to the toilet. In addition to this she presented feeding difficulties, restless sleep, temper tantrums, enuresis, and occasional soiling. The maternal great-grandmother, maternal grandmother, and mother all had a history of chronic constipation, although the mother's constipation ceased when her interest was directed toward her daughter's bowels. This suggested to the mother that the child's constipation was inherited. She had, however, developed other theories to explain the constipation, the latest of which was an etiologic connection between the constipation and a malformation of one of her nipples which she felt should not have been used in nursing. Constipation had been the chief topic of conversation in the home for years, and it was said that the father was tired of it all and tired of the mother. The child had been given hundreds of enemas, innumerable purgatives and gallons of mineral oil, which she hated and fought. An attempt was made to dispel the mother's notions and to persuade her to give the child's bowels a chance to function normally. The girl was placed for a time in a summer camp, where her bowels moved normally from the start, and about a year later it was reported that she was getting along well.

Fear seems to have played an important part in the case of H. E., a white boy, six years, nine months old, of average intelligence, and physically healthy except for infected tonsils and carious teeth, who was referred because he was failing in school, had night terrors, walked in his sleep, wandered away from home, was afraid to go to the bathroom even in the daytime, and, since a car accident at the age of four years in which he was not seriously hurt, had been afraid of cars, had wet his clothes frequently, and had soiled his clothes twice a week. He was found to have a reading disability and in the next few months was given reading training. His tonsils were removed and he received dental care. The father, an uneducated chronic alcoholic, who did not support his family adequately, was in the habit, during sprees, of telling the boy blood-curdling tales at bedtime. Social work with the family came to a standstill because of the father's indifference and laziness. As part of the psychiatric study, Dr. J. H. Conn,[11] in order to determine the child's attitude toward the soiling, and his imagination associated with it, placed the child in a play situation in which dolls were used. In a number of such sessions over a period of about eighteen months, the boy explained that he was afraid to go to the bathroom because he feared that spooks, bogy men, ghosts, and kidnappers might cut off his penis and otherwise hurt him. He also feared that a mouse might chew off his penis. Later he identified the ghosts with his father. As his fears were brought out into the open and discussed sensibly, he gradually lost them. His enuresis stopped, the soiling decreased in frequency from twice a week to once in three weeks, and at the last interview (May 22, 1937) he had not soiled for three weeks, was going to the bathroom regularly alone, and talked as if his fears were things of the past.

A jealousy situation played an important part in the behavior of D. D., a seven-year-old white boy (I.Q. 106), who was brought by his mother with the complaints that he banged his head when he awakened in the morning or if aroused at night, giggled at everything whether it was funny or not, was slow in performing tasks, soiled his clothes about 3 or 4 times a month the past two years, teased his little brother, and was a "cry-baby." His school teacher complained that he did not apply himself or finish his work, acted silly, and was annoying, dependent, and a "disorganizing force" in the classroom. The patient had been a well-behaved child until the age of two years when an older sister died. The mother, greatly upset by this, allowed the child to get the upper hand. The encopresis began after the birth of a brother. In the play situation the child explained that when he bumped his head he imagined that he was rocking himself to sleep like a baby. He wet and soiled his pants because he wanted to be like a baby. He hurt his little brother because his mother scolded him and did not scold his little brother. He wanted his mother not to scold him and he wanted to play with his mother like a baby. The child was also found to have a potential reading disability and was given reading training. The mother was advised to praise good behavior and to ignore, as much as possible, undesirable behavior. The boy was sent to a convalescent home where he was frequently mixed up in some teasing and pounding scrape. He sat around much of the time with his mouth open as if in a daze, and the children considered him "no good." The encopresis stopped after two months, and about a year later the mother reported that he was behaving better and doing better in school.

One eight-year-old girl who soiled her clothes irregularly said she did it because she did not like her mother and wanted to be bad. In explaining the motives of a doll who was assumed to be enuretic and encopretic she said, "She is trying not to do what her mother tells her to. She doesn't want to listen to her mother. She worries her mother when she makes number 1 in her pants." Another little girl doll was brought into the situation and was supposed to ask her why she didn't listen to her mother. She said, "I want to be sassy." (Why?) "I want to be bad 'cause I don't like my mother." (Why doesn't she like her mother?) "She hits her." (Does she think her mother loves her?) "No sir, her mother likes her father better than her." (What does she say?) "I'm going to be sassy. I am going to be mad with you. I am going to make number 1 in my pants.'' This little girl (I.Q. 107) was the younger of two unwanted children of a superstitious, hypochondriacal mother of borderline intelligence, and a reticent, sensitive, immature father. After years of domestic friction and economic strain which brought the mother to a psychiatrist, the parents separated and the mother found some happiness in the attentions of a forty-one-year-old "boy friend" who was a widower with 5 children. As would be expected, there were other behavior disturbances. The child was enuretic, had a poor appetite, was irregular in her sleep habits, had complaints of pains here and there, and in the past had had night terrors. Except for chronically infected tonsils and dental caries she was physically healthy. She has been under treatment about three months and in this period has soiled on two occasions.

Eighteen of the 25 intellectually adequate children of school age presented school difficulties. Eleven were doing poorly in school work; of these 4 had failed at least once. Ten presented behavior problems in school. One child was expelled from school because his teacher "could do nothing with him." One little boy who started to school before he was mentally quite ready for it came home from school frequently with his clothes soiled; he had not soiled before.

It is interesting that 5 boys with encopresis had some degree of reading disability. The most striking case was that of R. S., an eight-year-old white boy of average intelligence (I.Q. 92) whose mother complained that he was very inattentive, didn't mind anything she said, was always squirming around, wouldn't eat, scratched his back "something terrible" at night, was afraid of the dark, was doing poorly in school; didn't like his teacher, and came home from school about twice a week with his clothes soiled. Physical examination revealed malnutrition, poor posture, evidence of old rickets, chronic upper respiratory infection, thick, scarred eardrums, mild conductive deafness, and scabies. In spite of all this the child said, "I feel pretty good but my mother thinks I'm sick. I make out I can't hear and she thinks I can't." In addition to pediatric care, the child was given special reading training. Two months later the mother exclaimed, "Doctor, there has been a great change in R— the last month and I don't know what causes it. He never soils himself." Six months later his teacher reported that although he still did not do well in reading, he was not such a problem in class.

In some cases, as has been mentioned, from the data available it was difficult to understand the causes of the encopresis, the motives behind it, and the purposes which it served, and such children sometimes did not respond well to treatment.

A. R., a normally intelligent, attractive, and sociable girl, who was nearly fifteen years old and who seemed physically healthy except for slight obesity and mild chronic sinusitis, began to soil her clothes at the age of twelve following a diarrhea which was variously diagnosed as diverticula of the rectum, spastic colitis, Hirschsprung's disease, amebic dysentery, and "nothing wrong organically." For three years she had discharged fecal matter both in the daytime and at night at home, at school, at camp, and in spite of supposedly regular bowel movements in the toilet twice a day. She was the older of two children of a hypochondriacal father and a "nervous, irritable," and domineering mother. She started out in life with feeding difficulties which persisted to her tenth year, slept poorly and had nightmares, was enuretic to the age of 10, and in early child-

172

hood had frequent bouts of diarrhea, frequent attacks of pyelitis, and repeated upper respiratory infections often complicated by otitis media. The mother was very considerate with her regarding the soiling. She never punished, called the occurrences accidents, praised and rewarded for clean periods, sent her to the country with a special nurse "for a change of environment," and, on one occasion, arranged a dramatic ritual of burning all her underwear in the incinerator and buying a complete new outfit of underclothing. It was remarkable that the girl discussed the matter without the slightest display of embarrassment. She stated that she did not think her accidents were beyond her control; if she made a little more effort she could easily overcome them. She accepted the offer of help as a "good idea," readily assented to returning for interviews, but gave no convincing expression of a need for help. During interviews the next three months she persisted in her superficial attitude and repeatedly said that she was much better, although her mother continued to find soiled garments hidden about the house. During this period she refused to submit to a rectal examination, and when she finally did a fecal impaction was found. X-ray and proctoscopic examinations revealed an enormously dilated rectum with no evidence of pathology in the sphincter area or in the rectum. Although the possibility of congenital megalorectum was considered, Dr. Thomas R. Brown expressed the opinion that presumably the whole picture was "due to increased accumulation with its associated progressive dilatation of the rectum, a behavioristic syndrome, possibly with bad intestinal habits over a long period of time in a very spoilt, difficult child."

Fifteen of the 33 intellectually adequate children were found to be physically healthy. Three were constipated. One had x-ray evidence of dilated rectum. In one, spina bifida was found by x-ray, but this was not associated with neurologic findings. Others had various physical findings which were not considered to be of direct etiologic significance in the encopresis.

TREATMENT

Treatment in these cases is not directed solely towards relieving a symptom, but is rather planned to help the child to make a better adjustment in whatever sphere there seems to be difficulty. In other words, the child, rather than the encopresis, is treated, and in many cases the course of the encopresis runs a close parallel to the improvement in the general adjustment of the child.

Each child, of course, should have a careful physical examination, and physical abnormalities should be corrected as far as possible. Even though such conditions as malnutrition, chronically infected tonsils, or constipation cannot be considered to be direct causes of the encopresis, they may contribute to the child's unhappiness and interfere with his ability to make adjustments.

If treatment is to be effective, it is essential that the physician have an understanding of the environmental situations to which the child is attempting to adjust. He needs information concerning the intellectual level, economic and moral standards, and emotional atmosphere of the home. Economic difficulties may require the aid of social agencies, mari-

173

tal maladjustment may need amelioration, physical illnesses or personality difficulties of the parents may require medical attention, and medical misinformation and superstition may need correction. Many of the parents need advice as to habit training. Bowel training may be neglected, carried out inconsistently, or interfered with by faulty disciplinary methods. Severe punishment, shaming, and humiliating seldom result in the desired effect, but rather tend to cause in some children feelings of guilt, anxiety, and loss of self-confidence; in others, resentment and spitefulness. Excessive leniency and overindulgence may encourage soiling to gain attention or to control the family. Lack of parental affection may result in encopresis as an attempt to win sympathy or as an expression of hostility. Parental favoritism may foster jealousy and result in soiling as an expression of resentment. When the home environment is seriously at fault and proves to be unmodifiable, placement of the child in a foster home or boarding school may offer the most hope of improvement. In many cases school adjustment needs consideration. Unhappiness often results when the child is placed beyond his intellectual capacity in school and pressure is brought to bear both at school and at home. Reading disability should be thought of in children with adequate intelligence who are failing in their work, and when this is found, it requires special reading training by one who is familiar with this type of handicap. Some of the children need help with their social adjustment. Adequate and supervised play, cultivation of friendships, and development of interests and hobbies may contribute to the child's happiness.

An important part of treatment is work with the child. A sympathetic and uncritical physician can often win the child's confidence so that the child will talk freely of his troubles, fears, and dissatisfactions. Occasionally, a child will be delighted to discover for the first time that he is not a victim of heredity or that he does not have some disease or weakness, or that he is not just bad or lazy. The physician may utilize the good feeling towards him to give the child understanding as to why he behaves as he does and to offer suggestions as to how he may solve his problems in ways personally more satisfying and socially more acceptable. The smaller child's cooperation in overcoming his soiling may often be obtained by having him keep a star chart and letting him work for a prize. Slight improvement should be generously praised, and the child thus learns that soiling is a habit which he can overcome if he really tries. When pride or fear prevents the child from discussing his soiling frankly, the use of play situations and the discussion of the soiling in the third person with the use of dolls sometimes serves the same purpose.

In many cases encopresis responds quite satisfactorily to such treatment. Five of the 33 intellectually adequate children stopped soiling immediately after the first visit to the clinic or after the recommendations were carried out; in 12 the encopresis stopped within six months; in 2 it persisted for about a year. Children from homes which are difficulty to modify because of lack of cooperation or personality inadequacies sometimes continue to soil for longer periods, and occasionally a child will be found who taxes to the utmost one's therapeutic resources. Five of the 33 children continue to soil for about two years, one for three and one-half years, and one child whose parents failed to carry out recommendations and did not return for further help was still soiling his clothes once or twice a week after five years. Five of the 33 children have been seen recently and are still under treatment.

SUMMARY

Encopresis, or involuntary defecation not directly due to organic illness, occurred in 70 or 2.9 per cent of the 2,406 children referred to the Psychiatric Clinic of the Harriet Lane Home for Invalid Children from Nov. 1, 1930 to March 11, 1937. Twenty-six of these encopretic children were feebleminded, 10 were of borderline intelligence, and 33 had I.Q.'s of 80 or above. Fifty-nine were boys, 11 were girls. In most cases the encopresis was one of a number of complaints. Outstanding etiologic factors are illustrated with brief case reports and treatment is discussed.

REFERENCES

1. Kanner, Leo: Child Psychiatry, Springfield, Ill., 1935, Charles C. Thomas, p. 224.
2. Weissenberg, S.: Ztschr. f. Kinderh. 40: 674-677, 1926. Quoted by Kanner.
3. Fowler, Geo. B.: Am. J. Obst. 15: 985, 1882.
4. Ostheimer, Maurice: Univ. Penn. Med. Bull. 17: 405, 1905.
5. Goodhart and Still: Diseases of Children, London, 1905, J. & A. Churchill, p. 492.
6. Morichau-Beauchant, R.: Paris med. 12: 83, 1923. Ab. J. A. M. A. 79: 1084, 1923.
7. Pearson, Gerald: Oxford Medicine, Vol. VII, Chapter II, pp. 172-173.
8. Hendrick, Ives: Facts and Theories of Psychoanalysis, New York, 1935, Alfred A. Knopf, p. 53.
9. Pototzky, C.: Psychogenese und Psychotherapie von Organsymptomen beim Kinde, Oswald Schwarz's Psychogenese und Psychotherapie körperlicher Symptome, Berlin, 1925. Quoted by Kanner.
10. Thom, Douglas A.: Everyday Problems of the Everyday Child, New York, 1934, D. Appleton-Century Company, Inc., pp. 101-102.
11. Conn, J. H.: For method, see Psychiatric Study of Car Sickness in Children, paper delivered before American Psychiatric Association in Pittsburgh, May, 1937.

WHY CHILDREN EAT THINGS THAT ARE NOT FOOD

Reginald S. Lourie
Emma M. Layman
Frances K. Millican

F OR THE PAST 8 years the Children's Hospital of the District of Columbia has been conducting studies of children with pica—a craving to eat bizarre substances not intended as food. The studies grew out of concern about an increasing number of cases of lead poisoning in preschool children.

The children with lead poisoning were treated with efficient methods of removing the lead from the body, and their parents were repeatedly warned not to permit their eating lead-containing substances, such as plaster and paint from walls. Nevertheless, many of the children were brought back to the hospital later with lead intoxication, some of them with growing evidence of resultant brain damage; some with already developed permanent convulsive patterns and severe mental retardation. Thus it became increasingly evident that lead ingestion was a public health problem, the solution of which would require investigation of why these children were eating these lead-containing substances in the first place.

Therefore, the hospital planned an investigation of pica in children, with five research goals:

1. To trace out the natural history of pica as a phenomenon.

2. To describe the emotional climate in which this condition develops and flourishes.

3. To determine the relationship of pica to nutritional disturbances in the affected children.

CHILDREN, 1963, Vol. 10, pp. 143-146.

4. To find out whether there are cultural aspects.

5. To delineate implications for prevention.

The investigations were carried out by an inter-professional research team consisting of a psychiatrist, pediatrician, psychologist, and social worker. They were assisted in investigating the prevalence of pica by the nurses of the District of Columbia Visiting Nurse Association, who inquired about the problem of all mothers of children from 1 to 6 into whose homes they went for any reason.

Ninety-five of the children from our pica clinic, 36 with lead poisoning, were studied intensively in the psychiatric phase of the research. However, the studies could not be completed on some of these children since their mothers failed to bring them back to the clinic even for medical followup. There is reason to believe that the children who were studied may represent milder cases of psychosocial pathology than those not included.

This phase of our investigations involved a control group of 27 normal children and 32 children with psychiatric diagnoses. It consisted of—

• Interviews with the mother and (in some instances) the father.

• Psychological testing of the child by the clinical psychologist.

• A playroom interview with the child by the psychiatrist.

• A Rorschach test of the mother if she was willing to participate; 115 of the 145 mothers of the subjects and the controls were willing.

• Interpretation to the parents by the psychiatrist after the research team had conferred to summarize the psychodynamics involved in the child's pica and to consider the most feasible ways of approaching the problems.

• Followup of a number of the children for several years after the original study through the pica clinic. In this followup, the medical, psychological, and social problems were reevaluated. The social worker provided casework service to some families over extended periods. Seventeen of the children with pica and seven of the children who were psychiatric controls received psychotherapy.

Nutritional studies were made on 78 children, 28 of whom were controls. They included a number of items pertaining to both social history and psychological data, where data comparable to the psychiatric studies were obtained. Observations made on the children at play through a one-way screen revealed not only whether or not they had pica and, if so, to what extent, but also verified some of the findings of the psychiatric study.

While stimulated by the medical problem of lead poisoning, the investigations soon revealed that children with lead poisoning represented only a small portion of those having pica. In fact, it was found that 50 percent of the children hospitalized for so-called accidental poisonings had persistent pica.

History and Incidence

Most children begin mouthing objects in the middle of their first year as part of the normal hand-to-mouth stage of development. Child development studies indicate that this type of activity subsides early in the second year of life. Its persistence as a major activity past 18 months of age may be considered in the abnormal range, but pica involves a further step—the developing of a craving for actual ingestion of a particular substance. The 500 children we studied with this condition habitually ate such substances as newspaper, toilet paper, cleansing tissue, dirt, plaster, wood, cigarettes, matches, starch, paint, powder, crayons, grass and leaves, soaps, bugs, and other objects. The craving for such unnatural "food" is symptomatic of an unmet need.

In a random survey of 859 children, it was found that pica as a symptom occurs chiefly in preschool children, the greatest incidence occurring in children between 18 months and 2 years of age. In lower socioeconomic groups the incidence among children in this age group is between 50 and 60 percent; in higher income families, about 30 percent.[1]

After 2 years of age, incidence drops. By 3 to 4 years of age the manifestation seems to be mostly given up as a persistent habit by children of the "private patient" economic level, while it continues to be evident in about 20 percent of the Negro children of lower economic status found with this condition. Pica does not usually occur in persons past 6 years of age, with notable exceptions such as organically damaged or schizophrenic children, pregnant

178

women, and women in some subcultural groups. It seems to be substituted for by other behavioral and somatic manifestations when the psychological need for symptoms persists.

The Emotional Climate

Through our various investigations we have come to see pica as a result of interaction between forces acting within the child and in the environment.

The dynamic forces within every child at birth include a very necessary investment in oral activity. This varies considerably in strength from child to child. Some children show more interest in mouth activity than others. Some children may have such interests enhanced by the way their mouth activities are dealt with by adults or even other children, particularly their siblings. Once there is an intense pressure for oral stimulation in the child, its fate and manifestations are determined by the way in which it is dealt with from the outside.

Since there is a normal tendency for mouth activity, mouthing and ingestion of all types of materials are to be expected on an experimental basis in the normal hand-to-mouth stage of development at younger age levels, which persist when there are extra pressures in this direction. Usually mothers are on the alert for this and will not allow the child to take harmful objects into the mouth, much less swallow them. However, among children with pica, the mothers usually have supplied inadequate patterns of control for these oral activities. The manifestation then may go on to become an internalized one in the child, with the craving often becoming quite specialized to one or a few materials which seem to have acquired specific meaning, usually symbolic to the child. In other words, the child has experienced no conflict between his inner pressures to mouth objects and the forces outside because the forces outside have been nonoperative.

In this frame of reference, our studies[2, 3] thus far indicate four ways in which pica may develop:

1. *Pica may be an attempt by a young child to solve the problem of meeting his oral needs when the mother is unavailable to him because of death or separation or because of personality disturbances in the mother.* In the latter instance, the personality disturbance lead-

179

ing to the mother's unavailability may be manifested as: (*a*) excessive passivity; (*b*) incapacity to relate to the child; (*c*) depression and withdrawal; (*d*) excessive dependency; (*e*) hostile feelings toward the child; (*f*) concern over marital conflicts.

2. *Pica may represent excessive oral gratification resulting from overstimulation by the mother.* This overstimulation may stem from: (*a*) conscious or unconscious maternal satisfaction in the oral activities and appetites of the child; (*b*) maternal disturbances in impulse control (in mothers who may have patterns of addiction themselves) so that the mother cannot deny the impulse satisfaction in the child; (*c*) the mother's expectation that the child will control the mother's own impulses; (*d*) the mother's handling of any anxiety manifested by her child by offering oral activity.

3. *Pica may represent aggression directed toward the mother as a continuation or displacement of early conflicts over feeding, especially around introduction of solid foods.*

4. *Pica may be accentuated or perpetuated by brain damage affecting perceptual and motor development.* This occurs when: the child uses his mouth as a supplementary sense organ to aid him in compensation for distortions in visual and auditory perception; or the mother fails to recognize or is unable to meet the exaggerated dependency needs of the organically damaged child.

In some families the father does the overstimulating which induces the pica. In others, the father prevents the pica by providing controls when conditions are otherwise conducive to pica.

Corrective approaches to these problems are of course based on differential diagnosis and bringing to bear appropriate measures. Except in the less frequent cases of the severely brain damaged child and where the pica is related to a psychosis or deep neurosis in the child, pica responds well and quickly to treatment of the mother through education or psychotherapy, usually carried out by the pediatrician or a social worker.

Of all the maternal personality syndromes conducive to pica, the one most frequently encountered is the combination of passivity and dependency. Mothers with this as an ingrained character pattern are frequently of low socioeconomic status and are rarely readily available to the treatment staff. Their passivity is so great that they cannot reach out to the clinic teams. Therefore, reaching them with appropriate treatment or education means abandoning our time-honored reliance on having mothers come to our clinic. The staff must go to them. Only if ways are found to meet the dependency needs of such mothers can they in turn meet those of the child.

Nutritional Factors

Many writers have assumed that a nutritional deficiency is the major etiological factor in pica. However, investigators at the Children's Hospital could find no correlation between the occurrence of nutritional deficiencies and of pica.[4] They did find, in repeating experiments originally carried out in the Union of South Africa, that intramuscular injections of iron cleared up pica. However, in a controlled experiment in which some children were given intramuscular injections of saline, the Children's Hospital team found as many children were cured with saline as with iron.

Another controlled study employing a multivitamin-mineral preparation showed this to be only as effective as a placebo in curing pica.[5]

Cultural Aspects

Early in our studies it became apparent that pica in the District of Columbia area is especially prevalent among children whose mothers have pica themselves and among children whose mothers have come from communities where clay eating and starch eating are a part of the cultural pattern. This early impression was borne out by the later controlled studies.[6] In general, mothers who came from communities where clay eating and starch eating were common, or who had engaged in pica as adults, tended to have a tolerant attitude toward pica in their children and some even encouraged it.

Geophagy, or clay eating, has been reported to exist in many parts of the world, particularly among primitive people, and is said to have been known among the North American Indians before the time of Columbus. Today it is still found among some poor people, Negroes and whites, in the southeastern

181

part of the United States. Clay eating was common among the slaves in pre-Civil War days, and may have been a custom they brought from Africa. On the other hand, some Negroes may have eaten clay in those days as a means of attempting suicide. The original significance of geophagy faded.

In order to learn more about the cultural aspects of pica, one of the research investigators held group interviews with 16 mothers of children with pica. The mothers were selected as having come from communities where clay eating occurs or as having had pica themselves.

From these interviews, we learned that in different parts of the South different kinds of clay are eaten. The most popular are red clay and white clay, but yellow, gray, and black clays are also regarded as edible.

Clay for eating is obtained from various sources. In some communities it is dug from a pit; in others it is taken from special places at the side of the road, from around the roots of a tree, or from a mine. Sometimes clay which has been used as mortar is dug out from between the bricks of a chimney or fireplace and eaten, its smoky flavor being considered especially good. In large cities clay for eating may be purchased by the sack, but in rural communities each person digs his or her own clay. Some people eat the clay as it comes from the ground, but many prefer to bake it in the oven until it is hard, then pound it into small pieces and eat it.

In the past clay eating was engaged in by both men and women, but now in the South it is a practice found almost exclusively among women and children. Why the habit has been largely abandoned by men is not clear, but some of the women report the impression that there may be more smoking and drinking among the men than among the women in the areas where clay eating is prevalent.

Some women do their clay eating when alone; others prefer to munch on the clay in the company of friends when they are engaging in some activity together, such as a quilting bee. There is general agreement among our informants that clay is not usually eaten because of hunger, for frequently it is enjoyed right after a meal. Many clay-eating women start the habit in childhood, in imitation of their mothers and grandmothers. Others start during pregnancy. Some of the women interviewed described *cravings* for the clay which they are unable to satisfy with any substitutes.

In this country in most places where clay eating is known, laundry starch also is commonly ingested. Some of the mothers whom we interviewed had never eaten clay but had eaten starch since childhood. Several mothers took up starch eating after moving to the District of Columbia, where their favorite clay was not available. One mother, however, gave up the starch eating in favor of smoking. Some who began starch eating during pregnancy stopped after the baby was born; others continued.

The studies of culturally based clay-eating and starch-eating habits and attitudes of mothers who have been unable to resist the cultural influences suggest that for some children these influences may be important in predisposing the child to develop pica rather than to manifest some other behavior problem. In such cases the model presented by the mother would make it easy for the child to learn these patterns, particularly when the mother's attitude toward pica is one of permissiveness or even one of enjoyment in sharing the habit with the child.

As to Prevention

No matter what the pica-genic characteristics in the child's background, pica in children represents a craving early in life which has many of the dynamic characteristics of the cravings which later in life form the basis for the common addictions. Studies are going on to explore such possible correlations. These might possibly lead to awareness of "addiction prone" families.

At the Children's Hospital the adoption of the routine of inquiring in all history-taking about whether the child ingests nonedible substances and of regarding all pica cases as presumptive lead poisoning has resulted in a 300-percent increase in the diagnosis of lead poisoning, mostly before the usual clinical symptoms have appeared.

What we really need, however, is to apply the concept of primary prevention. This means identifying the types of families that are "pica prone" and,

183

long before symptoms can develop, to apply corrective emotional and sociocultural approaches.

[1] Millican, Frances K.; Layman, Emma M.; Lourie, Reginald S.; Takahashi, Lily Y.; Dublin, Christina C.: The prevalence of ingestion and mouthing of nonedible substances by children. *Clinical Proceedings of the Children's Hospital of the District of Columbia*, August 1962.

[2] Lourie, Reginald S.; Layman, Emma M.; Millican, Frances K.: A study of the etiology of pica in young children, an early pattern of addiction. *In* Problems of addiction and habituation. Paul H. Hoch and Joseph Zubin, eds. Grune & Stratton, New York. 1958.

[3] ————: Emotional factors in the etiology and treatment of lead poisoning. *A.M.A. Journal of Diseases of Children*, February 1956.

[4] Gutelius, Margaret F.; Millican, Frances K.; Layman, Emma M.; Cohen, George J.; Dublin, Christina C.: Nutritional studies of children with pica. I. Controlled study evaluating nutritional status. II. Treatment of pica with iron given intramuscularly. *Pediatrics*, June 1962.

[5] ————: The treatment of pica with vitamin and mineral supplement. *American Journal of Clinical Nutrition*, May 1963.

[6] Layman, Emma M.; Millican, Frances K.; Lourie, Reginald S.; Takahashi, Lily Y.: Cultural influences and symptom choice—clay-eating customs in relation to the etiology of pica. *Psychological Record*, July 1963.

OBSERVATIONS ON CHILDREN WHO HAVE BEEN PHYSICALLY ABUSED AND THEIR PARENTS

This report summarizes observations gathered over the past five years on young children who had been admitted to the Children's Hospital Medical Center, Boston, because of physical illness due to parental abuse. Psychiatric consultation, which was part of the management of these cases, afforded the opportunity to observe the responses of the children and to study the psychodynamics of their abusing parents. Interest in this syndrome stemmed from an earlier study of young children who displayed a failure to thrive in the absence of any demonstrable organic disease. Certain of these cases were subsequently admitted because of physical abuse.

This syndrome is but one of the several disorders of the function of parenthood. *Physical abuse* should be distinguished from *parental neglect*. Many abused children are well-fed and cared for. It is striking to see a young child, covered with welts and bruises, all decked out in a fresh pinafore. Similarly, these cases should be distinguished from those of *deliberate punishment* which occur in older children whose verbal and motor development afford a potential for the provocation of parental ire.

The abused children ranged in age from 3 months to 3-and-one-half years, with the largest group between 6 and 18 months of age. None of them had sufficient verbal or motor skills to be considered capable of realistically provocative behavior, to know the nature of their thoughts and acts.

An average of 12 patients per year has been so diagnosed. Doubtless this is a minimum figure. Physicians are reluctant to consider the diagnosis of parental abuse because it is personally abhorrent, it threatens to burden them with the role of accuser, there is a fear of retaliatory litigation and there is a sense of great futility about the ultimate management of such cases.

Once considered, the diagnosis is relatively readily established. There are few other diseases that produce the clinical picture of fresh and old bruises with new and healed fractures. Bleeding disorders and disorders of bone metabolism can be easily ruled out. Furthermore, such disease processes are seldom associated with the marked decrease in appetitive behavior which the abused child usually displays.

In describing the clinical material a composite picture may be illustrative. A young child is brought to the emergency ward by both parents who provide a brief history of easy bruisability or trauma inflicted by a sibling. Depending upon the site of the signs the child is admitted to a medical, surgical or orthopedic ward with the admitting diagnosis of "Malabsorption Syndrome —Failure to Thrive," "Bleeding Disorder" or "Fracture due to Accident." The parents leave quickly and seldom visit the child.

Often the possibility of parental abuse is raised by the radiologist who reports old, healed fractures of the ribs, skull or head of the humerus as an incidental finding.

In its extreme forms the behavior these children display initially is fairly characteristic, a fact which can be helpful in establishing the diagnosis. Some children manifest extreme fright upon any and all contact, whimpering and attempting to hide under the sheets. Others show a profound apathy to the point of apparent stupor, although they do withdraw from tactile stimuli. These children resemble cases of "shell-shock" in adults. They display a profound blunting of all the external manifestations of inner life. They sit or lie motionless, devoid of facial expression and unresponsive to all attempts at evoking recognition of the external world. They differ markedly from the autistic or schizophrenic child, whose behavior is bizarre. It appears not

AMERICAN JOURNAL OF PSYCHIATRY, 1965, Vol. 122, pp. 440-443.

185

so much that their inner psychic life is distorted or idiosyncratic, but rather that it has been completely suspended.

The treatment of these patients includes the initial management of their more pressing medical and surgical needs, while deferring all elective procedures. Infection and dehydration should be treated promptly and vigorously. The correction of malnutrition is dependent upon the nursing care they receive, for the blunting of appetite renders nutrition a major problem. No other patients demonstrate as dramatically as do these children the extent to which the expression of appetite can be influenced by the quality of relations with another human.

As in many hospitals, the relative shortage of nursing personnel has made the maintenance of a one-to-one relationship difficult. However, experience has suggested that with these children it is less important that the nursing care be constant than that it be provided by women who are comfortable in offering the type of contact which these children are able to utilize.

Initially the children are left unbothered on the ward. As they begin to indicate some awareness of the environment by means of facial expression and voice, some bodily contact is proffered. When the child responds, the nurse or aide offers more and for several days the child may be carried about the ward by one or another nurse who furnishes the maximum amount of bodily contact. The child will lie inertly in the nurse's arms as she goes about her business, occasionally humming or speaking to the child.

Gradually the child moves from total passivity to increasingly active behavior. It is at this stage that a change in personnel occasionally is indicated. Often the children are unappealing, and their early activity may be offensive. The nurse who is comfortable with an inert child is not necessarily comfortable with a child who tries to poke fingers up her nose or bites. The goal is to find a person who can adjust her own responses to the changing needs of the child as he moves from total passivity towards awkward activity. It is at this stage that the child begins to eat. The expression of appetite for food appears to be inextricably linked with an appetite for contact with the nurse, as though they were the same.

None of these children has been kept in the hospital for more than two months. Two died within two weeks of admission, having failed to make any improvement. One had been noted to have poked his finger into the stoma of his feeding gastrostomy shortly before his death, though no cause for death was determined at postmortem.

In recovery from the acute phase, some of the children continue to display extreme anxiety by clinging indiscriminately to any and all persons. Others show an improvement in their nutritional state coupled with striking growth of their ego skills such that they leave the hospital at a more mature level of development.

Others make a satisfactory physical recovery but continue to display a striking absence of appetitive behavior. They do not play with toys, initiate contacts or speak. It is not that they are unable to do so; with sufficient encouragement they do respond. Rather, it appears that these activities are devoid of pleasure for the child. The ego skill remains but the exercise of the particular function provides insufficient gratification to mobilize its spontaneous expression.

In summary, these observations suggest that the capacities of the various ego skills of early childhood present in accordance with a timetable that is relatively independent of experience. The exercise and development of these capacities are highly contingent upon the quantity and quality of gratification which the child can obtain from his experience, particularly with other humans.

When a child does not receive sufficient gratification from his experience over a prolonged period of time, he fails to exercise and develop the various specific ego skills. This can result in an atrophy of disuse whereby the capacity for the specific ego skill becomes irretrievably lost.

There is no particular ethnic, social or economic distribution to the case material of this study. In general the parents interviewed were young and of limited financial means and education. In only a few instances did gross poverty or ignorance appear, and in a few cases the parents were of upper middle-class background.

A major reversal in the traditional roles of the parents was a significant feature. Many of the fathers were unemployed or worked part-time, often alternating with their wives who also worked. The wife cared for the child part of the time and worked the rest, relegating the care of the child to the husband or a babysitter. In appearance and demeanor many of the women were quite masculine and their husbands correspondingly passive and retiring.

This trend can be understood as an attempt to cope with the psychological distress occasioned in the parent by the child. In a number of instances, the actual assault followed upon a breakdown in the arrangements. In one case the mother was forced to give up work as a result of another pregnancy and her husband's desire to return to school. She was forced into much closer contact with her ten-month-old son whom she subsequently beat because she experienced his cries as "so demanding."

It is in their choice of terms to describe the child that these parents most vividly illustrate their psychopathology. They speak of the child as if he were an adult with all the adult's capacity for deliberate, purposeful and organized behavior. Thus, one mother spoke of her three-year-old daughter, "Look at her give you the eye! That's how she picks up men—she's a regular sexpot." This woman brought in a photo of the girl at age two in which the child had been posed by the mother with her hands rigidly held in front to prevent masturbation.

A sergeant in the military police spoke of his nine-month-old son whose skull he had split, "He thinks he's boss—all the time trying to run things—but I showed him who is in charge around here!"

In these cases, as in most, the parents then proceeded to spontaneously associate their reactions to the child with personages and experiences from their own childhood. The mother told with great feeling of her loss through adoption of her only other daughter, born out of an illegitimate pregnancy when she was 16. Clearly she saw in the child she beat and accused of promiscuity all her own former guilt and loss.

The father told of his own alcoholic father who had beaten and tyrannized him in his childhood and who so dominated his mother that she took him and left the father whom he had never seen again. This man saw his son as the embodiment of his childhood relationship with his father.

In the extremity of their ambivalence, these parents perceive the child they assault as a hostile, persecutory adult. The child, by its presence alone, evokes affects in the parents which they find to be intolerable. Initially they attempt to deal with these emotions by withdrawing from the child and relegating its care to the other parent or someone else. It is usually upon the breakdown of this arrangement with the consequent confrontation of the parent with the child that the actual assault occurs.

Guilt and remorse often ensue, and there may be some intellectual awareness of the inappropriateness of the act. It is of little avail in constraining the parents, for the intensity of their ambivalence is such as to obscure the reality. The parents' normal narcissistic endowment of the child with the anticipated attributes of an adult is heavily contaminated with a residue of hostility from the past, distorting their perception of the child. Whereas most parents see their children *as if* they promised to reveal certain qualities in the future, these parents see the child as actually presenting these attributes of an adult here and now.

Thus the syndrome can be understood as the result of a transference psychosis in which there is a gross but circumscribed distortion in the perception of a particular child at a particular stage in its development. It should be emphasized that most of these parents are otherwise free from the major symptoms of psychotic illness.

Management of these cases requires early and active intervention, with emphasis upon the parents' misperception of the child. It has been found helpful to tell them initially and repeatedly that their perception has been erroneous and discolored by their own past experience, and to urge that they review their memories to ferret out any possible sources of such feelings. Such a recommendation serves to shift the focus of parental attention to their own unsettled past, where it properly belongs.

It is important to recognize the quality of their ambivalence. These are not simply rejecting or neglectful parents. None will-

phrenic or autistic. To whatever extent these conditions are determined by emotional climate, it appears that the developing ego is more likely to thrive in the warmth of wrath and to suffer blight in the chill of indifference.

ingly placed an abused child for adoption, and a number vigorously opposed even the temporary removal of the child from the home. Often the child they beat was the object of great love as well as great hatred.

None of the children observed was schizo-

PARENT-CHILD SIMILARITIES IN PERSONALITY DISTURBANCES

E. LAKIN PHILLIPS

INTRODUCTION

The purpose of this paper is to bring additional evidence to bear on one basic tenet in clinical work with parents and children, viz., that children's psychological difficulties grow out of and reflect the parent's psychological difficulties. The general possibility of such a relationship existing between parents and children is most reasonable when we consider the parent-child relationships in such variables as intelligence (6, 8), trait measurements (8, 14), the gross number of mother's fears and the gross number of children's fears (5), plus the fact that children are in many ways the products of their parent's biological and cultural backgrounds (2, 3, 9).

Representative clinical studies (1, 4, 10, 12) attest, also, to the parent-child relationships in personality characteristics where problem children and their parents are considered. Among the findings in these research studies, one finds: Mothers with unhappy childhoods have children with a variety of neurotic traits (4); children who were nagged, criticized, punished and supervised strictly by their parents were judged by their classmates as being quarrelsome, disobedient, quick-tempered and nervous (1); the child of dominant parents tends to be nonaggressive and insecure, while children of submissive parents tend to be rebellious and aggressive (12). As early as 1909, Jung observed the subtleness of parent-child relationships, regarding the developing child, "What most influences him is the peculiarly affective state which is totally unknown to his parents and educators. The concealed discord between parents, the secret worry, the repressed hidden wishes, all these produce in the individual a certain affective state which slowly but surely, though unconsciously, works its way into the child's mind, producing therein the same conditions and hence the same reactions to external stimuli . . . " (7, p. 246). Sperling found among twenty children suffering from psychosomatic illnesses that, "Mother and child represented a psychological unit in which the child reacted to the unconscious need of the mother with correspondingly unconscious obedience; it was as though the child were given a command to get sick, which meant in reality, to stay dependent and helpless" (10, p. 377). Thompson (13) remarks broadly on interpersonal relations theory and, along with Sullivan (11), offers some theoretical discussions which cover the parent-child configuration as well as other two-person relationships.

METHOD

The files of the Arlington (Va.) Guidance Center were examined over a period covering the past two years and fifty-two cases, from among over one-hundred cases, were found which included relatively complete psychological studies of the children and records of extensive psychiatric interviews with the parents of these children. These data included a battery of psychological tests, play-sessions, and interviews with the children; and a series of interviews by social workers and psychiatrists with the parents. Of the 52 cases, 25 were boys between ages 5 and 13, and 27 were girls of the same age range. All children were at least normal in intelligence, and none of the children came from families earning less than $3,000.00 per year.

RESULTS

These data were treated in two ways. First, in terms of the presenting complaints (symptoms) culled from all the data on parents and children. In all, there

JOURNAL OF CLINICAL PSYCHOLOGY, 1951, Vol. 7, pp. 188-190.

were 42 symptoms which occurred 132 times among the children and 81 and 52 times, respectively, among the mothers and fathers of the children. Seventy-one percent of the symptoms showed overlap (communality) among mother-child pairs, and 48 percent of them showed father-child communality.

The second way in which these data were treated was to compare the parents and children on the basis of the main complaints which the parent(s) saw in the child. On this basis, 40 out of the 52 families (77 percent) showed striking similarities. This finding covers an important qualitative result which cannot be quantified on the basis of the present data: The complaints regarding the child which bothered the parents most (their own evaluations), and which probably constituted the real basis for referring the child, were centered around the unresolved psychological difficulties which the parents had from their own histories. Three brief case histories will illustrate this point.

"Tom" age six, was referred because of his enuresis, and this was the behavior which concerned the mother most. The interviews finally brought out that the mother had been enuretic until she began to menstruate, that " . . . people used to kid me about it." The mother recalled in this context that as a child she had been so afraid that she would wet the bed that she refused to go to bed at night, or when she did go to bed she would lie awake for long periods of time disturbed over possible bed-wetting.

The mother referred "Curley," a girl of seven, around problems of discipline and control. In play-sessions, Curley showed much concern for orderliness, keeping her skirt spread out neatly when she sat down " . . . so it would not bunch up underneath me." In her doll-play, she said, "I have just ten minutes to cook dinner . . . just five minutes left!" And " . . . they (the dolls) can play for only one hour . . . I must tell Susan (the doll) when its time to do everything," and " . . . there, that's the way I want her to sleep!" The mother was extremely compulsive in her household chores, chastising herself in the interview for not keeping the house clean at all times, for not having meals ready on time, etc. Trouble with the child, then, was centered around the mother's demands on the child which were highly inappropriate for a seven year old, but which also reflected the mother's problem at the same time. The compulsive and irrational controls she placed on herself were communicated to the child and disrupted the child's behavior, thus making her a "problem" child in the mother's eyes.

"Karen," age eight, was aggressive, hostile and defiant, in her mother's and the school's reports. Karen repeatedly stated that she was "mad as the dickens," and was going to "tell off" everyone. In response to the S-B item, Opposite Analogies (L, VII, 5), "The point of a cane is blunt; the point of a knife is ——," Karen said, "Sharp enough to cut somebody's head off with!" with great vehemence. The interview series between the social worker and the mother showed how the mother dealt with threats in the same way, thus, "If I don't like people, I don't care how I treat them," and "I just spit out whatever comes in my mind."

DISCUSSION AND CONCLUSIONS

These data and the brief case materials illustrate the hypothesis on which this paper is based: Parent-child psychological difficulties arise out of a context of unresolved difficulties from the parent's behavioral history. The child's problems are apparently 'created,' not out of a context which defers to the question, "What's wrong with my child?" but out of a context in which the parent's disturbances in various areas of living are communicated to the child and get the child involved in problem behavior in his own right. Stated another way, we may say that children have to use their parents as models for adjusting to the multitudinous demands of living; if the parents are disturbed in some of their living relationships, this increases the burden the child carries and increases the likelihood that he will be involved in problem behavior in the same areas and in the same ways as his parents.

REFERENCES

1. ANDERSON, J. P. *A Study of the Relationship Between Certain Aspects of Parental Behavior and Attitudes and the Behavior of Junior High School Students.* New York: Bureau of Publications, Teachers College, Columbia University, 1940.

2. DAVIS, ALLISON. Child Training and Social Class. In Barker, Kounin, and Wright (Editors), *Child Behavior and Development.* New York: McGraw-Hill, 1943.

3. DAVIS, ALLISON AND HAVIGHURST, ROBERT S. *Father of the Man.* Boston: Houghton-Mifflin, Co., 1947.

4. FIELD, M. Maternal Attitudes Found in Twenty-Five Cases of Children with Primary Behavior Disorders. *Amer. J. Orthopsychiat.*, 1940, 10, 293-310.

5. HAGMAN, R. R. A Study of Fears of Children of Pre-School Age. *J. Exp. Educ.*, 1932, 1, 110-130.

6. HURLOCK, ELIZABETH B. *Child Development.* New York: McGraw-Hill, 1950.

7. JUNG, CARL. *The Association Method. Amer. J. Psychol.*, 1910, 21, 219-269.

8. OLSON, WILLARD C. *Child Development.* Boston: Heath & Co. 1949.

9. PHILLIPS, E. L. Intellectual and Personality Characteristics Associated with Social Class Attitudes Among Junior High School Students. (In press, *J. Genet. Psychol.*, 1950).

10. SPERLING MELITTA. The Role of the Mother in Psychosomatic Disorders in Children. *Psychosomatic Medicine*, 1949, 11, 377-385.

11. SULLIVAN, HARRY S. The Meaning of Anxiety in Psychiatry and in Life. *Psychiatry*, 1948, 11, 1-13.

12. SYMONDS, PERCIVAL. *The Psychology of Parent-Child Relations.* New York: D. Appleton-Century, 1939.

13. THOMPSON, CLARA. *Psychoanalysis: Evolution and Development.* New York: Hermitage House, 1950.

14. THORPE, L. P. *Child Psychology and Development.* New York: Ronald Press, 1946.

Family Dynamics and Origin of Schizophrenia

STEPHEN FLECK, M.D.

AN INTENSIVE STUDY of the families of young upper-class schizophrenic patients, initiated by Dr. Theodore Lidz in 1952, is now in its seventh year (not counting the first year's pilot study by Drs. Lidz and Beulah Parker.*) The team whose research is reported here consisted of two and occasionally more psychiatrists, a social worker, a psychologist, and research assistants. We selected families in which at least the mother and one sibling were available for the study. In most of our families both parents have been available because the bias in our sample has been intentionally directed toward better organized families than would be provided by a random sample of the families of schizophrenics.[31, 52] By dealing mostly with structurally intact

From the Department of Psychiatry, Yale University School of Medicine, New Haven, Conn.

The research reported here has been supported by grants from the National Institute of Mental Health and from the Social Research Foundation.

Presented in part at the program honoring Dr. John C. Whitehorn during the Meeting of the Johns Hopkins Medical and Surgical Association, Feb. 27, 1959, Baltimore, Md.

*Other collaborators: Alice Cornelison, M.S.S., Dorothy Terry, Ph.D., Daniel X. Freedman, M.D., Eleanor Kay, M.A., and Sarah Schafer, M.A.

families unencumbered by serious economic problems, we hoped to eliminate some of the more extraneous disorganizing factors that beset so many lower-class families.[24]

Contact with some of the families has been maintained through most of the research period and with all at least over many months. Interviews, held weekly in many cases, most commonly have involved the social worker and a family member.[9] Several parents, however, have been seen by one of the psychiatrists for long periods, although usually not at weekly intervals. Also, we often sought out and interviewed other relatives, especially grandparents, friends, and sometimes former servants. Home visits by the social worker have been made at least once in almost every instance. In addition, all available members of each nuclear family have been given a battery of psychological tests.[47] We have found it more useful not to record interviews verbatim but to dictate them as promptly as possible after a session. Even this condensed raw material on some families extends to several volumes of typed material. When satisfied that we had learned as much as we were likely to about a family, or when the patient had been discharged, we summarized the material in 50–100 type-written pages. We feel that the data for 16 families are at this time reasonably complete.

On one level, the findings can be stated quite simply. No family that functioned or had ever functioned in a way that could be characterized as wholesome or normal or as falling within the usual range of family life has been found. All were severely disturbed, distorted by conflict, and beset by role uncertainties of family members other than the patient. I recognize that such a statement is methodologically not very satisfactory, but the team has been more concerned with describing and delineating the difficulties and disturbances that characterize these families than with an attempt to establish some sort of controlled study. I shall, however, attempt to spell out some of these differences between the study families and other families later on. We have been encouraged in the pursuit of our approach by the concordant findings of other groups who have studied families of schizophrenics in recent years, such as the National Institute of Mental Health,[5, 53] the group under Drs. Don Jackson and Gregory Bateson in Palo Alto,[3, 22, 26] and in particular, by similar findings abroad.[2, 10] Notably, Alanen of Finland has made a statement almost identical with the above: All but 16 of 100 mothers of schizophrenic patients he studied suffered from a clear neurosis or more serious psychopathologic disturbance, but each of these 100 families had to be considered severely disturbed.[2]

It is not easy, however, to list and delineate the abnormalities in family function that we have discerned manifest in disturbed family interaction and in the personalities of its members. In part, such a list encompasses the titles of previous publications, each only a fragment of the total reconstruction of family histories and the histories of the persons in it. This presentation also can deal only with some segments of the unexpectedly rich and complicated

material that we have accumulated so far. Despite a multifaceted approach, we are by no means certain that we have as yet grasped the total picture of all the essentials of interaction in these families that have been studied from months to many years, or for that matter, of family dynamics in general. Our task is further complicated by the absence of a set of concepts (or a communication model for group interaction) that would simultaneously convey both a cross section of transactions at a given time and a longitudinal historical dimension.

The family is a unique type of group and operates under more complicated dynamics than do the synthetic groups usually studied in detail by sociologists or psychologists. Our traditional psychodynamic concepts alone are not suited to the description and analysis of the family-group process over a period of time. We have borrowed from social anthropologists and sociologists,[6] especially from Parsons,[42, 43] Kluckhohn,[28] and group psychologists[44] in an effort to place some of our work in a suitable frame of reference.[7, 16, 21, 48, 49] Without their work and that of many others in allied disciplines, we would have no suitable models to answer our needs at least in part.[12, 20] As I seek to describe some of our findings, it must be emphasized that different methods of abstraction as well as different conceptual approaches have been employed in describing different phases of the disturbed family milieu.

Certain facets of the disturbed family interaction we have observed have been separated out rather artificially, but the respective areas of interaction blend and, in actuality, of course, occur together. For the psychiatrist it is naturally easier to describe individual personal characteristics. In this work, however, impressive as the abnormalities of each family member often are, not to mention those of the patient, we have found that family interaction and the interlocking roles and role shifts appear to have more bearing upon the development of schizophrenia in one member than the characteristics of individual parents or siblings.

Parental Personalities

At the start it became obvious to us, as it has to others, that many mothers of schizophrenic patients appear severely disturbed, often bordering on the psychotic.[1, 2, 23, 34, 40, 45, 46] Many such personal characteristics of these mothers have been described by others, notably by Dr. Trudi Tietze[51]. We are not yet prepared, however, to amplify these earlier descriptions or to render them more inclusive but should note that none of them applies to all the mothers we have studied. We have found a wider range of disturbances, and no one personality type has emerged. At least half the mothers of our patients were psychotically disturbed. We are in the process of examining the characteristics of mothers in various ways, including the use of a sorting technique employing several hundred items, a modification of a similar study undertaken by Don Jackson and his colleagues.[26] Some of the disturbed interaction patterns and irrational rearing techniques of these mothers will become evident in later sections; here, I note our conclusion that in any analysis of material personalities and in searching for common characteristics, the mothers of schizophrenic sons and of schizophrenic daughters must be considered separately.[38]

We realized soon that the intrapsychic disturbances of the mothers were not nearly as relevant to what happened to one or more children in the family (especially to the child who became schizophrenic) as was the fact that these women were paired with husbands who would either acquiesce to their many irrational and bizarre notions of how the family should be run or who would constantly battle with and undermine an already anxious and insecure mother.[34,35] Furthermore, half the families were dominated by an equally irrational, often paranoid father paired with a submissive, acquiescing spouse, or at least by a disturbed husband who clashed with a constantly nagging and depreciating wife. Our first communication therefore concerned the characteristics of some of these fathers.[33] We have noted that while no characteristic type of disturbed father occurred in our series, many were so caught up in their personal problems—very often conscious and unconscious concerns about their masculinity—that they could not function in a parental fashion. Some used the child to gratify their narcissistic needs for admiration or completion of their selves quite as much as has been observed in the mother-child relationships of schizophrenic patients.[23, 32] Still others abdicated parental roles in the face of hostile, chronically nagging, and domineering spouses but might possibly have fulfilled parental functions more adequately if they had married supportive, less disturbed women. The reverse can also be said of some mothers, as Lidz and Lidz noted many years ago.[31] As far as the development of schizophrenia in an offspring is concerned, we now believe that more typical profiles for either parent may emerge if we group them according to the patient's sex.[38, 40]

Parental Interaction

We have discerned and attempted to describe the disturbed interaction as certain patterns seemed to become understandable. These patterns, we believe, have a significant impact upon our patients' development and seem pertinent to symptomatology, if not to the basic illness. We have documented these intrafamilial disturbances with detailed examples in a number of papers and in this paper summarize them only briefly.

Schismatic Families

Schismatic families are beset by chronic strife and controversy, primarily between the parents. The friction may focus on specific issues such as religion or the family's social status, and these topics are constantly dragged into family discussion and interaction. Usually, however, such specific contents are only the outward symptom of a basic distrust and often hatred of one spouse for the other.[35]

The Readings were such a family. A paranoid, grandiose, and autocratic father dominated it. After 20 yr. of marriage he had remained emotionally closer to his mother than to his wife. He was very intelligent and productive, but he resisted his wife's burning ambition to rise in the social scale—a source of constant open controversy between them. However, any issue was apt to produce a fight, and when the older of their two daughters became schizophrenic at 21, the illness, the hospitalization, and the treatment all offered more opportunities for mutual nagging, for undermining the other's plans and hopes, and for holding each other responsible for this disaster. The patient spent most of her time in catatonic muteness, possibly the only way open to her to remove herself from the family battlefield.

The topic of her illness and its relation to the family dynamics will receive further comment in a following section.

The schismatic families in which the parents undermine each other's worth, despising each other as man or woman, depriving each other of much needed support (often a narcissistic need in at least one of the parents), can create insurmountable identity problems for their offspring. To be like one parent incurs the wrath or disparagement of the other, and neither parent may be very self assured about his gender to begin with. We can trace in this way some of the identity problems of schizophrenics and also can appreciate that young people raised in such families break down just at a time when a sense of identity essential to a more independent social role outside the home is expected of them in early adulthood.[37, 39]

Skewed Families

Another form of distorted family milieu has been designated as skew. Such families differ from schismatic ones in that the marriage itself may be peaceful and mutually satisfactory because the spouses have overtly or covertly reached a compromise concerning a serious personality defect in one or the other. Usually one partner had given in to the more disturbed and domineering one, but peace between them may be maintained at the expense of the children because the parental alliance also preempts their emotional resources, and then truly parental obligations suffer.[35]

Mr. Lamb, for instance, was a very successful business man but a most inadequate parent. As a young adult he had been an outstanding athlete but had to leave his school for disciplinary reasons. Soon after marriage he began to drink heavily, and by the time his wife became pregnant for the first time, he was an alcoholic. From the time of the son's conception on, he made every possible effort to retain all of his wife's attention and affection, and to keep her away from his son, who later was our patient. Mr. Lamb was much less competitive with a subsequent daughter. His wife largely acceded to his demands and wishes although she was aware of her son's unfulfilled needs. Instead of standing up to the father and objecting to his behavior, she tended to look at times to the son for emotional support that the husband could not give her. Moreover, she encouraged the talented son to fulfill her own artistic tendencies. These were entirely lost on her husband, who openly criticized the son as effeminate, weak, and unathletic, after having thwarted the son's earlier efforts to be physically active by sneering at the child's performance in games or sports.

At 20 the son indeed showed all these characteristics. But he had absorbed more from the parental interaction. The father drank, and yet both spouses maintained that he was not an alcoholic. He was unfaithful, and this also remained masked except for one occasion on which it became a community-wide scandal. Cheating and lying caused the patient's removal from school prior to his hospitalization, and prevarication remained a serious handicap in his therapeutic relationship for a long time. During the first year of his hospitalization he also lorded it over the staff, as well as his mother, treating everybody like an underling, as his father had often done at home.

The father had been a sham from the son's point of view. Instead of a father he

195

was a competitor; the lack of integrity in his personal life could not be concealed, despite the parental conspiracy to deny the obvious. The concealment and deceit were reflected in the patient's symptoms and behavior in schizophrenic form.

Knowing the family history thoroughly and from many different vantage points, one is at a loss to find a position at any time to which this youngster could have regressed in order to re-experience some degree of security or satisfaction. Only autistic withdrawal seemed open to him. To live up to his father's "expectations" he had to be weak and passive in one sense, and an athlete in another; to please his mother he had to be artistic; but to assume a male role in any area carried the threat of incestuous closeness to his mother and indeed constituted a threat to his father's shaky masculinity. Thus, in this type of family also we can observe that the patient in his personality development is confronted with irreconcilable identity prototypes.

As far as these identity problems in young schizophrenics are concerned, we find that equivalent phenomena have been pointed out in a more general way by Erickson in his writings on identity crisis.[11, 37] We shall return to this topic later in connection with sexual problems.

The skew in the family can exist in another form: The dominant emotional dyad may be one parent and one offspring.[39] In these latter families the assignment to either group becomes somewhat arbitrary. Not only may a parental schism lead to hostile pairings or camps in the family, but one of these couplings may pre-empt the family's emotional resources just as importantly as the parental coalition illustrated above.

The Irrationality of the Family Milieu and Symptom Formation

Another skewed family may illustrate this important process observed in many of our families—the transmission of irrationality or, one might almost say, the learning of symptoms.[8, 14, 36]

Young Dollfuss came to us from another hospital, to which he had been admitted following a serious suicide attempt. Although relatively compliant and cooperative at first, he soon became increasingly resistant to hospital routines, spoke less and less with anybody, neglected his appearance, grew a beard, and would not allow his hair to be cut, so that long locks soon framed his shoulders. Being unusually tall, he not only looked like the Messiah but was indeed preoccupied with strange mystical religions—seemingly of his own invention. As if this appearance were not bizarre enough in the setting of an unbelievably messy room in which he hoarded food, a typical daily scene showed him almost naked, sitting on his toilet, studying stock quotations in the *Wall Street Journal*. It may be noted in passing that he showed a typically schizophrenic phenomenon, exhibiting severe psychotic and delusional behavior, unable to have any comfortable human contact, while still able to select a stock portfolio for his therapist that he predicted correctly would increase 40 per cent on the market in a year's time—a coexistence of abnormal and normal high-order mentation never encountered in any known organic brain disorder.

As we began to learn about the family background, it became clear that the patient conducted his hospital life in the same autocratic, pompous, and captious manner in which the father had governed the parental household. Mr. Dollfuss was an ingenious and successful foreign-born manufacturer, but at home he ruled his roost like an Eastern potentate, a role for which he also claimed divine sanction and inspiration via a special mystical cult that he shared only with a very few select friends. The patient would permit only a chosen few of the staff into his sanctum, just as the father had secluded himself in his bedroom during most of the time that he spent at home, with only his wife and the children's governess permitted to enter and attend to his needs. Mr. Dollfuss, successful inventor and merchant, would sit there in his underclothes reading religious books by the hour. The entire household participated in the religious rites, the mother sharing his beliefs completely and continuing to do so even after his death, which according to the cult meant continuing life in a different form; the widow did not dare to disavow his teachings, because she believed he would know of it.

More than imitation and caricaturization of the father's behavior was involved. Both the patient and his only sister were emotionally deprived children who were isolated from the parents *and* from the surrounding community because the family milieu was so aberrant. Thus, when not mute, the patient often consented to communicate only in foreign languages, as if to emphasize his and the family's estrangement from the surroundings. He "communicated" his sense of deprivation by hoarding food, and during one stage of his illness by devising a complicated airline system designed exclusively for transporting and distributing food supplies in such a way that his needs would be gratified from all over the world.

This case provides a striking example of the irrationality of the parental relationship that came to pervade the entire household and of the aberrant patterns that the child had to cope with and ultimately learn himself, in order to live within the family. To question the bizarre family milieu, as he became aware that people outside did live and perceive the world differently, might have endangered his place as a child, leading to further distance from the parents or others in the household, all of whom shared or seemed to share the abnormal mode of life. To live outside this family the child had to learn other ways of living, if he could—and our patient could not.

Violation of Generation Boundaries

We were further impressed that in both skewed and schismatic families, one child might perceive that in reality he was more important to one or the other parent than was the spouse. In schismatic families, loyalty to one parent, often seductively engendered by that parent, might invite hostility and derogation from the other, just as the spouse to whom the child was

close was despised by the partner. In addition to the obvious difficulties this created for the child who sought or needed to identify with one parent, such disregard of the familial generation boundaries had important bearing on the sexual confusions and panics from which practically all schizophrenics suffer.[15] Finally, by being all-important to one parent, or to both as a pawn of battle, the patient became predisposed to symptoms of grandiosity.

The skew in some families, as already described, might consist of a close, erotically colored continuing relationship between one parent and a child. Typically this kind of bond was highly charged with anxiety, since the two individuals never could find a comfortable distance or closeness in their interaction.[53] Therefore, the catatonic issue, "If I make one move, something terrible is going to happen—somebody will be harmed if I initiate a move," was a reality chronically confronting patients who grew up in such families.

We have discovered—especially in connection with the issue of institutionalization itself—that some parents were truly incapable of living without the child and could not tolerate the separation imposed by hospitalization;[13] this conclusion confirms earlier reports by the Lidzes,[32] Hill,[23] and others,[5, 18] based on findings in individual therapy that the so-called symbiotic tie between patient and parent may be more essential to the parent's existence than to that of the patient. When a mother a thousand miles away awakens every morning at 6 A.M. because this is 7 A.M. Eastern time and the moment when her schizophrenic son receives his insulin injection and continues to experience the insulin injection vicariously through the morning over all this distance, day after day, we can appreciate that she cannot leave her son long in the hands of his therapists. We can also understand why the son is right in claiming that every move he makes is of world-shaking consequence because, indeed, it is so to his mother, whose anxiety he in turn heightened by letting her know in detail "how the insulin softened his brain."

We have described in another communication a skewed family containing twins, one of whom became our patient.[39] The birth of these twins was the mother's longed-for triumph over her own nonidentical twin sister, and the twins became the center of her life as well as the masters of the family's existence. Shortly after their birth the father was evicted from his wife's bed and bath rooms and, together with the older son, was relegated literally to inferior roles in the house, being permitted, for example, to use only the basement lavatory. One day when the mother, who was given to temper tantrums, received a spanking from one of the twins, the father tried to intercede, but the mother forbade him to interfere. Most of the violations of the generation boundaries we have noted are somewhat less bizarre and drastic, but not necessarily less damaging to a child's need to find a child's role and position in the family, on the basis of which further personality development and socially adaptive growth can proceed.[15, 37, 42, 43]

Sexual Problems

In connection with the Lamb case we have referred to the serious impediments such a family situation can represent to the development in a child of a sense of identity, and also how difficult it may be for an offspring to find in two warring parents suitable prototypes for identification. Whether fighting with each other or supporting each other at the expense of adequate reality presentation to their offspring, most of our parents were usually also very insecure about their own sexuality.

During visiting hours one of our patients, Dora Nussbaum, suddenly ran from her room in greater panic than observed ever before during several months of hospitalization. On investigation it was learned that she suddenly panicked while sitting on her bed with her father. We knew already that the patient had often fallen asleep in her father's arms. The mother had told us of her disgust over these intimacies between father and daughter, which bothered Mrs. Nussbaum all the more because of the absence of any physical intimacies between herself and her husband. This was a schismatic family in which the parents had become irreconcilably estranged because of a feud between their respective primary families, to whom both spouses were still very much attached. Dora's older brother and the mother had a workable if not close relationship, but Dora was disliked by the mother and preferred by the father, a condition that resulted in a rather incestuous bond between them. In adolescence, Dora began to object to his habit of frequently sleeping on her bed, out of fear that she would become pregnant (we have no evidence of actual incestuous behavior). However, frequent close physical contact was resumed during Dora's psychosis at times when the father tried to calm her. One of Dora's early psychotic manifestations was fear that she would be raped while at the same time she behaved promiscuously with strangers. The father claimed to be impotent but tried to make his wife and daughter believe that he had a mistress. Whether true or not, it bespeaks his insecure masculinity, also expressed in other effeminate, narcissistic tendencies.

Thus one can discern the roots of a schizophrenic patient's sexual and incestuous problems and their close relationship to panic states, symptoms which become understandable through scrutiny of the family background and dynamics.[15, 37]

Another father, who never achieved satisfactory sexual relations with his wife, promoted both homosexual and incestuous tendencies in his schizophrenic son. He often spoke to him about arranging dates for him, specifically mentioning an actress who, he pointed out, resembled his mother very strongly. The father also arranged for a friend whom he knew to be homosexual to share the boy's bedroom, besides taking showers himself with the son, comparing the size of their genitals or rubbing each other's backs. During therapy it was learned that one of the patient's tenacious symptoms—a magical need to repeat certain figures—was specifically related to conscious efforts to keep incestuous ideas in abeyance.

In the Reading family, which was split into two camps (page 336), the patient was also aware of the incestuous potential. Her suspicious, cantankerous father, who preferred her over the sister—not to mention his wife, whom he blamed for the illness—also was highly critical of the hospital, as well as suspicious that we were giving him "a run for his money." Realistically, she made no progress, possibly at least in part because of the father's disapproval of our efforts, a parallel to his undermining the mother's social and educational ambitions for her daughters. There were many threats to remove the patient from the hospital, and this he finally did. Once he proposed the following therapeutic solution: the family should split up, the mother and the patient's sister, who formed one faction, would live together, and he would live with and look after the patient himself. When the patient learned of this plan, she made one of her few excursions into reality from her state of catatonic muteness and stated, "I'll do anything for my father, but he can't have me that way."

We have spelled out in more detail in two other communications the nature of the many areas of family dysfunction that we have observed and their possible specific implications for the development of conscious incestuous and homosexual conflicts on the part of patients.[15, 39] The entire family interaction may promote such conscious preoccupations rather than further repression in offspring and parents alike. The continuation of incestuous impulses may be an index of family disorganization, a view supported by Parson's psychosocial formulations.[42, 43] We found that Parson's essential prerequisites of family life, which must exist if a child is to de-eroticize his parental attachments, acquire a sexual identity, and prepare for sociocultural adaptation, are often absent in the families

we have studied.[11, 16, 43] Among the prerequisites that most, if not all, of our parents failed to observe were the maintenance of generation boundaries, a personal sense of security in each as to sexual, parental, and social roles, a certain degree of marital harmony, the ability to share or compromise on cultural values, and a capacity for role reciprocity.[37, 49]

Sociocultural Isolation

We have illustrated how some of our families do not maintain differential roles in the sense of parents who nurture and lead as against children who are dependent and learn; that sexuality in these families is not limited to parental activity; that the parents, although often competent in their jobs or professions, are rigid, inflexible, and uncompromising in their intrafamilial behavior, and that many provide a home life quite deviant from the surrounding culture. The social life of these families often appears very limited, except that some families are still anchored in the patient's grandparental families or in one of the parent's collateral sibling families. There is failure to form a nuclear family of their own. This we found in six of our schismatic families; in a sense, this failure also constitutes another form of violating generation boundaries—at least in modern America.

Individual parental pathologic traits and role deficiencies aside, it is therefore the irrational and idiosyncratic environment that these families create which seems most important and which has led us to speak of *"folie à famille"* in situations like that of the Dollfusses.[14] Furthermore, not only does the transmission of aberrant percepts seem specifically related to the later development of schizophrenic manifestations, but the feedback between the children and parents creates a self-perpetuating, irrational, and ambivalence-laden atmosphere. The interaction circuit may be one of axe-grinding between parents, or of a parent and child alternating between avoiding anxiety-arousing closeness — incestuous closeness—and efforts to overcome icy distance, but whichever it is, all family members must adapt to it in different roles.

Even if these family environments were not as deviant from the surrounding culture as many are, one gets the impression that intrafamilial life of the kinds described may absorb so much energy that but little emotional investment seems possible for learning and socializing tasks outside the home. Moreover, in many of these families the tools, especially the communication tools essential to the establishment of meaningful relationships outside the family, are simply not furnished.[14, 38] Thus, a vicious cycle exists because the aberrant family environment is self perpetuating unless corrected from the outside. But the isolating nature of the pathological forces within the family deprives its members of meaningful contacts with the outside world, and, therewith, of the potential corrective impact of intimate interaction with people outside the family circle. For instance, the incest issue may arouse enough guilt feelings in one or the other member to render difficult any other friendships; but in the absence of cathected relationships outside the family, those within become all the more intense and conflictful. The child caught in the special bind with a parent is most crucially affected. Seeking friends outside the bond endangers the very essential tie to the parent, and the absence of other ties renders the bond to that parent more intense and more ambivalent.

General Comment

Although the evidence is impressive, even from the fraction of our material presented, that the families discussed are unusually disturbed, we cannot state with certainty the extent to which the families are distinctive in structure and *modi operandi*. The nature of the abnormalities and the distortions of family life that we have ob-

served fall into behavioral categories such as personal, interpersonal, group dynamics, and psychology, and their specific relevance to the development of schizophrenia remains to be documented in detail by further search and study.

We do not intend to promulgate an environmental interpersonal approach as against a genetic or biochemical path to the etiology of schizophrenia. Our material is not suited to settle questions of causation, as we are not searching for a particular cause but have been exploring essentially uncharted territory. This material, pertinent to schizophrenia, may also help us to understand better the mode of transmission from generation to generation of the highest cerebral functions, in particular all those specifically human functions concerned with interpersonal communication through complicated, abstract, verbal and nonverbal symbols, whether normal or schizophrenic. Thus, the study of schizophrenia leads us to the problems of personality development in the human and to the broad question of how meaning and logic and a sense of identity are acquired.

We have previously stated that schizophrenia can be viewed as one possible outcome of personality development, or as Sullivan phrased it, a "way of life."[50] This view does not exclude organic determinants, as genetic and nongenetic physiochemical influences obviously underlie and impinge upon the learning processes through which every individual must pass to acquire an identity and to develop his intellectual and sociocultural adaptive capacities. The psysiological aspects of learning processes are only partially understood, but the development and the integration of symbolic processes and behavior occur after birth, whereas only simple reflexlike response patterns can be acquired prenatally.[25, 30] It seems fruitful, therefore, to scrutinize postnatal interactional phenomena, and such studies indeed render a great deal of this learning or transmission of behavior and attitudes, whether schizophrenic or not, more understandable, even if done retrospectively. This was expressed by Adolf Meyer 50 yr. ago: "We are, I believe, justified in directing our attention to the factors which we see at work in the life history of so-called dementia praecox. We are justified in emphasizing the process of crowding-out of normal reactions, of a substitution of inferior reactions some of which determine a cleavage along distinctly psychological lines incompatible with reintegration."[41] I am not citing these words because they may be truer or more appealing than other statements, but rather because if one rereads Bleuler,[4] Kraepelin,[29] Jung,[27] Meyer,[41] Freud,[19] and others who worked in this field half a century or more ago, recent studies of others and our own data seem to bear out Meyer's admonition above all others.

To explain bizarre behavior such as that of our Christ-like patient who sat in his bathroom with the *Wall Street Journal,* we neither have to fall back on or search for obscure pathological tissue processes on the one hand, nor do we have to speculate about all the possible symbolic meanings of such an activity, which is not to say that either consideration is irrelevant. Nor must we inject some psychotomimetic drug or postulate some sudden regressive break in the personality make-up to find explicable some of the other symptoms we described. To understand how items of behavior developed, however, is not necessarily to understand causality — certainly not the causality of as complicated a condition or process, whichever it may be, as schizophrenia. As long as there is no physical or chemical indicator for schizophrenia, we are left essentially with a conglomerate of clinical manifestations in making a diagnosis and are no better off today in this respect than was Bleuler half a century ago,[4] when he stressed that diagnosis rests on the psychological manifestations. In our day we prefer a still less limited area of diagnostic criteria by considering the patient's interpersonal behavior.

How can we be certain that the family interactions we have observed are pathological? Can we or anybody undertake "control studies?" If so, what variables should be controlled? We have designedly put this problem aside. It has taken months and years to arrive at reasonably plausible and congruous reconstructions of fewer than 20 families in terms of the personalities involved and their interaction patterns. Our data in themselves and even for the same family differ in reliability in that we have direct evidence about some phenomena from several sources and only plausible conjectures concerning other observations. Obviously, to duplicate such a study in detail would be an enormous task and open to question from the beginning if done by a different team because of the different personalities involved. We have undertaken recently to study also families of upper-class delinquents—not to compare variables, but to see how, if at all, these families differ, in the hope that we can sharpen our conceptualizations.[38]

Another question is: How are the phenomena described related to schizophrenia? Obviously we have not explained or made understandable all possible schizophrenic manifestations, nor is it likely that all of them are rooted in family interaction. Our data indicate, however, that the study of these families sheds much light on many schizophrenic manifestations, and that aspects of the parental personalities and of intrafamilial behavior of all members determine much of what we consider characteristic or pathognomonic of schizophrenia when we, as diagnosticians, approach a patient.

Another question that seemed formidable at first concerned the presence of "normal" and schizophrenic siblings in the same family. We have been working on this problem recently and have found it to be much less difficult. The patients' siblings are not unaffected by the abnormal environment. But when the entire family situation is known and the respective roles are understood, the development of the siblings' personalities, whether more nearly schizophrenic or more nearly normal, also fits into the total family pattern.[2a, 38]

Summary

In summary, some of the characteristic forms of family dysfunction related to schizophrenic manifestations that we observed are: (1) failure to form a nuclear family in that one or both parents remain primarily attached to one of his or her parents or siblings; (2) family schisms due to parental strife and lack of role reciprocity; (3) family skews when one dyadic relationship within it dominates family life at the expense of the needs of other members; (4) blurring of generation lines in the family, e.g., (a) when one parent competes with children in skewed families, (b) when one parent establishes a special bond with a child giving substance to the schizophrenic's claim that he or she is more important to a parent than the spouse, and (c) when continued erotization of a parent-child relationship occurs; (5) pervasion of the entire family atmosphere with irrational, usually paranoid, ideation; (6) persistence of conscious incestuous preoccupation and behavior within the group; (7) sociocultural isolation of the family as a concomitant of the six preceding conditions; (8) failure to educate toward and facilitate emancipation of the offspring from the family, a further consequence of points 1–5. (9) handicapping of a child in achieving sexual identity and maturity by the parents' uncertainty over their own sex roles; and (10) presentation to a child of prototypes for identification that are irreconcilable in the necessary process of consolidating his own personality.

Intensive work with these families has therapeutic implications which transcend our research plans as such and therewith the scope of this presentation. Other investigators of family dynamics have focused more on this aspect of the schizophrenia problem. The further development of rational psychotherapy, whether with the patient alone or with the family group, will depend upon better understanding and clarification of the complex interrelatedness of family dynamics, ego development, and identity formation. Thus, the study of schizophrenia and the quest for its origins leads us to the question of human development, and better understanding of the latter may illuminate the nature of schizophrenia as well as facilitate the treatment of schizophrenic patients.

References

1. ABRAHAMS, J., and VARON, E. J. *Maternal Dependency and Schizophrenia: Mother and Daughter in a Therapeutic Group.* New York, Internat. Univ. Press, 1953.
2. ALANEN, Y. O. The mothers of schizophrenic patients. *Acta psychiat. et neurol. scandinav.* Suppl. 124, 1958.
2a. ALANEN, Y. O. Work in progress.
3. BATESON, G., JACKSON, D. D., HALEY, J., and WEAKLAND, J. Towards the theory of schizophrenia. *Behavioral Sc.* 1:251, 1956.
4. BLEULER, E. Dementia Praecox oder Gruppe der Schizophrenien. In ASCHAFFENBURG, G., Ed. *Handbuch der Psychiatrie.* Leipzig & Wien, 1911.
5. BOWEN, M. Family relationships in schizophrenia. Presented at Hawaiian Divisional Meeting of American Psychiatric Association, May, 1958.
6. BOTT, E. *Family and Social Network.* London, Tavistock Publications, 1957.
7. BUELL, B., et al. *Classification of Disorganized Families for Use in Family Oriented Diagnosis and Treatment.* New York, New York, Community Research Associates, Inc., 1953.
8. CAMERON, N. The paranoid pseudo-community revisited. *Am. J. Sociology* 65:52, 1959.
9. CORNELISON, A. Casework interviewing as a research technique in a study of families of schizophrenic patients. *Ment. Hyg.*, in press.
10. DELAY, J., DENIKER, P., and GREEN, A. Le milieu familial des schizophrenics. *Encéphale* 46:189, 1957.
11. ERIKSON, E. The problem of ego identity. *J. Am. Psychoanalyt. A.* 4:56, 1956.
12. FISHER, S., and MENDELL, D. The communication of neurotic patterns over two and three generations. *Psychiatry* 19:41, 1956.
13. FLECK, S., et al. The intrafamilial environment of the schizophrenic patient. III. Interaction between hospital staff and families. *Psychiatry* 20:343, 1957.
14. FLECK, S., et al. The intrafamilial environment of the schizophrenic patient. V. The understanding of symptomatology through the study of family interaction. Presented at meeting of

the American Psychiatric Association, May 15, 1957.

15. FLECK, S., *et al.* The intrafamilial environment of the schizophrenic patient. Incestuous and homosexual problems. In MASSERMAN, J. H., Ed. *Science and Psychoanalysis: Individual and Familial Dynamics.* New York, Grune, 1959, vol. II.

16. FLUGEL, J. C. *Man, Morals and Society: A Psychoanalytic Study.* New York, Internat. Univ. Press, 1955.

17. FRAZEE, H. E. Children who later become schizophrenics. *Smith Coll. Studies in Social Work 23:*125, 1953.

18. FROMM-REICHMANN, F. Notes on the mother role in the family group. *Bull. Menninger Clin. 4:*132, 1940.

19. FREUD, S. Neurose and Psychose (1924). In *Gesammte Werke.* London, Imago, 1940, vol. XIII.

20. GERARD, D. L., and SIEGEL, J. The family background of schizophrenia. *Psychiat. Quart. 24:* 47, 1950.

21. GOLDBERG, E. M. Experiences with families of young men with duodenal ulcer and "normal" control families: Some problems of approach and method. *Brit. J. M. Psychol. 26:*204, 1953.

22. HALEY, J. The family of the schizophrenic: A model system. *J. Nerv. & Ment. Dis.,* in press.

23. HILL, L. *Psychotherapeutic Interaction in Schizophrenics.* Chicago, Univ. Chicago Press, 1955.

24. HOLLINGSHEAD, A. B., and REDLICH, F. *Social Class and Mental Illness.* New York, Wiley, 1958.

25. HOOKER, D. Unpublished address to medical sociology seminar, Yale University, 1958.

26. JACKSON, D. D. The question of family homeostasis. *Psychiat. Quart. Suppl. 31:*79, 1957.

27. JUNG, G. *The Psychology of Dementia Praecox.* New York, Nerv. & Ment. Dis. Publ. Co., 1936.

28. KLUCKHOHN, F. *Variants in Value Orientations.* Evanston, Ill., Row Peterson, 1957.

29. KRAEPELIN, E. Zur Diagnose und Prognose der Dementia Praecox. *Allg. Ztschr. Psychiatrie. 56:*254, 1899.

30. LANGWORTHY, O. R. *Development of Behavior Patterns and Myelinization of the Nervous System in the Human Fetus. Contributions to Embryology No. 124.* Washington, D. C., Carnegie Institute, 1933.

31. LIDZ, R. W., and LIDZ, T. The family environment of schizophrenic patients. *Am. J. Psychiat. 106:*332, 1949.

32. LIDZ, R. W., and LIDZ, T. Therapeutic considerations arising from the intense symbiotic needs of schizophrenic patients. In BRADY, G., and REDLICH, F., Eds., *Psychotherapy with Schizophrenics.* New York, Internat. Univ. Press, 1952.

33. LIDZ, T., *et al.* The intrafamilial environment

of the schizophrenic patient. I. The father. *Psychiatry 20:*329, 1957.

34. LIDZ, T., *et al.* The intrafamilial environment of the schizophrenic patient. IV. Parental personalities and family interaction. *Am. J. Orthopsychiat. 28:*764, 1958.

35. LIDZ, T., *et al.* The intrafamilial environment of schizophrenic patients. II. Marital schism and marital skew. *Am. J. Psychiat. 114:*241, 1957.

36. LIDZ, T., *et al.* The intrafamilial environment of the schizophrenic patient. VI. The transmission of irrationality. *A.M.A. Arch. Neurol. & Psychiat. 79:*305, 1958.

37. LIDZ, T., and FLECK, S. Schizophrenia, human integration and the role of the family. In *The Etiology of Schizophrenia,* New York, Basic Books, p. 323, 1960.

38. LIDZ, T., and FLECK, S. Studies in progress.

39. LIDZ, T., *et al.* The intrafamilial environment of the schizophrenic patient: VII. The differentiation of personalities and symptoms in identical twins. Unpublished.

40. MARK, J. D. The attitudes of mothers of male schizophrenics towards child behavior. *J. Abnorm. & Social Psychol. 48:*185, 1953.

41. MEYER, A. The dynamic interpretation of dementia praecox. *Am. J. Psychol. 21:*385, 1910.

42. PARSON, T. The incest taboo in relation to social structure and the socialization of the child. *Brit. J. Sociology 5:*101, 1954.

43. PARSONS, T. Social Structure and the Development of Personality. *Psychiatry 21:*321, 1958.

44. PARSONS, T., *et al. Family, Socialization and Interaction.* Glencoe, Ill., Free Press, 1955.

45. PROUT, C. T., and WHITE, M. A. A controlled study of personality relationships in mothers of schizophrenic male patients. *Am. J. Psychiat. 107:*251, 1951.

46. REICHARD, S., and TILLMAN, C. Patterns of parent-child relationships in schizophrenia. *Psychiatry 13:*247, 1950.

47. SOHLER, D. T., *et al.* The prediction of family interaction from a battery of projective tests. *J. Proj. Tech. 21:*199, 1957.

48. SPIEGEL, J. P. The resolution of role conflict with the family. *Psychiatry 20:*1, 1957.

49. SPIEGEL, J., *et al. Integration and Conflict in Family Behavior. Report 27.* Topeka, Kan., Group for the Advancement of Psychiatry, 1954.

50. SULLIVAN, H. S. *The Interpersonal Theory of Psychiatry (Part III).* Edited by PERZ, H. S., and GAVEL, M. L. New York, Norton, 1953.

51. TIETZE, T. A study of mothers of schizophrenic patients. *Psychiatry 12:*55, 1949.

52. WAHL, C. W. Antecedent factors in family histories of 392 schizophrenics. *Am. J. Psychiat. 110:*668, 1954.

53. WYNNE, L. C., *et al.* Pseudo-mutuality in the family relations of schizophrenics. *Psychiatry 21:*205, 1958.

Children as Agents in Socializing Parents

GERALDINE M. DEVOR

When the lay person hears the word "agent," more than likely he visualizes a somewhat shadowy figure dealing in foreign intrigue. The sociologist, on the other hand, may readily recognize the word as an abbreviation for the sociological concept "agent of socialization." The connotations may have some degree of similarity but the contexts in which the concepts function are worlds apart.

An agent of socialization is most frequently defined in terms of a force acting upon the individual causing him to adjust his attitudes, values, or mode of living. In the relevant literature, for example, the parent almost universally is described as the major agent of socialization for the child. (Bossard and Boll, 1966; Havighurst, 1962; Hollingshead, 1961; Ritchie and Koller, 1964; and, Tyler, 1967) Indeed, the most important function of parenthood is that of preparing children to become competent members of society. It is primarily through parents that children

learn the culture, e.g., language, behavior, attitudes, values, and standards, of the society to which they belong. The child also receives from his parents other more subtle kinds of education, perhaps even more influential in the development of his personality. Among these learnings are the child's particular perception of the world in which he lives, his characteristic mode of emotional response to stimuli from that world, and an individual mental "set" for coping with problems that come his way.

The term "socialization" is considered here as a dynamic, ongoing process. Inasmuch as culture itself is constantly in a state of change, an individual is never completely socialized to a culture. Furthermore, there are many forces or agents acting upon the individual with different times, e.g., family, other significant people in his life, mass media, and institutions such as government and education. In other words, when one speaks of a person becoming socialized, he does not mean that the person

FAMILY COORDINATOR, 1970, Vol. 19, pp. 208-212.

has achieved a particular state which he retains the remainder of his life.

Purpose

The idea explored in this study was that the child acts as a socializing agent for the parent as well. This possibility had been suggested as an area of research for the future in the more recent professional journals and books.

Probably one of the most obvious controlling influences within the family upon the parent has been most neglected in parent education. This is the influence of the child upon the parent, arising from the fact that the child himself has rights and legitimate modes of control regarding his relations with his parents. Each parent-child relation is different, and in the course of interaction over time certain norms arise which determine what is legitimate behavior on the part of *both* parent and child. . . . But beyond a given age, probably age two, the parent is influenced by the child's receptivity to changes which the parent attempts to introduce into his child-rearing practice. (Brim, 1959, 68)

What follows in this paper is the report of a preliminary investigation designed to examine the ways in which parents perceive themselves being socialized by their children.

Method
Subjects

This research was conducted in conjunction with a larger study using the same subjects and their children. The subjects in this study were 107 mothers enrolled in 25 Child Observation Classes sponsored by the Los Angeles City Board of Education. The classes consisted of two sections: the first, in which the preschool children participated in planned nursery school activities while the mothers observed them; and, the second, where the mothers met in planned parent education discussion groups to relate what they had observed and learned in class to their own children, to child development patterns, and to their own family living.

The subjects were divided into four

TABLE 1. DISTRIBUTION OF SUBJECTS BY RACE AND SOCIAL CLASS

	Caucasian	Negro	Totals
Middle class	43	10	53
Lower Class	33	21	54
Totals	76	31	107

groups on the basis of social class and race. (See Table 1.) The middle class groups, Caucasian middle class (CM) and Negro middle class (NM), lived in neighborhoods identified as middle to upper middle class and the primary occupations of the fathers were professional and managerial. The lower class groups, Caucasian lower class (CL) and Negro lower class (NL), lived primarily in neighborhoods identified as disadvantaged and the fathers were predominantly engaged in unskilled or semi-skilled occupations.

Procedure

In the larger study of which this research was a part, the investigator had occasion to question the mothers individually regarding their childrens' ages, periods of attendance in the class, fathers' occupation, etc. The situation was structured so that it was necessary for each mother to wait a brief period of time for her child to complete another task in an adjoining area. During this interval, the researcher engaged in casual, informal conversation with the parent. After some preliminary social remarks, the researcher asked each parent if she could think of any way her attitudes or way of living may have been changed because of her children. To assure spontaneous opinions, no attempt was made to elicit complete responses. The answers to the questions were recorded after the parents left the room.

Results
Response Categories

Perhaps the greatest difficulty in analyzing the wealth of data obtained was in classifying the variety of responses into discrete categories. For the purpose of this study,

205

	CM	CL	NM	NL	Totals
Child-rearing Attitudes	6	8	4	3	21
Parental Personality	10	3	0	4	17
Husband-wife Relationship	2	1	2	1	6
Recreation	1	3	1	0	5
Miscellaneous	12	4	0	2	18
No Change	12	14	3	11	40

six areas of children's influence on parents were selected: child-rearing attitudes, parental personality, husband-wife relationships, recreation, miscellaneous, and no change.

Twenty-one of the total of 107 mothers indicated modification of child-rearing attitudes resulting from interaction with their children. These are illustrated by remarks as: ". . . relaxing my idea of discipline;" "My child doesn't *always* need to obey me;" "I gave my child more opportunities for independence;" "I'm stricter than I thought I would be;" "I'm beginning to like children;" and "I don't want any more children."

Changes occurring in their own personalities which they attributed to the influence of their children was perceived by seventeen mothers. Some of the comments included: "I'm more social;" ". . . gave me confidence;" "I'm learning to hold my own," "I'm more energetic;" ". . . more efficient;" and "I'm more confused."

Six parents interviewed noted an effect on their relationships with their husbands because of the presence of children in the home: "We don't fight in front of the children;" "We're trying to have a more democratic family life;" and "We have more in common, the children."

Contrary to expectation, the influence of children on family recreation was less salient. The responses of five mothers included: "No more nightclubbing;" "We read different things;" "We enjoy watching 'Lassie' on TV;" and "Our taste in music seems to be changing."

The most frequent response listed under the miscellaneous category was: "Many ways, can't put my finger on any one

thing." Others included in this category were: "Can't work any more;" and "The kids made us change the church we went to."

Forty mothers did not perceive any changes in themselves or their mode of living resulting from the influence of children. Table 2 shows the breakdown of this category by socio-racial groupings as well as the other selected categories of perceived influence by children.

Data Analyses

Chi square was used as the non-parametric statistic to test the relationships between socio-racial group position and parental perception of children's socializing influence upon them. Specifically, comparisons were made between middle and lower class Caucasians and middle and lower class Negroes. The analyses of data of this method revealed no significant difference between the four socio-racial groupings relative to the amount of influence wielded by children from these families. Other analyses dealing solely with the race variable (classes combined) and with the social class variable (races combined), also, revealed no significant differences.

One may conclude, therefore, from the total population of mothers interviewed, that there is a tendency for parents to perceive of their children as agents of socialization for them. Middle class mothers of both races were particularly conscious of this influence.

Discussion

As one would expect, a pilot study of this broad nature raises many more questions than it answers. For example, the investigator was careful to define the socialization process as that which was "perceived" by the parents. Pertinent questions which may have affected the findings include: the awareness of parents of their children's influence, i.e., the child may influence the parent without the parent realizing it; the willingness of parents to admit to these influences; the casual structure of the interview; and, the limited amount of time for thought before the mothers responded.

Another limitation to the study was the age level of the children whose mothers were questioned. An hypothesis that children older than two-and-one-half to five years would be stronger agents of socialization in the family would appear to be reasonable. As the child matures and moves away from the nuclear family, he acquires new repertories of behavior and attitudes which furnish him with the ammunition to express his individuality and, thus, enhance his attempts to influence his family.

Although the attitudes and knowledge that the child gains from the family often aid him in making the transition into other systems, his roles in these other systems may require much more of him . . . he may find that participation in non-family social systems impose strange, new and conflicting demands upon him. Whatever his social background, as the child moves into these new situations, his values, attitudes, knowledge and skills are almost certain to be modified and enlarged. (Ritchie and Koller, 1964, 43)

Relevant at this point, also, is the discussion by Schiller and Leik (1963) of family role adjustment in terms of the acquisition of universals of society. These universals are defined as entities that become a frame of reference within which the person views the situation or object. The number of universals varies with societies and is acquired through experiences of the individual. Therefore, the more experience the person has, the more universals he may acquire. The "bargaining power" of children in the society is increased and their influences as socializing agents enhanced because they are part of a "youth culture" as well as an "adult culture;" they have more opportunities to learn universals and, consequently, a greater range of role patterns at their disposal.

Differences in social class appear to be a factor in the receptivity of the family to their children's efforts to effect change. This conclusion is supported by studies reported by Strodtbeck (1964) and Maas. (1951) The essence of the hidden curriculum in the middle class home, according to Strodtbeck, may lie in the interaction within a democratic atmosphere occurring between child and parent which brings about consensus. "The patent familiarity of this process sometimes hides the recognition that very complicated social behavior is involved." (Strodtbeck, 1964, 12) Although the greater power of middle class parents is recognized, it is only in rare circumstances that full mobilization of power is required. Some inferences which may be drawn from these conclusions are that middle class parents are more secure in their roles in the culture, thus allowing for openness and flexibility. Furthermore, this flexibility could facilitate the socializing influence of the child on the parent.

In a study proposing a reinterpretation of some social behavioral patterns of preadolescents and early adolescents in lower class and core-culture families, Maas concludes that middle class children experience a more flexible and open parent relationship. Lower class children, on the contrary, reported a closed and quite rigid relationship with their parents. Because lower class parents are particularly vulnerable to unpredictable threat, the power of the child in a social interaction situation is minimized. One, therefore, may conclude from this analysis that the lower class child is in a weaker position than the middle class child to serve as an agent of socialization for the parent.

Bronfenbrenner (1961), however, suggests that social class may be becoming a less salient variable in this kind of research. After an extensive review of the literature over the past 20 years, he drew the conclusion that the gap between social classes in patterns of child-rearing is narrowing. The most important causes of this development are mass communication and increasing mobility of the society. Another factor may be the effect of the middle class schoolroom on the lower class child and its subsequent influence in the parent-child interaction situation.

Implications

In conclusion, this pilot study demonstrates that the socializing influence of children upon parents is, indeed, a promising area for further study. With the results obtained from this investigation, guideposts which give tentative direction to further research have been suggested. Parent educators, particularly, will be interested to learn more of the ramifications of the parent-child interaction situation. Certainly, the more sensitive the parents are to the influence of their child-agents, the better they will be equipped to fulfill their roles as mothers and fathers. On the other hand, an awareness by parent educators of the potential influence of children on parents will increase their understanding of family structure and functioning as well as enhance their effectiveness as counselors.

The influence of classroom teachers as socializing agents may reach into the home by way of children. This influence can be seen as a positive force in the society in areas such as attitudes toward minority groups, sources of factual information which may clarify the issues of the day and, in general, reinforcers of the society's standards and values. Although this increases the responsibility of the teacher, it enhances that role in society by recognizing teachers as figures of authority.

REFERENCES:

Bossard, J. H. and E. S. Boll, *The Sociology of Child Development*. New York: Harper & Row, 1966.

Brim, O. G. *Education for Child-Rearing*. New York: Russell Sage Foundation, 1959.

Bronfenbrenner, U. The Changing American Child —A Speculative Analysis. *Merrill-Palmer Quarterly*, 1961, **7**, 2, 73-84.

Havighurst, R. J. and B. Neugarten. *Society and Education*. Boston: Allyn & Bacon, 1962.

Hollingshead, A. B. *Elmtown's Youth*. New York: John Wiley, 1961.

Maas, H. S. Some Social Class Differences in the Family Systems and Group Relations of Pre- and Early Adolescents. *Child Development*, 1951, **22**, 145-152.

Ritchie, O. W. and M. R. Koller. *Sociology of Childhood*. New York: Appleton-Century-Crofts, 1964.

Schiller, J. A. and R. K. Leik. Symbolic Interaction and Family Role Adjustment. *The Pacific Sociological Review*, 1963, **6**, 1, 30-36.

Strodtbeck, F. L. The Hidden Curriculum in The Middle Class Home. Paper from The Social Psychology Laboratory, University. of Chicago, September, 1964.

Tyler, L. E. *The Psychology of Human Differences*. New York: Appleton-Century-Crofts, 1956.

THE ROLE OF THE FAMILY IN THE DEVELOPMENT
OF PSYCHOPATHOLOGY

As psychopathology came to be viewed as the consequence of the emotional experiences to which the individual was exposed, interest was focused on the earliest of such experiences, those that occur in the family. The human infant is born incapable of sustaining its own life for a considerable length of time following birth, and is, in consequence, dependent upon the mother or a mother substitute for its very existence. There is no wonder, therefore, that the mother-child relationship is a close one and is expected to be influential with regard to the psychological development of the child. Some explanations for the development of psychopathology have therefore focused on this particular relationship as the major etiological factor. Levy (1931, 1932, 1937, 1943) has described a pattern centering around "maternal overprotection," involving a constellation of attitudes which he felt contributed to the development of neurotic disorders, and Despert (1938) focused on a kind of mother-child relationship which seemed to her to be closely associated with the development of schizophrenia, a pattern which has come to be termed the "schizophrenogenic mother."

The hypothesis that the emotional climate of the interpersonal relationships within the family—and between the child and its mother in particular—has a decisive part in the development of the personality of the child would seem to have face validity. In part,

support for this hypothesis may be gleaned from the data demonstrating the devastating effects of being brought up in the extreme interpersonal isolation that comes from *not* having a family (Beres & Obers, 1950; Brodbeck & Irwin, 1946; Goldfarb, 1943a, 1943b, 1943c, 1945a, 1945b; Lowrey, 1940; Spitz, 1945) or extreme social isolation within a family (Bartmeier, 1952; Davis, 1940). Moreover, it has been demonstrated that various specific emotional behaviors of the child seem to be correlated causally with factors in the home. For example, children who could be described as emotionally immature, who are dependent, fearful, negativistic, emotionally labile, etc., have had mothers described as worriers (Pearson, 1931), overattentive (Hattwick, 1936; Hattwick & Stowell, 1936), or punitive (McCord, McCord, & Howard, 1961; Sears, Whiting, Nowlis, & Sears, 1953; Watson, 1934). Children who were described as being overly aggressive were described as having come from homes where mothers were seen as overcontrolling (Bishop, 1951) or punitive (McCord et al., 1961; Sears, 1961).

The evidence thus far suggests that there is, in fact, a correlation between events in the parent-child relationship and resultant personality *traits*. The question arises as to whether there is evidence which supports the hypothesis that there is a correlation between events in the parent-child relationship and

PSYCHOLOGICAL BULLETIN, 1965, Vol. 64, pp. 191-205.

the resultant complex patterns of behavior which have been termed personality. More specifically, in light of the theories which relate personality development to social, (i.e., interpersonal) learning, the question is raised as to whether there is any consistent relationship between the emotional experience the child may have in the home and the development of personality pathology, that is, schizophrenia, neurosis, and behavior disorders. Towards this end, the findings of the research that has explored the psychological characteristics of the parents of these people will be analyzed in order to isolate those consistent characteristics of the parents that may emerge from study to study. The analysis will be done with regard to each major type of psychopathology as a group. Moreover, because psychological test data might yield different information than case history analysis, or direct observation of familial interaction as compared to attitudes as elicited by questionnaire, an attempt will be made to analyze the information gleaned from the studies in terms of the method of data collection within the specific psychopathological groupings.

SCHIZOPHRENIA

Case History

One of the classical methods of data collection in the study of psychiatric illness is the case history, the information for which has generally been gathered by other professionals. The individual conducting a piece of research notes the material in the folders and draws conclusions from the collation of these observations.

In so doing, Despert (1938) observed that approximately 50% of the mothers of a sample of schizophrenic children, generally between the ages of 7 and 13, had been described as aggressive, overanxious, and oversolicitous and were considered to be the dominant parent. Clardy (1951) noted that 50% of the 30 cases of children between the ages of 3 and 12 diagnosed as schizophrenic had families characterized as overprotective and yet basically rejecting. Frazee (1953) noted the presence of this constellation particularly when the families of schizophrenics were compared with the families of

children diagnosed as behavior disorders. Canavan and Clark (1923) and Lampron (1933) noted that 30% of the children of psychotics were themselves emotionally disturbed. Huschka (1941) and Lidz and Lidz (1949) noted that over 40% of their sample of schizophrenics had parents who were psychotic or neurotic. Bender (1936, 1937) and Frazee (1953) noted the high incidence of psychopathology in the children of psychotic parents. Preston and Antin (1932), on the other hand, found no significant differences in the incidence of psychosis and neurosis as a function of parents who were psychotic as compared to parents who were "normal," and Fanning, Lehr, Sherwin, and Wilson, (1938) found that 43% of the children of mothers who were psychotic were observed to be making an adequate social and personal adjustment, with only 11% of that sample classified as maladjusted.

Lidz and Lidz (1949) found that 40% of their sample of schizophrenic patients were deprived of one parent by divorce or separation before they were 19. Plank (1953) found that 63% of his sample of schizophrenics had families where one parent was absent either due to death or marital separation. Wahl (1954, 1956) found that there was a greater incidence of parental loss and rejection early in life for schizophrenics as compared to normals, and Barry (1936) found that from the case histories of 30 rulers adjudged, post facto, insane, 80% of them had lost one of their parents by the time they were 18. However, Barry and Bousfield (1937) found that the incidence of orphanhood in a psychiatric population (19 out of 26) was not much different from the incidence of orphanhood in a normal population (19 out of 24). Moreover, Oltman, McGarry, and Friedman (1952) found that the incidence of broken homes and parental deprivation in the families of schizophrenics (34%) was not very different from that found in the families of hospital employees (32%), alcoholics (31%), and manic-depressives (34%); indeed, in their sampling, neurotics (49%) and psychopaths (48%) showed a greater incidence. Other studies have found that the incidence of broken homes in the history of neurotics is between

210

20% (Brown & Moore, 1944) and 30% (Madow & Hardy, 1947; Wallace, 1935), and Gerard and Siegel (1950) found no particular incidence of broken homes in the family history of their sample of schizophrenics.

Psychiatric Interview

Another classical method of obtaining information regarding the individual with whom patients have been living is by having interviews with them directly. The quality of the mother-child relationship is then inferred from what the interviewee says. From this research, an overwhelming number of studies (Despert, 1951; Gerard & Siegel, 1950; Guertin, 1961; Hajdu-Gimes, 1940; Kasanin, Knight, & Sage, 1934; Lidz, Cornelison, Fleck, & Terry, 1957a, 1957b, 1957c; Lidz, Cornelison, Terry, & Fleck, 1958; Lidz & Lidz, 1949; Lidz, Parker, & Cornelison, 1956; Tietze, 1949; Walters, 1938) describe a familial pattern characterized by a dominant, overprotective, but basically rejecting mother and a passive, ineffectual father. Yet the data in the study by Schofield and Balian (1959) reflected similarity rather than differences in the families of schizophrenic and nonpsychiatric (general medical) patients, and the data of Gerard and Siegel (1950) indicated that the schizophrenics in their study, according to interpretation of the data gleaned from the interviews, received adequate breast feeding, had no history of particularly difficult toilet training or of obvious feeding problems, did not come from broken homes, and apparently were not unduly rejected or punished. Another factor which seems to emerge from the studies is that a dominant characteristic of the family life of schizophrenics is a quality of inappropriateness of thinking and behaving which seems to infiltrate the entire atmosphere (Fleck, Lidz, & Cornelison, 1963; Lidz et al., 1957b, 1957c; Stringer, 1962). Meyers and Goldfarb (1962), however, found that only 28% of the mothers of 45 children diagnosed as schizophrenic and only 12% of the fathers were themselves manifestly schizophrenic.

Psychological Evaluation

Attitude Questionnaires. One of the most widely used questionnaires in this area of research has been the Shoben (1949) Parent-Child Attitude Survey. The Shoben scale consists of 148 items which measure the dimensions of parental rejection, possessiveness, and domination. From the administration of this attitude survey, Mark (1953) and Freeman and Grayson (1955) reported significant differences in attitudes toward child rearing between mothers of schizophrenics and mothers of normal children. In comparison with the mothers of the control subjects, the mothers of schizophrenic patients (Mark, 1953) were revealed as inconsistent in their methods of control. They described themselves as being, at times, overrestrictive and controlling of behavior, but in some instances lax. They frowned on sex play and tended to keep information regarding sex from their children; they also seemed to frown on friends for their children. Their relationship to their children appeared inconsistent; they described what could be interpreted as excessive devotion and interest in the child's activities while at the same time revealing a notable degree of "cool detachment." Freeman and Grayson (1955) found that in comparison to mothers of students in an undergraduate course, mothers of 50 hospitalized schizophrenics (ages 20 to 35) tended to reveal themselves to be somewhat more possessive, but inherently rejecting of their children, and particularly disturbed about sexual behavior in their children. However, according to these same data, the mothers of schizophrenic patients did not reveal themselves to be more dominant, dogmatic, or inconsistent in their attitude than the controls. But most important was the fact that item analysis of these data revealed that the attitudes of the mothers of the schizophrenics and of the controls were distinguished on only 14 of the items, and then, in general, there was so much overlap that even on these items the statistical significance was contributed by a small percentage of each group. Freeman, Simmons, and Bergen (1959) included four items from the Shoben scale among a larger sample of questions posed to parents. These items had been derived from a previous study (Freeman & Simmons, 1958) and were included in the second study because they were the only ones in the first study which were found to discriminate between the attitudes of mothers of schizophrenic patients and those of mothers of normals. The items are:

1. Parents should sacrifice everything for their children.
2. A child should feel a deep sense of obligation always to act in accord with the wishes of his parents.
3. Children who are gentlemanly or lady-like are preferable to those who are tomboys or "regular guys."
4. It is better for children to play at home than to visit other children.

Freeman et al. (1959) found no capacity for these items to differentiate the attitudes of the mothers of schizophrenics from those of other individuals with severe functional disorders.

Zuckerman, Oltean, and Monashkin (1958) utilized another attitude scale, the Parental Attitude Research Inventory (PARI, developed by Schaefer and Bell in their work at the Psychology Laboratory at NIMH). The PARI was administered to mothers of schizophrenics, and it was found that only one item distinguished between their attitudes and those of mothers of normal children. The mothers of schizophrenics tended to describe themselves as being stricter than did the mothers of nonschizophrenic children.

The minimal discrimination value of the several attitude scales should be noted. This would seem to reflect either minimal capacity of the scales to make such distinctions or little in the way of measurable differences between the groups. In either case, it is very difficult to evaluate the meaning of these data since the attitudes of the mothers of schizophrenics seemed to be distinguished from the attitudes of the mothers of neurotics on only a few items (the obtained number of differences did not even exceed that expected by chance alone).

Projective Tests. Several studies presented Rorschach data on the mothers of schizophrenic patients (Baxter, Becker, & Hooks, 1963; Prout & White, 1950; Winder & Kantor, 1958). In comparison to those of the mothers of normals, the Rorschach protocols of the mothers of the schizophrenic patients were undistinguished as regards the general

degree of immaturity (Winder & Kantor, 1958) and the use of defences which are essentially reality distorting, namely, denial and projection (Baxter et al., 1963).[1] However, Prout and White did find more pure color without form and less human and animal movement and shading responses in the Rorschach protocols of mothers of schizophrenic boys as compared to the mothers of a comparable group of boys randomly selected from the community. Perr (1958) found that the parents of schizophrenic children gave responses to the Thematic Apperception Test (TAT) little distinguished from those of parents of normal children, and Fisher, Boyd, Walker, and Sheer (1959) found that the TAT and Rorschach protocols of the parents of schizophrenic patients were measurably different from those of the parents of nonpsychiatric (general medical) patients, but they were not distinguishable from the protocols of the parents of neurotic patients. The mothers of the schizophrenics revealed a higher degree of perceptual rigidity, greater incidence of indicators of maladjustment on the Rorschach, and less definitely conceived parental images on the TAT than the mothers of the normals.

Direct Observation of Interpersonal Behavior. Attempts have been made to study the interpersonal behavior of families of schizophrenics *in vivo;* some investigators

---

[1] The conclusion that the Rorschach protocols of the mothers of schizophrenics were undistinguished from the Rorschach protocols of the mothers of normals (as in the research by Winder & Kantor, 1958, Baxter et al., 1963) is an interpretation of the results made by the present author. In fact, in both of these articles, the authors conclude that there *are* significant differences. However, in the article by Winder and Kantor, the mean rating of the degree of maturity of personality development for the mothers of the schizophrenics was 2.89, for the mothers of the normals, 2.43. In the article by Baxter et al., the means of the ratings of the degree of utilization of psychologically immature defenses on the Rorschach by the parents of poor premorbid schizophrenics, good premorbid schizophrenics, and neurotics are, respectively, 19.43, 19.62, and 19.49. Though in both of these investigations valid statistical significance was demonstrated between the obtained means, the actual means, in both researches, are so similar to each other that the interpretation of *psychologically* significant differences between groups on the basis of the obtained *statistically* significant differences seemed a highly doubtful conclusion.

have gone into the home, others have brought the family into a hospital setting and observed the interaction between family members for an hour or so at a time, others have brought the family into a laboratory setting (National Institute of Mental Health) where the family lives under actual but known conditions for months at a time.

In the study of the interpersonal relationships in the actual home setting, Behrens and Goldfarb (1958) observed that the personality of the mother seemed to set the tone of the family milieu and that there seemed to be a direct relationship between the degree of pathology that could be seen in the family setting and the degree of psychopathology demonstrated by the child. The homes they observed appeared physically deteriorated and crowded. There was a basic isolation between the mother and father, and the fathers were basically passive. Confusion and disorganization characterized the family atmosphere, with the family demonstrating inadequate mechanisms to handle emotional flareups. The intensive observation of one mother-child interaction (Karon & Rosberg, 1958) yielded the observation that the mother was unempathic. She blocked verbalizations of emotions and tended to live vicariously through the child, but her relationship to the child appeared to involve a basic, though unconscious, hostility and rejection. The mother was an obsessive-compulsive personality, dominated the home, and was unable to accept herself as a woman. The intensive observation of 51 families (Donnelly, 1960) tends to confirm this finding. Observing the mother-child interaction in the home, utilizing the Fels Parent Behavior Scales, Donnelly found that mothers treated a psychotic child differently than their other nonpsychotic children. To the psychotic child, the mother was generally less warm, less accepting, less empathic, more punitive, more controlling, and more overprotective. The father was passive, but more rational than the mother in relation to the child. Psychotic children tended to come from homes characterized as less well adjusted, full of discord, and low in sociability. However, in comparing the family interaction of schizophrenic patients with those of normal controls, both Perr (1958)

and Meyers and Goldfarb (1961) found little that could stand as a valid measure of distinction between the two groups of families. Perr found that the parents of schizophrenics tend to show more self-deception and to describe themselves as being more hostile. Meyers and Goldfarb found that the mothers of schizophrenic children appeared less capable of formulating a consistent definition of the world for the child.

A method of directly assessing the interpersonal behavior of husband and wife was introduced by Strodtbeck (1951). He posed questions to each parent individually, then he brought them together and had them discuss those points where their attitudes differed. Farina and his associates (Bell, Garmezy, Farina, & Rodnick, 1960; Farina, 1960; Farina & Dunham, 1963) utilized this method to study the families of schizophrenic patients. The questionnaire they used was the PARI. They found that they could distinguish the interpersonal behavior of schizophrenics otherwise described as having good or poor premorbid adjustment. In these studies, mother dominance was discerned in the families of the poor premorbid group only, with interpersonal conflict greatest in that group. In comparing the family interaction of the schizophrenic patient with those of normal controls, Bell et al. (1960) found that in the family constellation of normals, authority tended to be shared by both parents, and parental conflict was at a minimum, although even here there was a trend towards maternal dominance.

Bishop (1951) reported a method of studying the mother-child interaction under live, yet controlled, conditions. The mother and child were brought into a play room where the interpersonal behavior was observed directly. In 1954, Bowen introduced the principle of this technique to the study of families of schizophrenics. Families were brought into what came to be known as the Family Study Section of NIMH (National Institute of Mental Health), and there they were observed living under actual but known conditions for long periods of time (6 months–2 years). Observations based on families living under these conditions revealed that the mothers of schizophrenics showed extremely domineering, smothering, close relationships with the child (Dworin & Wyant, 1957), with the mothers utilizing threat of deprivation to control the child. Bowen, Dysinger, and Basamanie (1959) observed the presence of marked emotional distance and intense conflict between the parents. The fathers were emotionally immature and unable to define their role in the family and unable to make decisions; the mothers were usually the dominant ones, affecting a close relationship with the child to the exclusion of the father. Brodey (1959) found that the behavior of the families of schizophrenics was characterized by a selective utilization of reality, particularly the use of externalization, and that the interpersonal relationships were highly narcissistic.

Perception of Parental Behavior by Patients. Several studies have indicated that schizophrenics tend to have experienced their mother as having been rejecting (Bolles, Metzger, & Pitts, 1941; Lane & Singer, 1959; Singer, 1954), and dominant, demanding, and overprotective (Garmezy, Clarke, & Stockner, 1961; Heilbrun, 1960; Kohn & Clausen, 1956; McKeown, 1950; Reichard & Tillman, 1950; Schofield & Balian, 1959). However, when one compares the perception of their mothers by normals (Garmezy et al., 1961; Heilbrun, 1960; Lane & Singer, 1959; Singer, 1954) the uniqueness of these attitudes toward the mothers of schizophrenics disappears. Recollections of dominance and overprotectiveness are common for both schizophrenics and normals. Although Heilbrun, Garmezy et al., and Bolles et al. report data which have shown that there is a greater incidence of a feeling of having been rejected on the part of a group of psychiatric patients when compared to medical-surgical controls, the actual incidence of this even in the psychiatric group was only 15% as compared to 1% in the controls. Moreover, Singer and Lane and Singer found that perception of parental relationships during childhood was more a function of the subjects' socioeconomic level than was psychopathology, paralleling a finding by Opler (1957) that familial patterns (parental dominance and attitudes) are a function of cultural factors (Italian versus Irish origin) rather than of psychopathology.

NEUROSIS

As compared to the research in the area of schizophrenia, investigations of the dynamics of the family life of neurotics are few and generally restricted to data gleaned from case histories. From these studies it appears that the neurotic behavior of the child is a direct function of the neurotic behavior of the mother (e.g., Fisher & Mendell, 1956; Ingham, 1949; Sperling, 1949, 1951; Zimmerman, 1930). Neurotic behavior in children has been seen to have been related to maternal overprotection (Holloway, 1931; Jacobsen, 1947; Zimmerman, 1930), maternal domination (Mueller, 1945), maternal rejection (Ingham, 1949; Newell, 1934, 1936; Silberpfennig, 1941), separation from the mother during the first 3 years of life (Bowlby, 1940; Ribble, 1941), and oral deprivation (Childers & Hamil, 1932). Neurotic involvement with the mother, where the mother needs the child for the satisfaction of her own needs and discourages the development of emotional separation between the child and herself, has been associated with the development in the child of psychosomatic disorders (Miller & Baruch, 1950; Sperling, 1949) and school phobia (e.g., Davidson, 1961; Eisenberg, 1958; Estes, Haylett, & Johnson, 1956; Goldberg, 1953; Johnson, Falstein, & Suzurek, 1941; Suttenfield, 1954; Talbot, 1957; van Houten, 1948; Waldfogel, Hahn, & Gardner, 1954; Wilson, 1955).

Neurosis in children has also been associated with such factors in the home as poverty (Brown & Moore, 1944; Holloway, 1931) and broken homes (Ingham, 1949; Madow & Hardy, 1947; Wallace, 1935). Silverman (1935), however, found that 75% of the children from broken homes were essentially "normal"; 16% were described as conduct disorders, and only 9% were classifiable as personality problems.

Of the studies that did not use the case history method of data collection, McKeown (1950) found that neurotic children perceive their mothers as demanding, antagonistic, and setting inordinately high standards for them to meet. Stein (1944) found that neurotics tended to perceive themselves as having been rejected, particularly as compared to the perception of their family life held by normals (Bolles et al., 1941). Although Kundert (1947) found that whether justified by experience or not (e.g., separation due to hospitalization of mother or child)', emotionally disturbed children, in general, fear being deserted by their mothers and cling to them compulsively. The Rorschach protocols of mothers of neurotics reveal that they tend to utilize psychological mechanisms which abrogate reality, for example, denial and projection (Baxter et al., 1963).

BEHAVIOR DISORDER

The research on the family background of individuals whose personality' problems take the form of antisocial behavior is scanty. Shaw and McKay (1932) found no differences in the incidence of broken homes from cases referred to Cook County Juvenile Court (36%) as compared to a random sample of children in the Chicago public school system (42%). Behavior disorders in children have been seen to have been related to neurotic behavior in their parents (Field, 1940; Huschka, 1941), primarily involving maternal rejection, overt and covert. In line with a social learning hypothesis, another interesting finding is that a correlation has been found between antisocial behavior in children and the children's perception of parents' antisocial behavior (Bender, 1937; K. Friedlander, 1945; Williams, 1932).

DISCUSSION

Let us now summarize what conclusions can be drawn from these data which illuminate the role of the family in the development of psychopathology. As regards the families of schizophrenics, from an overview of the research which has investigated the pattern of parent-child interaction of this pathological group considered without reference to any other pathological or control group, several factors emerge which seem to characterize this group, regardless of the method of data collection, that is, whether by case history, interview, psychological test, or direct observation. Families of schizophrenics seem to be characterized by mothers who are dominant, fathers who are passive,

and considerable family disharmony. The mother is overprotective, overpossessive, and overcontrolling, yet basically, albeit unconsciously, rejecting. These mothers frown on sex, are inconsistent in their methods of discipline, and introduce modes of thinking, feeling, and behaving which are not reality oriented. In light of the fact that these patterns emerge as a function of almost all methods of data collection, these results seem very impressive. Had our review of these data stopped here, we would have had apparent verification of the thesis that certain kinds of mother-child relationships and family atmospheres indeed account for the development of schizophrenia in the offspring. However, when each of these parental characteristics is compared with those which emerge from the analysis of the family situation of the normal (apparently nonpsychiatrically-involved) individual, each characteristic that is found to be typical of the families of schizophrenics is found to exist in the families of the controls as well. Furthermore, research which has attempted to make direct comparisons between the families of children in different categories of psychopathology (e.g., Baxter et al., 1963; Fisher et al., 1959; Frazee, 1953; Freeman et al., 1959; D. Friedlander, 1945; Inlow, 1933; McKeown, 1950; Oltman et al., 1952; Pollack & Malzberg, 1940; Pollack, Malzberg, & Fuller, 1936) reveals no significant or consistent differences in the psychological structure of the families.

The results are the same with regard to the families of the neurotics as well. At first glance, it appears that the mother's neurotic involvement with the child is causally associated with the neurotic behavior of the child. However, the essential characteristics of this involvement—maternal overprotectiveness, maternal domination, maternal rejection, deprivation and frustration, and the mothers fostering an almost symbiotic relationship between themselves and their children—are basically the same as those found in the families of schizophrenics and of children with behavior disorders. Moreover, in many respects, it would be hard, on blind analysis, to distinguish the family which produced an emotionally disturbed child from that which produced the so-called normal or well-adjusted child.

It seems apparent that the major conclusion that can be drawn from these data is that there is no such thing as a schizophrenogenic or a neurotogenic mother or family. At least these data do not permit of the description of a particular constellation of psychological events within the home and, in particular, between mother and child that can be isolated as a unique factor in the development of one or the other kind of personality disorder. If one is looking for *the* factor to account for the development of neurosis or schizophrenia, that one factor does not appear to exist as a clear cut finding in the research.

It is incumbent upon us to wonder why the research literature does not permit support of a hypothesis regarding parental influence on the psychological development of children in the manner we hypothesized. One of the major problems with which we must contend is that human behavior is a very complicated event, determined by many factors, and not clearly understood out of the context in which it occurs, and, in this regard, not everyone reacts in a like manner to similar life experiences. For example, strict discipline is reacted to differently when this occurs in a "warm" or "cold" home atmosphere (Sears, 1961); maternal rejection is reacted to differently where the father is accepting and warm (McCord et al., 1961) as well as where the father can be a buffer between the child and the overprotective mother (Witmer, 1933). Emphasizing the multivariate aspect of the determinants of behavior, one notes that Madow and Hardy (1947) reported that of the soldiers who broke down with neurotic reactions there was a high incidence of those coming from broken homes. Amongst those soldiers who did not break down, the incidence of coming from a broken home was 11–15%; the incidence of broken homes in the history of soldiers who did break down was 36%. Statistically, there is a significant difference between these percentages; however, even the 36% datum leaves 64% of the soldiers who broke down *not* coming from a broken home. Huschka (1941) reported that the incidence of neurotic mothers

of problem children is high (42%); however, this leaves 58% of the group *not* accounted for by this factor. Brown and Moore (1944) commented that the incidence of excessive poverty, drunkenness, and family conflict in soldiers who broke down was significant, but this accounted for only 20% of the cases. Although between 30% (Canavan & Clark, 1923; Lampron, 1933) and 40% (Huschka, 1941; Lidz & Lidz, 1949) of the children born to mothers who are psychotic become psychotic themselves, these percentages do not account for the majority of children born to these mothers. Indeed, Fanning et al. (1938) found that 43% of the children born to mothers who were psychotic were observed to be making an adequate social and personal adjustment; only 11% of that sample of children was not. It should be noted that only half of the samples of mothers studied by Despert (1938) and Clardy (1951) resembled the traditional pattern of what has come to be known as the "schizophrenogenic mother." Finally, Beres and Obers (1950) observed that there is a wide reaction to an experience of emotional deprivation (in this instance, institutionalization) ranging from the development of a schizoid personality to schizophrenia itself, and including neurotic reactions and character disorders. Indeed, 25% of their sample of children who were brought up in institutions appeared to be making a satisfactory adjustment in spite of this ostensibly devastating experience.

Over and above the complexity of human behavior contributing to the inconclusiveness of the results, one must look at the way in which these data have been collected. It might be that the criterion measure, that is, the diagnosis, did not provide the investigator with meaningful groupings of subjects so that consistent findings *could* be obtained. As regards the method of data collection: Case histories may be inadequate in providing basic data; Information can be gross and/or inaccurate; The informant has to rely on memory, and this memory might be consciously or unconsciously selective, or the informant might not be aware of the import of or feel shame in giving certain data. Yet, despite the many limitations of this mode

216

of data collection, some of the primary research in schizophrenia has utilized this method, and almost all of the data with respect to the family life of neurotics and behavior disorders were gathered in this way. These same limitations apply to data that are gathered when the informant is asked to fill out an attitude questionnaire. Surely the data on parents elicited from the children are susceptible to distortion even when given by normal children, no less those who already tend to consciously or unconsciously confound their perception of reality with fantasy. The psychiatric interview is a much more sensitive procedure than the case history or attitude questionnaire. Either structured or open-ended interviews enable the interviewer to follow up leads and possibly detect where information is being omitted for one reason or another. The problem here, however, is that there is always the possibility that distorted or inaccurate data are gathered by the interviewer, either through the kinds of questions asked, or the perception of the answer or of the individual being interviewed. For example, it is interesting to note that although the majority of psychiatric interviewers experienced the mothers of schizophrenics as matching the model of the schizophrenogenic mother—the dominant, overprotective, but basically rejecting mother who induces inappropriateness of thinking in her children—the psychological test evaluation of mothers of schizophrenics failed to confirm these findings. One explanation for this is that the interviewer, already acquainted with the literature regarding the mother of schizophrenics, anticipating to experience the mothers in terms of the ideas about schizophrenogenic mothers, did, indeed, experience them in that way, whereas a more objective evaluation of the patterns of thinking and feeling of these mothers did not confirm the more subjective impression.

In order to try and avoid the pitfalls inherent in data gleaned through case history or interview, investigators hypothesized that direct observation of the mother-child interaction might yield more valid information. Unfortunately, here, too, limitations inherent in the mode of data collection become apparent. Observations of the mother-child interaction in the home or in an observation room in a hospital or clinic are generally restricted to a limited time segment, for example, 1 hour once a week. This factor, in and of itself, limits the observations to a fairly restricted aspect of the spectrum of the interaction between mother and child. Here, too, the behavior to which the observer is exposed may be influenced by the conscious or unconscious attitudes and motives of the parent being observed. It is not too difficult for the parent to present only that behavior which, for one reason or another, she feels it safe to display and to control the presence of other behaviors. Direct observation of the family for extensive periods of time, that is, months, and under controlled but as natural as possible living conditions (as in the Family Study Section of NIMH) avoids the restrictiveness and overcomes, to one degree or another, the artificiality of the relatively brief observation. However, the family is still aware that they are being observed and may, to one degree or another, be unable to act "natural." Moreover, unless the observations are independently made by several people whose reliability of observation has already been established, they may also be influenced by the *Zeitgeist* and perceive the family as being "schizophrenogenic" whether it is or not, mutually reinforcing each other's expectations. A more pressing consideration in evaluating the validity of these kinds of observations is the fact that the interaction, no matter how natural, takes place after the development of the psychopathology. It is quite possible that the aspects of the interpersonal relationship within the family, or between the mother and child in particular, that eventuated in the development of the patterns of thinking, feeling, and behaving characteristic of the schizophrenic or the neurotic, are no longer present; they may have occurred at a time of the child's life long since past and/or under conditions of intimacy not even accessible to the observer. There is no reason to assume that the etiological factors are still functioning or that they will be available to the trained observer even over the course of 6 months. Of course, it might be that whatever differentiates the psychological existence of the schizophrenic from that of the neurotic or of the normal might be so subtle that it is imperceptible to the participants themselves or even the trained observer and, hence, escape notice. Here, one is reminded of Freud's comment that "the years of childhood of those who are later neurotic need not necessarily differ from those who are later normal except in intensity and distinctness [Freud, 1938 (Orig. publ. 1910), p. 583]."

Theorizing about the etiology of psychopathology has characteristically been of the either/or variety. Nineteenth century scientists sought explanations for neurotic and psychotic disorders in the hereditary background of their patients, working from the assumption that many directly inherited the neurotic or psychotic "illness." On the other hand, the scientist of the twentieth century has sought explanations for psychopathology in the experiential aspect of man's life, in his emotional and interpersonal learning. As with most events in our life, the truth is probably somewhere in between these two positions. Indeed, in spite of the emphasis that is placed on the role of experience in the development of personality in psychoanalysis, Freud did not think, at least as regards the etiology of psychopathology, in such categorically black and white terms. He was able to bridge the gap between the nature-nurture extremes:

We divide the causes of neurotic disease into those which the individual himself brings with him into life, and those which life bring to him—that is to say, into constitutional and accidental. It is the interaction of these as a rule first gives rise to illness [Freud, 1950b (Orig. publ. 1913), p. 122].

Let us bear clearly in mind that every human being has acquired, by the combined operation of inherent disposition and of external influences of childhood, a special individuality in the exercise of his capacity to love—that is, in the conditions which he sets up for loving, in the impulses he gratifies by it, and in the aims he sets out to achieve in it. ... We will here provide against misconceptions and reproaches to the effect that we have denied the importance of the inborn (constitutional) factor because we have emphasized the importance of infantile impressions. Such an accusation arises out of the narrowness with which mankind looks for causes, inasmuch as one single causal factor satisfies him, in spite of the many commonly underlying the face of reality. Psycho-Analysis has said much about the "accidental" component in aetiology and

little about the constitutional, but only because it could throw new light upon the former, whereas of the latter it knows no more so far than is already known. We deprecate the assumption of an essential opposition between the two series of aetiological factors; we presume rather a perpetual interchange of both in producing the results observed [Freud, 1950a (Orig. publ. 1912), p. 312].

Other psychoanalysts have followed Freud in the presumption of an inherent, predetermined characteristic functioning of the nervous system of the human organism which determines reactions to stimuli pre- and postnatally (e.g., Greenacre, 1941).

Augmenting the clinical observations of psychoanalysis, one must juxtapose the experimental evidence in psychology which indicates that (a) individuals reflect characteristic patterns of autonomic activity which are stable and which are typical of them as individuals (Grossman & Greenberg, 1957; Lacey, 1950; Richmond & Lustman, 1955; Wenger, 1941), (b) the characteristic patterns of neural activity are identifiable prenatally and are consistent with the patterns of activity observable postnatally (Richards & Newbery, 1938, (c) these characteristic patterns of autonomic activity consistently emerge in a factor of lability and balance in which specific personality factors are consistently highly loaded (Darling, 1940; Eysenck, 1956; Eysenck & Prell, 1951; Theron, 1948; van der Merwe, 1948; van der Merwe & Theron, 1947), (d) there is greater similarity of autonomic reactivity between identical twins than fraternal twins or ordinary siblings (Eysenck, 1956; Eysenck & Prell, 1951; Jost & Sontag, 1944), and (e) there is a selective influence on personality functioning due to the sex of the individual per se. For example, generally boys outnumber girls 2–1 in being referred for psychological help (Bender, 1937; Wile & Jones, 1937). Sears (1961) found a significant difference in the basic mode of self-reported expression of aggression between boys and girls: Girls appeared higher in socially acceptable forms of aggression and high in anxiety regarding hostility, while boys were significantly higher in aggression that was directed against social control. Sears also found that the more punitive the mother is, the more dependent the son becomes but the less dependent the daughter becomes. Newell (1936) found that maternal rejection affected males more than females: Marked increase in aggressive behavior was noted in the boys who experienced rejection, not so with the females. Baruch & Wilcox (1944) noted that interparental tensions lead to different reactions in boys as compared to girls; in boys, it led to ascendance-submission problems, in girls, to an experience of lack of affection.

We end this survey by concluding that we have not been able to find any unique factors in the family of the schizophrenic which distinguishes it from the family of the neurotic or from the family of controls, who are ostensibly free from evidence of patterns of gross psychopathology. In short, we end by stating that the assumption that the family is *the* factor in the development of personality has not been validated. It is interesting to note that Orlansky (1949), in his review of the literature exploring the relationship between certain childhood experiences, for example, feeding, toilet training, thumb-sucking, the degree of tactile stimulation by the mother, etc., upon the development of personality characteristics, was also forced to conclude that the data failed to confirm an invariant relationship between the experience in infancy and the resultant personality. Of course, it might well be that the reality of the family is not the important dimension in determining the child's reactions; rather, it might be the perception of the family members, and this might often have little or no relation to the people as they really are. This would mean, then, that in many instances the important variables in the development of psychopathology might be factors which the child brings to the family, the functioning of the nervous and metabolic systems and the cognitive capacity to integrate stimuli into meaningful perceptual and conceptual schema. Indeed, we are left to wonder, as do the psychoanalysts, whether the proclivity towards fantasy distortion of reality might not be *the* factor in the development of psychopathology, and this proclivity might not be always determined by the child's experiences per se.

Obviously, questions regarding the etiology of patterns of personality behavior which are regarded as pathological, unadaptive, or unadjusted cannot be met with simple answers. Apparently, the factors which play a part in the development of behavior in humans are so complex that it would appear that they almost defy being investigated scientifically and defy one's attempts to draw meaningful generalizations from the exploration which has already been done. It is, of course, conceivable that human behavior is so complex that it cannot be reduced to simple terms or be expected to yield unalterable patterns of occurrences. It might also be that what produces psychopathological reactions in one individual does not in another. All this would be understandable in light of the complexity that is the human being, neurologically as well as socially, but it is unfortunate as regards research endeavors. In 1926, Freud wrote:

Anxiety is the reaction to danger. One cannot, after all, help suspecting that the reason why the affect of anxiety occupies a unique position in the economy of the mind has something to do with the essential nature of danger. Yet dangers are the common lot of humanity; they are the same for everyone. What we need and cannot lay our fingers on is some factor which will explain why some people are able to subject the affect of anxiety, in spite of its peculiar quality, to the normal workings of the mind, or which decides who is doomed to come to grief over the task [Freud, 1936, p. 64].

We end this review of forty years of research without being able to feel that we are any closer to an answer than was Freud.

REFERENCES

AYER, MARY E., & BERNREUTER, R. G. A study of the relationship between discipline and personality traits in little children. *Journal of Genetic Psychology*, 1937, 50, 165–170.

BARRY, H. Orphanhood as a factor in psychoses. *Journal of Abnormal and Social Psychology*, 1936, 30, 431–438.

BARRY, H., & BOUSFIELD, W. A. Incidence of orphanhood among fifteen hundred psychotic patients. *Journal of Genetic Psychology*, 1937, 50, 198–202.

BARTMEIER, L. H. Deprivations during infancy and their effects upon personality development. *American Journal of Mental Deficiency*, 1952, 56, 708–711.

BARUCH, DOROTHY W., & WILCOX, J. ANNIE. A study of sex differences in preschool children's adjustment coexistent with inter-parental tensions. *Journal of Genetic Psychology*, 1944, 64, 281–303.

BAXTER, J. C., BECKER, J., & HOOKS. W. Defensive style in the families of schizophrenics and controls. *Journal of Abnormal and Social Psychology*, 1963, **66**, 512–518.

BEHRENS, MARJORIE L., & GOLDFARB, W. A study of patterns of interaction of families of schizophrenic children in residential treatment. *American Journal of Orthopsychiatry*, 1958, **28**, 300–312.

BELL, R. Q., GARMEZY, N., FARINA, A., & RODNICK, E. H. Direct study of parent-child interaction. *American Journal of Orthopsychiatry*, 1960, **30**, 445–452.

BENDER, LAURETTA. Reactive psychosis in response to mental disease in the family. *Journal of Nervous and Mental Disease*, 1936, **83**, 143–289.

BENDER, LAURETTA. Behavior problems in the children of psychotic and criminal parents. *Genetic Psychology Monographs*, 1937, **19**, 229–339.

BERES, D., & OBERS, S. J. The effects of extreme deprivation in infancy on psychic structure in adolescence: A study in ego development. *Psychoanalytic Study of the Child*, 1950, **5**, 212–235.

BISHOP, BARBARA M. Mother-child interaction and the social behavior of children. *Psychological Monographs*, 1951, **65**(11, Whole No. 328).

BOLLES, MARJORIE M., METZGER, HARRIET F., & PITTS, MARJORIE W. Early home background and personal adjustment. *American Journal of Orthopsychiatry*, 1941, **11**, 530–534.

BOWEN, M., DYSINGER, R. H., & BASAMANIE, BETTY. The role of the father in families with a schizophrenic patient. *American Journal of Psychiatry*, 1959, **115**, 1017–1020.

BOWLBY, J. The influence of early environment in the development of neurosis and neurotic character. *International Journal of Psychoanalysis*, 1940, **21**, 154–178.

BRODBECK, A. J., & IRWIN, O. C. The speech behavior of infants without families. *Child Development*, 1946, **17**, 145–156.

BRODEY, W. M. Some family operations in schizophrenia. *Archives of General Psychiatry*, 1959, **1**, 379–402.

BROWN, W. T., & MOORE, M. Soldiers who break down—family background and past history. *Military Surgeon*, 1944, **94**, 160–163.

CANAVAN, MYRTELLE M., & CLARK, ROSAMOND. The mental health of 463 children from dementia-praecox stock. *Mental Hygiene*, 1923, **7**, 137–148.

CHILDERS, A. T., & HAMIL, B. M. Emotional problems in children as related to the duration of breast feeding in infancy. *American Journal of Orthopsychiatry*, 1932, **2**, 134–142.

CLARDY, E. R. A study of the development and course of schizophrenic children. *Psychiatric Quarterly*, 1951, **25**, 81–90.

DARLING, R. P. Autonomic action in relation to personality traits of children. *Journal of Abnormal and Social Psychology*, 1940, **35**, 246–260.

DAVIDSON, SUSANNAH. School phobia as a manifestation of family disturbance: Its structure and treatment. *Journal of Child Psychology and Psychiatry*, 1961, **1**, 270–287.

DAVIS, K. Extreme social isolation of a child. *American Journal of Sociology*, 1940, **45**, 554–565.

DESPERT, LOUISE J. Schizophrenia in children. *Psychiatric Quarterly*, 1938, **12**, 366–371.

DESPERT, LOUISE J. Some considerations relating to the genesis of autistic behavior in children. *American Journal of Orthopsychiatry*, 1951, **21**, 335–350.

DONNELLY, ELLEN M. The quantitative analysis of parent behavior toward psychotic children and their siblings. *Genetic Psychology Monographs*, 1960, **62**, 331–376.

DWORIN, J., & WYANT, O. Authoritarian patterns in mothers of schizophrenics. *Journal of Clinical Psychology*, 1957, **13**, 332–338.

EISENBERG, L. School phobia: A study in the communication of anxiety. *American Journal of Psychiatry*, 1958, **114**, 712–718.

ESTES, H. R., HAYLETT, CLARICE H., & JOHNSON, ADELAIDE M. Separation anxiety. *American Journal of Psychotherapy*, 1956, **10**, 682–695.

EYSENCK, H. J. The inheritance of extraversion-introversion. *Acta Psychologica*, 1956, **12**, 95–110.

EYSENCK, H. J., & PRELL, D. B. The inheritance of neuroticism: An experimental study. *Journal of Mental Science*, 1951, **97**, 441–465.

FANNING, ANEITA, LEHR, SARA, SHERWIN, ROBERTA, & WILSON, MARJORIE. The mental health of children of psychotic mothers. *Smith College Studies in Social Work*, 1938, **8**, 291–343.

FARINA, A. Patterns of role dominance and conflict in parents of schizophrenic patients. *Journal of Abnormal and Social Psychology*, 1960, **61**, 31–38.

FARINA, A., & DUNHAM, R. M. Measurement of family relationships and their effects. *Archives of General Psychiatry*, 1963, **9**, 64–73.

FIELD, MINNA A. Maternal attitudes found in twenty-five cases of children with primary behavior disorders. *American Journal of Orthopsychiatry*, 1940, **10**, 293–311.

FISHER, S., BOYD, INA, WALKER D., & SHEER, DIANNE. Parents of schizophrenics, neurotics, and normals. *Archives of General Psychiatry*, 1959, **1**, 149–166.

FISHER, S., & MENDELL, D. The communication of neurotic patterns over two and three generations. *Psychiatry*, 1956, **19**, 41–46.

FLECK, S., LIDZ, T., & CORNELISON, ALICE. Comparison of parent-child relationships of male and female schizophrenic patients. *Archives of General Psychiatry*, 1963, **8**, 1–7.

FRAZEE, HELEN E. Children who later became schizophrenic. *Smith College Studies in Social Work*, 1953, **23**, 125–149.

FREEMAN, R. V., & GRAYSON, H. M. Maternal attitudes in schizophrenia. *Journal of Abnormal and Social Psychology*, 1955, **50**, 45–52.

FREEMAN, H. E., & SIMMONS, O. G. Mental patients in the community: Family settings and performance levels. *American Sociological Review*, 1958, **23**, 147–154.

FREEMAN, H. E., SIMMONS, O. G., & BERGEN, B. J. Possessiveness as a characteristic of mothers of schizophrenics. *Journal of Abnormal and Social Psychology*, 1959, **58**, 271–273.

220

FREUD, S. *Inhibitions, symptoms, and anxiety.* London: Hogarth Press, 1936.

FREUD, S. Three contributions to the theory of sex. In A. A. Brill (Ed.), *The basic writings of Sigmund Freud.* (Orig. Publ. 1910) New York: Modern Library, 1938. P. 583.

FREUD, S. The dynamics of the transference. (Orig. publ. 1912) In, *Collected papers.* Vol. 2. London: Hogarth Press, 1950. Pp. 312–322. (a)

FREUD, S. The predisposition to obsessional neurosis. (Orig. publ. 1913) In, *Collected papers.* Vol. 2. London: Hogarth Press, 1950. Pp. 122–132. (b)

FRIEDLANDER, D. Personality development of twenty-seven children who later became psychotic. *Journal of Abnormal and Social Psychology*, 1945, 40, 330–335.

FRIEDLANDER, KATE. Formation of the antisocial character. *Psychoanalytic Study of the Child*, 1945, 1, 189–203.

GARMEZY, N., CLARKE, A. R., & STOCKNER, CAROL. Child rearing attitudes of mothers and fathers as reported by schizophrenic and normal patients. *Journal of Abnormal and Social Psychology*, 1961, 63, 176–182.

GERARD, D. L., & SIEGAL, L. The family background of schizophrenia. *Psychiatric Quarterly*, 1950, 24, 47–73.

GOLDBERG, THELMA B. Factors in the development of school phobia. *Smith College Studies in Social Work*, 1953, 23, 227–248.

GOLDFARB, W. The effects of early institutional care on adolescent personality (graphic Rorschach data). *Child Development*, 1943, 14, 213–223 (a)

GOLDFARB, W. Infant rearing and problem behavior. *American Journal of Orthopsychiatry*, 1943, 13, 249–266. (b)

GOLDFARB, W. The effects of early institutional care on adolescent personality. *Journal of Experimental Education*, 1943, 12, 106–129. (c)

GOLDFARB, W. Psychological deprivation in infancy. *American Journal of Psychiatry*, 1945, 102, 19–33. (a)

GOLDFARB, W. Psychological privation in infancy and subsequent adjustment. *American Journal of Orthopsychiatry*, 1945, 15, 247–255. (b)

GREENACRE, PHYLLIS. The predisposition to anxiety. *Psychoanalytic Quarterly*, 1941, 10, 66–94.

GROSSMAN, H. J., & GREENBERG, N. H. Psychosomatic differentiation in infancy. I. Autonomic activity in the newborn. *Psychosomatic Medicine*, 1957, 19, 293–306.

GUERTIN, W. H. Are differences in schizophrenic symptoms related to the mother's avowed attitudes toward child rearing? *Journal of Abnormal and Social Psychology*, 1961, 63, 440–442.

HAJDU-GRIMES, LILLY. Contributions to the etiology of schizophrenia. *Psychoanalytic Review*, 1940, 27, 421–438.

HATTWICK, BERTA W. Interrelations between the preschool child's behavior and certain factors in the home. *Child Development*, 1936, 7, 200–226.

HATTWICK, BERTA W., & STOWELL, MARGARET. The relation of parental over-attentiveness to children's work habits and social adjustment in kindergarten and the first six grades of school. *Journal of Educational Research*, 1936, 30, 169–176.

HEILBRUN, A. B. Perception of maternal childbearing attitures in schizophrenics. *Journal of Consulting Psychology*, 1960, 24, 169–173.

HOLLOWAY, EDITH. A study of fifty-eight problem children, with emphasis upon the home situation as a causative factor in producing conflict. *Smith College Studies in Social Work*, 1931, 1, 403.

HUSCHKA, MABEL. Psychopathological disorders in the mother. *Journal of Nervous and Mental Disease*, 1941, 94, 76–33.

INGHAM, H. V. A statistical study of family relationships in psychoneurosis. *American Journal of Psychiatry*, 1949, 106, 91–98.

INLOW, RUBY S. The home as a factor in the development of the psychosis. *Smith College Studies in Social Work*, 1933, 4, 153–154.

JACOBSEN, VIRGINIA. Influential factors in the outcome of treatment of school phobia. *Smith College Studies in Social Work*, 1947, 19, 181–202.

JOHNSON, ADELAIDE M., FALSTEIN, E. I., SZUREK, S. A., & SVENDSEN, MARGARET. School phobia. *American Journal of Orthopsychiatry*, 1941, 11, 702–711.

JOST, H., & SONTAG, L. W. The genetic factor in autonomic nervous system function. *Psychosomatic Medicine*, 1944, 6, 308–310.

KARON, B. P., & ROSBERG, J. Study of the mother-child relationship in a case of paranoid schizophrenia. *American Journal of Psychotherapy*, 1958, 12, 522–533.

KASANIN, J., KNIGHT, ELIZABETH, & SAGE, PRISCILLA. The parent-child relationship in schizophrenia. *Journal of Nervous and Mental Disease*, 1934, 79, 249–263.

KOHN, M. L., & CLAUSEN, J. A. Parental authority behavior and schizophrenia. *American Journal of Orthopsychiatry*, 1956, 26, 297–313.

KUNDERT, ELIZABETH. Fear of desertion by mother. *American Journal of Orthopsychiatry*, 1947, 17, 326–336.

LACEY, J. I. Individual differences in somatic response patterns. *Journal of Comparative and Physiological Psychology*, 1950, 43, 338–350.

LAMPRON, EDNA M. Children of schizophrenic parents. *Mental Hygiene*, 1933, 17, 82–91.

LANE, R. C., & SINGER, J. L. Familial attitudes in paranoid schizophrenics and normals from two socioeconomic classes. *Journal of Abnormal and Social Psychology*, 1959, 59, 328–339.

LEVY, D. M. Maternal overprotection and rejection. *Archives of Neurology and Psychiatry*, 1931, 25, 886–889.

LEVY, D. M. On the problem of delinquency. *American Journal of Orthopsychiatry*, 1932, 2, 197–211.

LEVY, D. M. Primary affect hunger. *American Journal of Psychiatry*, 1937, 94, 643–652.

LEVY, D. M. *Maternal overprotection.* New York: Columbia Univer. Press, 1943.

221

LIDZ, T., CORNELISON, ALICE R., FLECK, S., & TERRY, DOROTHY. The intrafamilial environment of the schizophrenic patient: I. The father. *Psychiatry*, 1957, 20, 329–342. (a)

LIDZ, T., CORNELISON, ALICE R., FLECK, S., & TERRY, DOROTHY. The intrafamilial environment of schizophrenic patients: II. Marital schism and marital skew. *American Journal of Psychiatry*, 1957, 114, 241–248. (b)

LIDZ, T., CORNELISON, ALICE R., FLECK, S., & TERRY, DOROTHY. The intrafamilial environment of the schizophrenic patient. *Psychiatry*, 1957, 20, 329–342. (c)

LIDZ, T., CORNELISON, ALICE, TERRY, DOROTHY, & FLECK, S. Intrafamilial environment of the schizophrenic patient: VI. The transmisison of irrationality. *Archives of Neurology and Psychiatry*, 1958, 79, 305–316.

LIDZ, RUTH W., & LIDZ, T. The family environment of schizophrenic patients. *American Journal of Psychiatry*, 1949, 106, 332–345.

LIDZ, T., PARKER, NEULAH, & CORNELISON, ALICE. The role of the father in the family environment of the schizophrenic patient. *American Journal of Psychiatry*, 1956, 113, 126–137.

LOWREY, L. G. Personality distortion and early institutional care. *American Journal of Orthopsychiatry*, 1940, 10, 576–585.

MADOW, L., & HARDY, S. E. Incidence and analysis of the broken family in the background of neurosis. *American Journal of Orthopsychiatry*, 1947, 17, 521–528.

MARK, J. C. The attitudes of the mothers of male schizophrenics toward child behavior. *Journal of Abnormal and Social Psychology*, 1953, 48, 185–189.

McCORD, W., McCORD, JOAN, & HOWARD, A. Familial correlates of aggression in nondelinquent male children. *Journal of Abnormal and Social Psychology*, 1961, 62, 79–93.

McKEOWN, J. E. The behavior of parents of schizophrenic, neurotic, and normal children. *American Journal of Sociology*, 1950, 56, 175–179.

MEYERS, D. I., & GOLDFARB, W. Studies of perplexity in mothers of schizophrenic children. *American Journal of Orthopsychiatry*, 1961, 31, 551–564.

MEYERS, D., & GOLDFARB, W. Psychiatric appraisals of parents and siblings of schizophrenic children. *American Journal of Psychiatry*, 1962, 118, 902–908.

MILLER, H., & BARUCH, D. A study of hostility in allergic children. *American Journal of Orthopsychiatry*, 1950, 20, 506–519.

MUELLER, DOROTHY D. Paternal domination: Its influence on child guidance results. *Smith College Studies in Social Work*, 1945, 15, 184–215.

NEWELL, H. W. The psycho-dynamics of maternal rejection. *American Journal of Orthopsychiatry*, 1934, 4, 387–401.

NEWELL, H. W. A further study of maternal rejection. *American Journal of Orthopsychiatry*, 1936, 6, 576–589.

OLTMAN, JANE E., McGARRY, J. J., & FRIEDMAN, S. Parental deprivation and the "broken home" in dementia praecox and other mental disorders. *American Journal of Psychiatry*, 1952, 108, 685–694.

OPLER, M. K. Schizophrenia and culture. *Scientific American*, 1957, 197, 103–110.

ORLANSKY, H. Infant care and personality. *Psychological Bulletin*, 1949, 46, 1–48.

PEARSON, G. H. Some early factors in the formation of personality. *American Journal of Orthopsychiatry*, 1931, 1, 284–291.

PERR, H. M. Criteria distinguishing parents of schizophrenic and normal children. *Archives of Neurology and Psychiatry*, 1958, 79, 217–224.

PLANK, R. The family constellation of a group of schizophrenic patients. *American Journal of Orthopsychiatry*, 1953, 23, 817–825.

POLLOCK, H. M., & MALZBERG, B. Hereditary and environmental factors in the causation of manic-depressive psychoses and dementia praecox. *American Journal of Psychiatry*, 1940, 96, 1227–1244.

POLLOCK, H. M., MALZBERG, B., & FULLER, R. G. Hereditary and environmental factors in the causation of dementia praecox and manic-depressive psychoses. *Psychiatric Quarterly*, 1936, 10, 495–509.

PRESTON, G. H., & ANTIN, ROSEMARY. A study of children of psychotic parents. *American Journal of Orthopsychiatry*, 1932, 2, 231–241.

PROUT, C. T., & WHITE, MARY A. A controlled study of personality relationships in mothers of schizophrenic male patients. *American Journal of Psychiatry*, 1950, 107, 251–256.

REICHARD, SUZANNE, & TILLMAN, C. Patterns of parent-child relationships in schizophrenia. *Psychiatry*, 1950, 13, 247–257.

RIBBLE, MARGARETHE A. Disorganizing factors of infant personality. *American Journal of Psychiatry*, 1941, 98, 459–463.

RICHARDS, T. W., & NEWBERY, HELEN. Studies in fetal behavior: III. Can performance on test items at six months postnatally be predicted on the basis of fetal activity? *Child Development*, 1938, 9, 79–86.

RICHMOND, J. B., & LUSTMAN, S. L. Autonomic function in the neonate: I. Implications for psychosomatic theory. *Psychosomatic Medicine*, 1955, 17, 269–275.

SCHOFIELD, W., & BALIAN, L. A comparative study of the personal histories of schizophrenic and nonpsychiatric patients. *Journal of Abnormal and Social Psychology*, 1959, 59, 216–225.

SEARS, R. R. Relation of early socialization experiences to aggression in middle childhood. *Journal of Abnormal and Social Psychology*, 1961, 63, 466–492.

SEARS, R. R., WHITING, J. W. M., NOWLIS, V., & SEARS, PAULINE S. Some child-rearing antecedents of aggression and dependency in young children. *Genetic Psychology Monographs*, 1953, 47, 133–234.

SHAW, C. R., & MCKAY, H. D. Are broken homes a causative factor in juvenile delinquency? *Social Forces*, 1932, **10**, 514–524.

SHOBEN, E. J. The assessment of parental attitudes in relation to child adjustment. *Genetic Psychology Monographs*, 1949, **39**, 101–148.

SILBERPFENNIG, JUDITH. Mother types encountered in child guidance clinics. *American Journal of Orthopsychiatry*, 1941, **11**, 475–484.

SILVERMAN, B. The behavior of children from broken homes. *American Journal of Orthopsychiatry*, 1935, **5**, 11–18.

SINGER, J. L. Projected familial attitudes as a function of socioeconomic status and psychopathology. *Journal of Consulting Psychology*, 1954, **18**, 99–104.

SPERLING, MELITTA. The role of the mother in psychosomatic disorders in children. *Psychosomatic Medicine*, 1949, **11**, 377–385.

SPERLING, MELITTA. The neurotic child and his mother: A psychoanalytic study. *American Journal of Orthopsychiatry*, 1951, **21**, 351–362.

SPITZ, R. A. Hospitalism: An inquiry into the genesis of psychiatric conditions in early childhood. *Psychoanalytic Study of the Child*, 1945, **1**, 53–74.

STEIN, LUCILLE H. A study of over-inhibited and unsocialized-aggressive children. *Smith College Studies in Social Work*, 1944, **15**, 124–125.

STRINGER, JOYCE R. Case studies of the families of schizophrenics. *Smith College Studies in Social Work*, 1962, **32**, 118–148.

STRODTBECK, F. L. Husband-wife interaction over revealed differences. *American Sociological Review*, 1951, **16**, 468–473.

SUTTENFIELD, VIRGINIA. School phobia: A study of five cases. *American Journal of Orthopsychiatry*, 1954, **24**, 368–380.

TALBOT, MIRA. School Phobia: A workshop: I. Panic in school phobia. *American Journal of Orthopsychiatry*, 1957, **27**, 286–295.

THERON, P. A. Peripheral vasomotor reaction as indices of basic emotional tension and lability. *Psychosomatic Medicine*, 1948, **10**, 335–346.

TIETZE, TRUDE. A study of mothers of schizophrenic patients. *Psychiatry*, 1949, **12**, 55–65.

VAN DER MERWE, A. B. The diagnostic value of peripheral vasomotor reactions in the psychoneuroses. *Psychosomatic Medicine*, 1948, **10**, 347–354.

VAN DER MERWE, A. B., & THERON, P. A. A new method of measuring emotional stability. *Journal of General Psychology*, 1947, **37**, 109–124.

VAN HOUTEN, JANNY. Mother-child relationships in twelve cases of school phobia. *Smith College Studies in Social Work*, 1948, **18**, 161–180.

WAHL, C. W. Some antecedent factors in the family histories of 392 schizophrenics. *American Journal of Psychiatry*, 1954, **110**, 668–676.

WAHL, C. W. Some antecedent factors in the family histories of 568 male schizophrenics of the United States Navy. *American Journal of Psychiatry*, 1956, **113**, 201–210.

WALDFOGEL, S., HAHN, PAULINE B., & GARDNER, G. E. A study of school phobia in children. *Journal of Nervous and Mental Disease*, 1954, **120**, 399.

WALLACE, RAMONA. A study of the relationship between emotional tone of the home and adjustment status in cases referred to a travelling child guidance clinic. *Journal of Juvenile Research*, 1935, **19**, 205–220.

WALTERS, JEAN H. A study of the family relationships of schizophrenic patients. *Smith College Studies in Social Work*, 1939, **9**, 189–191.

WATSON, G. A. A comparison of the effects of lax versus strict home training. *Journal of Social Psychology*, 1934, **5**, 102–105.

WENGER, M. A. The measurement of individual differences in autonomic balance. *Psychosomatic Medicine*, 1941, **3**, 427–434.

WILE, I. S., & JONES, ANN B. Ordinal position and the behavior disorders of young children. *Journal of Genetic Psychology*, 1937, **51**, 61–93.

WILLIAMS, H. D. Causes of social maladjustment in children. *Psychological Monographs*, 1932, **43**(1, Whole No. 194)

WILSON, MARGARET J. Grandmother, mother, and daughter in cases of school phobia. *Smith College Studies in Social Work*, 1955, **25**, 56–57.

WINDER, C. L., & KANTOR, R. E. Rorschach maturity scores of the mothers of schizophrenics. *Journal of Consulting Psychology*, 1958, **22**, 438–440.

WITMER, HELEN L. Parental behavior as an index to the probable outcome of treatment in a child guidance clinic. *American Journal of Orthopsychiatry*, 1933, **3**, 431–444.

ZIMMERMAN, ANNA C. Parental adjustments and attitudes in relation to the problems of five- and six-year-old children. *Smith College Studies in Social Work*, 1930, **1**, 406–407.

ZUCKERMAN, M., OLTEAN, MARY, & MONASHKIN, I. The parental attitudes of mothers of schizophrenics. *Journal of Consulting Psychology*, 1958, **22**, 307–310.

Parent Group Discussions:
A Preventive Mental Health Technique

HELEN A. DeRosis

Background

The approach to be described here has been developed in the context of mental health rather than that of mental illness. In 1966 the author began working as a psychiatric consultant to a public school in New York City. Although the school personnel were needful of direct psychiatric services for the large numbers of children who were disturbed both academically and socially, efforts began to be directed toward an attempt to reduce the incidence of disease in children who might require these services in the future. Energies were therefore turned toward direct preventive services.

Studies revealed the need for, and the method of, prevention in industry, the military, the community and groups in general. An excellent collection is found in a Walter Reed Army Medical Center Publication of 1957. Other papers deal more with a sense of frustration regarding prevention. ". . . these (preventive) truths are too diffuse for scientific application to human beings in a democracy." (Action for Mental Health, 1961) In 1958, Robert Hunt stated, "Our hopes of preventing mental illness by mental health education and child guidance clinics have been disappointed. . ."

Also, in 1958, Abraham Kardiner stated that the greatest responsibility of psychoanalysis lay in "prophylaxis." Much later, in 1967, Geoffrey Esty stressed the necessity of underscoring wellness, and how to achieve and/or maintain it. He coined a new *specialty of wellness* which might be the joint responsibility of medicine and public health.

Following some consultative work, a preventive program was initiated in two Manhattan West Side schools. It had a threefold purpose: (1) to demonstrate that a preventive service could be rendered to school children by having their parents attend group discussions in the school every week. The approach was an educative one and the discussions were geared to effect changes in parental attitudes; (2) to train school personnel (i.e., guidance counselors) so that they could conduct parent groups in their own schools, thereby broadening the effect of preventive procedures; (3) To demonstrate that psychiatrists and psychoanalysts could shift their skills and training as therapists into useful tools for use in a new *educational psychiatry*. This program has already been described elsewhere and will not be detailed here. (DeRosis, 1968) The methodology which evolved was not only a simple one to apply in a group, but it seemed to be

FAMILY COORDINATOR, 1970, Vol. 19, pp. 329-334.

applicable to different groups, regardless of educational, social, or economic backgrounds. Further, it could be easily demonstrated in a group, could be conveyed to the parents as a do-it-yourself technique, and could be taught to guidance and other school personnel. The person who conducts the groups is called the *group coordinator*.

The simplified group technique used in preventive mental health work with parents involves three major elements: identification, planning, and action.

Identification

To identify the actual is to state the facts and not the fantasy of the matter. This refers to a knowledge of something, and can be best explained by an example. Mrs. B., the mother of a fourteen-year-old boy, complained to the group that her son never talked with her. She found it increasingly difficult to initiate a conversation and felt that the boy was becoming more and more estranged from her. She attributed this to the fact that he was fourteen years old and that he was "rebelling" as all good teenagers are supposed to do. Nevertheless, she took small comfort in this fact and expressed a measure of despair with the situation. Her identification of this situation included the following: (1) her son was fourteen, (2) he was therefore rebelling, and (3) he never talked with her. The group coordinator accepted these statements only as an incomplete identification, and began to help the parent with further identification. The following dialogue took place. (GC will refer to group coordinator.)

GC: You say he never talks to you?
Parent: Well, hardly ever.
GC: When does he speak to you?
Parent: Oh, he never does.
GC: Does he talk with you in the morning?
Parent: He's pretty grumpy in the morning.
GC: Did he talk with you this week?
Parent: Oh, I don't remember, He just doesn't seem to want to talk with me.
GC: You haven't talked with him all week, then?
Parent: Oh yes, we've talked sometime.
GC: When?
Parent: I don't remember.
GC: Did you talk yesterday?

Parent: Well, he comes bursting in after school and he's starved and so full of everything. So I give him some milk and cookies and he starts to tell me all about school. I'm usually busy then, so I tell him to tell me later.

When she gave this latter bit of information, the other group members seemed surprised. They had been following the above dialogue with increasing interest, not fully believing that this son never spoke with his mother, yet not fully convinced that it was not true. Her description of the boy's behavior after school revealed that the boy was eager to relate the happenings of the day in an enthusiastic outburst while they were still fresh, and while he was still very much involved with them. It was clear that she had no interest in what he had to say to her. She was asked by a group member, (GM):

GM: Then what happens?
Parent: He eats and goes out, or does his homework. Then later on, after dinner when I'm finished with the dishes and the kitchen, I ask him to tell me what he wanted to say earlier. 'Aw, forget it' he says, and no matter how much I try to get him to talk, he just won't.

At this point the other parents pointed out that this boy did talk with her, and wanted to talk with her, but that the timing seemed to be off. He wanted to talk at 3:30 and she wanted to talk at 9:30. She was not interested in what he had to say at 3:30 and he was not interested in saying anything at 9:30.

It might be well to mention here that at no time is a critical, derogatory attitude assumed on the part of the coordinator. As for the group members, they usually follow the cue of the coordinator. The questions raised are for the purpose of fact finding. The group members do not attack each other for evading, for being insensitive, nor do they behave in the hostile ways which are often in evidence in a group which seeks as its primary goal a therapeutic outcome. Since this is a *prevention* group (and only incidentally therapeutic), no member feels compelled to be treated or to contribute to the treatment of any other member. The general feeling tone of the group is one of curiosity and discovery. There is no high level of tension or anxiety, and most of the parents refer to the group as enjoyable and helpful. As for the technique, as soon as the trainee grasps the concept of fact finding in this particular context, he does not feel that he must be an authority of any kind. He merely co-ordinates the findings of the group members. These are elicited by simple, but relevant questioning. This coordinating process provides the rationale for the title of coordinator.

Mrs. B. was then asked if she wanted to find out more about the situation. She agreed and the identification procedure continued. A particular day was settled upon when the boy had come home and she had rejected his "talking." On that day, Mrs. B. was preparing something for dinner and was putting away some groceries. The question was raised regarding her ability to do this work and to listen to him at the same time. It appeared that this was possible. When asked what else she was doing, she replied that she was thinking. This "thinking" that a woman does while she is cooking, or cleaning, or doing any household chore can very well be thinking in fantasy form, and often is. This is not something which is easily relinquished by her because of the role it plays in her daily living.

Because of her own needs, then, Mrs. B. is not able to accept her son on his terms (when he wants to talk). Thus the identification of the actual facts in this situation were the following. (1) It was not true that the boy never spoke to his mother. (2) For her own reasons, she had no interest in his school activities and, therefore, none in him in relationship to these activities. However, this point cannot usually be made to the parent, because it would arouse more guilt than that with which she already comes burdened. The GC must recognize this point, but need not necessarily state it explicitly. For the parent to appreciate the poor timing of her show

of interest is usually enough for a preventive move to be initiated. No conclusion need be reached at that time. If the parent goes through only a show of interest when the youngster is ready, two things may occur. (1) The boy may find it pleasurable that his parent listens to him for a change. (2) The parent may find it pleasurable that her boy is talking to her. Although this exchange may lack the basic interest of the parent in the subject matter, there is no doubt that because of her effort, this exchange contains the beginnings of interest in establishing a communication with the son. This is enough for a start. This kind of 'practice' may make it possible for both son and parent to move closer to the goal of a mutually satisfying relationship.

The first phase, then, can be referred to by many names. The GC uses these many names in the group in order to familiarize the members with the process in as many ways as he can. Identifying the specific facts is also referred to as seeing them, or understanding them, or knowing them, or stating them, or underscoring them. This first step is the *what* of the situation. And it is clearly repeated over and over that while identification is necessary to any shift in attitude, it is only one part of a constellation of moves.

Planning

After identification takes place, the next phase begins to develop among the group members. Questions are raised, and possible alternatives are suggested and discussed. The repeated verbal participation on the part of the group members is the feature of this program which differentiates it from other educative approaches and which is crucial to its effectiveness. Although only one example may be given during the meeting, this example becomes a common denominator for each parent in the group. Each parent then is not merely listening to a member talk about something unrelated to him. As the one member speaks, each group member is often thinking of a similarity to his own situation. When the latter offers a suggestion, he is speaking for himself as well as for the other. Because of his interest, he is open to other comments made, perhaps even more open than the parent who produced the original material being discussed. This kind of involvement leads to a keener interest. This interest leads to more openness and involvement in the subject at hand. As in any learning process, more learning takes place by doing than by listening. In this case, the parent is 'doing' by his active, repeated participation in the group.

In this situation, the question was put to Mrs. B.: Why do you complain about something in which you have no interest? Mrs. B. insisted that even if she could not be genuinely interested in her boy's school news, she had to listen to him because it was necessary to his sense of self-importance. One Spanish-speaking mother stated flatly in understandable English, "So, if you decide to listen, you have to do it when he wants to talk, or else you won't have anything to listen to!" No one could deny the validity of this assessment. By now, the mother had come to the realization of the remarkable fact that she had been completely unaware of the quality of inattentiveness which she had manifested toward her son. Very often, the group discussion can be dropped at this point, either because some other point is made which is then pursued, or because the GC feels that there has been enough attention centered on this point for the time being. In any event, this focusing has been worth while, for it is unlikely that some of the discussion will not remain with the parent, and perhaps in the future it will enhance her awareness of her son's need at 3:30 in the afternoon, rather than at 9:30 in the evening. If this occurs, a preventive move has been instituted and its ramifications would be difficult to predict.

The alternatives which are discussed in this second stage depend entirely upon the content of the group discussion. A common problem which is discussed is the matter of children's bedtime and its accompanying irritations. Many parents are plagued with the child who takes one, two, or more hours to settle down each night. These are usually fairly young children. But the example may be used to illustrate the principle of the use of alternatives.

The first thing which has to be done in this context is to identify (1) the desire of the parent to get the child "out of the way" at bedtime after a long day and (2) the parent's mounting irritability when this activity is prolonged. The parents who have this problem often exclaim, "I've tried everything!" Everything usually refers to a set of activities which are gone through in a regular consecutive order, and include games, drinks, etc.

All the while the principle of permissiveness is being applied. But this application is often an ungrounded one because true permissiveness with children of any age can be only a condition of inner responsiveness to the child's demand. Either the child's behavior is "all right" with the parent, or it is not. If it is not, then any show of permissiveness is a pretense. When the parent is applying the principle of permissiveness without feeling permissive, then there is no permissiveness. A permissive state is an inner feeling state, or attitude, which is manifested by certain actions or lack of them. One cannot behave permissively without being permissive, and when one is permissive, there is very often no need to do anything. Permissiveness is not for everyone, simply because not everyone can have a permissive attitude.

Having to go through the above procedure almost every night, the parent indeed feels that he has been through "everything." The group members begin to discuss other ways of handling the problem. Although many parents have a similar problem, they are often much more clear-sighted regarding some other people's children than their own. Some spontaneous suggestions include: no stimulation before bedtime (no playing games, TV, etc.), warm bath and bed, a glass of water on the night table with ice in it (to anticipate the complaint that the water is not cold enough), etc. Other suggestions come: talking it over with the spouse, with relatives, with neighbors, with pediatrician, seeing a psychiatrist to find out if both parents are working together on the problem, or are subtly undermining each other, not feeling guilty if the permissive attitude is not adapted, etc. These various parental strategies may or may not be of use to some members. Whether they are workable or not remains to be demonstrated. But the important thing is the parent's opening awareness to the rich variety of alternatives that are available, and that he has, in all probability, not tried everything. The particular method tried will be the one that is most suitable for any particular family, and is not important in and of itself. Of greater importance is the family's identification of the problem as it exists in fact, and then learning to plan for alternative methods of dealing with it. Too often the parents resign themselves to a pattern of behavior in the child which causes distress to the entire family. In this case, no relief can be achieved. It is unlikely that continued efforts to change these conditions would meet with failure in the majority of cases. Consistent, relevant efforts to establish a different pattern for the child have to be made. Failure is sometimes due to the lack of this kind of effort, and not to any inherent failure factor. When the parent grasps the idea that there is no *one* way of handling this situation, he can often see the applicability of this principle in other areas of parental concern.

The planning phase, then, is that phase where the focus is on the seeking of other possibilities. These other possibilities are referred to as *alternatives*. In the context of the group, the member has the opportunity to observe how alternatives are arrived at. Any idea may be considered as an alternative course, although it may not necessarily be applicable to all group members. The member can practice this searching for alternatives in the group setting, so that when he is at home with his family he may be able to follow this procedure when a stressful situation arises. This planning phase is the thinking phase. As the identification phase exposes the *what* of the situation, this phase reveals to the parent the *how* of the situation.

Action

Talk is cheap. The parent, therefore, has to be helped to realize that planning must be followed by action. Action may consist of a verbalization of one of the possibilities discussed in the group. The effort to utter these few words, however, must be made definitively. Without these words (if such be the need), all remains in the realm of fantasy, with the continuous sop: "I'm going to try that tomorrow." Two lengthy examples of such action were described elsewhere by the author. (DeRosis, 1968)

There are no guarantees that such action will bring about the desired result. But there is the guarantee that without a new action, nothing new can happen. Sometimes the action may be a non-action (i.e., not doing something, or keeping quiet). But anyone who does something habitually (i.e., criticize, nag, remind, etc.) which he realizes is destructive to a relationship, knows how difficult it is not to criticize, nag, etc. It takes a deliberate effort to keep quiet under these circumstances. This may be considered action also.

In action there are always risks. The most inhibiting one is the risk of failure. If one identifies and plans and does not act, there is no clear-cut failure evident. But as soon as one performs an act, be it word or deed, then he can judge it as a success or failure.

When a parent is distressed by a way of being of his offspring, very often he can only be patient and wait for the child to outgrow that particular phase. Later on, the characteristics which surface are often likely to be more lasting, and have to be met therefore with acceptance and respect, if not approval.

The action phase, then, is the phase of doing, where the information gleaned and the possible alternatives discovered and mulled over become aspects of a definite course of action, for better or worse. This is where the actual effort beyond that of group discussion and thinking is required. This might be called the *when* phase of this three step procedure. After the *what* of phase one, and the *how* of phase two have been considered, the when is *now*. This is the basic message to the parent. He cannot only think, worry, or complain about his children. If the parent does not sometimes succeed, he must continue his efforts, in spite of his discouragement. Objective, trained professionals are the ones who must provide the encouragement the parent requires to continue these efforts. If one believes that the parent is *the primary preventive agent in a program for prevention,* one cannot afford to permit his bouts of discouragement to be lasting. He must be constantly receiving support. It is a formidable responsibility and perhaps the greatest challenge which has ever faced the helping professions.

REFERENCES:

DeRosis, H. A Preventive Community Psychiatry Project and Its Relationship to Psychoanalytic Principles, *American Journal of Psychoanalysis.* 1968, 28, 129-138.

Esty, G. W. The Prevention of Psychosocial Disorders of Youth: A Challenge to Mental Health, Public Health, and Education. *The Journal of School Health,* 1967, 37, 19-23.

Joint Commission on Mental Illness and Health. *Action for Mental Health.* New York: Basic Books, 1961.

Kardiner, A. New Horizons and Responsibilities of Psychoanalysis. *American Journal of Psychoanalysis.* 1958, 18, 115-126.

Walter Reed Army Medical Center and National Council. Symposium on Preventive and Social Psychiatry. Walter Reed Army Institute of Research, 1957.

MOTHERS AS BEHAVIOR THERAPISTS FOR
THEIR OWN CHILDREN

ROBERT G. WAHLER , GARY H. WINKEL, ROBERT F. PETERSON and
DELMONT C. MORRISON

Two reviews of the literature on behavior therapy (Bandura, 1961; Grossberg, 1964) reveal a large number of systematic attempts to apply principles of learning theory to psychotherapy. It would appear that many investigators, working within the conceptual frameworks of respondent and operant learning, have produced practical changes in the deviant behavior of both adults and children.

Typically, these investigators have implied that stimuli making up the adult's or child's natural environments are responsible for development and maintenance of the deviant behaviors involved. That is, through unfortunate contingencies between stimuli, or between stimuli and behavior, deviant behavior is produced and maintained. However, while most investigators have assumed that this is true, few have accepted the full implications of this position. Instead of changing "faulty" contingencies involving the natural environment, most research therapists have placed their subjects in artificial environments, designed to modify the deviant behavior through extinction, punishment, and/or reinforcement of responses which are incompatible with the deviant behavior. Although these techniques have produced some remarkable changes in the deviant behavior within the artificial environments—and in some cases within the natural environments—one wonders about the effect that the unmodified natural environments would eventually have on the behavior changes; logically, it would be expected that the deviant behavior would again be strengthened, and behavior developed in the artificial environments would be weakened.

From the standpoint of methodology there is good reason for the behavior therapists' failure to deal with the natural environment. Since the efficacy of their techniques depends upon control of specific contingencies between stimuli, or between stimuli and behavior, they have typically chosen to work in settings that are highly contrived. However, the extent of this methodological problem is, in large part, correlated with the patient's age. Undoubtedly, the natural environment of the young child is far less complex than that of

BEHAVIOR RESEARCH AND THERAPY, 1965, Vol. 3, pp. 113-124.

an adolescent or an adult, and it therefore should present fewer difficulties in systematic control. One might conclude that attempts to develop therapeutic techniques for the control of natural environments should initially utilize children as patient–subjects.

Most psychotherapists assume that a child's parents compose the most influential part of his natural environment. It is likely, from a learning theory viewpoint, that their behaviors serve a large variety of stimulus functions, controlling both the respondent and operant behaviors of their children. It then follows that if some of the child's behavior is considered to be deviant at a particular time in his early years, his parents are probably the source of eliciting stimuli and reinforcers which have produced, and are currently maintaining this behavior. A logical procedure for the modification of the child's deviant behavior would involve changing the parents' behavior. These changes would be aimed at training them both to eliminate the contingencies which currently support their child's deviant behavior, and to provide new contingencies to produce and maintain more normal behaviors which would compete with the deviant behavior.

Techniques of parent-child psychotherapy have been investigated by several researchers (Prince, 1961; Russo, 1964; Straughan, 1964). However, the procedures used in these studies did not permit assessment of variables which were maintaining the children's deviant behavior, nor did they permit analyses of those variables which were responsible for changing the deviant behavior. While the investigators concluded that changes in the children's deviant behavior were probably a function of changes in the parents' behavior, these conclusions could not be clearly supported. Thus, in the further study of parent–child therapeutic techniques it would be of value to utilize procedures which will provide information concerning those stimulus events provided by the parents which function to maintain deviant classes of the child's behavior. Once these controlling stimulus events are detected, it might prove feasible to modify the occurrence of these events in ways which will produce predictable and clinically significant changes in the child's behavior.

The present experiment was an attempt to modify the deviant behavior of three children by producing specific changes in the behavior of their mothers. The major purposes of the study were: (1) to experimentally analyze the mother–child interbehaviors in an effort to specify those variables (i.e. reinforcement contingencies) which may function to maintain the deviant behavior of the children; (2) to eliminate these variables in an effort to modify the children's deviant behavior. Therefore, the focus of the study was not on producing long term changes in the children, but rather to discover how their deviant behavior is maintained and how appropriate changes may be brought about.

METHOD

Subjects and apparatus

Subjects were three boys varying in age from four to six years and their respective mothers. While the children's behavior problems would probably be considered moderate by most clinical standards, all had exhibited behavior which was sufficiently deviant to motivate their parents to seek psychological help. More detailed information on the children and their mothers will be presented in a later section.

The apparatus was located in the Gatzert Child Development Clinic of the University of Washington. The equipment consisted of a playroom with two adjoining observation rooms which were equipped for visual and auditory monitoring of behavior in the playroom. Each observation room contained a panel with three microswitches which were connected to a Gerbrand six-channel event recorder; depression of the microswitches by observers activated selected channels of the event recorder. In addition, the playroom was equipped with a signal light which could be illuminated by the experimenter in one of the observation rooms.

General procedure

Prior to the behavior therapy sessions, the parents of each child were seen in interviews aimed at obtaining descriptions of the behavior which created problems at home and/or at school. The interviewer also asked the parents to describe their typical reactions to these behavior patterns whenever they occurred.

All mother–child cases were seen separately for approximately twenty-minute sessions, held once or twice weekly in the playroom. The mother and her child were always the sole occupants of the playroom.

Classification of mother–child interbehavior. For the first two sessions, the mother was instructed, "Just play with——as you might at home". These instructions were modified for one of the cases when a later analysis of the data revealed little or no evidence of what the parents had earlier described as deviant behavior. In this case the mother was given other instructions, based on her description of her typical behavior at home.

During these sessions, two observers, working in separate observation rooms, obtained complete written records of the child's and the mother's behavior. Analysis of these records began with a selection of the child's deviant behavior. This selection was based upon similarities between the recorded behavior and the behavior which the parents reported to create problems at home. A second classification of the child's behavior was made to establish a class of behavior which the experimenter regarded as incompatible with the deviant behavior. Later, strengthening of this class was used in eliminating the deviant behavior.

A second analysis of the written records involved a description of the mother's ways of reacting to her child's deviant behavior, and to his incompatible behavior. Essentially, this analysis provided a description of possible reinforcers provided by the mother for the two classes of the child's behavior.

Observer reliability and baseline measures of behavior. Following the classification sessions, instructions to the mother were the same; however, the observers now recorded only three classes of behavior—two for the child (deviant behavior and incompatible behavior) and one for the mother (her reactions to her child's behavior classes). This was done by depressing selected microswitches every five seconds for any of the previously classified deviant or incompatible behavior patterns which occurred during the five-second intervals. Another microswitch was reserved for any behavior of the mother's which occurred immediately after the child's two classes of behavior. Essentially, this system was a time-saving device which eliminated the laborious procedure of writing down behavior and then classifying it. Thus, once the child's deviant and incompatible behaviors, and the mother's reactions to them were defined and labeled by the experimenter, the observers' attention in further sessions was focused only on these behavior patterns.

The observational records obtained from the above sessions were also analysed for observer reliability. For each behavior class an agreement or disagreement was tallied for every five-second interval. The percentage of agreements for observers was then computed for each behavior class, for each session. Observer agreement of ninety per cent or better was considered to be adequate; once this agreement was obtained on all behavior classes the baseline sessions were begun. Essentially, the baseline sessions provided a measure of the strength or rate of occurrence of the child's deviant or incompatible behavior, and a measure of how frequently the mother responded to them. These sessions were continued until both mother and child showed fairly stable behavioral rates.

Before the baseline sessions were begun, one of the observers was arbitrarily chosen to record the data, and the other observer served only as a reliability check. In all cases reliability checks showed observer agreement of ninety per cent or better.

Behavior modification procedures. Following the baseline sessions, E made systematic attempts to change the mother's reactions to her child's behavior. These attempts involved the use of instructions to the mother before and after the playroom sessions, plus signal light communications to her during the sessions. During initial sessions, E used the signal light as a cueing system, essentially to tell the mother when and how to behave in response to her child's behavior. As the mother improved in her ability to follow instructions, E eventually changed the function of the signal light from cueing system to reinforcement system. The mother was now required to discriminate and respond appropriately to her child's behavior without E's cueing. E used the signal light to provide immediate feedback to the mother concerning her correct and incorrect discriminations, thus teaching her appropriate discrimination responses.

Instructions and the coded significance of the signal light were determined from the baseline data and principles of operant learning theory. In general, the aim was to eliminate possible reinforcers provided by the mother for her child's deviant behavior, but to have her produce them following the child's incompatible behavior. It was thus hoped to train the mother to weaken her child's deviant behavior through a combination of extinction, and by reinforcement of behavior which would compete with the deviant behavior. To accomplish these goals, the mother was first shown the baseline data and given a complete explanation of it; she was also given numerous examples of her child's deviant behavior and his incompatible behavior. She was then told that in further sessions she must completely ignore her child's deviant behavior and respond in any approving way only to his incompatible behavior. The signal light was described to her as an aid which would help her to carry out the instructions. She was told to keep an eye on the light and to respond to her child *only* if it was illuminated; otherwise she was to sit in a chair, ostensibly reading a book and make no verbal or non-verbal contact with her child. E, of course, illuminated the light only following the child's incompatible behavior. In one case, where the child's deviant behavior proved to be ususually resistant to extinction, the mother was trained in the use of a punishment technique as well as the differential reinforcement procedure.

When the observational data revealed that the mother was responding appropriately to the signal light, she was told that in later sessions she must make her own decisions to respond or not respond to her child. She was again told to keep an eye on the light, since it would now be illuminated following her correct decisions.

Experimental demonstration of mother's control. As later results will indicate, the behavior modification procedures appeared to be effective in producing expected changes in the behavior of the mothers and their children. However, there yet remained the task of demonstrating that modification of the child's behavior was solely a function of the mother's ways of reacting to him. In further sessions the mother was instructed to react to her child as she had done during the baseline sessions; that is, to again be responsive to the deviant behavior. If the mother's reactions to her child during the behavior modification sessions had been responsible for weakening his deviant behavior, one would expect that this procedure would strengthen the deviant behavior. Once this test for control had been made, the mother was instructed to again make her reinforcement contingent only upon the incompatible behavior, thus resuming her "therapeutic" ways of reacting to him.

RESULTS

Case number one

Danny was a six-year old boy who was brought to the Child Development Clinic by his parents, because of his frequent attempts to force then to comply with his wishes. According to the parents, he virtually determined his own bedtime, foods he would eat, when the parents would play with him, and other household activities. In addition, he frequently attempted, with less success, to manipulate his teacher and peers. His parents reported they were simply "unable" to refuse his demands, and had rarely attempted to ignore or punish him. On the few occasions when they had refused him, they quickly relented when he began to shout or cry.

During the classification and baseline sessions, Danny's mother reported that she was extremely uncomfortable, because of Danny's behavior and her knowledge that she was

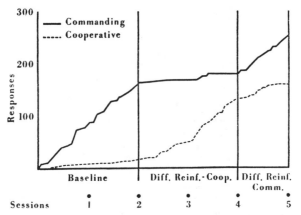

Fig. 1. Rate measures of Danny's commanding and cooperative behavior over baseline and therapy sessions.

being observed. Figure 1 shows cumulative records of Danny's deviant and incompatible behaviors during all therapy sessions. His deviant behavior was labelled as "commanding behavior" during the classification sessions, and was defined as any verbal or non-verbal instructions to his mother (e.g. pushes his mother into a chair; "Now we'll play this;" "You go over there and I'll stay here;" "No, that's wrong. Do it this way."). The incompatible behavior, labelled as "cooperative behavior", was defined as non-imperative

234

statements or actions or by questions. Note the marked difference in rate between the deviant and incompatible behaviors during the two baseline sessions. Figure 2 shows

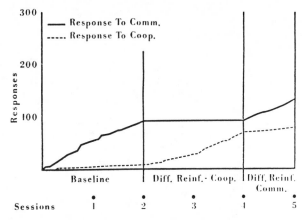

FIG. 2. Rate measures of Mother's general responses to Danny's commanding and cooperative behavior over baseline and therapy sessions.

cumulative records of the mother's general reactions to Danny's two behavior classes during the therapy sessions. Her reactions usually consisted of following Danny's instructions and such verbal comments as "Okay, if that's what you think; am I doing it right now?"

Following the baseline sessions the mother was instructed to be responsive to Danny's cooperative behavior but to completely ignore his commanding behavior. Reference to Fig. 2 indicates that she was successful in following these instructions. During the first two differential reinforcement sessions her rate of response to his commanding behavior dropped to zero, while her response to his cooperative behavior increased steadily in rate. (Use of the signal light as a cueing system was discontinued for the second differential reinforcement session.) Danny's behavior during the differential reinforcement sessions is shown in Fig. 1. Note that his rate of commanding behavior dropped considerably compared to the baseline sessions, while his cooperative behavior increased sharply in rate. Interestingly enough, Danny's mother reported that she was much more comfortable with him during the last of these sessions.

The test of Mother's control was performed following the first two differential reinforcement sessions. This one session demonstration involved instructing the mother to behave as she had done during the baseline sessions. As the rate of response curves in Figs. 1 and 2 indicate, change in the mother's behavior was again correlated with the expected change in Danny's behavior; his rate of commanding behavior increased compared to the previous two sessions, and his cooperative behavior declined in rate. Thus, the finding that Danny's commanding and cooperative behaviors could be weakened when his mother's reactions to these classes were eliminated, and strengthened when they were replaced, points with some certainty to the fact that her behavior changes were responsible for the changes in Danny's behavior.

Further sessions were planned to reinstate the contingencies of the first differential reinforcement sessions. Again the mother was instructed to reinforce only the cooperative behavior; unfortunately, administrative problems made it necessary to terminate this case before the sessions could be conducted.

Case number two

Johnny, age four, was brought to the Clinic by his parents because of what they termed "very dependent" behavior. In addition, they were concerned about a nursery-school teacher's report that he frequently hit or kicked his peers and teacher when they were inattentive to him. According to his mother, Johnny rarely showed this behavior at home, but instead tended to follow her around the house much of the day, asking questions and requesting her help for various tasks. She, in turn, tended to be very responsive to this behavior and also tended to interrupt him when he played alone or with his peers. When asked why she behaved in these ways, she reported that she was quite concerned about the possibility that he might break things in the house or get into trouble with his playmates; she felt much more comfortable when he was at her side or at least within sight.

Johnny's teachers felt that his aggressive behavior in nursery school was related to his "dependence on others for direction and support". They stated that if he was told what to do, or if a teacher watched him or played with him, the hitting and kicking was not likely to occur. However, it was also apparent from the teacher's report that, inadvertently, they may have been providing social reinforcement for his aggressive behavior.

Following an analysis of the classification session, two classes of Johnny's behavior were defined; the deviant class was labeled "dependent behavior," which included such behavior as questions and non-verbal requests for help (e.g. bringing a toy to her following a request for her to play with it or to show him how it works). Aggressive behavior, such as hitting or kicking did not occur. Behavior considered incompatible with the deviant class was labeled "independent behavior." This class included any behavior in which he played alone, with no verbal comment to his mother.

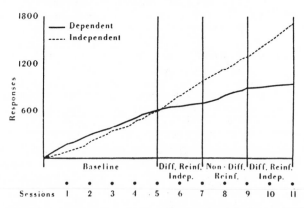

FIG. 3. Rate measures of Johnny's dependent and independent behavior over baseline and therapy sessions.

Figure 3 shows comulative records of Johnny's dependent and independent behaviors during all therapy sessions. Note that the response rates for his two behavior classes during the baseline sessions are roughly comparable. Figure 4 shows cumulative records of

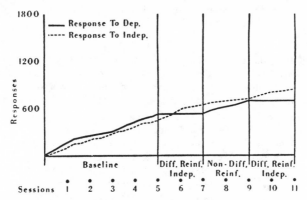

Fɪɢ. 4. Rate measures of Mother's general responses to Johnny's dependent and independent behavior over baseline and therapy sessions.

mother's general reactions to Johnny's two behavior classes during the therapy sessions. Her reactions to his dependent behavior usually involved answering his questions or granting his requests for help. Consistent with her self observations, Mother's reactions to Johnny's independent behavior almost always involved interrupting his play with imperative statements or non-verbal interference such as taking a toy away from him.

During the differential reinforcement sessions, Johnny's mother was instructed to ignore his dependency behavior and respond approvingly to his independent behavior. Reference to the differential reinforcement sessions shown in Fig. 4 indicate that she was successful in following these instructions, even following elimination of the cueing system after the first session. As the rate of response curves show, her rate of response to his independent behavior increased, and for his dependent behavior it dropped to zero. Correlated with his mother's behavior changes, Johnny's behavior changed in the expected ways. The rate of response curve for his dependent behavior, seen in Fig. 3, dropped compared to the baseline sessions, while his independent behavior increased in rate.

Following the two differential reinforcement sessions, the test of mother's control was performed. She was now instructed to resume her baseline behavior, and as the data indicate, she was successful in following these instructions; her response rates shown in the non-differential reinforcement sessions in Fig. 4, were roughly similar, and comparable to her baseline rates.

Again, correlated with these changes in Mother's behavior, Johnny's behavior changed in the expected ways. Reference to the non-differential reinforcement sessions of Fig. 3 shows that his response rates for the two behavior classes are comparable to his baseline rates.

The final two sessions involved reinstatement of Mother's differential reinforcement contingencies without use of the cueing system. The response rates shown in the last two sessions of Figs. 3 and 4 indicate that this procedure was effective. Therefore, as was true in case number one, the finding that Johnny's deviant and incompatible behavior patterns could be weakened when his mother's reactions to these classes were eliminated, and strengthened when they were replaced, supports the contention that her behavior changes were responsible for the changes in Johnny's behavior.

Case number three

Eddie, age four, was brought to the Clinic because of what his parents referred to as "extreme stubbornness." According to the parents, this behavior occurred only in the presence of Eddie's mother. Essentially, this "stubbornness" involved ignoring her commands and requests or doing the opposite of what he was told or asked to do.

She reported that her reactions to this behavior usually involved pleas, threats, and spankings, none of which appeared to be effective. It also became clear that most of her interactions with him were restricted to his oppositional behavior; she rarely played games with him, read to him, or talked to him. She did however, attempt to respond approvingly to his infrequent cooperative behavior. When asked why she was so selective in her interactions with him, she reported that because of his opposition, she felt "frustrated with him" and "angry with him" most of the time. She was convinced that he opposed her because he "liked" to get her angry.

During the classification sessions it became necessary to modify the instructions to Eddie's mother. Initially she was told to "just play with Eddie as you would at home." However, as might have been expected, mother and child ignored each other. The instructions were then changed to require mother to ask Eddie to play with a different toy every sixty seconds. These instructions were in effect throughout all therapy sessions. Eddie's behavior was classified as either oppositional (not complying with mother's request) or cooperative (complying).

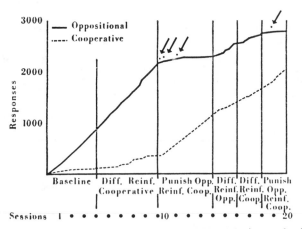

FIG. 5. Rate measures of Eddie's oppositional and cooperative behavior over baseline and therapy sessions.

Figure 5 shows cumulative records of Eddie's oppositional and cooperative behaviors during all therapy sessions Note that his rate of oppositional behavior during the baseline sessions is far greater than his rate of cooperative behavior Figure 6 shows cumulative records of Mother's general reactions to Eddie's two behavior classes Her reactions to his oppositional behavior almost always involved threats or repetition of her request. Following his few cooperative responses, she either ignored him or stated her approval in a low voice without smiling.

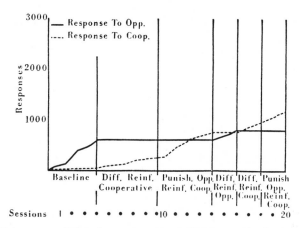

FIG. 6. Rate measures of Mother's general responses to Eddie's oppositional and cooperative behavior over baseline and therapy sessions.

During the differential reinforcement sessions, Eddie's mother was instructed to ignore his oppositional behavior and respond enthusiastically and with a smile to his cooperative behavior. As the differential reinforcement sessions shown in Fig. 6 indicate, she was successful in following the instructions and use of the cueing system was discontinued after the second session. Reference to the same sessions in Figure 5 indicates that the expected changes in Eddie's behavior occurred gradually as the sessions progressed. However, note that the increase in his rate of cooperative behavior was not marked, and it declined during the fourth and fifth differential reinforcement sessions. Because of this problem, E decided to instruct Mother in the use of a punishment procedure which could be combined with the differential reinforcement technique. She was instructed to isolate Eddie in an empty room (adjacent to the playroom) immediately following any of his oppositional responses. She was also told to leave him alone in this room for five minutes, unless he exhibited other undesirable behavior such as temper tantrums; if this type of behavior occurred, he remained in the room until it terminated.

Eddie's behavior during the punishment-reinforcement sessions is shown in Fig. 5. The arrows indicate those instances in which Mother was signaled via the cueing system, to initiate the punishment procedure. Note the marked change in Eddie's oppositional and cooperative behavior; his oppositional behavior declined sharply in rate while his rate of cooperative behavior increased markedly. As these records also indicate, modifications in

Eddie's behavior were maintained during the last two punishment-reinforcement sessions by Mother's use of differential reinforcement alone. Interestingly enough, Eddie's mother reported, following one of these latter sessions, that she "actually enjoyed being with him".

The test of Mother's control of Eddie's behavior was complicated by the fact that she had used two procedures in the course of the therapy sessions. As a result, two questions had to be answered: (1) Was Mother responsible for the changes in Eddie's behavior? (2) Was one of her procedures more important than the other in producing these changes? To answer these questions, Mother was first instructed to respond only to Eddie's oppositional behavior. The differential-reinforcement-oppositional sessions of Fig. 6 revealed that she was successful in following these instructions. Correlated with these changes in Mother's behavior, Eddie's oppositional behavior (Fig. 5) increased in rate, while his cooperative behavior declined in rate. Thus, it seemed certain that Mother was responsible for the earlier changes in Eddie's behavior. To determine whether Mother's differential reinforcement or differential reinforcement *plus* punishment had produced these changes, she was instructed in one set of sessions to resume her differential reinforcement of Eddie's cooperative behavior; in another set of sessions she was instructed to differentially reinforce the cooperative behavior and punish the oppositional behavior. Mother's success in following these instructions is shown in the last two sessions of Fig. 6 and by the arrow in the last session of Fig. 5. As Fig. 5 also indicates, the expected changes in Eddie's behavior occurred only during the last set of sessions, thus demonstrating that Mother's combined use of differential reinforcement and punishment was responsible for the modifications in Eddie's behavior.

DISCUSSION

The data from two of the cases reported in this study indicate that a mother's social behavior may function as a powerful class of positive reinforcers for her child's deviant as well as his normal behavior. Experimental analysis of case number one revealed that Danny's mother was maintaining his commanding and cooperative behavior patterns through her reactions to these two response classes. A similar experimental analysis of case number two showed that Johnny's mother was maintaining his dependent and independent behavior through her reactions to these response classes. In both of these cases the response rates of the children's deviant and incompatible behavior patterns were weakened when their mothers' contingent behavior was eliminated, and strengthened when they were replaced. It would thus seem beyond a reasonable possibility of coincidence that the children's behavior classes were under the control of their respective mothers. However, this conclusion could not be supported by the data from case number three. It will be recalled that little rate change occurred in Eddie's oppositional and cooperative behavior following manipulation of the contingencies between these response classes and his mother's behavior; not until his mother utilized a punishment procedure did dramatic rate changes occur. Thus, little can be said concerning variables in Eddie's natural environment which were responsible for maintaining his deviant and incompatible behavior.

The data reported in this study are also of interest in terms of the modification of deviant child behavior. In all cases it proved possible to train the mothers in the effective use of behavior modification techniques based upon principles of operant learning theory. In two of the cases (Danny and Johnny) the techniques simply involved instructing the mothers to change the usual contingencies between their behavior and their children's deviant and incompatible behavior. Since it had been experimentally demonstrated with these cases that the mothers were providing social reinforcement for their children's deviant behavior, the next logical step would involve training the mothers to ignore these behavior patterns and to provide their reinforcers for behavior which was incompatible with the deviant behavior. As the data indicate, this differential reinforcement procedure was quite effective within the confines of the experimental setting.

Selection of the behavior modification technique used for the third case (Eddie) required more reliance on past research findings than on information gained from an analysis of mother-child interbehavior. Since E was unable after five sessions to determine the source of control of Eddie's deviant behavior, it was decided to stop the search for controlling stimulus events and concentrate on finding the most practical means of eliminating his deviant behavior. Past research (Wolf *et al.*, 1964) has shown that social isolation may function as a highly effective punishment technique for deviant child behavior. As the data indicate, Eddie's mother made very effective use of this technique.

The design of this study did not permit assessment of the generality of the changes in the children's behavior. One would expect that since the mothers were responsible for the changes which were produced, the question of generality would in part be a question of how well the mothers' "therapeutic" behaviors were maintained outside the experimental setting. That is, were their newly learned reactions to their children effective in obtaining reinforcement from the natural environment as well as from the experimental setting? Further research is planned to provide answers to this question.

REFERENCES

BANDURA A. (1961) Psychotherapy as a learning process. *Psychol. Bull.* **58,** 143–149.
GROSSBERG J. N. (1964) Behavior therapy: A review. *Psychol. Bull.* **62,** 73–88.
PRINCE G. S. (1961) A clinical approach to parent–child interaction. *J. child psychol. psychiat.* **2,** 169–184.
RUSSO S. (1964) Adaptations in behavioral therapy with children. *Behav. Res. Ther.* **2,** 43–47.
STRAUGHAN J. H. (1964) Treatment with child and mother in the playroom. *Behav. Res. Ther.* **2,** 37–41.
WOLF M. M., RISLEY T. and MEES H. (1964) Application of operant conditioning procedures to the behavior problems of an autistic child. *Behav. Res. Ther.* **1,** 305–312.

A MEANS OF INVOLVING FATHERS IN FAMILY TREATMENT: GUIDANCE GROUPS FOR FATHERS

HERBERT S. STREAN

Of the many institutions in our society that have changed their perspective on the father's participation in the family, psychiatric clinics have been among the most prominent. Currently, an attempt is being made to involve more fathers in various treatment procedures. This paper deals with the writer's experience in working with a group of fathers, each of whom refused to participate in a one-to-one treatment relationship. While described as passive, weak, and poor treatment candidates they all responded positively to a Fathers' Guidance Group. Feeling that their pathology would not be intensively explored, they could discuss their conflicts and frequently resolve them within a sympathetic male group.

THE ROLE OF THE FATHER in our society has been difficult to grasp. As customs, beliefs, thought, and knowledge change, the father's role assumes new forms.

Our Victorian stereotype of the distant, taciturn, and stern father has been undergoing modification. The more modern picture of the father is that of a gregarious young man interested in his wife and children, who likes his home and likes to work around it. He enjoys helping his wife with household duties and with the routine of child care (3).

We should like to believe that our current conception of the modern father is a realistic one, and that he is replacing the older types. Unfortunately, facts seem to show that society in general, and fathers in particular, find it extremely difficult to define the role of the contemporary father (1, p. 63).

Of the many institutions in our society that have changed their perspective on the father's participation in the family, mental hygiene clinics, family agencies,

The author would like to thank Mr. Leslie Rosenthal, Consultant, Group Therapy Department, Jewish Board of Guardians, for his many suggestions and valuable assistance.

AMERICAN JOURNAL OF ORTHOPSYCHIATRY, 1962, Vol. 32, pp. 719-725.

and child guidance clinics are among the most prominent. In contrast to earlier years, when clinics and social agencies tended to work largely with the mother, or with the mother and child, there is evidence that a new trend is in operation. Currently, an attempt is being made to involve more and more fathers in various types of treatment procedures (2).

While the literature is replete with case examples showing the soundness of various treatment methods as they pertain to fathers, to this writer's knowledge few attempts have been made to describe the processes inherent in the simultaneous treatment of several fathers in a guidance group.[1]

The aim in a guidance group is to increase the parent's adequacy of functioning in his day-to-day relationship with the child. Theoretically, this aim is achieved by involving fathers in a group where discussion is held mainly on father-child relationships and father-child conflicts.

This paper, therefore, will deal with the writer's experience in treating several fathers through the medium of a guidance group. The question to be answered is: Do guidance groups help fathers, and, if so, how do they help create a more favorable family climate for their members?

In attempting to examine the writer's experience with this group, several areas will be investigated: 1) the group composition—the men themselves, their backgrounds, their families, their motivations for joining the group; 2) content of the sessions—what the fathers talked about, how they related to each other and to the therapist; and 3) an attempt

by the therapist to demonstrate how he related to the material brought out in the sessions.

The group met at the Madeleine Borg Child Guidance Institute of the Jewish Board of Guardians for a little over a year. The men met once every two weeks in the evening for an hour and a half and participated in approximately 20 sessions.

When the group was initiated in January 1957, it consisted of six men. Each was the father of two children, of whom at least one had been in treatment from two to three years. The wives of all of the men had been in treatment for approximately the same length of time as the children.

In June 1957, two fathers already in individual treatment joined the group and the membership then totaled eight. The attendance at meetings, however, remained around five.

Most of these men were described by intake workers as passive, weak, defeated fathers, but they were very strongly resistant to treatment for themselves. They felt that the wife made the major decisions, particularly in the area of child rearing. They, the fathers, did not have time for, or interest in, getting involved with the agency. It seemed equivalent to invading the women's world, of which they wanted no part. At intake they frequently provoked rejection or hostility and emerged as outsiders in the treatment of their families. It is important to emphasize that these very fathers, who were described as passive, weak and not very active in participating in their own families, became in each case nonparticipants in the treatment of their respective families.

---

[1] S. R. Slavson introduced the procedure of guidance groups for parents. The background of his work is described in a recent book (4).

The case of Mr. A provides a good illustration. A mild but constant depreciator of his wife and children's behavior, Mr. A's major contributions to the family were his salary and an occasional exhibition of his athletic prowess to his daughters. He delegated all family decisions and child rearing to Mrs. A. Resentful of Mr. A's disinterest and apathy, she felt compelled to fill the vacuum left by her husband. Though there were constant arguments between the parents over Mr. A's emotional isolation, the mother consistently ruled with an iron hand and the father nodded to her decisions.

The A children's reactive behavior disorders complicated the tenuous family balance and their hyperactive and frequently contemptuous behavior only added insult to the injurious family relationships.

Though against psychotherapy, Mr. A apprehensively went along with Mrs. A's initiation of treatment for their daughters. Mr. A came for only one intake interview during the two years his "three girls" (wife and two daughters) were in treatment. This family situation is quite typical of many under discussion.

Though united in their resistance against treatment, the fathers in the group varied widely in occupations and in family constellations. Among them were a commercial artist, a jewelry-store owner, a mailman, a salesman, and the owner of a religious goods store. Most of the fathers were in their forties, and their children ranged in age from 3 to 20 years.

As indicated, all of these fathers were threatened by the prospect of treatment for themselves but responded to the idea of a guidance group. Why should this happen? To answer this question, some of the men's comments may serve as a clue. "If I want to talk, I can talk. If I want to listen, I listen. If I want to shut up, I shut up" . . . "What a good way to get away from the wife and kids for the night, smoke a cigar and relax" . . . "It's always good to know that other guys have troubles too" . . . "I wanted to be part of the plan here but they weren't too eager to have me" . . . "In a group you won't get to that unconscious stuff" . . . "It's good to be with men and men only."

It seemed then that the idea of group treatment was less disturbing to these men than individual treatment. The fear of having their own pathology explored was allayed. The opportunity to discuss universal problems and to leave their children for an evening was a possible reason for the unanimous response to the idea of a group. Evidently, too, the guidance group was perceived by some as a further opportunity to insulate themselves from the rest of the family.

It should be mentioned that the group therapist had several ideas in mind when interviewing all the prospective members individually. The group was presented as strictly voluntary and experimental, and each individual's defensive structure was supported. The man reluctant to talk in groups was told that we would be interested in evaluating what the group could offer to one who remained solely a listener. The father who bragged about how he handled his son skillfully was told that here might be an opportunity to be an advice-giver. The men were further told that we would be talking about father-child relationships principally and would not be directly concerned with marriage, in-laws, etc.

Of the men available as potential candidates for the guidance group, none could be described as overtly destructive in the family constellation. On the contrary, they seemed psychologically unavailable as fathers and unavailable as treatment candidates.

In reviewing the first four or five sessions of the group, we found that the continual theme appeared to be how tough it is to be a father and how much more fun it is to be a child. The fathers all agreed that the demands placed on them were enormous and extremely difficult if not impossible to fulfill. The following were typical reactions to their children's demands: "I have to give him more money for an allowance than I ever got" . . . "They keep wanting to watch television all the time and I never get my turn" . . . "If you give one kid attention, the other one hollers, so you quit after a while" . . . "It's too much. You'd think they'd realize that I had a hard day and I'm entitled to some rest."

The men drew a strong contrast between the way children in this generation seek to be indulged and the firm and punitive way the fathers themselves had been handled by their own parents. The memory of the "lockshen strap"[2] was revived on more than one occasion.

When the members were confronted with the fact that from time to time children need limits and are capable of arousing legitimate and honest anger in adults, most members of the group expressed great surprise. Defensive maneuvers were erected to protect themselves from seeing children any differently. "He's my child; I have to love him and give him everything," said one father.

Although the therapist tried very hard to support the defenses and resistances of the fathers by allowing them to express resentment about their burdens, and although he suggested that they did not have to meet every one of their children's demands, he was still seen as an ungiving person. He was attacked for not giving more information on techniques in child rearing. He was told that he was too withdrawn and passive a person, and it was suggested that perhaps he could serve the men beer or cookies and coffee.

Evidently these fathers wanted to be fed more than the therapist was feeding them. Though they complained bitterly that their children made too many demands on them, which they felt incapable of meeting, they put themselves in exactly the same demanding position in regard to the therapist. Their behavior in the group was certainly in many instances a repetition of their children's behavior at home.

Mr. A, a humorous depreciator of his wife's interaction with the children, made fun of events that other fathers described. Mr. T, a self-righteous moralist who insisted on adult-like behavior from his son, frowned upon any display of regression in the group. Mr. S, a very provocative man in his relationship with his son, aroused so much hostility in the other men that they tried their best to get him to withdraw from the group. His methods of withdrawal from the group were very similar to those he used in withdrawing psychologically from his own home. Finally, Mr. L, who was Mother's Little Helper at home, always insisted on helping the therapist in as many ways as he could find.

It can be concluded that the group was for many of its members a symbolic family. The men used each other and the therapist to act out neurotic problems in old and current relationships. Though the men obviously protected themselves from freely interacting with each other by various defensive maneuvers, their need to establish themselves as members of a symbolic family was ever-present.

Frequently the therapist emerged as the object to cathect unresolved problems. He might be loved and hated as

---

[2] A strap with appendages at the end, traditionally used by many European Jewish families to punish children.

were the members' parents or siblings in the past. For example, at about the sixth session when the men were beginning to report some changes—"giving my son what he needs rather than what he wants" . . . "allowing myself to be really annoyed at my daughter and not feeling so guilty afterwards"—they openly attacked the therapist for being incompetent.

When the therapist asked what was wrong with him and why they thought he was a poor therapist, the men said he made them work too hard, that he did not supply solutions to perplexing questions, or give them enough theoretical data. This experience of seeing the therapist subject the members' complaints to examination turned out to be a key session and changed the tone of the next several meetings. The fathers began to acknowledge openly in the group their own personal limitations as people, as husbands, and as fathers. They started to allow themselves to admit directly personal as well as interpersonal problems.

It is suggested that when the therapist allows himself to be subjected to examination, the group members will eventually subject themselves to a similar examination. Typical statements made by the fathers after the session referred to above are the following: "I asked my son what is going on between us since we can't get along very well and we had a great discussion" . . . "Johnny wasn't going to bed on time and there was a fight every night. I looked at myself and saw that I really wanted him to stay up."

Whether a group therapist allows himself to be subjected to examination or not, inevitably he will be. The nature of a therapeutic group is such that the group will respond to the therapist's unconscious. At the seventh session, when the therapist's position in the agency was in doubt, the group chose to discuss separation anxiety.

At about the thirteenth session, the therapist out of his own needs called a very early meeting right after Labor Day. The men spent most of their time talking about their hard-working youthful days and competed to see who got paid the least.

It was interesting too that, after one of these sessions, a father exclaimed: "Sometimes kids know exactly what's on your mind. You don't even have to say anything; they pick up the subtleties."

Although the group was structured to discuss solely parent-child conflicts, they began to discuss marital problems, conflicts with their own parents, and in-laws. Actually this evolved very interestingly. After criticizing their children, they attacked and criticized the therapist. Next they criticized their wives, then each other and finally themselves. This changed the classic structure of the traditional guidance group. Under the stimulation of the psychiatric consultant for this group, and with the group therapy consultant concurring, it was decided to let the group be an arena for all feelings in all relationships instead of limiting discussions to parent-child relationships.

Coupled with a growing open ventilation of individual problems were various attempts to test the therapist. The members wanted to see if he was really honest in his convictions. Around the fourteenth session, after the therapist had supported statements of the members regarding the importance of their own individual pleasures, and they had begun to limit their children appropriately, they started to dawdle and stay beyond the time allotted for the meetings. When the therapist was forced to say that he wanted to go home and relax because he had had a hard day, the fathers were quite impressed and later gave examples of having allowed themselves to "take it easy" at home.

Another phenomenon which seemed to evolve in this group was a developmental scheme. During the early sessions there was much discussion on oral problems such as thumb-sucking and excessive eating. After a while discussion turned to anal problems: toilet-training, problems of controlling, saving and withholding.

Not only were oral and anal problems discussed as such, but the men's behavior toward each other and toward the therapist showed what level they were operating on. Still later, phallic and genital problems were discussed, such as masturbation and sexual relations. The discussions in the group went back and forth without giving the therapist much opportunity to predict what would happen next.

This developmental sequence offers us another clue to the members' perception of the group. Frequently the group fosters growing up. Having demanded to be "fed," the members in turn often "fed" the surrogate parent by developing better controls and demonstrating more mature behavior. After this type of experience, the men should be in a better position to help their own children develop.

Perhaps, at this point, an attempt can be made to answer the question: "Do guidance groups help fathers, and if so, how do they provide a better family climate for their members?"

To the first part of the question, "Do guidance groups help fathers?" the writer's answer is "Yes and no." There are men who have attended group meetings very infrequently, and they have provided much information on some of the negative aspects of a guidance group.

One man said, "You don't talk enough about wives; that's my problem —I've got to get that fixed up." This man is being helped toward individual treatment and perhaps that is what should have occurred in the first place. Another father said, "I don't like all men in groups. We need women in here, too." In other words, a fathers' group may arouse in some men so much homosexual anxiety that they withdraw. Moreover some men find more aggression than they can tolerate; they become panicky and also withdraw.

In a fathers' group the major focus is on guidance, although in the group described this was somewhat modified. To some men discussion in this medium does not affect underlying pathology sufficiently and hence their relationships at home are not altered appreciably.

On the positive side, a guidance group for fathers can provide a sympathetic male audience. This can offer strength, understanding, and support. New techniques on child rearing are picked up, tried and often integrated. A guidance group offers members the opportunity to feel "I'm not so alone in this world; other guys have troubles too." Offered a chance to regress in the group, they often show mature behavior on the outside. After one member had brought out a tremendous amount of hostility toward his wife and daughters, which was subjected to considerable analysis in the group, he asked his wife, "How can I learn to understand you better?"

Many fathers who are outsiders in the family, if offered an opportunity to participate in the treatment plan, can mobilize a greater willingness to participate as members of their own families. Participation in a symbolic family can pave the way for participation in a real family.

The aim in a guidance group is to increase the parents' adequacy of functioning in the day-to-day relationship with their children. While there is some evidence that the children often react positively when the father is increasingly sensitized to their needs, further collaboration is needed with the workers treating other members of the family. It is important to have more impressions and observations of the advantages and disadvantages that accrue after a father enters a guidance group.

All too frequently a child guidance clinic or family agency is confronted with a strong, seemingly powerful, controlling mother and a threatened, weak, passive, defeated father. Fearful of treatment for himself, the father retires once more and becomes a withdrawn outsider. A guidance group may be a means of uniting him with his family, giving him some strength to cope with the burdens of being a parent, and helping him to enjoy some of its potential pleasures.

REFERENCES

1. BURGESS, ERNEST W., and HARVEY J. LOCKE. *The Family.* Chicago: American Book Co., 1947.

2. *Editorial Notes.* Soc. Casewk., 35: 354-355, 1954.

3. ENGLISH, O. SPURGEON. *The Psychological Role of the Father in the Family.* Soc. Casewk., 35: 323-329, 1954.

4. SLAVSON, SAMUEL R. *Child-Centered Group Guidance of Parents.* New York: Internat. Univ. Press, 1958.